GENDER AND CRIME

Critical Concepts in Criminology

Other titles in this series:

Crime Reduction
Edited and with a new introduction by Kate Moss
4-volume set

Surveillance
Edited and with a new introduction by Benjamin Goold
4-volume set

Restorative Justice
Edited and with a new introduction by Carolyn Hoyle
4-volume set

Organized Crime
Edited and with a new introduction by Federico Varese
4-volume set

GENDER AND CRIME

Critical Concepts in Criminology

Edited by
Sandra Walklate

Volume I
Sex and Crime or Gender and Crime?

Routledge
Taylor & Francis Group
LONDON AND NEW YORK

First published 2012
by Routledge
2 Park Square, Milton Park, Abingdon, Oxon OX14 4RN

Simultaneously published in the USA and Canada
by Routledge
711 Third Avenue, New York, NY 10017

Routledge is an imprint of the Taylor & Francis Group, an informa business

British Library Cataloguing in Publication Data
A catalogue record for this book is available from the British Library

Library of Congress Cataloging in Publication Data
Gender and crime : critical concepts in criminology / edited by Sandra Walklate.
v. cm.
Includes bibliographical references and index.
Contents: v. 1. Sex and crime or gender and crime? – v. 2. Gender, crime, and criminal victimisation – v. 3. Gendered experiences of the criminal justice process – v. 4. Gender, crime, and punishment.
ISBN 978-0-415-61963-9 (set : alk. paper) – ISBN 978-0-415-61964-6 (volume 1 : alk. paper) – ISBN 978-0-415-61965-3 (volume 2 : alk. paper) – ISBN 978-0-415-61967-7 (volume 3 : alk. paper) – ISBN 978-0-415-61968-4 (volume 4 : alk. paper)
1. Crime–Sex differences. 2. Feminist criminology. 3. Women–Crimes against. 4. Criminology. 5. Sex discrimination in criminal justice administration. I. Walklate, Sandra.
HV6158.G454 2012
364.081–dc23

2011049494

ISBN: 978-0-415-61963-9 (Set)
ISBN: 978-0-415-61964-6 (Volume I)

Typeset in 10/12pt Times NR MT
by Graphicraft Limited, Hong Kong

Publisher's Note
References within each chapter are as they appear in the original complete work

MIX
Paper from responsible sources
FSC
www.fsc.org
FSC® C004839

Printed and bound in Great Britain by the MPG Books Group

CONTENTS

VOLUME II GENDER, CRIME, AND CRIMINAL VICTIMISATION

VOLUME III GENDERED EXPERIENCES OF THE CRIMINAL JUSTICE PROCESS

CONTENTS

VOLUME IV GENDER, CRIME, AND PUNISHMENT

ACKNOWLEDGEMENTS

The publishers would like to thank the following for permission to reprint their material:

Wiley for permission to reprint Carol Smart, 'Criminological theory: its ideology and implications concerning women', *British Journal of Sociology*, 28, 1, 1977, pp. 89–100.

Wiley for permission to reprint Frances Heidensohn, 'The deviance of women: a critique and an enquiry', *British Journal of Sociology*, 19, 2, 1968, pp. 160–75.

Taylor & Francis for permission to reprint Beverley Brown, 'Women and crime: the dark figures of criminology', *Economy and Society*, 15, 3, 1986, pp. 355–402.

Open University Press for permission to reprint Maureen Cain, 'Realist philosophy and standpoint epistemologies or feminist criminology as a successor science', in L. Gelsthorpe and A. Morris (eds), *Feminist Perspectives in Criminology* (Milton Keynes: Open University Press, 1990), pp. 124–40.

Open University Press for permission to reprint Carol Smart, 'Feminist approaches to criminology or postmodern woman meets atavistic man', in L. Gelsthorpe and A. Morris (eds), *Feminist Perspectives in Criminology* (Milton Keynes: Open University Press, 1990), pp. 70–84.

Sage for permission to reprint Dana M. Britton, 'Feminism in criminology: engendering the outlaw', *The Annals of the American Academy of Political and Social Science*, 571, September, 2000, pp. 57–76.

Sage for permission to reprint Tony Jefferson, 'Muscle, "hard men" and "iron" Mike Tyson: reflections on desire, anxiety and the embodiment of masculinity', *Body and Society*, 4, 1, 1998, pp. 77–98.

Rowman & Littlefield Publishers, Inc. for permission to reprint James Messerschmidt, 'Varieties of "real men"', in J. Messerschmidt, *Masculinities and Crime* (Maryland: Rowman and Littlefield, 1993), pp. 119–53.

Oxford University Press for permission to reprint Joachim Kersten, 'Culture, masculinities and violence against women', in T. Jefferson and P. Carlen (eds), *Masculinities, Social Relations and Crime, Special Issue of the British Journal of Criminology*, 36, 3, 1996, pp. 381–95.

Sage for permission to reprint Robert W. Connell and James W. Messerschmidt, 'Hegemonic masculinity: rethinking the concept', *Gender and Society*, 19, 6, 2005, pp. 829–59.

Sage for permission to reprint Kathleen Daly, 'Different ways of conceptualizing sex/gender in feminist theory and their implications for criminology', *Theoretical Criminology*, 1, 1, 1997, pp. 25–51.

Sage for permission to reprint Amanda Burgess-Proctor, 'Intersections of race, class, gender, and crime: future directions for feminist criminology', *Feminist Criminology*, 1, 1, 2006, pp. 27–47.

Sage for permission to reprint Meda Chesney-Lind, 'Patriarchy, crime, and justice: feminist criminology in an era of backlash', *Feminist Criminology*, 1, 1, 2006, pp. 6–26.

Disclaimer

Chronological table of reprinted articles and chapters

Date	*Author*	*Title*	*Source*	*Vol.*	*Chap.*
1878	Frances Power Cobbe	Wife torture in England	J. Radford and D. Russell (eds), *Femicide: The Politics of Woman Killing*, Milton Keynes: Open University Press, 1992, pp. 46–52.	II	29
1968	Frances Heidensohn	The deviance of women: a critique and an enquiry	*British Journal of Sociology*, 19:2, 160–75.	I	3
1973	Meda Chesney-Lind	Judicial enforcement of the female sex role: the family court and the female delinquent	*Issues in Criminology*, 8:2, 51–69.	III	47
1973	Dorie Klein	The etiology of female crime	*Issues in Criminology*, 8:2, 3–30.	I	1
1975	Susan Brownmiller	Women fight back	K. Evans and J. Jamieson (eds), *Gender and Crime: a Reader*, McGraw-Hill/Open University Press, 2008, pp. 51–64.	II	30
1977	Gail Armstrong	Females under the law—'protected' but unequal	*Crime and Delinquency*, 23 (April), 109–20.	III	48
1977	Carol Smart	Criminological theory: its ideology and implications concerning women	*British Journal of Sociology*, 28:1, 89–100.	I	2
1979	Susan E. Martin	*Police* women and police *women*: occupational role dilemmas and choices of female officers	*Journal of Police Science and Administration*, 2, 314–23.	III	38
1983	Meda Chesney-Lind and Noelie Rodriguez	Women under lock and key: a view from the inside	*The Prison Journal*, 63:2, 47–65.	IV	67
1983	Charles E. Frazier, E. Wilbur Bock and John C. Henretta	The role of probation officers in determining gender differences in sentencing severity	*Sociological Quarterly*, 24:2, 305–18.	III	44
1983	Diana E. Russell and Nancy Howell	The prevalence of rape in the United States revisited	*Signs*, 8:4, 688–95.	II	31
1985	Mark Warr	Fear of rape among urban women	*Social Problems*, 32:3, 238–50.	II	16

Chronological table continued

Date	*Author*	*Title*	*Source*	*Vol.*	*Chap.*
1986	Beverley Brown	Women and crime: the dark figures of criminology	*Economy and Society*, 15:3, 355–402.	I	4
1986	Frances Heidensohn	Models of justice: Portia or Persephone?: some thoughts on equality, fairness and gender in the field of criminal justice	*International Journal of the Sociology of Law*, 14:3–4, 287–98.	III	52
1987	Hilary Allen	Rendering them harmless: the professional portrayal of women charged with serious violent crimes	P. Carlen and A. Worrall (eds), *Gender, Crime and Justice*, Milton Keynes: Open University Press, pp. 81–94.	III	49
1987	Roland Chilton and Susan K. Datesman	Gender, race, and crime: an analysis of urban arrest trends, 1960–1980	*Gender and Society*, 1:2, 152–71.	III	37
1987	Liz Kelly	The continuum of sexual violence	J. Hamner and M. Maynard (eds), *Women, Violence and Social Control*, London: Macmillan, pp. 46–60.	II	19
1987	Anne Worrall	Sisters in law?: women defendants and women magistrates	P. Carlen and A. Worrall (eds), *Gender, Crime and Justice*, Milton Keynes: Open University Press, pp. 108–24.	III	50
1988	Elizabeth A. Stanko	Fear of crime and the myth of the safe home: a feminist critique of criminology	K. Yllo and M. Bograd (eds), *Feminist Perspectives on Wife Abuse*, London: Sage, pp. 75–89.	II	17
1989	Edna Erez	Gender, rehabilitation, and probation decisions	*Criminology*, 27:2, 307–26.	III	45
1990	Maureen Cain	Realist philosophy and standpoint epistemologies or feminist criminology as a successor science	L. Gelsthorpe and A. Morris (eds), *Feminist Perspectives in Criminology*, Milton Keynes: Open University Press, pp. 124–40.	I	5
1990	Carol Brooks Gardner	Safe conduct: women, crime, and self in public places	*Social Problems*, 37:3, 311–28.	II	18

1990	Marcia Rice	Challenging orthodoxies in feminist theory: a black feminist critique	L. Gelsthorpe and A. Morris (eds), *Feminist Perspectives in Criminology*, Milton Keynes: Open University Press, pp. 57–70.	I	12
1990	Carol Smart	Feminist approaches to criminology or postmodern woman meets atavistic man	L. Gelsthorpe and A. Morris (eds), *Feminist Perspectives in Criminology*, Milton Keynes: Open University Press, pp. 70–84.	I	6
1992	Mary E. Gilfus	From victims to survivors to offenders: women's routes of entry and immersion into street crime	*Women and Criminal Justice*, 4:1, 63–89.	IV	57
1992	Carol Smart	The woman of legal discourse	*Social and Legal Studies*, 1, 29–44.	III	53
1992	Sari Van der Poel	Professional male prostitution: a neglected phenomenon	*Crime, Law and Social Change*, 18:3, 259–75.	II	24
1993	Jane Caputi	The sexual politics of murder	P. B. Bart and E. G. Moran (eds), *Violence Against Women: The Bloody Footprints*, London: Sage, pp. 5–25.	II	26
1993	James Messerschmidt	Varieties of 'real men'	J. Messerschmidt, *Masculinities and Crime*, Maryland: Rowman and Littlefield, pp. 119–53.	I	9
1993	Diana Scully and Joseph Marolla	'Riding the bull at Gilley's': convicted rapists describe the rewards of rape	P. B. Bart and E. G. Moran (eds), *Violence Against Women: The Bloody Footprints*, London: Sage, 26–46.	II	32
1993	Elizabeth A. Stanko and Kathy Hobdell	Assault on men: masculinity and male victimization	*British Journal of Criminology*, 33:3, 400–15.	II	35
1993	Sandra Walklate	Policing by women, with women, for women?: is the Equal Opportunities policy depriving the service of skills more likely to be found in female officers?	*Policing*, 9:2, 101–16.	III	41

Chronological table continued

Date	*Author*	*Title*	*Source*	*Vol.*	*Chap.*
1994	Pat Carlen	Why study women's imprisonment?: or anyone else's?: an indefinite article	*British Journal of Criminology*, 34:1, 131–40.	IV	68
1994	Nigel Fielding	Cop canteen culture	T. Newburn and E. Stanko (eds), *Just Boys Doing Business*, London: Routledge, pp. 46–63.	III	42
1994	Frances Heidensohn	'We can handle it out here': women officers in Britain and the USA and the policing of public order	*Policing and Society*, 4:4, 293–303.	III	39
1994	Joe Sim	Tougher than the rest: men in prison	T. Newburn and B. Stanko (eds), *Just Boys Doing Business*, London: Routledge, pp. 100–17.	IV	71
1996	Joachim Kersten	Culture, masculinities and violence against women	T. Jefferson and P. Carlen (eds), *Masculinities, Social Relations and Crime, Special Issue of the British Journal of Criminology*, 36:3, 381–95.	I	10
1997	Kathleen Daly	Different ways of conceptualizing sex/gender in feminist theory and their implications for criminology	*Theoretical Criminology*, 1:1, 25–51.	I	13
1997	Jo Goodey	Boys don't cry: masculinities, fear of crime and fearlessness	*British Journal of Criminology*, 37:3, 401–18.	II	20
1997	Sue Lees	Male rape	S. Lees, *Ruling Passions: Sexual Violence, Reputation and the Law*, Milton Keynes: Open University Press, pp. 89–109.	II	33
1998	Tony Jefferson	Muscle, 'hard men' and 'iron' Mike Tyson: reflections on desire, anxiety and the embodiment of masculinity	*Body and Society*, 4:1, 77–98.	I	8
1998	Christopher Uggen and Candace Kruttschnitt	Crime in the breaking: gender differences in desistance	*Law & Society Review*, 32:2, 339–66.	IV	59

1999	Stephanie J. Funk	Risk assessment for juveniles on probation: a focus on gender	*Criminal Justice and Behavior*, 26:1, 44–68.	IV	62
2000	Dana M. Britton	Feminism in criminology: engendering the outlaw	*The Annals of the American Academy of Political and Social Science*, 571 (September), 57–76.	I	7
2000	Joanna Phoenix	Prostitute identities: men, money, and violence	*British Journal of Criminology*, 40:1, 37–55.	II	25
2001	Jan Jordan	Worlds apart?: women, rape and the police reporting process	*British Journal of Criminology*, 41:4, 679–706.	III	40
2002	Stephanie Allen	Male victims of rape: responses to a perceived threat to masculinity	C. Hoyle and R. Young (eds), *New Visions of Crime Victims*, Oxford and Portland, OR: Hart Publishing, pp. 23–45.	II	34
2003	Pamela A. Davies	Is economic crime a man's game?	*Feminist Theory*, 4:3, 283–303.	II	22
2003	Belinda Morrissey	Inconceivable survivors: battered women who kill	B. Morrissey, *When Women Kill: Questions of Agency and Subjectivity*, London: Routledge, pp. 67–100.	II	28
2003	Ngaire Naffine	Who are law's persons?: from Cheshire Cats to responsible subjects	*Modern Law Review*, 66:3, 346–67.	III	54
2003	Laureen Snider	Constituting the punishable woman: atavistic man incarcerates postmodern woman	*British Journal of Criminology*, 43:2, 354–78.	IV	69
2004	R. Emerson Dobash, Russell P. Dobash, Kate Cavanagh and Ruth Lewis	Not an ordinary killer – just an ordinary guy: when men murder an intimate woman partner	*Violence Against Women*, 10:6, 577–605.	II	27
2004	Russell P. Dobash and R. Emerson Dobash	Women's violence to men in intimate relationships: working on a puzzle	*British Journal of Criminology*, 44:3, 324–49.	II	36

Chronological table continued

Date	*Author*	*Title*	*Source*	*Vol.*	*Chap.*
2004	Judith Rumgay	Scripts for safer survival: pathways out of female crime	*The Howard Journal*, 43:4, 405–19.	IV	61
2005	Susan Batchelor	Prove me the bam!: victimisation and agency in the lives of young women who commit violent offences	*Probation Journal: The Journal of Community and Criminal Justice*, 52:4, 358–75.	IV	58
2005	Alex Campbell	Keeping the 'lady' safe: the regulation of femininity through crime prevention literature	*Critical Criminology*, 13:1, 119–40.	II	21
2005	Robert W. Connell and James W. Messerschmidt	Hegemonic masculinity: rethinking the concept	*Gender and Society*, 19:6, 829–59.	I	11
2006	Amanda Burgess-Proctor	Intersections of race, class, gender, and crime: future directions for feminist criminology	*Feminist Criminology*, 1:1, 27–47.	I	14
2006	Kerry Carrington	Does feminism spoil girls?: explanations for official rises in female delinquency	*The Australian and New Zealand Journal of Criminology*, 39:1, 34–53.	II	23
2006	Meda Chesney-Lind	Patriarchy, crime, and justice: feminist criminology in an era of backlash	*Feminist Criminology*, 1:1, 6–26.	I	15
2006	Kathleen Daly and Julie Stubbs	Feminist engagement with restorative justice	*Theoretical Criminology*, 10:1, 9–28.	IV	72
2006	Emily Gaarder and Lois Presser	A feminist vision of justice?: the problems and possibilities of restorative justice for girls and women	D. Sullivan and L. Tift (eds), *Handbook of Restorative Justice*, London: Routledge, pp. 483–94.	IV	75
2006	Ruth Graham	Male rape and the careful construction of the male victim	*Social and Legal Studies*, 15:2, 187–208.	III	55
2006	Patricia Gray	Women's experiences of incarceration in Hong Kong: doing time, doing choice, doing class-gender-culture	*International Journal of the Sociology of Law*, 34, 89–104.	IV	70

2006	Kelly Hannah-Moffat	Pandora's box: risk/need and gender-responsive corrections	*Criminology and Public Policy*, 5:1, 183–92.	IV	63
2006	Barbara Hudson	Beyond white man's justice: race, gender and justice in late modernity	*Theoretical Criminology*, 10:1, 29–47.	III	56
2006	Mary P. Koss	Restoring rape survivors: justice, advocacy, and a call to action	*Annals New York Academy of Sciences*, 1087, 206–34.	IV	74
2007	Marisa Silvestri	'Doing' police leadership: enter the 'new smart macho'	*Policing and Society*, 17:1, 38–58.	III	43
2007	Julie Stubbs	Beyond apology?: domestic violence and critical questions for restorative justice	*Criminology and Criminal Justice*, 7:2, 169–87.	IV	73
2008	Gillian Balfour	Falling between the cracks of retributive and restorative justice: the victimization and punishment of Aboriginal women	*Feminist Criminology*, 3:2, 101–20.	IV	76
2008	Dermot Feenan	Women judges: gendering judging, justifying diversity	*Journal of Law and Society*, 35:4, 490–519.	III	51
2008	Carolyn Hoyle	Will she be safe?: a critical analysis of risk assessment in domestic violence cases	*Children and Youth Services Review*, 30, 323–37.	IV	66
2009	Janet T. Davidson and Meda Chesney-Lind	Discounting women: context matters in risk and need assessment	*Critical Criminology*, 17, 221–45.	IV	65
2009	Amanda L. Robinson and James Rowlands	Assessing and managing risk among different victims of domestic abuse: limits of a generic model of risk assessment?	*Security Journal*, 22:3, 190–204.	IV	64
2009	Anne Worrall and Loraine Gelsthorpe	'What works' with women offenders: the past 30 years	*Probation Journal*, 56:4, 329–45.	III	46
2010	Eileen Baldry	Women in transition: from prison to . . .	*Current Issues in Criminal Justice*, 22:2, 253–67.	IV	60

PREFACE

Preparing these four volumes has been both interesting and a challenge: interesting insofar as it has afforded a very thought-provoking opportunity to reflect upon what kinds of readings to choose and on what basis to make that choice and a challenge for precisely those same reasons. I have endeavoured here to offer a flavour, both historically and contemporarily of some of the key interventions that have been made addressing the question of gender for both criminology and victimology. I have endeavoured to be as wide-ranging in the choices made as possible but have obviously been constrained by space (yes, even in a four-volume set of this kind), and availability of material that could be made accessible to a wider audience. I am indebted to Dominic Shryane for inviting me to take on this task and to Maria Barrow for her unfailing editorial support. I hope that those of you who dip into these volumes learn something from the choices that I have made.

Sandra Walklate
Eleanor Rathbone Chair of Sociology
University of Liverpool, UK
November 2011

INTRODUCTION

Criminologists have been interested in the differences between the sexes in criminal behaviour for a long time. From the work of Lombroso and Ferraro (1895) in the late nineteenth century to the more recent work of Braithwaite in the twentieth century, the disproportionate offending behaviour of males as compared to females is a criminological 'fact' that every criminological theory needs to be able to address (Braithwaite 1989: 44–49). This volume of readings explores this enduring criminological pre-occupation, the feminist response to it, and the extent to which the discipline has been changed as a consequence. Before we consider the questions which this volume of readings encourages us to think about, it is important to be clear about the difference between sex and gender. Put simply, sex is a biological given. A person is either male or female. Whilst there might be some confusion about the nature of this biological given for a small percentage of people, being male or being female is a *biologically* ascribed attribute. Gender, on the other hand, refers to the *socially* achieved attributes of being male or female, that is, being a man or a woman. More specifically, the concept of gender alludes to socially constructed understandings of masculinity and femininity. So, whilst we are all biologically either male or female, sociologically, being male or being female does not necessarily equate with being masculine or being feminine. These latter attributes refer to the social expectations associated with biological characteristics that may vary over time and place. Moreover, it is important to remember that the term 'gender', by implication, refers to both men and women.

Gender, as opposed to sex, raises all kinds of questions about, and for, criminology not only in terms of who is the subject matter of criminology but also about how that subject matter is studied and what kind of concepts are used to make sense of that subject matter. This volume is concerned to trace the way in which the questions of sex and crime, and gender and crime have evolved since the work of Lombroso and Ferraro in 1895.

Part 1: Challenging criminology's domain assumptions

Gouldner (1973) observed that all disciplines reflect assumptions that are so deeply embedded in the way in which they view the world that they are taken as 'given'. These he referred to as 'domain' assumptions. Gender is one of these 'domain' assumptions for criminology. Put another way, historically criminology has been 'gender blind': that is, as a discipline it could not see men and women. Early feminist interventions within criminology were concerned with this gender blindness, that is, with the extent to which criminological theories and explanations operated with the assumption that the human world was an androgynous world. This early work challenged this view and asked the question: to what extent is it possible to make the assumption that the term 'human' accurately conveys the world experiences of males and females both of whom are attributed with masculine and feminine qualities. Brown (included in this volume) expressed this problem in this way:

> The more one seeks to show that male criminologists take leave of their senses when the question Woman looms on the agenda, the more one implies that they are in their right minds when they talk about male crime.

By implication this observation demands that criminology not only includes women but also that the discipline is thinking critically about men in its theorising and explanatory potential. As both Wootton (1959) and Cain (1989) have commented, separated by thirty years, men and the maleness of crime have largely been absent from the criminological gaze. Part of the reason for this lies within the deeply embedded hold that positivism has had on criminology. This is typified in the work of both the biological positivists and the sociological positivists, which, when taken together, presumed that sex differences explained male and female offending behaviour. The power of these presumptions is illustrated in the readings offered here by Klein, Smart and Heidensohn, all of whom, in their different ways, point to the prevailing criminological assumptions that female criminality had been largely associated with women's (legitimate) endeavours to find a mate or to sustain a relationship with a man. These presumptions made it impossible for criminology to see women as aggressive or violent, for example, since this challenged the ideal of femininity that was so deeply embedded in criminological work (Naffine, 1987). In her later work Heidensohn (1985) went on to develop this critique by suggesting that one way of understanding female criminality was to situate such behaviour within the wider context of women's lives as a whole and ask the questions, how and when they were under control (by men), out of control (offending the prevailing norms of femininity), or increasingly in control (by having achieved a degree of economic independence through entering the workplace). All of these questions centred the power that men had over women and the implicit failure of criminology to ask questions about the nature and impact of that power. However, as the feminist voice gained momentum it became clear that not all feminists were asking the same kinds of questions about criminology. Whilst the early interventions by Klein, Smart and Heidensohn were informed by radical feminism and an awareness of the overarching power that patriarchal social relationships had over women's lives, in due course other feminist voices emerged that tempered the totalising explanatory tendencies inherent in this approach. In this volume it is possible to appreciate a flavour of these other feminist voices presented here in the later work of Cain and Smart. Cain, influenced by socialist feminism, and Smart, who in her later work was influenced by post-modern feminism, each in their own way challenged the viability of a discipline that failed to take gender seriously within the specificities of time and place. This is a failure still evident in the commentary offered by Brittan. The questions raised by feminism did provoke a response. This response endeavoured to render men and masculinity problematic for the criminological enterprise.

The criminological response: problematising men and masculinity

One of the major achievements of the feminist intervention in criminology was to place the maleness of criminal behaviour alongside the maleness of the criminal justice professions and processes. Many (male) criminologists looked to the seminal work of Connell (1987, 1995) as offering a conceptual way forward in understanding this problem. According to Connell (1987) the expression of masculinity in contemporary society reflects the cultural power of normative heterosexuality. This cultural power expects (normal) men to see themselves as different from women and at the same time to desire women. The power of this cultural expectation is found in all aspects of social life: the man as 'breadwinner', the criminalisation of homosexuality, women as objects in pornography. Such expectations define the structure and form of manhood that individual men are expected to live up to. Of course within this cultural expectation there is also a presumption of whiteness. The white heterosexual male sits at the top of a hierarchy of masculinity that in comparison downgrades ethnicity, other forms of sexuality and, of course, femininity. This Connell termed hegemonic masculinity: 'The set of ideas, values, representations and practices associated with "being male" which is commonly accepted as the dominant position in gender relations in a society at a particular historical moment' (Jefferson, 2006: 199). The extract from Messerschmidt relates these ideas to three different locations: the street (the pimp); the home (male sexual propriety and violence); and the workplace (sexual harassment and sharp business practices of the white collar executive). All of these examples for Messerschmidt illustrate the different ways that men demonstrate their masculinity to themselves and others through crime whilst simultaneously putting women 'in their place'.

The influence of this way of thinking about the maleness of crime is clearly evident in how criminologists began to think differently about all aspects of the crime experience, from the fear of crime (covered in Volume II), to understanding the nature and impact of the criminal justice process (addressed in Volume III) to an appreciation of routes in and out of crime (considered in Volume IV) and stands as testimony to the way in which feminist thought pushed the boundaries of the discipline. However, putting masculinity to the fore was not without it critics. Hood-Williams (2001: 44) captured the essence of such criticisms. He asked:

> The question remains, however, why it is that only a minority of men need to produce masculinity through crime rather than through other non-criminal means?

This question reminds us of the deep-seated drive within criminology to search for a variable or an explanation for *all* crime, and as others, along with Hood-Williams argued, overlooked the question as to when and under what circumstances gender was the salient variable. We consider some of that work in the readings produced in Part 3 of this volume.

The aftermath: the salience of gender and the problem of backlash

As has already been mentioned, feminism does not comprise of one coherent voice or one theoretical perspective, but a number of different voices. The influence of post-modernism in particular created the space in which some of those different voices could be heard. If there was one question that appeared amongst those different voices, it was the question of whether or not the term Woman could stand for all women. Consequently criminologists became increasingly concerned to trace the diversity between different women's experiences of crime and the criminal justice system as well as their similarities. The readings in the third and final part of this volume capture some of these concerns. The readings by Rice, Daly and Carlen each in their different way call for a more finely tuned appreciation of difference and similarity, with Carlen's intervention particularly encouraging a consideration of the ways in which class, race and gender (as variables) might differently interact with one another in different global contexts. Proctor-Burgess also takes up this issue. Yet, despite nearly four decades of debate, criminology still struggles with taking the gender question seriously, so much so that, as Chesney-Lind suggests, some would argue that we are now in a era of backlash. So what have these interventions achieved?

It is possible to discern supportive evidence for Chesney-Lind's analysis (in this volume) that within criminology there is today a 'repression of dissent'. She is, of course, referring in particular to the United States. Yet, as policies, policy makers and commentators increasingly substitute the word 'gender' for 'sex' (sometimes appropriately and sometimes not) it is possible to suggest a groundswell of opinion that on the one hand the work of feminism is 'done' and on the other a subtle reframing of social problems, including that of crime, that assumes that changing the word sex for gender solves 'the problem'. However as the readings included here, and those that are to come in the subsequent volumes, clearly indicate, this is not the case. So what has changed and what has remained the same as a result of the work captured in this volume?

Firstly it is important to note that the central criminological agenda has been fundamentally transformed as a result of raising the sex-gender question. Criminology's understanding of what counts as crime, who the victims of crime are, and who does what to whom, is substantially different in the twenty-first century from its understanding of these questions in the nineteenth century. For example, men's violence towards women is now a central feature of any criminological textbook and indeed in many criminal justice systems' responses to crime. The central importance of this substantive issue has inevitably carried with it implications for how offenders are defined, understood and responded to. This does not mean that either criminology or criminal justice policy is 'gender proofed' (Gelsthorpe 2006: 242). It does mean that there is still much work to be done. Carlen (see Volume IV) reminds us that if we are committed to working within criminology, and all that implies about the discipline's intimate relationship with criminal justice policy, then we need to be brave enough to tackle both the contradictions and the specificities that men and women's relationship with crime draws us into. Embracing this call will ensure that criminology, and its debates about the salience of gender, will continue to be as vibrant and exciting a discipline for the next hundred years as it has been for the last.

References

Braithwaite, J. (1989) *Crime, Shame and Reintegration.* Cambridge: Cambridge University Press.

Cain, M. (1989) 'Feminists transgress criminology', in M. Cain (ed.) *Growing up Good.* London: Sage.

Connell, G. W. (1987) *Gender and Power*. Oxford: Polity Press.

Connell, G. W. (1995) *Masculinities.* Oxford: Polity Press.

Gelsthorpe, L. (2006) 'COUNTERBLAST: women and criminal justice: saying it again, again and again.' *The Howard Journal of Criminal Justice* 45, 4, pp. 421–424.

Gouldner, A. (1973) *For Sociology: Renewal and Critique in Sociology Today.* Harmondsworth: Penguin.

Heidensohn, F. (1985) *Women and Crime.* London: Macmillan.

Hood-Williams, J. (2001) 'Gender, masculinities and crime.' *Theoretical Criminology* 5, 1, pp. 37–60.

Jefferson, T. (2006) 'Hegemonic masculinity', in E. McLaughlin and J. Muncie (eds) *The Sage Dictionary of Criminology* (2/e). London: Sage.

Lombroso, C. and Ferraro, W. (1895) *The Female Offender.* London: T. Fisher Unwin.

Naffine, N. (1987) *Female Crime*. Sydney: Allen and Unwin.

Wootton, B. (1959) *Social Science and Social Pathology*. London: George, Allen and Unwin.

Part 1

FEMINISM CHALLENGES CRIMINOLOGY'S DOMAIN ASSUMPTIONS

1

THE ETIOLOGY OF FEMALE CRIME

Dorie Klein

Source: *Issues in Criminology*, 8:2 (1973), 3–30.

Introduction

The criminality of women has long been a neglected subject area of criminology. Many explanations have been advanced for this, such as women's low official rate of crime and delinquency and the preponderance of male theorists in the field. Female criminality has often ended up as a footnote to works on men that purport to be works on criminality in general.

There has been, however, a small group of writings specifically concerned with women and crime. This paper will explore those works concerned with the etiology of female crime and delinquency, beginning with the turn-of-the-century writing of Lombroso and extending to the present. Writers selected to be included have been chosen either for their influence on the field, such as Lombroso, Thomas, Freud, Davis and Pollak, or because they are representative of the kinds of work being published, such as Konopka, Vedder and Somerville, and Cowie, Cowie and Slater. The emphasis is on the continuity between these works, because it is clear that, despite recognizable differences in analytical approaches and specific theories, the authors represent a tradition to a great extent. It is important to understand, therefore, the shared assumptions made by the writers that are used in laying the groundwork for their theories.

The writers see criminality as the result of *individual* characteristics that are only peripherally affected by economic, social and political forces. These characteristics are of a *physiological* or *psychological* nature and are uniformly based on implicit or explicit assumptions about the *inherent nature of women*. This nature is *universal*, rather than existing within a specific historical framework.

Since criminality is seen as an individual activity, rather than as a condition built into existing structures, the focus is on biological, psychological and social factors that would turn a woman toward criminal activity. To do this, the writers create two distinct classes of women: good women who are 'normal' non-criminals, and bad women who are criminals, thus taking a moral position that often masquerades as a scientific distinction. The writers, although they may be biological or social determinists to varying degrees, assume that individuals have *choices* between criminal and non-criminal activity. They see persons as atomistically moving about in a social and political vacuum; many writers use marketplace models for human interaction.

Although the theorists may differ on specific remedies for individual criminality, ranging from sterilization to psychoanalysis (but always stopping far short of social change), the basic thrust is toward *individual adjustment*, whether it be physical or mental, and the frequent model is rehabilitative therapy. Widespread environmental alterations are usually included as casual footnotes to specific plans for individual therapy. Most of the writers are concerned with *social harmony* and the welfare of the existing social structure rather than with the women involved or with women's position in general. None of the writers come from anything near a 'feminist' or 'radical' perspective.

In *The Female Offender*, originally published in 1903, Lombroso described female criminality as an inherent tendency produced in individuals that could be regarded as biological atavisms, similar to cranial and facial features, and one could expect a withering away of crime if the atavistic people were prohibited from breeding. At this time criminality was widely regarded as a physical ailment, like epilepsy. Today, Cowie, Cowie and Slater (1968) have identified physical traits in girls who have been classified as delinquent, and have concluded that certain traits, such as bigness, may lead to aggressiveness. This theme of physiological characteristics has been developed by a good number of writers in the last seventy years, such as the Gluecks (Glueck and Glueck, 1934). One sees at the present time a new surge of 'biological' theories of criminality; for example, a study involving 'violence-prone' women and menstrual cycles has recently been proposed at UCLA.[1]

Thomas, to a certain degree, and Freud extend the physiological explanation of criminality to propose a psychological theory. However, it is critical to understand that these psychological notions are based on assumptions of universal *physiological* traits of women, such as their reproductive instinct and passivity, that are seen as invariably producing certain psychological reactions. Women may be viewed as turning to crime as a *perversion of* or *rebellion against* their *natural feminine roles*. Whether their problems are biological, psychological or social-environmental, the point is always to return them to their roles. Thomas (1907, 1923), for example, points out that poverty might prevent a woman from marrying, whereby she would turn to prostitution as an alternative to carry on her feminine service role. In fact, Davis (1961) discusses prostitution as a parallel illegal institution to marriage. Pollak (1950) discusses how women extend their service roles into criminal activity due to inherent tendencies such as deceitfulness. Freud (1933, Jones, 1961) sees any kind of rebellion as the result of a failure to develop healthy feminine attitudes, such as narcissism, and Konopka (1966) and Vedder and Somerville (1970) apply Freudian thought to the problem of female delinquency.

The specific characteristics ascribed to women's nature and those critical to theories of female criminality are uniformly *sexual* in their nature. Sexuality is seen as the root of female behavior and the problem of crime. Women are defined as sexual beings, as sexual capital in many cases, physiologically, psychologically and socially. This definition *reflects* and *reinforces* the economic position of women as reproductive and domestic workers. It is mirrored in the laws themselves and in their enforcement, which penalize sexual deviations for women and may be more lenient with economic offenses committed by them, in contrast to the treatment given men. The theorists accept the sexual double standard inherent in the law, often noting that 'chivalry' protects women, and many of them build notions of the universality of *sex repression* into their explanations of women's position. Women are thus the sexual backbone of civilization.

In setting hegemonic standards of conduct for all women, the theorists define *femininity*, which they equate with healthy femaleness, in classist, racist and sexist terms, using their assumptions of women's nature, specifically their sexuality, to justify what is often in reality merely a defense of the existing order. Lombroso, Thomas and Freud consider the upper-class white woman to be the highest expression of femininity, although she is inferior to the upper-class white man. These standards are adopted by later writers in discussing femininity. To most theorists, women are inherently inferior to men at masculine tasks such as thought and production, and therefore it is logical that their sphere should be reproductive.

Specific characteristics are proposed to bolster this sexual ideology, expressed for example by Freud, such as passivity, emotionalism, narcissism and deceitfulness. In the discussions of criminality, certain theorists, such as Pollak, link female criminality to these traits. Others see criminality as an attempt away from femininity into masculinity, such as Lombroso, although the specifics are often confused. Contradictions can be clearly seen, which are explained by the dual nature of 'good' and 'bad' women and by the fact that this is a mythology attempting to explain real behavior. Many explanations of what are obviously economically motivated offenses, such as prostitution and shoplifting, are explained in sexual terms, such as prostitution being promiscuity, and shoplifting being 'kleptomania' caused by women's inexplicable mental cycles tied to menstruation. Different explanations have to be made for 'masculine' crimes, e.g., burglary, and for 'feminine' crimes, e.g., shoplifting. Although this distinction crops up consistently, the specifics differ wildly.

The problem is complicated by the lack of knowledge of the epidemiology of female crime, which allows such ideas as 'hidden crime', first expressed by Pollak (1950), to take root. The problem must be considered on two levels: women, having been confined to certain tasks and socialized in certain ways, are *in fact* more likely to commit crime related to their lives which are sexually oriented; yet even nonsexual offenses are *explained* in sexual terms by the theorists. The writers ignore the problems of poor and Third World women, concentrating on affluent white standards of femininity. The experiences of these overlooked women, who *in fact* constitute a good percentage of women caught up in the criminal justice system, negate the notions of sexually motivated crime. These women have real economic needs which are not being met, and in many cases engage in illegal activities as a viable economic alternative. Furthermore, chivalry has never been extended to them.

The writers largely ignore the problems of sexism, racism and class, thus their work is sexist, racist and classist in its implications. Their concern is adjustment of the woman to society, not social change. Hence, they represent a tradition in criminology and carry along a host of assumptions about women and humanity in general. It is important to explore these assumptions and traditions in depth in order to understand what kinds of myths have been propagated around women and crime. The discussions of each writer or writers will focus on these assumptions and their relevance to criminological theories. These assumptions of universal, biological/psychological characteristics, of individual responsibility for crime, of the necessity for maintaining social harmony, and of the benevolence of the state link different theories along a continuum, transcending political labels and minor divergences. The road from Lombroso to the present is surprisingly straight.

Lombroso: 'there must be some anomaly . . .'

Lombroso's work on female criminality (1920) is important to consider today despite the fact that his methodology and conclusions have long been successfully discredited. Later writings on female crime by Thomas, Davis, Pollak and others use more sophisticated methodologies and may proffer more palatable liberal theories. However, to varying degrees they rely on those sexual ideologies based on *implicit* assumptions about the physiological and psychological nature of women that are *explicit* in Lombroso's work. Reading the work helps to achieve a better understanding of what kinds of myths have been developed for women in general and for female crime and deviance in particular.

One specific notion of women offered by Lombroso is women's physiological immobility and psychological passivity, later elaborated by Thomas, Freud and other writers. Another ascribed characteristic is the Lombrosian notion of women's adaptability to surroundings and their capacity for survival as being superior to that of men. A third idea discussed by Lombroso is women's amorality: they are cold and calculating. This is developed by Thomas (1923), who describes women's manipulation of the male sex urge for ulterior purposes; by Freud (1933), who sees women as avenging their lack of penis on men; and by Pollak (1950), who depicts women as inherently deceitful.

When one looks at these specific traits, one sees contradictions. The myth of compassionate women clashes with their reputed coldness; their frailness belies their capacity to survive. One possible explanation for these contradictions is the duality of sexual ideology with regard to 'good' and 'bad' women.[2] Bad women are whores, driven by lust for money or for men, often essentially 'masculine' in their orientation, and perhaps afflicted with a touch of penis envy. Good women are chaste, 'feminine', and usually not prone to criminal activity. But when they are, they commit crime in a most *ladylike* way such as poisoning. In more sophisticated theory, all women are seen as having a bit of both tendencies in them. Therefore, women can be compassionate *and* cold, frail *and* sturdy, pious *and* amoral, depending on which path they choose to follow. They are seen as rational (although they are irrational, too!), atomistic individuals making choices in a vacuum, prompted only by personal, physiological/psychological factors. These choices relate only to the *sexual* sphere. Women have no place in any other sphere. Men, on the other hand, are not held sexually accountable, although, as Thomas notes (1907), they are held responsible in *economic* matters. Men's sexual freedom is justified by the myth of masculine, irresistible sex urges. This myth, still worshipped today, is frequently offered as a rationalization for the existence of prostitution and the double standard. As Davis maintains, this necessitates the parallel existence of classes of 'good' and 'bad' women.

These dual moralities for the sexes are outgrowths of the economic, political and social *realities* for men and women. Women are primarily workers within the family, a critical institution of reproduction and socialization that services such basic needs as food and shelter. Laws and codes of behavior for women thus attempt to maintain the smooth functioning of women in that role, which requires that women act as a conservative force in the continuation of the nuclear family. Women's main tasks are sexual, and the law embodies sexual limitations for women, which do not exist for men, such as the prohibition of promiscuity for girls. This explains why theorists of female criminality are not only concerned with sexual violations by female offenders, but attempt to account for even *non-sexual* offenses, such as prostitution, in sexual terms, e.g., women enter prostitution for sex rather than for money. Such women are not only economic offenders but are sexual deviants, falling neatly into the category of 'bad' women.

The works of Lombroso, particularly *The Female Offender* (1920), are a foremost example of the biological explanation of crime. Lombroso deals with crime as an atavism, or survival of 'primitive' traits in individuals, particularly those of the female and non-white races. He theorizes that individuals develop differentially within sexual and racial limitations which differ hierarchically from the most highly developed, the white men, to the most primitive, the non-white women. Beginning with the assumption that criminals must be atavistic, he spends a good deal of time comparing the crania, moles, heights etc. of convicted criminals and prostitutes with those of normal women. Any trait that he finds to be more common in the 'criminal' group is pronounced an atavistic trait, such as moles, dark hair, etc., and women with a number of these telltale traits could be regarded as potentially criminal, since they are of the atavistic type. He specifically rejects the idea that some of these traits, for example obesity in prostitutes, could be the *result* of their activities rather than an indicator of their propensity to them. Many of the traits depicted as 'anomalies', such as darkness and shortness, are characteristic of certain racial groups, such as the Sicilians, who undoubtedly comprise an oppressed group within Italy and form a large part of the imprisoned population.

Lombroso traces an overall pattern of evolution in the human species that accounts for the uneven development of groups: the white and non-white races, males and females, adults and children. Women, children and non-whites share many traits in common. There are fewer variations in their mental capacities: 'even the female criminal is monotonous and uniform compared with her male companion, just as in general woman is inferior to man' (1920: 122), due to her being 'atavistically nearer to her origin than the male' (1920: 107). The notion of women's mediocrity, or limited range of mental possibilities, is a recurrent one in the writings of the twentieth century. Thomas and others note that women comprise 'fewer geniuses, fewer lunatics and fewer morons' (Thomas, 1907: 45); lacking the imagination to be at either end of the spectrum, they are conformist and dull . . . not due to social, political or economic constraints on their activities, but because of their innate physiological limitations as a sex. Lombroso attributes the lower female rate of criminality to their having fewer anomalies, which is one aspect of their closeness to the lower forms of less differentiated life.

Related characteristics of women are their passivity and conservatism. Lombroso admits that women's traditional sex roles in the family bind them to a more sedentary life. However, he insists that women's passivity can be directly traced to the 'immobility of the ovule compared with the zoosperm' (1920: 109), falling back on the sexual act in an interesting anticipation of Freud.

Women, like the lower races, have greater powers of endurance and resistance to mental and physical pain than men. Lombroso states: 'denizens of female prisons . . . have reached the age of 90, having lived within those walls since they were 29 without any grave injury to health' (1920: 125). Denying the humanity of women by denying their capability for suffering justifies exploitation of women's energies by arguing for their suitability to hardship. Lombroso remarks that 'a duchess can adapt herself to new surroundings and become a washerwoman much more easily than a man can transform himself under analogous conditions' (1920: 272). The theme of women's adaptability to physical and social surroundings, which are male initiated, male controlled, and often expressed by saying that women are actually the 'stronger' sex, is a persistent thread in writings on women.

Lombroso explains that because women are unable to feel pain, they are insensitive to the pain of others and lack moral refinement. His blunt denial of the age-old myth of women's compassion and sensitivity is modified, however, to take into account women's low crime rate:

> Women have many traits in common with children; that their moral sense is deficient; that they are revengeful, jealous . . . In ordinary cases these defects are neutralized by piety, maternity, want of passion, sexual coldness, weakness and an undeveloped intelligence.
>
> (1920: 151)

Although women lack the higher sensibilities of men, they are thus restrained from criminal activity in most cases by lack of intelligence and passion, qualities which *criminal* women possess as well as all *men*. Within this framework of biological limits of women's nature, the female offender is characterized as *masculine* whereas the normal woman is *feminine*. The anomalies of skull, physiognomy and brain capacity of female criminals, according to Lombroso, more closely approximate that of the man, normal or criminal, than they do those of the normal woman; the female offender often has a 'virile cranium' and considerable body hair. Masculinity in women is an anomaly itself, rather than a sign of development, however. A related notion is developed by Thomas, who notes that in 'civilized' nations the sexes are more physically different.

> What we look for most in the female is femininity, and when we find the opposite in her, we must conclude as a rule that there must be some anomaly . . . Virility was one of the special features of the savage woman . . . In the portraits of Red Indian and Negro beauties, whom it is difficult to recognize for women, so huge are their jaws and cheekbones, so hard and coarse their features, and the same is often the case in their crania and brains.
>
> (1907: 112)

The more highly developed races would therefore have the most feminized women with the requisite passivity, lack of passion, etc. This is a *racist* and *classist* definition of femininity – just as are almost all theories of *femininity* and as, indeed, is the thing itself. The ideal of the lady can only exist in a society built on the exploitation of labor to maintain the woman of leisure who can *be* that ideal lady.

Finally, Lombroso notes women's lack of *property sense*, which contributes to their criminality.

> In their eyes theft is . . . an audacity for which account compensation is due to the owner . . . as an individual rather than a social crime,

> just as it was regarded in the primitive periods of human evolution and is still regarded by many uncivilized nations.
>
> (1920: 217)

One may question this statement on several levels. Can it be assumed to have any validity at all, or is it false that women have a different sense of property than men? If it is valid to a degree, is it related to women's lack of property ownership and non-participation in the accumulation of capitalist wealth? Indeed, as Thomas (1907) points out, women are considered property themselves. At any rate, it is an interesting point in Lombroso's book that has only been touched on by later writers, and always in a manner supportive of the institution of private property.

Thomas: 'the stimulation she craves'

The works of W. I. Thomas are critical in that they mark a transition from purely physiological explanations such as Lombroso's to more sophisticated theories that embrace physiological, psychological and social-structural factors. However, even the most sophisticated explanations of female crime rely on implicit assumptions about the *biological* nature of women. In Thomas's *Sex and Society* (1907) and *The Unadjusted Girl* (1923), there are important contradictions in the two approaches that are representative of the movements during that period between publication dates: a departure from biological Social-Darwinian theories to complex analyses of the interaction between society and the individual, i.e., societal repression and manipulation of the 'natural' wishes of persons.

In *Sex and Society* (1907), Thomas poses basic biological differences between the sexes as his starting point. Maleness is 'katabolic', the animal force which is destructive of energy and allows men the possibility of creative work through this outward flow. Femaleness is 'anabolic', analogous to a plant which stores energy, and is motionless and conservative. Here Thomas is offering his own version of the age-old male/female dichotomy expressed by Lombroso and elaborated on in Freud's paradigm, in the structural-functionalist 'instrumental-expressive' duality, and in other analyses of the status quo. According to Thomas, the dichotomy is most highly developed in the more civilized races, due to the greater differentiation of sex roles. This statement ignores the hard physical work done by poor *white* women at home and in the factories and offices in 'civilized' countries, and accepts a *ruling-class* definition of femininity.

The cause of women's relative decline in stature in more 'civilized' countries is a subject on which Thomas is ambivalent. At one point he attributes it to the lack of 'a superior fitness on the motor side' in women (1907: 94); at another point, he regards her loss of *sexual freedom* as critical, with the coming of monogamy and her confinement to sexual tasks such as wifehood and motherhood. He perceptively notes:

> Women were still further degraded by the development of property and its control by man, together with the habit of treating her as a piece of property, whose value was enhanced if its purity was assured.
> (1907: 297)

However, Thomas's underlying assumptions in his explanations of the inferior status of women are *physiological* ones. He attributes to men high amounts of sexual energy, which lead them to pursue women for their sex, and he attributes to women maternal feelings devoid of sexuality, which lead *them* to exchange sex for domesticity. Thus monogamy, with chastity for women, is the *accommodation* of these basic urges, and women are domesticated while men assume leadership, in a true market exchange.

Why, then, does Thomas see problems in the position of women? It is because modern women are plagued by 'irregularity, pettiness, ill health and inserviceableness' (1907: 245). Change is required to maintain *social harmony*, apart from considerations of women's needs, and women must be educated to make them better wives, a theme reiterated throughout this century by 'liberals' on the subject. Correctly anticipating a threat, Thomas urges that change be made to stabilize the family, and warns that 'no civilization can remain the highest if another civilization adds to the intelligence of its men the intelligence of its women' (1907: 314). Thomas is motivated by considerations of social integration. Of course, one might question how women are to be able to contribute much if they are indeed anabolic. However, due to the transitional nature of Thomas's work, there are immense contradictions in his writing.

Many of Thomas's specific assertions about the nature of women are indistinguishable from Lombroso's; they both delineate a biological hierarchy along race and sex lines.

> Man has, in short, become more somatically specialized an animal than woman, and feels more keenly any disturbance of normal conditions with which he has not the same physiological surplus as woman with which to meet the disturbance . . . It is a logical fact, however, that the lower human races, the lower classes of society, women and children show something of the same quality in their superior tolerance of surgical disease.
> (1907: 36)

Like Lombroso, Thomas is crediting women with superior capabilities of survival because they are further down the scale in terms of evolution. It is significant that Thomas includes the lower classes in his observation; is he implying that the lower classes are in their position *because* of their natural unfitness, or perhaps that their *situation* renders them less sensitive to pain? At different times, Thomas implies both. Furthermore, he agrees with Lombroso that women are more nearly uniform than men, and says that they have a smaller percentage of 'genius, insanity and idiocy' (1907: 45) than men, as well as fewer creative outbursts of energy.

Dealing with female criminality in *Sex and Society* (1907), Thomas begins to address the issue of morality, which he closely links to legality from a standpoint of maintaining social order. He discriminates between male and female morality:

> Morality as applied to men has a larger element of the contractual, representing the adjustment of his activities to those of society at large, or more particularly to the activities of the male members of society; while the morality which we think of in connection with women shows less of the contractual and more of the personal, representing her adjustment to men, more particularly the adjustment of her person to men.
>
> (1907: 172)

Whereas Lombroso barely observes women's lack of participation in the institution of private property, Thomas's perception is more profound. He points out that women *are* property of men and that their conduct is subject to different codes.

> Morality, in the most general sense, represents the code under which activities are best carried on and is worked out in the school of experience. It is preeminently an adult and male system, and men are intelligent enough to realize that neither women nor children have passed through this school. It is on this account that man is merciless to woman from the standpoint of personal behavior, yet he exempts her from anything in the way of contractual morality, or views her defections in this regard with allowance and even with amusement.
>
> (1907: 234)

Disregarding his remarks about intelligence, one confronts the critical point about women with respect to the law: because they occupy a *marginal* position in the productive sphere of exchange commodities outside the home, they in turn occupy a marginal position in regard to 'contractual' law which regulates relations of property and production. The argument of differential treatment of men and women by the law is developed in later works by Pollak and others, who attribute it to the 'chivalry' of the system which is lenient to women committing offenses. As Thomas notes, however, women are simply not a serious *threat* to property, and are treated more 'leniently' because of this. Certain women do become threats by transcending (or by being denied) their traditional role, particularly many Third World women and political rebels, and they are *not* afforded chivalrous treatment! In fact, chivalry is reserved for the women who are least likely to ever come in contact with the criminal justice system: the ladies, or white middle-class women. In matters of *sexual* conduct, however, which embody the double standard, women are rigorously prosecuted by the law. As Thomas understands, this is the sphere in which women's functions *are* critical. Thus it is not a matter of 'chivalry' how one is handled, but of different forms and thrusts of social control applied to men and women. Men are engaged in productive tasks and their activities in this area *are* strictly curtailed.

In *The Unadjusted Girl* (1923), Thomas deals with female delinquency as a 'normal' response under certain social conditions, using assumptions about the nature of women which he leaves unarticulated in this work. Driven by basic 'wishes', an individual is controlled by society in her activities through institutional transmission of codes and mores. Depending on how they are manipulated, wishes can be made to serve social or antisocial ends. Thomas stresses the institutions that socialize, such as the family, giving people certain 'definitions of the situation'. He confidently – and defiantly – asserts:

> There is no individual energy, no unrest, no type of wish, which cannot be sublimated and made socially useful. From this standpoint, the problem is not the right of society to protect itself from the disorderly and antisocial person, but the right of the disorderly and antisocial person to be made orderly and socially valuable . . . The problem of society is to produce the right attitudes in its members.
> (1923: 232–3)

This is an important shift in perspective, from the traditional libertarian view of protecting society by punishing transgressors, to the *rehabilitative* and *preventive* perspective of crime control that seeks to control *minds* through socialization rather than to merely control behavior through punishment. The autonomy of the individual to choose is seen as the product of his environment which the state can alter. This is an important refutation of the Lombrosian biological perspective, which maintains that there are crime-prone individuals who must be locked up, sterilized or otherwise incapacitated. Today, one can see an amalgamation of the two perspectives in new theories of 'behavior control' that use tactics such as conditioning and brain surgery, combining biological and environmental viewpoints.[3]

Thomas proposes the manipulation of individuals through institutions to prevent antisocial attitudes, and maintains that there is no such person as the 'crime prone' individual. A hegemonic system of belief can be imposed by sublimating natural urges and by correcting the poor socialization of slum families. In this perspective, the *definition* of the situation rather than the situation *itself* is what should be changed; a situation is what someone *thinks* it is. The response to a criminal woman who is dissatisfied with her conventional sexual roles is to change not the roles, which would mean widespread social transformations, but to change her attitudes. This concept of civilization as repressive and the need to adjust is later refined by Freud.

Middle-class women, according to Thomas, commit little crime because they are socialized to sublimate their natural desires and to behave well, treasuring their chastity as an investment. The poor woman, however, 'is not immoral, because this implies a loss of morality, but amoral' (1923: 98). Poor women are not objectively driven to crime; they long for it. Delinquent girls are motivated by the desire for excitement or 'new experience', and forget the repressive urge of 'security'. However, these desires are well within Thomas's conception of *femininity*: delinquents are not rebelling against womanhood, as Lombroso suggests, but merely acting it out illegally. Davis and Pollak agree with this notion that delinquent women are not 'different' from non-delinquent women.

Thomas maintains that it is not sexual desire that motivates delinquent girls, for they are no more passionate than other women, but they are *manipulating* male desires for sex to achieve their own ulterior ends.

> The beginning of delinquency in girls is usually an impulse to get amusement, adventure, pretty clothes, favorable notice, distinction, freedom in the larger world . . . The girls have usually become 'wild' before the development of sexual desire, and their casual sex relations do not usually awaken sex feeling. Their sex is used as a condition of the realization of other wishes. It is their capital.
>
> (1923: 109)

Here Thomas is expanding on the myth of the manipulative woman, who is cold and scheming and vain. To him, good female sexual behavior is a protective measure – 'instinctive, of course' (1907: 241), whereas male behavior is uncontrollable as men are caught by helpless desires. This is the common Victorian notion of the woman as seductress which in turn perpetuates the myth of a lack of real sexuality to justify her responsibility for upholding sexual mores. Thomas uses a market analogy to female virtue: good women *keep* their bodies as capital to sell in matrimony for marriage and security, whereas bad women *trade* their bodies for excitement. One notes, of course, the familiar dichotomy. It is difficult, in this framework, to see how Thomas can make *any* moral distinctions, since morality seems to be merely good business sense. In fact, Thomas's yardstick is social harmony, necessitating *control.*

Thomas shows an insensitivity to real human relationships and needs. He also shows ignorance of economic hardships in his denial of economic factors in delinquency.

> An unattached woman has a tendency to become an adventuress not so much on economic as on psychological grounds. Life is rarely

> so hard that a young woman cannot earn her bread; but she cannot always live and have the stimulation she craves.
>
> (1907: 241)

This is an amazing statement in an era of mass starvation and illness! He rejects economic causes as a possibility at all, denying their importance in criminal activity with as much certainty as Lombroso, Freud, Davis, Pollak and most other writers.

Freud: 'beauty, charm and sweetness'

The Freudian theory of the position of women is grounded in explicit biological assumptions about their nature, expressed by the famous 'Anatomy is Destiny'. Built upon this foundation is a construction incorporating psychological and social-structural factors.

Freud himself sees women as anatomically inferior; they are destined to be wives and mothers, and this is admittedly an inferior destiny as befits the inferior sex. The root of this inferiority is that women's *sex organs* are inferior to those of men, a fact *universally* recognized by children in the Freudian scheme. The girl assumes that she has lost a penis as punishment, is traumatized, and grows up envious and revengeful. The boy also sees the girl as having lost a penis, fears a similar punishment himself, and dreads the girl's envy and vengeance. Feminine traits can be traced to the inferior genitals themselves, or to women's inferiority complex arising from their response to them: women are exhibitionistic, narcissistic, and attempt to compensate for their lack of a penis by being well dressed and physically beautiful. Women become mothers trying to replace the lost penis with a baby. Women are also masochistic, as Lombroso and Thomas have noted, because their *sexual* role is one of receptor, and their sexual pleasure consists of pain. This woman, Freud notes, is the *healthy* woman. In the familiar dichotomy, the men are aggressive and pain inflicting. Freud comments:

> The male pursues the female for the purposes of sexual union, seizes hold of her, and penetrates into her . . . by this you have precisely reduced the characteristic of masculinity to the factor of aggressiveness.
>
> (Millett, 1970: 189)

Freud, like Lombroso and Thomas, takes the notion of men's activity and women's inactivity and *reduces* it to the sexual level, seeing the sexual union itself through Victorian eyes: ladies don't move.

Women are also inferior in the sense that they are concerned with personal matters and have little social sense. Freud sees civilization as based on repression of the sex drive, where it is the duty of men to repress their strong instincts in order to get on with the worldly business of civilization. Women, on the other hand,

> have little sense of justice, and this is no doubt connected with the preponderance of envy in their mental life; for the demands of justice are a modification of envy; they lay down the conditions under which one is willing to part with it. We also say of women that their social interests are weaker than those of men and that their capacity for the sublimation of their instincts is less.
>
> (1933: 183)

Men are capable of sublimating their individual needs because they rationally perceive the Hobbesian conflict between those urges and social needs. Women are emotional and incapable of such an adjustment because of their innate inability to make such rational judgements. It is only fair then that they should have a marginal relation to production and property.

In this framework, the deviant woman is one who is attempting to be a *man*. She is aggressively rebellious, and her drive to accomplishment is the expression of her longing for a penis; this is a hopeless pursuit, of course, and she will only end up 'neurotic'. Thus the deviant woman should be treated and helped to *adjust* to her sex role. Here again, as in Thomas's writing, is the notion of individual accommodation that repudiates the possibility of social change.

In a Victorian fashion, Freud rationalizes women's oppression by glorifying their duties as wives and mothers:

> It is really a stillborn thought to send women into the struggle for existence exactly the same as men. If, for instance, I imagined my sweet gentle girl as a competitor, it would only end in my telling her, as I did seventeen months ago, that I am fond of her, and I implore her to withdraw from the strife into the calm, uncompetitive activity of my home . . . Nature has determined woman's destiny through beauty, charm and sweetness . . . in youth an adored darling, in mature years a loved wife.
>
> (Jones, 1961: 117–18)

In speaking of femininity, Freud, like his forebears, is speaking along racist and classist lines. Only upper- and middle-class women could possibly enjoy lives as sheltered darlings. Freud sets hegemonic standards of femininity for poor and Third World women.

It is important to understand Freudianism because it reduces categories of sexual ideology to explicit sexuality and makes these categories *scientific*. For the last fifty years, Freudianism has been a mainstay of sexist social theory. Kate Millett notes that Freud himself saw his work as stemming the tide of feminist revolution, which he constantly ridiculed:

> Coming as it did, at the peak of the sexual revolution, Freud's doctrine of penis envy is in fact a superbly timed accusation, enabling masculine sentiment to take the offensive again as it had not since the disappearance of overt misogyny when the pose of chivalry became fashionable.
>
> (Millett, 1970: 189)

Freudian notions of the repression of sexual instincts, the sexual passivity of women, and the sanctity of the nuclear family are conservative not only in their contemporary context, but in the context of their own time. Hitler writes:

> For her [woman's] world is her husband, her family, her children and her home . . . The man upholds the nation as the woman upholds the family. The equal rights of women consist in the fact that in the realm of life determined for her by nature, she experience the high esteem that is her due. Woman and man represent quite different types of being. Reason is dominant in man . . . Feeling, in contrast, is much more stable than reason, and woman is the feeling, and therefore the stable, element.
>
> (Millett, 1970: 170)

One can mark the decline in the position of women after the 1920s through the use of various indices: by noting the progressively earlier age of marriage of women in the United States and the steady rise in the number of children born to them, culminating in the birth explosion of the late 1940s and 1950s; by looking at the relative decline in the number of women scholars; and by seeing the failure to liberate women in the Soviet Union and the rise of fascist sexual ideology. Freudianism has had an unparalleled influence in the United States (and came at a key point to help swing the tide against the women's movement) to facilitate the return of women during the depression and postwar years to the home, out of an economy which had no room for them. Freud affected such writers on female deviance as Davis, Pollak and Konopka, who turn to concepts of sexual maladjustment and neurosis to explain women's criminality. Healthy women would now be seen as masochistic, passive and sexually indifferent. Criminal women would be seen as *sexual* misfits. Most importantly, *psychological* factors would be used to explain criminal activity, and social, economic and political factors would be ignored. Explanations would seek to be *universal*, and historical possibilities of change would be refuted.

Davis: 'the most convenient sexual outlet for armies . . .'

Kingsley Davis's work on prostitution (1961) is still considered a classical analysis on the subject with a structural-functionalist perspective. It employs assumptions about 'the organic nature of man' and woman, many of which can be traced to ideas proffered by Thomas and Freud.

Davis sees prostitution as a structural necessity whose roots lie in the *sexual* nature of men and women; for example, female humans, unlike primates, are sexually available year-round. He asserts that prostitution is *universal* in time and place, eliminating the possibilities of historical change and ignoring critical differences in the quality and quantity of prostitution in different societies. He maintains that there will always be a class of women who will be prostitutes, the familiar class of 'bad' women. The reason for the universality of prostitution is that sexual *repression*, a concept stressed by Thomas and Freud, is essential to the functioning of society. Once again there is the notion of sublimating 'natural' sex urges to the overall needs of society, namely social order. Davis notes that in our society sexuality is permitted only within the structure of the nuclear family, which is an institution of stability. He does not, however, analyse in depth the economic and social functions of the family, other than to say it is a bulwark of morality.

> The norms of every society tend to harness and control the sexual appetite, and one of the ways of doing this is to link the sexual act to some stable or potentially stable social relationship . . . Men dominate women in economic, sexual and familial relationships and consider them to some extent as sexual property, to be prohibited to other males. They therefore find promiscuity on the part of women repugnant.
>
> (1961: 264)

Davis is linking the concept of prostitution to promiscuity, defining it as a *sexual* crime, and calling prostitutes sexual transgressors. Its origins, he claims, lie not in economic hardship, but in the marital restraints on sexuality. As long as men seek women, prostitutes will be in demand. One wonders why sex-seeking women have not created a class of male prostitutes.

Davis sees the only possibility of eliminating prostitution in the liberalization of sexual mores, although he is pessimistic about the likelihood of total elimination. In light of the contemporary American 'sexual revolution' of commercial sex, which has surely created more prostitutes and semi-prostitutes rather than eliminating the phenomenon, and in considering the revolution in China where, despite a 'puritanical' outlook on sexuality, prostitution has largely been eliminated through major economic and social change, the superficiality of Davis's approach becomes evident. Without dealing with root economic, social and political factors, one cannot analyse prostitution.

Davis shows Freudian pessimism about the nature of sexual repression:

> We can imagine a social system in which the motive for prostitution would be completely absent, but we cannot imagine that the system

> will ever come to pass. It would be a regime of absolute sexual freedom with intercourse practiced solely for pleasure by both parties. There would be no institutional control of sexual expression . . . All sexual desire would have to be mutually complementary . . . Since the basic causes of prostitution – the institutional control of sex, the unequal scale of attractiveness, and the presence of economic and social inequalities between classes and between males and females – are not likely to disappear, prostitution is not likely to disappear either.
>
> (1961: 286)

By talking about 'complementary desire', Davis is using a marketplace notion of sex: two attractive or unattractive people are drawn to each other and exchange sexual favors; people are placed on a scale of attractiveness and may be rejected by people above them on the scale; hence they (*men*) become frustrated and demand prostitutes. Women who become prostitutes do so for good pay *and* sexual pleasure. Thus one has a neat little system in which everyone benefits.

> Enabling a small number of women to take care of the needs of a large number of men, it is the most convenient sexual outlet for armies, for the legions of strangers, perverts and physically repulsive in our midst.
>
> (1961: 288)

Prostitution 'functions', therefore it must be good. Davis, like Thomas, is motivated by concerns of social order rather than by concerns of what the needs and desires of the women involved might be. He denies that the women involved are economically oppressed; they are on the streets through autonomous, *individual* choice.

> Some women physically enjoy the intercourse they sell. From a purely economic point of view, prostitution comes near the situation of getting something for nothing . . . Women's wages could scarcely be raised significantly without also raising men's. Men would then have more to spend on prostitution.
>
> (1961: 277)

It is important to understand that, given a *sexual* interpretation of what is an *economic* crime, and given a refusal to consider widespread change (even equalization of wages, hardly a revolutionary act), Davis's conclusion is the logical technocratic solution.

In this framework, the deviant women are merely adjusting to their feminine role in an illegitimate fashion, as Thomas has theorized. They are *not* attempting to be rebels or to be 'men', as Lombroso's and Freud's positions suggest. Although Davis sees the main difference between wives and prostitutes in a macrosocial sense as the difference merely between legal and illegal roles, in a personal sense he sees the women who *choose* prostitution as maladjusted and neurotic. However, given the universal necessity for prostitution, this analysis implies the necessity of having a perpetually ill and maladjusted class of women. Thus oppression is *built into* the system, and a healthy *system* makes for a sick *individual.* Here Davis is integrating Thomas's notions of social integration with Freudian perspectives on neurosis and maladjustment.

Pollak: 'a different attitude toward veracity'

Otto Pollak's *The Criminality of Women* (1950) has had an outstanding influence on the field of women and crime, being the major work on the subject in the postwar years. Pollak advances the theory of 'hidden' female crime to account for what he considers unreasonably low official rates for women.

A major reason for the existence of hidden crime, as he sees it, lies in the *nature* of women themselves. They are instigators rather than perpetrators of criminal activity. While Pollak admits that this role is partly a socially enforced one, he insists that women are inherently deceitful for *physiological* reasons.

> Man must achieve an erection in order to perform the sex act and will not be able to hide his failure. His lack of positive emotion in the sexual sphere must become overt to the partner, and pretense of sexual response is impossible for him, if it is lacking. Woman's body, however, permits such pretense to a certain degree and lack of orgasm does not prevent her ability to participate in the sex act.
> (1950: 10)

Pollak *reduces* women's nature to the *sex act*, as Freud has done, and finds women inherently more capable of manipulation, accustomed to being sly, passive and passionless. As Thomas suggests, women can use sex for ulterior purposes. Furthermore, Pollak suggests that women are innately deceitful on yet another level:

> Our sex mores force women to conceal every four weeks the period of menstruation . . . They thus make concealment and misrepresentation in the eyes of women socially required and must condition them to a different attitude toward veracity than men.
> (1950: 11)

Women's abilities at concealment thus allow them to successfully commit crimes in stealth.

Women are also vengeful. Menstruation, in the classic Freudian sense, seals their doomed hopes to become men and arouses women's desire for vengeance, especially during that time of the month. Thus Pollak offers new rationalizations to bolster old myths.

A second factor in hidden crime is the roles played by women which furnish them with opportunities as domestics, nurses, teachers and housewives to commit undetectable crimes. The *kinds* of crimes women commit reflect their nature: false accusation, for example, is an outgrowth of women's treachery, spite or fear and is a sign of neurosis; shoplifting can be traced in many cases to a special mental disease – kleptomania. Economic factors play a minor role; *sexual-psychological* factors account for female criminality. Crime in women is *personalized* and often accounted for by mental illness.

Pollak notes:

> Robbery and burglary . . . are considered specifically male offenses since they represent the pursuit of monetary gain by overt action . . . Those cases of female robbery which seem to express a tendency toward masculinization come from . . . [areas] where social conditions have favored the assumptions of male pursuits by women . . . The female offenders usually retain some trace of femininity, however, and even so glaring an example of masculinization as the 'Michigan Babes,' an all woman gang of robbers in Chicago, shows a typically feminine trait in the modus operandi.
>
> (1950: 29)

Pollak is defining crimes with economic motives that employ overt action as *masculine*, and defining as *feminine* those crimes for *sexual* activity, such as luring men as baits. Thus he is using circular reasoning by saying that feminine crime is feminine. To fit women into the scheme and justify the statistics, he must invent the notion of hidden crime.

It is important to recognize that, to some extent, women *do* adapt to their enforced sexual roles and may be more likely to instigate, to use sexual traps, and to conform to all the other feminine role expectations. However, it is not accidental that theorists label women as conforming even when they are *not*; for example, by inventing sexual motives for what are clearly crimes of economic necessity, or by invoking 'mental illness' such as kleptomania for shoplifting. It is difficult to separate the *theory* from the *reality*, since the reality of female crime is largely unknown. But it is not difficult to see that Pollak is using sexist terms and making sexist assumptions to advance theories of hidden female crime.

Pollak, then, sees criminal women as extending their sexual role, like Davis and Thomas, by using sexuality for ulterior purposes. He suggests that the condemnation of extramarital sex has 'delivered men who engage in such conduct as practically helpless victims' (1950: 152) into the hands of women blackmailers, overlooking completely the possibility of men blackmailing women, which would seem more likely, given the greater taboo on sex for women and their greater risks of being punished.

The final factor that Pollak advances as a root cause of hidden crime is that of 'chivalry' in the criminal justice system. Pollak uses Thomas's observation that women are differentially treated by the law, and carries it to a sweeping conclusion based on *cultural* analyses of men's feelings toward women.

> One of the outstanding concomitants of the existing inequality . . . is chivalry, and the general protective attitude of man toward woman . . . Men hate to accuse women and thus indirectly to send them to their punishment, police officers dislike to arrest them, district attorneys to prosecute them, judges and juries to find them guilty, and so on.
>
> (1950: 151)

Pollak rejects the possibility of an actual discrepancy between crime rates for men and women; therefore, he must look for factors to expand the scope of female crime. He assumes that there is chivalry in the criminal justice system that is extended to the women who come in contact with it. Yet the women involved are likely to be poor and Third World women or white middle-class women who have stepped *outside* the definitions of femininity to become hippies or political rebels, and chivalry is *not* likely to be extended to them. Chivalry is a racist and classist concept founded on the notion of women as 'ladies' which applies only to wealthy white women and ignores the double sexual standard. These 'ladies', however, are the least likely women to ever come in contact with the criminal justice system in the first place.[4]

The legacy of sexism

A major purpose in tracing the development and interaction of ideas pertaining to sexual ideology based on implicit assumptions of the inherent nature of women throughout the works of Lombroso, Thomas, Freud, Davis and Pollak, is to clarify their positions in relation to writers in the field today. One can see the influence their ideas still have by looking at a number of contemporary theorists on female criminality. Illuminating examples can be found in Gisela Konopka's *Adolescent Girl in Conflict* (1966), Vedder and Somerville's *The Delinquent Girl* (1970) and Cowie, Cowie and Slater's *Delinquency in Girls* (1968). The ideas in these minor works have direct roots in those already traced in this paper.

Konopka justifies her decision to study delinquency in girls rather than in boys by noting girls' *influence* on boys in gang fights and on future generations as mothers. This is the notion of women as instigators of men and influencers on children.

Konopka's main point is that delinquency in girls can be traced to a specific emotional response: loneliness.

> What I found in the girl in conflict was . . . loneliness accompanied by despair. Adolescent boys too often feel lonely and search for understanding and friends. Yet in general this does not seem to be the central core of their problems, not their most outspoken ache. While these girls also strive for independence, their need for dependence is unusually great.
>
> (1966: 40)

In this perspective, girls are driven to delinquency by an emotional problem – loneliness and dependency. There are *inherent* emotional differences between the sexes.

> Almost invariably her [the girl's] problems are deeply personalized. Whatever her offense – whether shoplifting, truancy or running away from home – it is usually accompanied by some disturbance or unfavorable behavior in the sexual area.
>
> (1966: 4)

Here is the familiar resurrection of female personalism, emotionalism, and above all, *sexuality* – characteristics already described by Lombroso, Thomas and Freud. Konopka maintains:

> The delinquent girl suffers, like many boys, from lack of success, lack of opportunity. But her drive to success is never separated from her need for people, for interpersonal involvement.
>
> (1966: 41)

Boys are 'instrumental' and become delinquent if they are deprived of the chance for creative success. However, girls are 'expressive' and happiest dealing with people as wives, mothers, teachers, nurses or psychologists. This perspective is drawn from the theory of delinquency as a result of blocked opportunity and from the instrumental/expressive sexual dualism developed by structural-functionalists. Thus female delinquency must be dealt with on this *psychological* level, using therapy geared to their needs as future wives and mothers. They should be *adjusted* and given *opportunities* to be pretty, sociable women.

The important point is to understand how Konopka analyses the roots of girls' feelings. It is very possible that, given women's position, girls may be in fact more concerned with dependence and sociability. One's understanding of this, however, is based on an understanding of the historical position of women and the nature of their oppression. Konopka says:

> What are the reasons for this essential loneliness in girls? Some will be found in the nature of being an adolescent girl, in her biological make-up and her particular position in her culture and time.
>
> (1966: 41)

Coming from a Freudian perspective, Konopka's emphasis on female emotions as cause for delinquency, which ignores economic and social factors, is questionable. She employs assumptions about the *physiological* and *psychological* nature of women that very well may have led her to see only those feelings in the first place. For example, she cites menstruation as a significant event in a girl's development. Thus Konopka is rooted firmly in the tradition of Freud and, apart from sympathy, contributes little that is new to the field.[5]

Vedder and Somerville (1970) account for female delinquency in a manner similar to that of Konopka. They also feel the need to justify their attention to girls by remarking that (while female delinquency may not pose as much of a problem as that of boys) because women raise families and are critical agents of socialization, it is worth taking the time to study and control them. Vedder and Somerville also stress the dependence of girls on boys and the instigatory role girls play in boys' activities.

Like Freud and Konopka, the authors view delinquency as blocked access or maladjustment to the normal feminine role. In a blatant statement that ignores the economic and social factors that result from racism and poverty, they attribute the high rates of delinquency among black girls to their lack of 'healthy' feminine narcissism, *reducing* racism to a psychological problem in totally sexist and racist terms.

> The black girl is, in fact, the antithesis of the American beauty. However loved she may be by her mother, family and community, she has no real basis of female attractiveness on which to build a sound feminine narcissism . . . Perhaps the 'black is beautiful' movement will help the Negro girl to increase her femininity and personal satisfaction as a black woman.
>
> (1970: 159–60)

Again the focus is on a lack of *sexual* opportunities for women, i.e., the Black woman is not Miss America. *Economic* offenses such as shoplifting are explained as outlets for *sexual* frustration. Since healthy women conform, the individual delinquents should be helped to adjust; the emphasis is on the 'definition of the situation' rather than on the situation.

The answer lies in *therapy*, and racism and sexism become merely psychological problems.

> Special attention should be given to girls, taking into consideration their constitutional biological and psychological differences, and

> their social position in our male dominated culture. The female offender's goal, as any woman's, is a happy and successful marriage; therefore her self-image is dependent on the establishment of satisfactory relationships with the opposite sex. The double standard for sexual behavior on the part of the male and female must be recognized.
>
> (1970: 153)

Like Konopka, and to some extent drawing on Thomas, the authors see female delinquents as extending femininity in an illegitimate fashion rather than rebelling against it. The assumptions made about women's goals and needs, including *biological* assumptions, lock women into a system from which there is no escape, whereby any behavior will be sexually interpreted and dealt with.

The resurgence of biological or physiological explanations of criminality in general has been noteworthy in the last several years, exemplified by the XYY chromosome controversy and the interest in brain waves in 'violent' individuals.[6] In the case of women, biological explanations have *always* been prevalent; every writer has made assumptions about anatomy as destiny. Women are prey, in the literature, to cycles of reproduction, including menstruation, pregnancy, maternity and menopause; they experience emotional responses to these cycles that make them inclined to irrationality and potentially violent activity.

Cowie, Cowie and Slater (1968) propose a *chromosomal* explanation of female delinquency that hearkens back to the works of Lombroso and others such as Healy (Healy and Bronner, 1926), Edith Spaulding (1923) and the Gluecks (Glueck and Glueck, 1934). They write:

> The chromosomal difference between the sexes starts the individual on a divergent path, leading either in a masculine or feminine direction . . . It is possible that the methods of upbringing, differing somewhat for the two sexes, may play some part in increasing the angle of this divergence.
>
> (Cowie et al., 1968: 171)

This is the healthy, normal divergence for the sexes. The authors equate *masculinity* and *femininity* with *maleness* and *femaleness*, although contemporary feminists point out that the first categories are *social* and the latter ones *physical*.[7] What relationship exists between the two – how femaleness determines femininity – is dependent on the larger social structure. There is no question that a wide range of possibilities exist historically, and in a non-sexist society it is possible that 'masculinity' and 'femininity' would disappear, and that the sexes would differ only biologically, specifically by their sex organs. The authors, however, lack this understanding and assume an ahistorical sexist view of women, stressing the *universality* of femininity in the Freudian tradition, and of women's inferior role in the nuclear family.[8]

In this perspective, the female offender is *different* physiologically and psychologically from the 'normal' girl.

The authors conclude, in the tradition of Lombroso, that female delinquents are *masculine*. Examining girls for physical characteristics, they note:

> Markedly masculine traits in girl delinquents have been commented on . . . [as well as] the frequency of homosexual tendencies . . . Energy, aggressiveness, enterprise and the rebelliousness that drives the individual to break through conformist habits are thought of as being masculine . . . We can be sure that they have some physical basis. (1968: 172)

The authors see crime as a *rebellion* against sex roles rather than as a maladjusted expression of them. By defining rebellion as *masculine*, they are ascribing characteristics of masculinity to any female rebel. Like Lombroso, they spend time measuring heights, weights, and other *biological* features of female delinquents with other girls.

Crime defined as masculine seems to mean violent, overt crime, whereas 'ladylike' crime usually refers to sexual violations and shoplifting. Women are neatly categorized no matter *which* kind of crime they commit: if they are violent, they are 'masculine' and suffering from chromosomal deficiencies, penis envy, or atavisms. If they conform, they are manipulative, sexually maladjusted and promiscuous. The *economic* and *social* realities of crime – the fact that poor women commit crimes, and that most crimes for women are property offenses – are overlooked. Women's behavior must be *sexually* defined before it will be considered, for women count only in the sexual sphere. The theme of sexuality is a unifying thread in the various, often contradictory theories.

Conclusion

A good deal of the writing on women and crime being done at the present time is squarely in the tradition of the writers that have been discussed. The basic assumptions and technocratic concerns of these writers have produced work that is sexist, racist and classist; assumptions that have served to maintain a repressive ideology with its extensive apparatus of control. To do a new kind of research on women and crime – one that has feminist roots and a radical orientation – it is necessary to understand the assumptions made by the traditional writers and to break away from them. Work that focuses on human needs, rather than those of the state, will require new definitions of criminality, women, the individual and her/his relation to the state. It is beyond the scope of this paper to develop possible areas of study, but it is none the less imperative that this work be made a priority by women *and* men in the future.

Notes

1 Quoted from the 1973 proposal for the Center for the Study and Reduction of Violence prepared by Dr Louis J. West, Director, Neuropsychiatric Institute, UCLA: 'The question of violence in females will be examined from the point of view that females are more likely to commit acts of violence during the pre-menstrual and menstrual periods' (1973: 43).

2 I am indebted to Marion Goldman for introducing me to the notion of the dual morality based on assumptions of different sexuality for men and women.

3 For a discussion of the possibilities of psychosurgery in behavior modification for 'violence-prone' individuals, see Frank Ervin and Vernon Mark, *Violence and the Brain* (1970). For an eclectic view of this perspective on crime, see the proposal for the Center for the Study and Reduction of Violence (note 1).

4 The concept of hidden crime is reiterated in Reckless and Kay's report to the President's Commission on Law Enforcement and the Administration of Justice. They note:

> A large part of the infrequent officially acted upon involvement of women in crime can be traced to the masking effect of women's roles, effective practice on the part of women of deceit and indirection, their instigation of men to commit their crimes (the Lady Macbeth factor), and the unwillingness on the part of the public and law enforcement officials to hold women accountable for their deeds (the chivalry factor).
>
> (1967: 13)

5 Bertha Payak in 'Understanding the Female Offender' (1963) stresses that women offenders have poor self-concepts, feelings of insecurity and dependency, are emotionally selfish, and prey to irrationality during menstruation, pregnancy, and menopause (a good deal of their life!).

6 See Theodore R. Sarbin and Jeffrey E. Miller, 'Demonism revisited: the XYY chromosomal anomaly', *Issues in Criminology* 5(2), (1970).

7 Kate Millett notes that 'sex is biological, gender psychological and therefore cultural . . . if proper terms for sex are male and female, the corresponding terms for gender are masculine and feminine; these latter may be quite independent of biological sex' (1970: 30).

8 Zelditch (1960), a structural-functionalist, writes that the nuclear family is an inevitability and that within it, women, the 'expressive' sex, will inevitably be the domestics.

References

Bishop, C. (1931) *Women and Crime*. London: Chatto and Windus.

Cowie, J., Cowie V. and Slater, E. (1968) *Delinquency in Girls*. London: Heinemann.

Davis, K. (1961) 'Prostitution', in R. K. Merton and R. A. Nisbet (eds), *Contemporary Social Problems*. New York: Harcourt Brace and Jovanovich. Originally published as 'The sociology of prostitution', *American Sociological Review*, 1937, 2(5).

Ervin, F. and Mark, V. (1970) *Violence and the Brain*. New York: Harper and Row.

Freud, S. (1933) *New Introductory Lectures on Psychoanalysis*. New York: W.W. Norton.

Glueck, E. and Glueck, S. (1934) *Four Hundred Delinquent Women*. New York: Alfred A. Knopf.

Healy, W. and Bronner, A. (1926) *Delinquents and Criminals: their Making and Unmaking*. New York: Macmillan and Company.

Jones, E. (1961) *The Life and Works of Sigmund Freud*. New York: Basic Books.

Konopka, G. (1966) *The Adolescent Girl in Conflict*. Englewood Cliffs, NJ: Prentice-Hall.

Lombroso, C. (1920) *The Female Offender* (trans.). New York: Appleton. Originally published in 1903.

Millett, K. (1970) *Sexual Politics*. New York: Doubleday.

Monahan, F. (1941) *Women in Crime*. New York: I. Washburn.

Payak, B. (1963) 'Understanding the female offender', *Federal Probation*, XXVII.

Pollak, O. (1950) *The Criminality of Women*. Philadelphia: University of Pennsylvania Press.

Reckless, W. and Kay, B. (1967) *The Female Offender*. Report to the President's Commission on Law Enforcement and the Administration of Justice. Washington, DC: U.S. Government Printing Office.

Sarbin, T. R. and Miller, J. E. (1970) 'Demonism revisited: the XYY chromosomal anomaly', *Issues in Criminology*, 5(2) (Summer).

Spaulding, E. (1923) *An Experimental Study of Psychopathic Delinquent Women*. New York: Rand McNally.

Thomas, W. I. (1907) *Sex and Society*. Boston: Little, Brown.

Thomas, W. I. (1923) *The Unadjusted Girl*. New York: Harper and Row.

Vedder, C. and Somerville, D. (1970) *The Delinquent Girl*. Springfield, Ill.: Charles C. Thomas.

West, J. (1973) *Proposal for the Center for the Study and Reduction of Violence*. Neuropsychiatric Institute, UCLA (10 April).

Zelditch, M. Jr (1960) 'Role Differentiation in the nuclear family: a comparative study', in N. Bell and E. Vogel (eds), *The Family*. Glencoe, Ill.: The Free Press.

2

CRIMINOLOGICAL THEORY

Its ideology and implications concerning women

Carol Smart

Source: *British Journal of Sociology*, 28:1 (1977), 89–100.

Abstract

Classical and contemporary criminology has largely overlooked female criminality. This neglect has produced a situation in which analyses of this phenomenon have met no theoretically informed body of criticism and ideologically informed studies have become 'leading' works by default. The ideological underpinnings of these studies are based upon common-sense, uncritical understandings of female behaviour and upon a belief that deviant behaviour is caused by individual pathology. The combination of these factors has had certain implications for our present knowledge and understanding of female criminality and for the 'treatment' of female offenders. In particular the transformation of Holloway Prison into a secure psychiatric hospital is symbolic of social attitudes towards female offenders who are presumed to be 'sick' and who need help to re-adjust to their appropriate, traditional role. This paper attempts to outline the prevailing ideologies inherent in the major works on female criminality and to point to their implications. By so doing it is hoped that more critical interest in this area will be generated so that female criminality will not remain of such marginal interest to the new schools of thought that are developing inside criminology as it has been to the traditional schools.

Criminological theories have rarely been concerned with the analysis of female criminality. Typically criminologists have either been content to subsume discussion of women offenders under 'general' theories, that is to say they have implicitly assumed the female is dealt with in discussing the male, or they have dealt with them exceptionally briefly in the way that other 'marginal' or 'special' categories are treated. The reason offered for this overwhelming lack of interest is that within the population of known offenders, female offenders constitute a statistically much smaller proportion than male offenders. With the exception of offences like shoplifting and soliciting, the number of female offenders nowhere exceed the numbers of male offenders known to the police. But this statistical 'insignificance' alone cannot fully explain why so little work has been attempted in this area. Rather the relative absence of work on crimes by women may be considered as symbolic of the nature of the discipline of criminology. Traditional criminology in both the UK and the USA has always had close links with social and penal policy-making bodies with the result that research has tended to be directed towards areas officially designated as social problems. Female criminality has not generally been treated as a particularly important or pressing social problem, not only because of its comparative rarity, but also because of the nature of the offences committed by women. Official statistics, which are themselves a problematic source of information in criminology,[1] indicate that women engage mostly in petty offences and, with the exception of prostitutes, most appearances by women in court are for first offences. Women do not seem to pose a serious recidivist problem therefore; nor a threat to society, and so fail to constitute a real problem to the agencies of social control. Failing to become a pressing social problem has meant that studies of female criminality have not received much official support or finance with the result that traditional 'control oriented' criminology has also shown a lack of interest in this area.

The lack of attention devoted to the question of crimes committed by women and their treatment has given rise to the present unsatisfactory understanding of female offenders and the offences they commit. There has been virtually no development of our knowledge in this area with the result that ostensibly scientific works predicated upon unexplicated ideologies have been allowed to stand uncriticized. Recognition of the under-development of criminology and sociology in this area is explicit in Ward's statement to the U.S. National Commission on Crimes of Violence that:

> Our knowledge of the character and causes of female criminality is at the same stage of development that characterised our knowledge of male criminality some thirty or more years ago.[2]

As a consequence of this lack of development the ideology and methodological limitation inherent in some of the classical works on female criminality still inform contemporary studies and, furthermore, are reflected in the treatment of female offenders.

This paper is therefore concerned to reveal the ideological foundations of the major theories of female criminality, in particular the culturally relative, common-sense conceptions of women on which they are based. I shall concentrate on the works of Lombroso and Pollak, whose theories are still influential, as well as the work of Cowie, Cowie and Slater whose analysis of female delinquents reveals the influence of the early theorists.[3] The second part of this paper will focus on the possible implications of the ideologies inherent in these studies of female criminality.

The ideology of theories of female criminality

The most significant ideology which informs both classical and contemporary accounts of female criminality is a sexist ideology. It is sexist not because it differentiates between the sexes but because it attributes to one sex socially undesirable characteristics which are assumed to be intrinsic or 'natural' characteristics of that sex. Such an ideology arises because the socially structured and culturally given nature of the assumptions informing these theories are not treated as subjects for analysis; rather common-sense understandings are taken for granted as a suitable platform from which to commence theorizing. Working within the natural attitude, adopting culturally given understandings of the nature of sexual differences and in particular the characteristics attributed to women, the theorists concerned provide merely a scientific gloss for common-sense understandings. Myths about the 'inherent' evil in women or their lack of intelligence and ability and their 'natural' passivity therefore abound in these studies and they are used uncritically to supply 'evidence' for either the greater or lesser involvement of women in crime.

An equally persuasive theme implicit in most accounts of female criminality, which also stems from the uncritical attitudes of the pioneers in this field, is that of biological determinism. Biological determinist accounts may take two forms, although they are rarely mutually exclusive. Firstly women who have committed offences are perceived to have been motivated by fundamental biological bodily processes. For example, menstruation or the menopause, by affecting the hormonal balance in the body, are taken to be precipitating factors leading some women to commit criminal acts. In such cases action is seen to be directly related to, or even directly produced by, hormonal or biological imbalance. Secondly, and more significantly, the female biology is perceived to determine the temperament, intelligence, ability and aggression of women. In this case it is usually argued that women are 'naturally' averse to crime and hence any involvement in criminal activities is treated as symptomatic of a fundamental physical (or more recently mental) pathology. As a consequence of biological factors assuming such a key status in studies of female criminality it has followed that female offenders have been treated as a homogeneous group. Such factors as class, status, power, age, culture and so on are not considered as pertinent to an understanding of female criminality even though these variables are now accepted as relevant to the study of male criminality. As a result, therefore, of both the creation of a narrow stereotypical perception of women which relies upon culturally constituted understandings of the nature of female sexuality and the belief in biological determination, those women who do commit offences are judged to be either criminal by nature[4] or pathological because they deviate from the 'true' biologically determined nature of woman which is to be law abiding.[5] The latter perspective which treats female offenders as pathological is prevalent in both classical and contemporary criminological theories, one consequence of this being the continuing implementation of policy decisions predicated upon an understanding that criminal activity by women is a product of pathology located within the individual rather than an exemplification of meaningful action. Indeed it has become a 'popular' belief that women who commit criminal offences are 'sick' and in need of psychiatric treatment; it is to a much lesser extent that this 'sick' analogy has been adopted in the treatment of men as men are generally assumed to be rationally responsible for their actions while women are not.

This theme of the biological basis of female criminality which has become so entrenched in official and academic explanations was first fully formulated by Lombroso in his work entitled *The Female Offender* published in 1895. It is of course true that Lombroso employed biological factors to account for male criminality but with few exceptions this school of thought has been repudiated. As Shoham maintains,

> Today . . . . . , the Lombrosian myth in criminology, and the few contemporary adherents to the biophysiological approach to the genesis of crime, are considered a sad episode which retarded the development of the field by almost half a century.[6]

This is undoubtedly the case with most of Lombroso's theories and yet the ideological content of his work on female criminality persists in contemporary explanations. In particular his assertion that most women, with the exception of the rare 'born' criminal, are 'congenitally . . . less inclined to crime' and his belief that women's 'natural' passivity and conservatism robs them of the initiative to break the law have become a predominent part of the ideology in contemporary criminological and sociological theories.

The work of Cowie, Cowie and Slater (1968) is perhaps the best exemplar of a modified form of the ideology inherent in Lombroso's work. In analysing the differences between male and female delinquency they state,

> Differences between the sexes in hereditary predisposition (to crime) could be explained by sex-linked genes. Furthermore the female mode of personality, more timid, more lacking in enterprise, may guard her against delinquency.[7]

Clearly, Cowie, Cowie and Slater and other theorists who adopt similar positions, have taken no cognizance of cross-cultural studies nor of historical data which reveal that, rather than there being only one 'female mode of personality' there are a multitude of culturally and historically based sets of attitudes and expectations that influence the consciousness or personalities of women, thus producing gender-related behaviour. To suggest, for example, that women are 'more lacking in enterprise', or in the case of Lombroso, lead more sedentary lives because of their genetic structure, is to ignore the social situation facing many women which gives no opportunity or outlet for active or creative behaviour.

Interestingly, Lombroso maintains that one sure sign of criminality in women is the lack of a maternal instinct. This deficiency was perceived to mean that 'psychologically and anthropologically' the delinquent woman belongs more to the male than the female sex. But this belief, which is echoed in Cowie's work, is based on not only biological determinism but also on a confusion between sex and gender. As Ann Oakley[8] has pointed out sex is a biological term and gender a social, cultural and psychological term such that for a woman to act in a socially defined 'masculine' way does not mean that she is sexually or biologically abnormal. However, where gender appropriate behaviour is seen as biologically determined women who adopt 'masculine' forms of behaviour become labelled 'masculine' themselves and this has connotations of 'maleness' which are seen to be linked to hormonal or genetic abnormalities. Cowie *et al.* in fact failed to distinguish between sex and gender at all, they state,

> Is there any evidence that *masculinity or femininity of bodily constitution* plays any part in predisposing to delinquency and in determining the form it takes?
>
> (Emphasis added.)

In response to this question they maintain,

> Delinquents of both sexes tend to be larger than controls, and overgrown by population standards . . . Markedly masculine traits in girl delinquents have been commented on by psychoanalytic observers. . . . *we can be sure that they have had some physical basis.*
>
> (Emphasis added.)[9]

The point is that female delinquents are not perceived to be merely adopting behaviour more usually associated with males, they are portrayed as being chromosomally or genetically abnormal. This means that the 'treatment' of such offenders becomes justifiable, the aims, intentionality and rationality of the deviant act are overlooked and the social and cultural conditions under which the act took place can be relegated to the vague status of 'environmnetal' factors whose only role is to occasionally 'trigger' the inherent pathology of the deviant. Crime and delinquency can thereby be treated as an individual, not social, phenomenon.

Inherent in this 'individual pathology' model is a control oriented ideology which serves to locate the causes of 'problems' in specific individuals and which supplies the relevant knowledge and understanding to develop the appropriate technologies and social policies for controlling deviant members. Criminological theorizing thereby becomes a means of providing new technologies for control or, failing that, a means of legitimating current policies which become justified as forms of treatment rather than punishment. Moreover, while such theorizing is not concerned to provide the subjects of its study with the means to change their social situation and status it does provide a damaging anti-intellectual diet for its consumers which in fact serves to mystify the social phenomenon under research. For example, the way in which Cowie, Cowie and Slater present their evidence is worth noting for they attempt to appeal to the reader's 'senses' rather than intellect or critical faculties. They have a tendency to invoke 'common-sense' and concepts of the 'natural' to support their claims rather than relying on credible, scientific evidence. Rather than reducing the influence of their work however, their anti-theoretical and anti-intellectual approach may be conducive to acceptance by policy-makers who perceive themselves to be concerned with 'practical' issues and not theoretical ones. For example, Cowie *et al.* state,

> *Common-sense* suggests that the main factors are somatic ones, especially hormonal ones . . . . .
>
> (Emphasis added.)

and again later,

> *It is more natural to suppose* that the male–female difference, both in delinquency rates and in the forms that delinquency takes, would be closely connected with the masculine or feminine pattern of development of personality.
>
> (Emphasis added.)[10]

This debunking of a theoretical and intellectual approach to the topic may be seen as the witting embrace of ideology.[11]

I have implied that the work of Pollak[12] is also of considerable significance to the present state of our knowledge of female criminality. His work is broadly within the same ideological tradition of Lombroso and Cowie but the conclusions he draws show some interesting variations. For example, he does not assume that fewer women than men commit crimes; in fact, he argues that women are the most able criminals as biologically and socially they are well equipped for lying, deceiving and trickery. Consequently, he argues that they commit heinous crimes but are never apprehended and he thereby gives considerable support to the theological and common-sensical view that women are inherently more evil than men. He maintains in fact that women instigate crimes and manipulate the gullible male sex into enacting them, in other words women are the cause of the downfall of others.[13] The ability to be manipulative is, according to Pollak, due to the physiologically based fact that women can conceal their 'positive emotion' during sexual intercourse while men cannot as they must achieve an erection. He argues,

> It cannot be denied that this basic physiological difference may well have a great influence on the degree of confidence which the two sexes have in the possible success of concealment and thus on their character pattern in this respect.[14]

Thus, rather than considering the implications of the sexual politics which produce a situation in which many women face sexual intercourse when they are neither aroused nor willing, Pollak takes this example as a basis for further assumptions about women's ambiguous attitude towards 'veracity' and deceit.

There are numerous other examples in Pollak's work where his uncritical, anti-feminist presuppositions lead him to make authoritative but unsubstantiated statements about the origins of female criminality. In this respect his work cannot be differentiated from other ideologically informed works like Lombroso's and Cowie's. Where he does offer an important variation however, which is uniquely significant in terms of its implication, is in relation to the treatment of female offenders by the Courts and police. He maintains that the chivalrous attitude of men towards women, which is based on a misconception of women as gentle and passive creatures, leads them to treat female offenders more leniently than their male counterparts. He states

> One of the outstanding concomitants of the existing inequality between the sexes is chivalry and the general protective attitude of man towards woman . . . . . Men hate to accuse women and thus indirectly to send them to their punishment, police officers dislike to arrest them, district attorneys to prosecute them, judges and juries to find them guilty and so on.[15]

Such beliefs are still extremely prevalent both in common-sense and criminological accounts,[16] in spite of evidence which reveals that in sentencing, magistrates are more likely to be influenced by a previous record or the seriousness of the offence than the sex of offender[17] and that in some cases, particularly in so-called moral offences, female offenders are actually treated more severely[18] than male offenders. The implications of this ideology of chivalry and male benevolence are discussed in the next section.

The implications of the ideological content of theories of female criminality

The implications of theorizing have frequently been overlooked by those sociologists or criminologists who perceive themselves merely to be observers or recorders of everyday life. Yet social theories do have indirect social implications either by confirming common-sense and culturally located beliefs or by altering the consciousness of people in their everyday lives through a criticism and demystification of accepted values and beliefs. Allen recognizes this when he argues that,

> Theories enter into the ideological process and emerge in an abbreviated, often vulgarized, sloganized form embedded in language and thought processes alike. They form the basis of common-sense attitudes. They are transmitted through the family, enter into folklore, get expression through the mass media. In a variety of subtle ways conventional theoretical explanations enter the conscious of individuals and provide them with instant explanations.[19]

Although this process by which theories are translated into common conceptual currency will influence the actors own perception of self, our concern here is more with the way in which particular 'scientific' theories of female criminality, operating with conceptions of social science which indicate an interest in technical control rather than emancipation or liberation and emphasizing the biological and pathological nature of criminal offences, may have influenced and/or legitimated the conceptualizations of policy makers such that female criminality is, or continues to be, interpreted as a biologically-rooted sickness.

Indeed there is a clear trend within the English penal system towards adopting a concept of 'treatment' for offenders rather than, or in association with, punishment. This development may be simply indicative of an 'official' recognition of more 'efficient' means of controlling criminals than have been available in the past but it may also indicate a change in the conception of the motivational basis of criminality away from the classical concept of responsibility to a more positivistic orientation which emphasizes individual pathology.

The development is most marked in penal policies relating to female offenders. For example one consequence of the adoption of the 'sick' analogy for understanding what is defined as criminal motivation, is the transformation of Holloway from a prison to a secure psychiatric hospital in which women will receive psychiatric treatment related to their perceived individual psychological 'needs' rather than to their offence.[20] The assumption underlying this policy is that to deviate in a criminal way is 'proof' of some kind of mental imbalance in women. This position is quite consistent with other assumptions about the mental instability of women in general employed to explain or account for the mental health statistics which indicate that women suffer from mental illness more frequently than men.[21] In fact mental illness has been perceived as an alternative to crime for women[22]—both crime and mental illness being treated as phenomena emerging from common 'causes' rather than as possible rational and logical action.[23] Nigel Walker lends some credence to this practice when he states that,

> Certainly in practice women offenders have a higher chance of being dealt with as mentally abnormal . . . We cannot however exclude the possibility that psychiatrists' diagnoses . . . are being influenced by the . . . proposition . . . that there is probably something abnormal about a woman delinquent.[24]

The implications of the adoption of the 'sick' analogy in the treatment of female offenders does not merely rest with the introduction of therapeutic methods and the removal and denial of responsibility for action. It in fact creates a situation in which realistic and potentially self-determining educational and vocational courses are intentionally excluded or reduced in importance. The women in the new Holloway will not be able to work, except for therapeutic or general domestic work. They will not be given the opportunity to learn skills which will fundamentally improve their life-chances, not only because the average stay in Holloway is so short, but also because it is not the principal aim of penal policy for women. In fact their typically dependent status will be confirmed and their ability to control or possibly change their lifestyles further damaged. Penal policy for female offenders is geared to preserving the typical female role, its intention is to make women and girls adapt to their pre-given passive social role which by definition is thought to preclude deviant behaviour. The criminological theories discussed in the preceding section (with the exception of Pollak's work) all provide a justification for this policy because they support common-sense understandings of the 'natural' role and behaviour of women. Even if it is impossible to show that these theories of female criminality have precipitated some of the changes in the treatment of female criminals it can still be argued that the ideological basis of such works offers a 'scientistic' legitimation of social policy oriented towards an adoption of the 'sick' analogy, the development of more effective techniques of control and the perpetuation of the subordinate position of women.

Lastly, in considering the implication of these ideologically informed theories of female criminality, we must return to the idea of chivalry and male benevolence propounded by Pollak. While it is possible that sexual discrimination plays an important part in differential arrest and sentencing policy, it is misleading to assume that this discrimination is always in favour of the female sex. In fact it is difficult to reconcile the view that the police and legal system are staffed by 'chivalrous' men with reports on the treatment of female political prisoners,[25] prostitutes[26] and raped women.[27] It would seem that if sexual discrimination is an influential factor in the treatment of women it is not a simple variable that always leads to greater leniency. However the belief in chivalry and leniency has become a part of our (mis)understanding of the operation of the legal system and it has served to conceal the existence of unfavourable attitudes towards female offenders and the real injustice often meted out in the name of benevolence and paternalism.[28] The very existence of chivalry is synonymous with an inequality of power between the sexes in which a woman must depend on a man for her protection. Women must deserve their protection however, and women and girls of a 'bad moral' character who lose their rights in this respect, leave themselves open to the full force of outraged morality. It should also be remembered that the morality co-existent with chivalry imposes double-standards on men and women, frequently condoning the same behaviour in one sex while punishing it in the other. As Chesney-Lind maintains,

> These labels (immoral, incorrigible) allow for the same abuses that characterize the labels of 'sick' or 'insane'—that is, the 'saving' or 'helping' of a girl often justifies more radical and severe 'treatment' than does the punishment of a male law violator.[29]

The practice of sending adolescent girls to Approved Schools (now community homes) for being found 'in need of care and protection' or for being in 'moral danger' is an example of the double-edged nature of chivalry and paternalism. The Home Office statistics for 1960 reveal that while 95 per cent of boys are sent to Approved Schools for committing offences, only 36 per cent of girls are similarly committed. Consequently 64 per cent of these girls are committed to penal institutions without having committed any criminal offence.[30] The justification for this discrimination is often couched in humanitarian terms, for example as a form of protection or as an opportunity for moral guidance, but in practice it would seem that juvenile girls are punished severely for behaviour which is usually overlooked in boys. A similar case can be made for prostitutes who are socially stigmatized and punished for their behaviour while their clients remain respected members of society. Such inequitable treatment finds its justification in the ideology which underpins most of the theories of female criminality. Once it is accepted that deviant females are sick individuals or that they are naturally inclined to wrongdoing and this is combined with a belief in the 'benefits' of chivalry and paternalism it is not surprising that Cowie can make the statement that,

> These girls had to be removed from society into the security of a residential school much more for their own sakes than to protect

> society. *And yet, if one looks at their deliquent acts, they are of a very petty and trivial kind.*
>
> (Emphasis added.)[31]

The frequent injustice and the severity of the 'treatment' of female offenders or adolescents involved in so-called sexual or moral deviations is therefore veiled in humanitarianism. Moreover because the courts and other agents of social control reflect the double-standards of morality implicit in our socio-sexual mores and because their attitudes towards women are informed by a common-sense understanding of what a 'natural' female should be, negative discrimination towards women in 'sexual' offences, including rape cases, is overlooked. Theories of female criminality have tended to preserve this mystification and to justify the differential treatment of male and female offenders in terms of unexplicated assumptions about the 'true nature' of men and women. They have in no way served to clarify our understanding of a complex issue. It is to be hoped that new trends in the sociology of deviance and criminology will not merely replicate the major limitations of existing studies of female criminality by treating this phenomenon as marginal to a general understanding of the nature of crime in contemporary society.[32]

Notes

1 B. Hindess, *The Use of Official Statistics in Sociology*, Macmillan, 1973; P. N. P. Wiles, 'Criminal Statistics and Sociological Explanations of Crime' in P. Wiles and W. G. Carson (eds), *Crime and Delinquency*, Martin Robertson, 1970.
2 D. Ward, 'Crimes of Violence by Women', *A Report to the National U.S. Commission on Crimes of Violence*, 1968.
3 C. Lombroso, *The Female Offender*, Fisher Unwin, 1895; O. Pollak, *The Criminality of Women*, University of Pensylvania Press, 1950 (Perpetua Edition, 1961); J. Cowie, V. Cowie and E. Slater, *Delinquency in Girls*, Heinemann, 1968.
4 O. Pollak, op. cit.
5 C. Lombroso, op. cit; J. Cowie, op. cit.
6 S. G. Shoham, *Society and the Absurd*, Basil Blackwell, 1974, p. 117.
7 J. Cowie, op. cit., p. 167.
8 A. Oakley, *Sex, Gender and Society*, Temple Smith, 1972.
9 J. Cowie, op. cit., pp. 171–2.
10 J. Cowie, op. cit., pp. 170–71.
11 For a further example of this sort of anti-intellectual approach see G. Konopka, *The Adolescent Girl in Conflict*, Prentice Hall, 1966.
12 O. Pollak, op. cit.
13 A contemporary version of the belief that women cause the downfall of others, particularly men, is embodied in the 'maternal deprivation' debate which argues that unloving or rejecting mothers cause the delinquency and criminality of the next generation. See, for example, T. C. N. Gibbens, 'Female Offenders' in *British Journal of Hospital Medicine*, vol. 6, 1971, p. 280.
14 O. Pollak, op. cit., p. 10.
15 O. Pollak, op. cit., p. 151.

16 See, for example, A. Smith 'The Woman Offender' in L. Blom-Cooper, *Progress in Penal Reform*, Clarendon Press, 1974.
17 N. Walker, *Crime and Punishment in Britain*, University of Edinburgh Press, 1973, p. 300.
18 M. Chesney-Lind, 'Judicial Enforcement of the Female Sex Role: the Family Court and the Female Delinquent' in *Issues in Criminology*, vol. 8, no. 2 (1973).
19 V. L. Allen, 'The Common-Sense Guide to Industrial Relations' in *University of Leeds Review*, vol. 17, no. 1 (1974), p. 10.
20 D. E. R. Faulkner, 'The Redevelopment of Holloway Prison' in *The Howard Journal of Penology and Crime Prevention*, vol. 12, no. 2 (1971).
21 There is a considerable debate about whether women 'really' suffer from mental illness more than men or whether a male-oriented health service merely diagnoses women as mentally ill more readily than men. For part of the debate see P. Chester, *Women and Madness*, Allen Lane, 1974; D. L. Phillips and B. E. Segal, 'Sexual Status and Psychiatric Symptoms', *American Sociological Review*, vol. 34 (1969).
22 M. A. Bertrand, 'The Insignificance of Female Criminality', First Conference of the European Group for the Study of Deviance and Social Control, Florence, 1973.
23 R. D. Laing, *The Politics of Experience*, Penguin, 1968.
24 N. Walker, op. cit., p. 302.
25 A. Davis, *If they come in the morning . . .* , Orbach and Chambers, 1971.
26 K. Millett, *The Prostitution Papers*, Paladin, 1975; K. Davis, 'Prostitution' in R. K. Merton and R. Nisbet (eds), *Contemporary Social Problems*, Harcourt Brace and World, 1966.
27 S. Griffin, 'Rape: the All-American Crime', *Ramparts*, Sept. 1971; K. Weis and S. Borges 'Victimology and Rape', *Issues in Criminology*, vol. 8, no. 2 (1973).
28 R. M. Terry, 'Discrimination in the Handling of Juvenile Offenders by Social Control Agencies' in P. G. Garabedian (ed.), *Becoming Delinquent*, Aldine Press, 1970; M. Chesney-Lind, op. cit.
29 M. Chesney-Lind, op cit., pp. 57.
30 H. J. Richardson, *Adolescent Girls in Approved Schools*, Routledge & Kegan Paul, 1969.
31 J. Cowie, op cit., p. 166.
32 There are some indications that the area of women and crime is being treated more critically now. See, for example, *Issues in Criminology*, vol. 8, no. 2 (1973); K. E. Rosenblum, 'Female deviance and the female sex role: a preliminary investigation', *Brit. J. Sociol.*, vol. 26, no. 2 (1975). C. Smart, *Women, Crime and Criminology: A Feminist Critique*, Routledge & Kegan Paul, 1977.

3

THE DEVIANCE OF WOMEN

A critique and an enquiry

Frances Heidensohn

Source: *British Journal of Sociology*, 19:2 (1968), 160–75.

The purpose of this paper is quite simple: it is to focus on an obscure and largely ignored area of human behaviour, namely deviance in women. It is suggested

(*a*) that the problems associated with this neglect may, in themselves, be interesting from a sociological point of view.
(*b*) that the topic has both intrinsic interest for the sociologist today and that it has wider relevance to, for example, aspects of social structure.
(*c*) that, in so far as it is an example of possibly curious counter-tendencies to certain widespread trends in deviance, it may be of especial interest.

The deviance of women is one of the areas of human behaviour most notably ignored in sociological literature. This apparent lack of interest is remarkable for a number of reasons:

(*a*) Deviance in general (i.e. in practice either male and female deviance together or simply male deviance alone) has long aroused considerable interest. Since Durkheim argued[1] that 'deviant' or 'pathological' behaviour has social as well as individual aspects, the sociology of deviance has been an important and developing field of sociological theorizing and enquiry. Therefore the general unconcern with the potential deviance of approximately half the members of any human society is surprising.
(*b*) Interest in the changing position of women as it has affected marriage, the family and the division of roles within it has been considerable and has been productive of a vast range of studies, from, moreover, almost every known 'type' of sociologist: from American functionalist theoreticians to the more empirically-minded British.[2]

(*c*) As will be indicated below, differences between the patterns and manifestations of male and of female deviance were long ago observed;[3] they were observed, moreover, to differ with that kind of regularity and uniformity which normally attract the attention of the social scientist.[4]

Nevertheless the focus of research has been very much away from this particular area, so that a wide-ranging selection of readings on the sociology of crime and delinquency, published in 1962, did not contain one extract on female criminality.[5] Despite this gap, this has remained an often crucial, although unacknowledged dimension of deviance.

Of course, one can advance simple, straightforward reasons for this gap in sociological literature. Women appear to have low rates of participation in deviant activities as measured by such indices as official criminal statistics,[6] the range and number of their socially disapproved sexual outlets,[7] suicide rates,[8] involvement in activities labelled as vagrant,[9] and, although with certain provisos,[10] when defined as mentally ill.

(Perhaps it should be made clear at this point that the activities here selected are not put forward in any sense as integrated components of a comprehensive definition of deviant behaviour; they simply represent a range of categories, commonly thought of as deviant.[11] They thus correspond to the concept defined by Howard S. Becker:[12]

> deviance is not a quality of the act the person commits, but rather a consequence of the application by others of rules and sanctions to an 'offender'. The deviant is one to whom that label has successfully been applied; deviant behaviour is behaviour that people so label.[13]

These modes of behaviour also correspond to Lemert's secondary deviance in that they largely receive institutional reinforcement as deviating behaviour and may become deviant careers[14] for individuals resorting to them.)

Not only do woman *appear* to be remarkably conformist,[15] they seem to have consistently lower rates of deviance than men, with a fairly constant ratio which remains despite fluctuations in rates over time. (There is some suggestion of a diminution of this ratio in recent years, but data for the U.K. do not, on the whole, support this view.) It is perhaps therefore inevitable that male delinquents and deviants should be studied in preference to females: there are more of them and they thus have greater social visibility, are more accessible because more widespread, and are much more likely to appear—and be defined as—a pressing social problem. The last mentioned factor will ultimately affect the research funds available for a particular type of project.[16]

These reasons to some extent explain the concentration on male deviance, but not the almost total *exclusion* of studies of females from serious literature. One might argue that there is a strong element of pragmatism in this (as in so many other) areas of sociological research. Current focal concerns of society and especially of its rulers and policy-makers have a way of becoming the consuming interests of sociologists.[17] (Note the number of sociologists in the U.K. listed in a recent survey as working on the sociology of education and compare this with involvement of successive governments in educational research and reform.) Certainly students of the sociology of deviance have been often closely (often inevitably, for purposes of data collection) involved with the operators of the social control system. At the very least most workers in this field tend to approach their subject with the dual purposes of investigating then eradicating what they term social 'disorganization' or 'pathology'.[18]

Given this orientation amongst social pathologists, it is interesting to observe, as Professor Mays[19] did recently in a critical review, that concern over a subject—and notably that of juvenile delinquency—is in almost directly inverse relationship to the efficacy of policy. It may well be that the very formulation of a mode of behaviour as a 'problem area' for study may draw public and press attention to it and hence, through greater likelihood of reporting, stepped up police vigilance etc., immensely increase its dimensions; it has been suggested[20] that in the case of the 'Teddy boys' of the nineteen-fifties the 'menace' existed in the public mind long before any activities of the teenagers concerned warranted it.[21] One need not go as far as to argue that high rates of sociological interest in a problem area produce appropriately high 'problem situation' responses; but one might well be forgiven for wondering whether the deviance of women is a non-problem both to the social scientist and to society in general, because so little effort has been devoted to studying it. On one of the very few occasions in recent years that the deviant behaviour of women became a matter for public concern, the reaction of the committee set up to investigate it was to suggest that the social visibility of the activities should be so reduced that the public concern could largely cease,[22] although the deviant behaviour would continue.[23]

As was suggested earlier, when certain factors are taken into account, the picture of deviance amongst women, certainly in the U.K. since the early years of this century, has been an increasingly calm and conforming one. Of course, this statement must be heavily qualified, not least by the view that deviant women may have benefited far more than their male counterparts by the extension of the concept of the sick role and its more widespread application, in that women who might once have been adjudged 'delinquent' may now be defined as 'sick' and are hence excluded from the population of 'deviants'. Nevertheless, whatever the caveats it is broadly true to say that, for example, the number of women convicted for offences of drunkenness has declined very markedly since 1900, and *much more* rapidly than has the equivalent rate for men.[24] Similarly, it seems to be widely agreed that the numbers and proportion of women involved in prostitution has declined. Undoubtedly the legislation introduced after the Wolfenden Committee reported was aimed at minimizing the social visibility (and hence society's awareness) of prostitution, but this decline seems to be a common international trend.[25] Where indictable offences are concerned, the picture is more complex, but it appears that the numbers of women convicted for, for example, violent offences against the person tended to decline between the wars and began to rise again only after 1945. Rates of convictions of women for indictable offences have increased since the war, but for most categories of offences the proportionate rise has kept pace with the parallel rise in rates of males convicted although rarely has it been as high. This suggests several interpretations, among them that increased willingness to report offences, greater police efficiency in certain directions and a decrease in tolerance of crime amongst the public have affected female offenders only as much but no more than males; again what may either be a general increase in the opportunities for certain types of crime[26] or simply an overall rise in criminal activity has involved women to no greater extent than men.

The most curious feature of this analysis is that one would expect a *more than proportionate* rise in the conviction rates for women over this period; as Barbara Wootton has pointed out,[27] given that the participation of women in social, business and industrial life has been increasing steadily, one might expect a commensurate development in their criminal activities. That this does not appear to be the case reflects significantly upon the deviant behaviour of women and, perhaps more importantly, upon the societal reaction to it.

In this context of societal reaction to female deviance the legislation based upon the recommendations of the Wolfenden Committee[28] was very curious. Basically it rationalized and strengthened statutes against open soliciting, by abolishing the requirement of proven 'annoyance' as a basis for prosecution; yet it retained the term 'common prostitute', thereby preserving a process of damning the accused before conviction, let alone sentence which is, to say the least, unusual in English Law.[29] Thus, contrary to most modern trends in the growth of devices for labelling deviants and the increase in the number of categories available,[30] although the old style term was retained, its potential use was much reduced. For there seems to be widespread agreement that an effect of the 1959 Act was by 'driving' prostitution off the streets (and indeed, any public place) to make it more difficult to observe and check trends and also to 'catch' prostitutes and reform them. This was *anticipated* in the Report, as it was that middlemen, taxi-drivers, hotel porters, café proprietors, would enter the 'game' and make matters more complex and difficult to control.[31] That a society is prepared, while keeping its formal, deviant-defining structure to reduce the toll of those so defined and, indirectly, to lose some possibility of controlling them, is surely remarkable.

Many more notable features in the trends of delinquency reported amongst women can be observed—for instance, the sharp rises during the two world wars. Other forms of deviance, while more difficult to study from this point of view, seem to display also certain interesting and often unexpected characteristics: thus it has been suggested that the rising rates of illegitimacy are especially amongst middle class girls[32] and this may in part represent a deviant phenomenon of some dimensions—in terms, for example, of its rejection both of the accepted sexual mores of the group and its 'rational' ethic in regard to birth control.

But the most remarkable common feature of all the varied data on female deviance is the way in which it largely lacks consideration in the appropriate literature. Yet by any standards there would appear to be sufficient grounds for such study, either the pragmatic ones of concern for social problems, or the simple natural-historical one of wishing to observe, measure, categorize and discuss. The answer to this mystery seems to lie not so much in the reasons listed above but in the fact that most theories of crime or deviance within a sociological framework have to make passing reference to female behaviour. Most studies at least begin with the framework imposed by the legal system, which imposes exact definitions of categories of behaviour, and these are often treated as discrete and meaningful groupings.[33] Except for certain specific instances, such as rape, most legal provisions are considered as applying with equal force to both sexes.[34] Behaviourial categories *not* dealt with by law usually follow parallel forms in referring both to male and female deviance from them *as deviant* (although perhaps not always treating the misbehaviour of the two sexes as equally heinous). Any hypotheses put forward, any theories offered as explanation or for understanding deviant forms of behaviour are thus bound to take account of both male and female behaviour. Given the ubiquitous nature of the sex differential in crime and in deviance in general, any generalizing theory must point to factors which operate with very different effects upon men and upon women or, alternatively, that their like deviance is dealt with in very different manners by facets of the social system.[35] Indeed whether a particular theory explains feminine delinquency as well as masculine and offers within its framework an explanation for the apparent difference in rates is often a useful touchstone of its validity. Most sociologists working in this field are aware, with perhaps some discomfort, of the sex based variation in modes of, and participation in, deviance and do try to allow for it, however awkwardly.

The very stability and ubiquity of the sex differential in crime rates and other forms of deviance already instanced have meant that sociologists involved in the study of deviance have had to put forward explanatory theories based on the male and on masculine forms of acting out behaviour in a social frame—whether the behaviour was genetically determined, culturally framed or an adaptation based on responses to dysfunctional features of industrial/capitalist society. The female side, since it loomed much less significantly, was fitted in as an aspect of such explanations. Early theorists of crime and typologists of criminal behaviour, such as Lombroso, tended to suggest modes of behaviour not formally recognized as crime, notably prostitution, as available to women, but not men, hence their lower participation rates in 'normal' crime. More recent approaches have, like Lombroso, seen deviant behaviour as a single meaningful category of action, but have insisted that in practice the sexes choose different responses or 'outlets' for deviance because of socially prescribed focal concerns and structural characteristics of the social framework. The following brief outline of a few of these approaches will indicate some of their weaker points and suggest that their inadequacies stem from a fundamentally awkward and misconceived approach to the subject.

One major grouping (although it includes Pollak, a more recent writer) may be labelled the 'female iceberg' theorists, since they deny our current perception of the deviant situation and suggest that women are only too deviant but in a different, or a more successfully concealed, manner.[36] Lombroso and Ferrero argued that women criminals are essentially occasional rather than habitual, although they, like their masculine counterparts, had certain allegedly atavistic features, notably unfeminine features and build and dark masculine hair (sic). Lombroso also argued[37] that women would appear to be as criminal as men were their prostitutive activities included in the criminal statistics. In other words, prostitution is the female functional equivalent of crime. This view may be challenged on many counts: first and simply that prostitution appears to be in secular decline, while 'male' crime manifestly is not. Secondly, if female behaviour as in prostitution is not characterized as crime (although being, as it were, an ethical equivalent) *why is* this so? Surely a topic of considerable interest in itself. Thirdly female delinquency, as defined by Lombroso, consists of acts by definition involving men, in fact many more men than women.[38] Fourthly, as Davis (op. cit.) shows, prostitution flourishes when family ties are strong and the status of women, especially wives, is low. Hence the decline of prostitution in modern society—with the emancipation of women and rise in status—to be replaced by 'free, mutually pleasurable intercourse'. Can this also be defined as deviant? Finally, of course, there is the question of how the facts of female deviance, particularly the predominance of property offences, notably larceny, fit into this view.

Otto Pollak[39] saw the problem of 'explaining' female deviance in terms of feminine deviousness. Like Lombroso, he argues that much female deviance goes unrecorded, but unlike Lombroso he claims that women commit the same types of offences as men—and indeed have certain special opportunities for theft and murder—but that they are both equipped biologically to dissemble and socialized into so doing. They thus deviate as much as males but take advantage of their talents of dissembling and concealment and their positions in home and family to avoid discovery, and hence social awareness, of the deviant behaviour. This interpretation, although ingenious, begs far too many questions; to select a few of the more obvious: is there any evidence that hidden female crime is much greater than hidden male crime (such as embezzlement, white collar crime, 'knocking-off' in factories, docks, etc., motoring offences). These are likely to be *as least* as frequent, or, alternatively, quite as immeasurable. Pollak does not explain why some female deviance does surface and is 'processed'. Nor does he, any more than Lombroso, answer the query as to what functional needs of society are fulfilled by tacitly permitting women to engage in deviance such as murdering their families, seducing children and stealing from employers and clients.

Modern neofunctionalist theory[40] has made serious attempts to include female deviance in its scheme. The functionalist approach, stressing as it does the impact of social structural features on individuals and groups and also the structuring of situations which lead to opportunities for deviance, has had enormous influence on modern studies of deviance, notably on studies of juvenile delinquency, but also on aspects of mental health and illness, and, rather less directly, on studies of institutions. The concern of this approach has been especially with the effect of certain societal goals (and the structural means, or lack of them, for attaining them) and their impact on specific social groups found, or forced, to be inadequate in these terms, such as lower socio-economic groups, ethnic minorities of low status. The reaction, it is argued,[41] will be into forms of deviance, criminal or retreatist perhaps, depending on the availability of such subcultural opportunities. In these discussions it is assumed that growing adolescent males accept as the focal point of their lives the occupational/financial syndrome and that their actions can be interpreted in this light. It is argued (e.g. by Parsons and by Cohen) of girls, whose 'focal concerns' are said to be sexual and marital, that female delinquency follows different lines. Women are not required in our society to perform the same instrumental functions in the labour market or in support and protection of their families; their role, on the contrary, is to act through men, through whom they acquire status and are related to the economic system. As a result, sex, and their ability to bargain with it becomes their major interest. As Kingsley Davis puts it: 'Women must depend on sex for their social position much more than men do.' Hence women are more likely to be involved in violating sexual mores than in delinquent activities. The fullest statement of this view appears in G. H. Grosser, *Juvenile Delinquency and Contemporary American Sex Roles* (unpublished Ph.D. thesis, Harvard, 1951), where male and female delinquents are equally fully considered. It is apparent that a number of subsequent writers have delved into Grosser's theoretical formulations and relied on his empirical data—Cohen for one acknowledges such a debt. Yet another curious footnote to this whole discussion might be to wonder why this seminal work has remained unpublished.

These theoretical approaches which have been briefly stated and it is hoped, with a minimum of distortion, pose several initial and straightforward problems. First they ignore, or cannot subsume, substantive knowledge about deviance: their assumptions that young girls find 'role expression' through sexual delinquency rather than other forms of deviance are not borne out by the data, for example, in the U.K. where property offences remain the single largest category of offences—and where, for example, over the age of seventeen, female shoplifters exceed males. The reasons for the lower observed rates of deviant participation are nowhere fully articulated. Are they the result perhaps of sexual success being comparatively easier to obtain than occupational achievement—success criteria in the former context being rapidly fulfilled by marriage, which once achieved is a fairly plateau-like position, there being no promotion available? If this is so, then 'wayward' behaviour in girls may be seen as parallel to delinquency in boys; except that it can hardly be regarded in Grosser's terms as the moral equivalent of stealing, since theft accepts legitimate ends—the acquisition of goods, enhancement of life style, etc.—but rejects the legitimate means of attaining them. Promiscuous behaviour is then much more akin to the negativistic, anti-utilitarian theft-and-vandalism syndrome described by Cohen[42] which rejects both legitimate means and ends. Now this exegesis of one aspect of female deviance is surely overcomplex. Difficulties arise because the masculine and feminine poles of deviance have to be forced on to a single axis. Yet it is quite clear that this leads to the denial of certain characteristics of female deviance and of the nature and meaning of the modes of activity which comprise it. Thus Grosser, who, with his concept of sex-role-expressive behaviour, perhaps comes nearest to success in explanatory hypotheses concerning female deviance, still adds to a central confusion about sexuality and the female role. He talks, for example, of a continuum of female sex offences from *prostitutive* to *impulsive*; but these points represent surely essentially different types of behaviour in terms of its meaning to the actor. A single shot attack on received values (both bourgeois and respectable working-class) with regard to sexual behaviour—chastity, monogamy, sex should be linked to (responsible) procreation, etc.—can hardly be equated, either in its subjectively perceived aspects, or its societal effects, with any form of prostitution, whether 'casual' or fully professional, where an economic gain is one of the major concerns. This failure to see that prostitution is a deviant career structure, with its own economic organization and even apprenticeships and fee-splitting,[43] leads to it being equated with hysterical gestures of sexual deviance and actual sexual inversion. Yet basically, all they have in common in terms of situational definitions, is that women are, in both instances, being deviant in what Grosser calls a role-expressive way. This is merely tautological and has little analytical value as regards the problems of female deviance.

Possibly the most fruitful source of interpretation and analysis of female deviance in recent thinking could have been that of what Jack P. Gibbs has called the 'new perspective' of the study of societal reactions to deviance.[44] Examples of this approach suggest (in summary) that in contrast to what Gibbs calls the 'biological' approach and 'analytic' approach of previous studies attention should focus on the process of definitions of deviance and the labelling of deviants by means of a complex of feedbacks and reinforcements through societal reaction.

Gibbs chooses for analysis and critique statements from Kitsuse, Erikson and Becker, but the present writer would suggest that much of the work done by, for instance, Lemert[45] could also be included, while the contribution of Wilkins[46] is important too and the recent book by Scheff probably represents this approach carried to its ultimate conclusion.[47]

Such a view would seem to have considerable potential in examining some of the problems posed by female deviance: clearly the fact that this approach focuses on the societal reaction to deviance should make it illuminate an area apparently much influenced by social definitions and attitudes. It is rather remarkable, then, that very little work in this field appears to have been done. One of the few exceptions to this is Lemert's chapter on prostitution in his *Social Pathology*. Although his stated aim in this study is to examine the way in which primary deviance becomes reinforced and redefined into secondary deviance through societal reactions and personal definitions, in fact, when dealing with prostitution he concentrates on structural aspects of prostitution: the socio-economic background of prostitutes, occupations associated with prostitution, ecological factors and red light districts. While he indicates the type of women likely to drift into prostitution (e.g. unskilled migrants to urban areas) and suggests that there may be a process of self-definition involved, his actual analysis does not differ markedly from the structural functionalist form taken by Davis.[48]

In a sense, Lemert exemplifies, through his own implicit attitudes which emerge in this article, the importance of societal reaction to, and attitudes towards, deviance, and the process of defining deviance and the deviant. For instance, he begins by regarding prostitution as an example of *sexual deviation.*[49] Now, while the activities of a prostitute clearly deviate from the mores laid down for sexual relations—that is monogamy and fidelity, affection and desire, rather than cash, as the basis for intercourse—nevertheless from her own point of view, they are a 'normal' (within the subculture) instrumental means of earning a living. Bryan,[50] for instance, has shown how a rudimentary apprenticeship system exists in prostitution as a recognized means for girls to learn the ways of the 'game'. Autobiographical accounts of the careers of prostitutes also lay stress on the professional aspects of prostitution: the narrator of *Streetwalker* describes her annoyance at being expected to respond to a leer 'out of business hours' and her account of her discussions and gossip with another young prostitute and her landlady (who has retired from the streets) bear all the marks of occupational 'intalk'. Wayland Young[51] has instanced the learning and association patterns connected with prostitution, the passing on of skills, tricks and techniques. Again, Jackman *et al.*,[52] in their small-scale study of the prostitute's self-image demonstrate the existence of various 'strategies' for managing a career in prostitution despite the status denigration of the occupation; these appear to consist of taking an essentially instrumental view of the prostitute's role and its relation to her existence.[53]

The foregoing somewhat limited account of a number of approaches to female deviance should serve to demonstrate their common inadequacy and inappropriateness for the topic. This is not, of course, to deny that considerable illumination has emerged through many of these works. The point at issue is rather that much more meaningful insight and understanding might be obtained by other approaches, and that distortion of the inherent characteristics of the material is often a consequence of trying to force it into an inappropriate schematic or conceptual framework. Major common flaws appear to be grounded in the laudable scholarly aim of intellectual economy. Thus the sex differential in reported deviance (and the cultural perception of women as generally more conformist in social behaviour) was so ubiquitously observed that all theories of deviance have had to take some cognizance of it; however, they have tended to do so by constructing single, homogeneous hypotheses which account for both male and female deviance and their apparent differences. Thus Lombroso saw atavistic hysterical females taking prostitution as an alternative to 'normal' crime; Pollak, concentrating on opportunity structures, argues that women commit at least as much crime as men but conceal it better; the neofunctionalists (Grosser, Cohen, Cloward and Ohlin) claim that the focal concerns of the male in modern society are occupational and financial, for the female they are primarily sexual, hence the difference in deviance and patterns of deviance. All these views acknowledge differences in the social-structural components of sex roles even if only implicitly; they tend to ignore on the one hand the empirical realities of the deviance of women—e.g. the recorded figures on crime which demonstrate that the most (statistically) typical offence for females is theft as it is for males and that so-called sex offences by females tend to be a result of concern over protection of adolescent girls on the one hand or behaviour by prostitutes on the other, of which the latter can just conceivably be so defined, but is probably more helpfully perceived as occupational deviance.

Thus a much more meaningful approach would take female deviance as an aspect of the female sex role and its relationship with social structure, rather than trying to make it conform to patterns apparently observed in the male role and its particular articulation with social structure. It would analyse components of the role, alternative role sets, opportunities for role playing in society, supportive agencies available for aid in role playing, and would view the deviance of women as related to and within this perspective.[54]

Lest this should seem as fruitless a task as some of the attempts mentioned above, it is perhaps useful here to point to two very important contributions to the study of deviant women which have appeared in the last two years and both of which consider social structure in institutions for women.[55] Both these illuminating studies take as their starting point the roles of women in society and the consequent adaptation necessary within a total institution. Their findings not only throw light on institutional life for women—in showing, for instance, that feminine adaptation and structuring of social relations within prison tends to be in terms of homosexual roles (Ward and Kassebaum) or in familial/homosexual clusters (Giallombardo) rather than in occupational or criminal/political terms as in men's prisons[56]—they also throw considerable doubt on many assumptions and assertions about the impact of total institutions and the structuring of inmate society.[57]

Any survey of the literature indicates that at present we barely possess the basic components for an initial analysis of the deviance of women. These are lonely, uncharted seas of human behaviour. We lack, for this area, the rich resources of past documentation and research that one can call upon in studying male juvenile delinquency or alcoholism, we have no equivalent of *The Jackroller, The Professional Thief*, still less is there a *Delinquent Girls*. We start very much from scratch, although a recent book by a journalistic writer using a penetrating case-study technique[58] illustrates the kind of initial data required and which, apart from a few studies of prostitutes, by themselves and others, scarcely exist.

Despite the considerable groundwork which has to be put in, there can be little doubt that this will be rewarded by an interesting and valuable outcome. As was suggested in the introduction to this paper, this area qualifies for study both in its own right as being characterized by certain unusual features such as lower levels of deviance participation, differential perception and definition of this deviance by the community, and countertrends to contemporary patterns of deviance. But further as we have seen, neglect of this area and misapprehension about it make it peculiarly interesting to the sociologist of sociology and could perhaps make one wonder about the 'ideology' of social pathologists on this point.[59]

Greater knowledge of the sociology of female deviance would enhance our knowledge of feminine behaviour, of sex roles—their characteristics, norms and socializing processes associated with them; it would broaden our view of deviance in general and especially would it make more meaningful the study of male deviance by freeing it from an embarrassing need to include problems of female deviance.[60]

To summarize, what seems to be needed in the study of female deviance is a crash programme of research which telescopes decades of comparable studies of males. First of all we do not even begin to have a 'natural history' of female deviance, our knowledge of its parameters,[61] its structure and substructures, the types and nature of activities which make it up, are all exceedingly limited. Even those few sources which exist, such as the autobiographical accounts of prostitutes, have nowhere been systematically analysed and studied. Then, as Mannheim has admirably put it, we need to[62] 'avoid the frequent mistake of studying the subject solely under . . . comparative aspects . . . An objective and scientific approach should try to treat female crime as a topic in its own right. Nor, should [we] try to understand female criminality exclusively from the sexual angle.' But it seems at the same time desirable and likely to prove fruitful to continue some aspects of modern approaches, to take, for example, descriptions of the structures of modern societies and analyse how these provide a framework within which certain roles are acted out, such as those of the adolescent girl or the adult woman and how deviance occurs, is reinforced (or not) and deviant career patterns and roles for women emerge. Eventually, no doubt, it will be possible to reintegrate the study of male and female deviance, not simply for reasons of intellectual economy, but because a sociology of deviance can only be fully developed if it takes as its field *all* deviant phenomena. But first, of course, these phenomena must have been properly studied within their own context. Where the deviance of women is concerned, there may be a syndrome of 'modification' of female deviance within the social system, rather than the 'amplification' of deviance amongst adolescent males,[63] due perhaps to certain factors of the female role in society and social perceptions of its importance. At present such a suggestion must await further developments in the study of the deviance of women before we have sufficient material to begin to formulate it into fully fledged hypotheses. I hope that in this brief critical enquiry I have indicated some of the features that this research should not have, a few which it could possess and above all, the grounds for deeming it both a proper, necessary and potentially most interesting field for sociological enquiry.

Notes

1 *The Rules of Sociological Method*, Chicago, University of Chicago, 1938 (English translation), ch. III.
2 T. Parsons and R. F. Bales, *Family Socialization and Interaction Processes*, London, Routledge & Kegan Paul, 1955. W. J. Goode, *After Divorce*, New York, Free Press, 1956, as contrasted with the works of the Institute of Community Studies on women and family life, e.g. M. Young and P. Willmott, *Family and Kinship in East London*, London, Routledge & Kegan Paul, 1957, or the book by H. Gavron, *The Captive Wife*, London, Routledge & Kegan Paul, 1966.
3 By, e.g., Quetelet, *Recherches sur le penchant au crime*, 1838, and by Durkheim, *Suicide*, bk. 3, ch. II.
4 See L. Radzinowicz, 'Variability of the Sex Ratio of Criminality, *Soc. Rev.*, vol. 29 (1937).
5 M. E. Wolfgang, L. Savitz and N. Johnston, *The Sociology of Crime and Delinquency*, London, John Wiley, 1962.
6 Radzinowicz, op. cit.; H. Mannheim, *Comparative Criminology*, London, Routledge & Kegan Paul, 1965, vol. II, ch. 26.
7 A. Kinsey *et al., Sexual Behaviour in the Human Female*, London, Saunders, 1953; M. Schofield, *The Sexual Behaviour of Young People*, London, Longmans, 1965.
8 Durkheim, op. cit.
9 See, e.g., Philip O'Connor, *Britain in the Sixties: Vagrancy*, London, Penguin Books, 1961.
10 But see A. N. Little 'An "Expectancy" Estimate of Hospitalization Rates for Mental Illness in England and Wales'. *Brit. J. Sociol.*, vol. 16, no. 3 (Sept. 1965).
11 The very fact that they have all been the subject of study within a 'social pathological' framework should support this assertion, plus, of course, evidence of popular reaction to such behaviour as evinced by the mass media, and, in some

of the cases, the formal sanctions imposed by the legal system and other normative frameworks.

12 H. S. Becker, *Outsiders*, London, Collier-Macmillan, 1963, ch. 1.

13 Becker acknowledges here the earlier statements of this view by F. Tannenbaum, *Crime and the Community*, New York, McGraw Hill, 1951, and E. M. Lemert, *Social Pathology*, New York, McGraw Hill, 1951: his formulation is used because of its comparative simplicity and conciseness.

14 E. M. Lemert, op. cit., and *Human Deviance, Social Problems and Social Control*, London, Prentice-Hall, 1967, ch. III.

15 This of course also is true of, among other things, their political behaviour (S. M. Lipset, *Political Man*, London, Heinemann, 1960, ch. V) and their conformity to social mores as measured through responses to psychological tests (D. Krech, R. S. Crutchfield and E. L. Ballachey, *Individual in Society*, London, McGraw Hill, 1962, ch. 14).

16 Perhaps also relevant here is the sex ratio among graduate students and researchers in the social sciences! This appears to be an inverse of that obtaining among undergraduates (H. Glennester *et al., Graduate School: a study of Graduate Work at the London School of Economics*, London, Oliver & Boyd, 1967). While from one scientific point of view it may be desirable that students confine themselves to subjects where their empathetic powers are likely to flourish, it may not be helpful for the total development of a subject.

17 Since sociology is essentially a value-relative discipline, whose practitioners are bound by the constraints and limits of their own society this is inevitable and hardly a cause for regret. Concern, however, may be felt when the frontiers of knowledge fail to be extended because of pragmatic considerations or when retrospective interest is baulked by the lack of previous research.

18 In *Soc. Rev.*, vol. 14, no. 3 (Nov. 1966).

19 C. Wright Mills, 'The Professional Ideology of Social Pathologists', *Amer. J. Sociol.*, vol. 44 (Sept. 1942).

20 By S. Cohen and P. E. Rock, 'The Teddy Boy, the Evolution of a Social Type' in V. Bogdanor and R. Skidelsky (eds.), *Britain in the Fifties* (forthcoming).

21 S. Cohen, in an earlier article, ('Mods, Rockers and the Rest', *Howard Journal*, March 1967) has pointed out the effect of mass media in stimulating artificial 'happenings' amongst young people and the syndrome of deviance 'amplification' which results. L. Yablonsky in *The Violent Gang*, London, Collier-Macmillan, 1962, illustrates the way in which the press can influence and distort community conception of delinquent acts.

22 *Report of the Departmental Committee on Homosexual Offences and Prostitution*, Command No. 274: 1956 (the 'Wolfenden Report').

23 It is notable that the work of the Wolfenden Committee produced little response from social scientists on the topic of prostitution, although a good deal was published on the social and moral aspects of male homosexuality. One which did appear *before* the Committee had completed its work was Rosalind Wilkinson, *Women of the Streets*, ed. C. H. Rolph, London, 1955. But the anonymous *Streetwalker*, 1959, was already out of date and of largely historical interest by the time it appeared.

24 In 1908, for instance, some 32,439 females were convicted of either 'simple' drunkenness or 'drunkenness with aggravations'. By 1938 the figure (including a further category of drunkenness at the same time as another offence) had fallen to 7,686, although the female population was of course larger. By 1962 the figure was 4,793 and the rate per 10,000 of population had fallen from 4.50 to 2.54 as compared with a *rise* for males from 30.51 to 45.95 between 1938 and 1962.

25 Most European countries, for example, have abolished their various forms of licensed prostitution since the war.
26 L. T. Wilkins has shown that the rise in the number convicted of taking and driving away vehicles is directly related to the increase in motor vehicle registrations issued: *Social Deviance*, London, Tavistock, 1964.
27 Baroness Wootton of Abinger, *Crime and the Criminal Law: Reflections of a Magistrate and Social Scientist* (15th Hamlyn Lectures).
28 Street Offences Act, 1959.
29 For a full discussion of the implications of this term, and of its retention, see J. E. Hall Williams, *Law and Contemporary Problems*, vol. 25 (Spring 1960)—issue on sex offences.
30 Through the sheer growth in the number and range of offences and the development of more elaborate and sophisticated policing, detecting, and processing and judicial apparatus, the likelihood that actors will be observed in acts of primary delinquency and reported is much greater. Further the spread of professional crime and the development of certain new features of the social structure (e.g. the sub-world of the hippies and the 'Underground') may well ensure a pattern of increased reinforcement in secondary deviance.
31 Revelations made after the Profumo scandal, indicate how complex indirect arrangements for private catering for sexual wants can become.
32 See, e.g., Clark E. Vincent, *Unmarried Mothers*, New York, Free Press, 1961, and Robert W. Roberts (ed.), *The Unwed Mother*, London, Harper & Row, 1966.
33 This is not to imply that these cannot be meaningful typologies and bases for sociological enquiry—as in Lemert's studies of cheque forging or Cressey's of embezzlers.
34 Under English Law one of the rare exceptions to this rule is the crime of infanticide, a sub-category of homicide which takes cognizance of the postpartum mental state of a mother who kills her own child.
35 Most sociological theorizing about crime and deviance falls, following the still-strong Lombrosian position, into the first category. For a discussion of the implications (and the flaws) of determinism, see David Matza, *Delinquency and Drift*, New York, John Wiley, 1964.
36 Lombroso and G. Ferrero, *La Donna Delinquente*, Torino, Roux, 1893.
37 Lombroso, *Crime, its Causes and Remedies*, Boston, 1911.
38 Of course Kingsley Davis has pointed out that society castigates the prostitute, but not her clients, as deviant, but he suggests that this is for practical not other reasons (K. Davis, 'The Sociology of Prostitution' in R. Merton and R. Nisbet (eds.), *Contemporary Social Problems*, London, Hart-Davis, 1963).
39 Otto Pollak, *The Criminality of Women*, Philadelphia, 1950.
40 As e.g., in Talcott Parsons, *Essays in Sociological Theory*, rev. edn., 1954; A. K. Cohen, *Delinquent Boys*, London, Routledge & Kegan Paul, 1955; R. A. Cloward and L. Ohlin, *Delinquency and Opportunity*, London, Routledge & Kegan Paul, 1960.
41 E.g. by A. K. Cohen in *Delinquent Boys* as a 'reaction formation' but also by R. Cloward and L. Ohlin in *Delinquency and Opportunity* as a straightforward reaction to a situation where the desired high-financial goal is only attainable through non-legitimate means.
42 A. K. Cohen, op. cit.
43 On this point see especially, James A. Bryan, 'Apprenticeships in Prostitution', *Social Problems* (Winter 1965) and also the anonymous *Streetwalker*, Bodley Head, 1959, and Wayland Young, *Eros Denied*, New York, Grove Press, 1964.
44 Jack P. Gibbs, 'Conceptions of Deviant Behaviour: the Old and the New', *Pacific Sociol. Rev.* (Spring 1966).

45 In, e.g., his *Social Pathology*, or more recently as expounded in *Human Deviance, Social Problems and Social Control*, New York, Prentice Hall, 1967. Lemert largely antedates the other writers, and is responsible for introducing the concept of secondary deviance into the debate. But see also Frank Tannenbaum, op. cit., above.
46 L. T. Wilkins, *Social Deviance*, op. cit.
47 Thomas J. Scheff, *Being Mentally Ill*, London, Weidenfeld and Nicholson, 1966.
48 K. Davis, op. cit.
49 He argues, in fact, that he could also have chosen homosexuality as his subject.
50 J. P. Bryan, op. cit.
51 Wayland Young, op. cit.
52 Norman R. Jackman, Richard O'Toole and Gilbert Grieg, 'The Self Image of the Prostitute', *Sociol. Quart.*, vol. 4, no. 2 (April 1963).
53 In such statements as 'I hope that my husband can find a job and gets to working steadily again so I can be an ordinary housewife', 'I figgered [sic] it was easy money . . . prostitution . . .'
54 For some recent studies of sex roles see, e.g., Biddle and Thomas, *Role Theory*, London, John Wiley, 1966, and E. Dahlström, *The Changing Roles of Men and Women*, London, Gerald Duckworth, 1967.
55 David A. Ward and Gene G. Kassebaum, *Women's Prison: Sex and Social Structure*, London, Weidenfeld and Nicholson, 1966; Rose Giallombardo, *Society of Women*, London, John Wiley, 1966.
56 Contrast with the 'tobacco barons' in an English prison, T. Morris and P. Morris, *Pentonville: the Sociology of an English Prison*, London, Routledge and Kegan Paul, 1963.
57 As stated in, e.g., Gresham Sykes, *Society of Captives*, Princeton, 1958.
58 Tony Parker, *Five Women*, London, Hutchinson, 1955.
59 Cf. C. Wright Mills, 'The Professional Ideology of Social Pathologists', *Amer. J. Sociol.*, vol. 49 (Sept. 1942).
60 It may well be, of course, that further study of female deviance in depth may involve some challenging of underlying assumptions about male deviance as instanced in the case of prison studies mentioned above.
61 As this article was being prepared for publication the Home Office Research Unit published a monograph on *Studies of Female Offenders*, A Home Office Research Unit Report, London, H.M.S.O., 1967, which collates and somewhat extends our knowledge in this area.
62 Mannheim, *Comparative Criminology*, London, Routledge & Kegan Paul, 1965, vol. I.
63 As discussed by S. Cohen and S. Cohen and P. E. Rock.

4

WOMEN AND CRIME

The dark figures of criminology

Beverley Brown

Source: *Economy and Society*, 15:3 (1986), 355–402.

Texts reviewed

Pat Carlen (ed.) and Jenny Hicks, Josie O'Dwyer, Diana Christina, Chris Tchaikovsky *Criminal Women: Autobiographical Accounts*, Polity Press in association with Basil Blackwell, 'Feminist Perspectives' series, 1985.

Frances Heidensohn *Women and Crime*, Macmillan, 'Women in Society' series, 1985.

Introduction: the project of a feminist criminology

> What is 'feminist' criminology? . . . Does a criminologist become a Marxist because she/he tangentially refers to the influence of class distinctions in the criminal justice process? Is the existence of feminist criminologists enough to constitute a 'feminist' criminology? Clearly feminism as a theoretical and political position must be more than the study of women, the discovery of discrimination or the existence of feminists inside the discipline.
>
> (Smart, 1981, p. 85)

> Since the mid-1970s, several collections of articles have been published with a feminist approach on women offenders. . . . They all contribute to the feminist critique of criminology without taking it beyond the initial outlines with which it began.
>
> (Heidensohn, p. 152)

> Yet attempts to establish a feminist criminology have not been very successful . . .
>
> (Carlen, p. 6)

It is now ten years since the publication of Carol Smart's *Women, Crime and Criminology*, in effect the official founding of 'feminist' criminology. At one level, it would be churlish to deny that such an area of work exists, however difficult it may be to define, and that by a variety of institutional and political tests, it has achieved a measure of success. The question of women and crime and the treatment of women by the criminal justice system is now obligatory as at least 'a topic' on the university curriculumn – indeed the growing bank of empirical documentation makes it difficult to contain within this limited space. Intellectually, feminist criminology can claim living connections with current debates in criminology, sociology, Marxist and feminist theory. Nor does this level of 'establishment' success seem to have drained feminist criminology of its political energies in either its task of providing accessible popular-political reading or its campaigning commitments for reforms of the criminal justice system.

The two books reviewed here exemplify these several virtues. Frances Heidensohn's *Women and Crime*, which will probably succeed Smart as the up-to-date textbook, contains current statistics and a review of the problems of interpreting them, accounts of the 'experiences' of women and crime linking together campaigns among prostitutes to resist legal encroachment with the protests of Greenham women against 'man-made' laws, descriptions of the processes of court and prison, and consideration of images of female deviance and sexuality, as well as an outline of the theoretical placing of women by traditional, modern and feminist criminology. She seeks to convey the variety of perspectives available in approaching women's relation to crime, as offenders and as victims. In particular, she emphasises the continuum between criminal-justice and social processes more widely, drawing on social control theories to understand the shaping of female regulation.

Pat Carlen's *Criminal Women*, by contrast, is in a rather different genre, more an ethnography, a dense description of the diverse lives of four women whose variety of lawbreaking actions – petty theft, grand larceny – brought them into relation to the criminal justice system and imprisonment. While less overtly academic, it is prefaced by a theoretically demanding and acute introduction, justifying Carlen's choice of the descriptive approach as the appropriate methodology of today's feminist criminology. Meanwhile, the political credentials of the book are attested not only by its style of 'letting women speak' but by its final pages, the manifesto of Women in Prison, a group of ex-prisoners seeking reforms of women's and men's prisons.

Yet, as the opening quotations indicate, these two books which exemplify the strengths of feminist criminology themselves express doubts about its past and future. They see themselves as making breaks with the failings of the past and offering distinctive new alternatives, fresh starts. For Heidensohn, feminist criminology must turn its attention to what she identifies as a hitherto neglected area, examining

> female conformity as much, if not more than, female deviance in looking at female criminality. Criminologists have in general looked too little at conformity but that neglect is particularly striking with regard to women.
>
> (Heidensohn, p. 174)

She seeks to indicate the 'subtly-woven web' of 'bonds, attachments and constraints' (p. 192) which constrain female conduct externally and internally.

Carlen's alternative consists of an approach which will bring out the diversity of women's lives and hence avoid the pre-given typifications of sexual difference and women's crime which, for her, inform even 'feminist' criminologies. There are no special women's troubles constituting a separate area of investigation. Rather, one can only examine

> how, under certain material and ideological conditions, either law-breaking and/or other forms of deviant protest may indeed comprise rational and coherent responses to women's awareness of the social disabilities imposed upon them by discriminatory and exploitative class and gender relations.
>
> (Carlen, p. 9)

As well as seeking fresh starts, these two books have other common themes. Both, for instance, employ a strong rhetoric of what one could call a feminist rationalism, deploying the language of choice and self-determination in describing female conduct and self-perception. For Heidensohn, the rationalist strand is more restrained, drawing on MacLeod to emphasise the economic rationality of prostitution, for instance, and stressing the milieu of constraint in which such choices are made. For Carlen, the rationalist streak is more pronounced, a strong oppositional rhetoric countering the endless depiction of women as victims – of biology, pathology, society, men, as prisoners of everything but genuine prisons. Also encompassed is the theme of the intelligibility and meaningfulness of female 'criminal' conduct, a coherence of experience perhaps unintelligible to the social controllers but manifest in the autobiographical form.

In both books, then, women's imprisonment is an important theme raising current critical issues. Heidensohn has doubts about the logic of complaining of the sexism of the 'soft' treatment of women by comparison with men, expressing fears that this implies a demand for greater female incarceration. Carlen in fact disputes whether this 'soft' image is in fact true of women's prisons at all, and two of the accounts in her book confirm reports from the Howard League and NACRO about the punitive element in women's prisons and the greater tendency to punish for disciplinary infractions. For Carlen it is important to attack the myth that 'women's prisons are not real prisons'.

What is the significance of these emerging themes and the search for new feminist projects? Are Heidensohn's and Carlen's fresh starts and diagnoses of past error comparable and compatible? Are there broad trends of development in the field over the past ten years? These are the issues which this review seeks to explore on the occasion of this tenth anniversary.

As indicated by Carol Smart's remarks cited earlier, this is not the first time that the project of a feminist criminology has been queried. In its *de facto* existence, this field of work can be constituted by a string of questions. What can be learned about female crime patterns through official statistics? Is the overall low participation rate of women in crime of any significance? Are there distinctively female crimes? Do women commit crimes for different reasons than men? Do women have different relations to deviant subcultures than men? Are women treated differently from men in the legal process? What difference to such questions does it make to understand women's position in society as part of a system of patriarchal social relations – does it reflect the understanding of female criminal conduct or their treatment by legal and paralegal agencies? Does womanhood and its images cross the boundary between offenders and victims, characterising both by sexual double standards?

These are the kinds of questions which feminist criminology has in fact addressed. But clearly such a list cannot constitute a necessary or sufficient specification of a distinctively feminist criminology. This was Smart's point. Such questions about female crime have been asked and answered by non-feminist criminologists in the past; analysing the sexism of these answers has indeed been a major industry. Nor is an awareness of feminist issues, even particular documentations of discrimination, enough to guarantee a feminist analytical project. Are there then no linking themes, by which one can identify an already existing feminist criminology? In practice, the identifiable unity has been largely derived from the project of *critique*, a diagnostic of past criminological theory and the allegedly corresponding treatment of women by the criminal justice system. Carol Smart's founding text was subtitled 'a feminist critique' and, as Heidensohn's opening quote indicates, much current work can be grouped under this heading. The influence of this critique, its key terms and its shaping of feminist alternatives will be a major theme of this review.

To understand the status of this critique, it is important to grasp the status of 'theory' in criminology. Here, more than in other disciplines, theories are attributed with immediate practical consequences or conversely seen as adopted primarily for practical efficacy – criminology has notoriously dirty hands in actually shaping penal institutions and correctionalist strategies. The 'pragmatism' of the discipline was a recurrent embarrassment in radical attacks on criminology in the 1960s and 1970s, assigned responsibility for a politically compromised outlook as well as theoretical crassness and eclecticism (see, for instance, Cohen, 1974). The corresponding theme in feminist criminology has been, crudely, that traditional criminology is the theory, Holloway – especially its psychiatric wing – the practice. An additionally cohesive force is added by feminist criminology's emphasis on the monotonous repetition of criminology's view of the female offender, a few basic themes reiterated from the opening shots fired in 1895 by Lombroso and Ferrero's *The Female Offender*. Whereas approaches to male criminality have acquired certain levels of sophistication or variety since Lombroso's day, the state of the Woman and Crime question within the discipline is said to be essentially a theoretical throwback – an atavism appropriate to a discipline which began by claiming that women were less evolved than men. Given these strongly unifying themes – the image of criminological theory as having an immediate cash value in practice and as consisting in a few symptomatic 'views' on women – the critique of this theory-and-practice has formed unified package by which feminist criminology can be recognised.

Heidensohn and Carlen have a somewhat ambiguous attitude to this critical package. Their disillusionment with the past ten years of feminist criminology moves them to reject particular elements and presumptions, to seek new approaches. Yet, at least at the level of rhetoric, they reproduce many of the established tropes. Heidensohn's book is announced in blindingly familiar terms:

> Female offenders have traditionally been largely ignored by academic (mainly male) criminologists. In *Women and Crime* Frances Heidensohn produces a long-overdue account and critique of previous criminological and sociological writings on women and crime.
>
> (back cover)

For Carlen

> Lombroso and Ferrero's book *The Female Offender* published in 1895 contained most of the stereotypical elements responsible for subsequent characterisations of women lawbreakers.
>
> (Carlen, p. 2)

To invoke this rhetoric is to invoke that powerful and epiphanous moment in which feminist criminology was announced, a moment of foundation and denunciation, indeed foundation-by-denunciation, when feminist criminology could simply constitute itself as *Critique* and the urgency of the question of Woman could stand self-evident in the manifest sexism of the discipline. When such familiar terms are summoned up by the present writers, it is difficult not to see this as an urge to put the clock back, to forget the problems of definition and debate thrown up over the past ten years and, by a powerful counterwish to be instantaneously transported back to that happy place outside criminology, pleasurably scandalised by the views of the founding fathers, and their sons, on the nature of women and women's crime.

It will be argued here that this critique has in fact been responsible for the failings and dead ends of feminist criminology. Whether or not the present authors entirely succeed in evading the grip of the critical package also remains to be seen.

The foundational critique

The foundational critique of feminist criminology begins with the depiction of women's place in 'male' criminology as ignored and maligned. Women are ignored in that the whole topic of female crime has been under-researched and neglected – to read a standard criminological text one would scarcely guess that there were any female offenders at all; protests from male criminologists that this is due to the low level of female crime or its specialised nature are to be regarded as over-motivated and defensive. But, worse, where the female criminal is acknowledged to exist at all, she is encapsulated in a series of offensive stereotypes which render her variously evil, passive, cunning, maternal, unmaternal, mad or simply unwitting. The figure Woman monotonously recurs as that impossibly split image, either the 'idealised' eternal-maternal Being above all reproachful hint of criminality (and too busy doing the housework anyway) or her monstrous shadow, the female criminal so perverted in her femininity that she is more male than female. The crime of the deviant woman is first and foremost a crime against her nature as a woman and only secondly against the state. Such themes have an ancient and a modern form for, while an immemorial, notably Biblical, sexism animates the whole project, the 19th century supplied a revitalising injection of biological positivism. To read the works of Lombroso and his son-in-law in crime is to know the whole story, for here one finds the superstition of yesterday alloyed with the pseudo-scientific superstitions of the modern age: biological determinism is the great 'phallacy' of the criminological approach to women.

Within this critique different reading stances can be distinguished, on the one hand an oppositional discourse of exposé political diagnostics and, on the other hand, substantive counter-argument addressing the errors of criminological theory and demonstrating its consequent policy implications for the treatment of the female offender. These reading stances frequently converge, particularly in the central and concerted attack on what is identified as the key symptomatic failing of traditional criminology, its belief in a biologically based female constitution. That women and not men are viewed in terms of their biology or other fixed and pre-social natural determinations is the central motif in the foundational critical package, as in the following representative sample from Heidensohn:

> writers on female crime seek to rationalise and to make intellectually respectable a series of propositions about women and their consequences for criminal behaviour. Women in this view are determined

> by their biology and their physiology. Their hormones, their reproductive role, inexorably determine their emotionality, unreliability and childishness, deviousness, etc. These factors lead to female crime. Even a superficial examination shows up the contradictions here.
>
> (Heidensohn, p. 112)

Read first through the spectrum of oppositional exposé, this biologism is subject to the tests of sexist bias and distortion, a reading by contrasts and comparisons which reveal the hidden, or not so hidden, values and presumptions, discriminations and moralisations of the discipline. As mere expressions of sexism, such 'theories' do not really deserve the name of 'theories' at all and their contradictions will reliably give them away. In the pictures of women they present nothing really distinguishes them from any other arena of sexist manifestation. Thus one may simply pull out from the texts contrasting statements – women are less evolved than men, more emotional, naturally weaker and inferior, inherently unequal. Such stereotypes may be further exposed by referring them to their social origins. Traditional criminology is little more than myth, mechanically reproducing widespread sexist images of women's 'inevitable' character and destiny, lies which do in fact correspond to the truth of female oppression, the roles they are forced to live out and the hypocritical moral values which police their everyday existence. Thus, Lombroso and Ferrero 'attempt to rationalise and justify the status quo, the existing position of women and the double standards of their day' (Heidensohn, p. 114)

To counter such manifest sexism it is enough to let it speak for itself. Misogyny, in its ancient or modern guise, may be combated by emphasis and irony, *sic*'d to death, shown even by a 'superficial examination' to be transparently illogical; such theories are always to be found 'contriving' and 'managing' to make sense out of their manifest prejudice.

However, biological and other positivisms are also to be taken more seriously as substantive and contestable claims about an innate and given female constitution, claims with a significant influence on the treatment of women by the law. Woman is falsely said to be closer to nature, more the fixed and mechanised creature of her reproductive role. Lombroso and Ferrero set the themes. She is a being at the mercy of her hormones for better or – in the case of the female offender – for worse. More modern contributors will 'up-date' a purely biological thesis with a range of psycho-sexual imperatives retaining the same basic logic of an inherently different female character, fixed and pre-social. Woman will be found to have special needs for love, critical vulnerabilities in her formation. W. I. Thomas's *The Unadjusted Girl* is usually cited as an influential account of female adolescent disturbance, bringing to the fore a further theme also initiated by Lombroso and Ferrero, the sexualisation of the female associated with some failure to make the normal transit from one inevitable station of the female life to the next. Adolescent female 'promiscuity' is the warning sign; what Lombroso calls 'precocity' is the typical response of she who cannot face wifehood-and-motherhood without flinching.

Hence female criminality, particularly in the young, is referred to the grid of mental norm and illness, with sexual conduct seen as a primary manifestation of this ambivalence about gender identity. Consequently, according to the critique, the girl will be seen as ill and 'maladjusted' where the boy is treated in more classical terms of guilt and responsibility. In this the junior delinquent merely displays in a more extreme form what Carlen calls the

> myth that female lawbreakers, rather than being serious and intentional criminals, are nothing more than deviants from what are *supposed* to be their natural biologically determined socio-sexual roles and destinies . . . rather than conceiving of little girls as being young female persons, conceives of them as being nothing more than embryo wives, mothers and sex objects.
>
> (Carlen p. 10)

Hence, the influence of criminological positivism on the legal treatment of women is, generally speaking, seen as an over-determined non-criminalisation of the female offender. Already, as woman, regarded as determined by an innate female nature as less rational and responsible, the female offender is further driven by a biology off the rails, her special pathology. Consequently, the law condemns by mitigation, seeking to avoid female imprisonment and instead targeting women for diversionary, social-work alternatives; women who are sent to gaol will find themselves prescribed a retraining in proper feminine role pursuits in institutions which are soft and psychiatric, not hard and punitive. But moral policing has its other side too, also demonstrated by the treatment of female adolescents. For precisely as sexual deviation, not strictly criminal conduct, becomes the warning sign of female 'disturbance', so the net of social control widens and the care orders are slapped down.

For the feminist critique, these positive propositions and their applications require substantive counter-argument and contestation. Their error must be demonstrated. In these counter-claims the term 'society' functions as the magic bullet (phallocentric imagery permitting) to show up the mistakes of criminology ancient and modern. With the invocation of this powerful word biology and psychology may be exiled, all determinisms vanquished in the name of social origins and social change. To expose the social origins of the 'normal' female role will simultaneously liberate her role-deviant criminal sister from her specialised pathology and regime of re-socialising 'treatment'. Women are made not born – it is society, not the individual which should change:

> Explanations of female crime have usually been given in terms of the failure of individual women to adapt themselves to their supposedly natural and/or socio-sexual destinies. The implication has been that it is individual women who should change – rather than the social formations which impose restrictive and exploitative roles upon all women.
>
> (Carlen, p. 1)

Thus, oppositional and substantive critical strands in the foundational critique converge on this central doctrine of biologism and hence on 'society' as the alternative diagnostics and cure of past criminology.

However, these forms of critique did not just fall from the sky, nor are they special *de novo* inventions of feminist criminology. To create this neat package, feminist criminology drew upon critical traditions in sociology and 'radical' criminology. The sex/gender distinction derives from modifications wrought in classical sociological theories of the family and social roles by adding an awareness of cross-cultural and historical variation. The fact that family forms and constructions of masculinity and feminity show considerable variation across the globe and over time was seen as an important counter to the inevitabilism of explicitly or implicitly biologistic theories that sex was destiny. 'Gender' is thus a way of asserting that what society has made, it can unmake. Allied to this development in role theory was a similar utilisation of ethnography and history by theorists of sexual deviance such as Gagnon and Garfinkel who used the cross-cultural matrix to query received notions of sexual norms and pathologies. Heterosexuality was not the universally prescribed cultural form; other cultures' acceptance of homosexuality or other forms of 'deviance' could be cited as evidence that there were was no inherent division between reproductive, natural and unnatural sexualities. The existence of social and cultural variation showed that Western patterns of gender and sexuality are social constructions and not fixed givens. Consequently, this social construction could itself be approached in a new light, as a process of ideological formation. Biologism and allied naturalisms could themselves be assessed not only as erroneous claimants to truth but, further, as mythologies, as modes of justifying exploitative and oppressive social systems.

Exposing such myths as power mechanisms could become an important move in a politics of social change. Recognising the non-fixity of social and sexual norms shows social reform to be both just and possible. For the sake of women in general, 'society must change'.

Criminological self-critique in the form of deviancy theory and radical criminology is the other main source of this invocation of 'society'. Here the term 'society' has a particular weight against the pathologisation of the individual offender, with biological and other positivisms singled out as the source of 'original sin'. Just as in feminist criminology, this involves a preamble of ritual degradation of Lombroso (this time minus Ferrero), a diagnosis of political bias and class distortion (parallel sexism) and the depiction of biological positivism as a legitimising pseudo-science, a rationalisation of the status quo of a class society in general and its criminalising routines in particular. The doctrine of a biologically fixed individual pathology is held responsible for the view that there are inherently different criminal types, pathologically fixed in their criminality, marked through and through by their 'otherness' and hence divided from the normal and law abiding by an absolute division. The correctionalist focus of criminal justice derives from such ancient positivisms and their more modern variants. For all, the focus has been on changing the individual, in regimenting him (for it is him) into the roles of an inherently unjust society.

Hence, pointing to 'society' involves, first, recognising social not individual causes of criminal conduct, economic disability and structural inequalities: the criminal is not an inherently different type of being in terms of motivation and goals – 'mindless and irrational' conduct can be shown to be intelligible. It is means and access which distinguish them and influence the criminal career. Second, the heading 'social' also emphasises the contribution of the criminalisation process itself to the construction of criminality. Here a range of differentiations is catalogued: the arbitrariness of criminal sanction in its choice of condemned behaviour, the element of social reaction rather than rationality, etc. Taken together, these arguments seek to show that there is no social pathology, no generically distinct category of harmful actions, just as there is no inherent individual pathology. To understand the production of that individual criminality one must also consider the effects of the criminalisation process on those persons picked up in its net, labelled perhaps from spheres well outside criminal justice as such and processed through the system. By such means the criminalisation process may be understood as a self-fulfilling prophecy, transforming the juridical subjects of individual acts of deviance into fully criminal beings. Thus – although engineered through an emphasis on meaning rather than causality – structural inequality combined with the criminalisation process, allows at least a rhetoric in which society may be held responsible for the very social and individual pathologies 'found', 'diagnosed' and 'treated' via the positivist tradition. It follows that, to eliminate crime and stop producing criminals, it is again society which should change, not the individual.

Women and crime – the feminist alternatives

Women, Crime and Criminology ended with the warning:

> it is not adequate to present a theory which is based solely on the negation of existing theories . . . a critique alone cannot constitute a new theoretical perspective.
>
> (Smart, 1977, p. 183)

But, for femininst criminology, critique *has* constituted the alternatives, not just in the never-finished denunciation of the past but, crucially, in framing the possibilities of new work and thinking. Corresponding to the two reading stances, it produced two basic lines of direction, a project of correcting the male bias of the discipline by various equalising remedies and an imperative to assert and investigate the social origins of gender and the social processes involved in the criminalisation process. Both of these projects were, by implication, to fulfil the more general feminist task of providing an approach informed by an awareness of the oppressive nature of the social conditions that governed women's lives, focused in the reiterated demand that 'society must change'. Minimally, this was a call for research, for more attention to be given to the placing and experiences of women inside and outside legality. More ambitiously, it was implied that some alternative feminist account of the question of women and crime could be produced.

Over ten years, various criticisms emerged, in which the disappointing results of this project have been registered. Broadly speaking, the criticisms amount to saying that feminist criminology ended up accepting the truth of the status quo, whether that be the fact of existing social relations or the concepts of criminology. Since criminology, with respect to women, was seen as reflecting patriarchal society anyway, the lies it told about women also counted as truths. Meanwhile the discipline was not really challenged in what it said about men; worse, this functioned, as did male imprisonment, as a sort of measure for assessing the status of women. The removal of oppression remained the outcome of tomorrow; in the meantime the analysis of power relations was construed largely in respect to criminal motivation. Could female crime be understood as protest against exploitation – if so, why wasn't there more female crime? Were social conditions the cause of female non-crime – how different was this from previous views of women? These are the problems which will be outlined here.

It would be difficult to identify a huge mass of reflective argument within feminist criminology. The two main critical articles appearing in 1980–81, will be outlined here. The first, by Victoria Greenwood, has been greeted largely with bafflement; the other, by Mark Cousins, taken up rather more. Cousins is a major referent for Carlen, but not for Heidensohn, who does, however, cite Greenwood's essay: she finds it 'puzzling' and does not mention its attack on social control theories such as her own. The other sources drawn upon here are also slightly peripheral to any 'tradition' of feminist criminology.

Reifying male criminology and criminality

The charge here is essentially that, in its wish to restore women to their place in criminology or to demonstrate their exclusion from it, feminist criminology has failed to be sufficiently critical of the discipline itself. Greenwood linked this failing to the monocular focus on sexism:

> For the feminists, the task has been to examine the sexism of the traditional theories. It is true that much of their work is riddled with sexist assumptions about the inherent nature of women. However, the way in which the trajectory is posed is that, if one could rid these theoreticians of their sexism, their theories might themselves be valid.
>
> (Greenwood, 1981, p. 77)

For Cousins:

> the thesis of a female criminality distorted by patriarchal relations perversely sets up male criminality as the norm by which reference is made to female criminality. For presumably patriarchal social relations permit male criminality to be adequately represented in court . . .
>
> (Cousins, 1980, p. 114)

Crudely, the criticism they are offering is that the more one seeks to show that male criminologists take leave of their senses when the question Woman looms on the agenda, the more one implies that they are in their right minds when they talk about male crime. This is obviously one dangerous effect of oppositional discourses, a congenital weakness of any argument from bias – distortion must show up by contrast with some measure of non-distortion and be corrected by applying 'the' standard uniformly.

More precisely, two sorts of dangers are indicated. First, one may be insufficiently critical of the 'givens' of criminology, especially as identified through the positivist origins of the discipline with its assumptions of a demarcated criminality awaiting investigation, a lack of awareness of the social construction of crime and the historically variable components in the criminalisation process. When Cousins refers to a presumed 'female criminality waiting in the wings' heretofore ignored or distorted by male criminology, and when Greenwood refers to the presumption that, sexism aside, criminological theories would be valid, these are the sorts of problems which are meant. The list of scepticisms can be extended but the point is general – one can hardly demand that female crime be simply accorded its 'proper' place in an era of criminological scepticisms about yesterday's proprieties.

The other risk is to accept implicit or explicit masculinities of criminality as the truth against which female crime is to be counted and female criminality properly rewarded. Is feminist criminology simply to demonstrate that female crime and criminality can literally or figuratively measure up to the male standard, to overturn the stereotypical depiction of the rare or timid female criminal in order to discover the truth of a female criminality imbued with a toughness and calculation hitherto reserved to the male? A fairly stunning example of this form of romance of crime is to be found in Chris Tchaikovsky's essay in *Criminal Women*, a heady access of tough talk which certainly proves that women can write prose like Micky Spillane crossed with Dick Hebdige. There is more than a whiff of sulphur in her 'Nietzschean' contempt for the bovine complacency of women at large, a contempt equalled only by her casual scorn for those men – and in her story that refers to all of them beginning with Father – who always fail one way or another to be minimally competent. Crime can still function as 'masculine' even if only women – a few of them at least – are up to it.

Greenwood found a similar set of cultural masculine attributes inscribed in the theoretical stance of New Criminology in the

> purposeful, rational, determined human being who is 'the criminal'... Such a perspective has all the nuances and tones which constitute the stereotype of the machismo male built into it.
>
> (Greenwood, 1981, p. 78)

Clearly, what Carlen calls the 'presumed masculinity of crime' is far wider and more subtle than a mere shopping list of explicit male actions or characteristics. Theories which depict the female criminal as 'social bandit' may well fall into this trap. More to the point, both Heidensohn's and more crucially Carlen's own usage of the feminist-rationalist rhetoric of free choice and self-determination (itself possibly borrowed from the New Criminology) could be criticised.

Other queries might be raised about 'abstract' standards of attention-worthiness in criminology, volume of crime and seriousness of offence. For feminist criminology to require that female crime not be ignored, need it justify this demand on these grounds or feel some implicit pressure to do so? Certainly the logic of opposition and fair dues would suggest such an obligation.

Reifying sexist stereotypes

Put at its most polemical, this critical strand is an attack on the sex/gender distinction, in use if not in essence. How successful is the attempt to evade the grip of functionalism and role theory? Does the sex/gender distinction merely substitute social for biological determinism? Do its categories homogenise and essentialise the category woman? Such criticisms come from different quarters, from work on female subcultures, from anti-functionalist sociology, and from the anti-essentialist feminist theory associated with Mark Cousins' article. Taken together, these positions accuse the sex/gender distinction of in practice conflating biology and society.

Angela McRobbie, investigating the question of adolescent female gangs, comments on the continuing 'masculinity' of this area of criminology. However, she sees this as not so much, or not only, due to continuing male self-preoccupation or disregard of feminism by alleged radicals. She also finds a not surprising reluctance of deviancy and subcultural theorists to tangle with the sociologically discredited functionalism lurking behind feminist accounts of the family and female social roles.

> It's no coincidence, for example, that while the Sociologies of Deviance and Youth were blooming in the early Seventies, the Sociology of the Family – still steeped in the structural functionalism of Talcott Parsons – was everybody's least favourite option . . . the sociology of Crime/Deviance/Youth Culture was one of the first areas from which the hegemony of Parsonianism was challenged.
>
> (MacRobbie, 1980, p. 39)

A similar argument comes from David Morgan, again commenting on the less than progressive effects of role theory in practice:

> The common approach to the study of men and women in society is through the use of the concept 'role'. There have been two opposite consequences of this common usage. In the first place, the concept 'role' implies some differentiation between culture and biology and hence serves to show the possibility of culture variation and change. . . . In practice, however, the opposite seems to have been the case and while clear differentiation between biology and culture are made, the concept of role has taken on the mandatory character of a biologically based determinism: instead of 'Biology is destiny', 'Role is destiny' . . .
>
> (Morgan, 1975, p. 135)

For Morgan, the substitution of society for biology retains two presumptions. First, that the categories masculine/feminine have a uniform content, fixed and unfluid cultural tropes. Second, there is a presumption that, through the iron grip of socialisation, the male and female populations will simply be the living embodiments of these stereotypes. Not only does this maintain the acceptance of fixed role contents as the truth of sexual difference, it also retains the implicit valuations of male and female. Women remain as inferior, deprived of skills and status, as incapable and over-emotional as if they had necessarily been born that way. All that is shifted is the blame, for it is society, not biology that has made us this way.

The anti-essentialist argument of Cousins similarly insists on both the multiplicity of discursively drawn sexual differences and the variety of positioning of individuals in relation to those classifications. By contrast, sociology's conceptualisation of sexual division whilst always protesting a social as opposed to biological origin, nonetheless can never derive its notion of a mutually exclusive and jointly exhaustive division between the sexes from social relations, and thus necessarily presupposes it, falling back on the given referents of the terms 'men' and 'women', the existing population. Thus, metaphysically, and all too physically, this concept of sexual division is inevitably given and pre-social. This argument is not, like Morgan's, concerned with an alleged social determinism; rather it is concerned with essentialism, its target is reductive theories of law and society as an expression of, ultimately, patriarchy.

Feminist criminology has a number of replies to these charges. After all, what was the purpose of cross-culturalism and the invocation of historical otherness but to escape the conventions of functionalism? Where functionalist theories of the family suppose a universal family form fulfilling universal social functions which are little but disguised biological imperatives, gender and family theory point to variation and multiplicity of forms. Or where unmitigated role theory has assumed some single universal female form, once again social, historical, cross-cultural variations in role-content challenge such inherent biologisms. Equally, variations of race and class insist on the multiplicity of femininity and masculinity and its lived realities. Non-universality equals non-biologism.

But how effective are these gestures? They may work against 'baby' functionalism which is indeed crudely universalistic and simple-minded in its alleged 'social' global functions of child-rearing and feeding. But they are not much use against Parsons, whose theory of the nuclear family is about non-universal family forms, indeed precisely concerned to demonstrate how the modern family evolves as a specialist institution to meet the needs of a complex industrialised society with its pluralism of values and stress on individual autonomy. For him the explanation of the specialised roles of parenting, as divided between instrumental and affective roles, is derived partly as a response to this particular complex of essentially new social needs and partly from the efficiencies of small group management. No critique based on charges of globalism, universalism and biologism of functions is going to be very effective here.

Similarly, one can demonstrate the limitations of the 'cross-cultural' gesture as a challenge to implied uniformities and instantiations of role-content. Recognising social, cultural, historical variation and the possibility of social change, or pointing to the variables of race and class within a culture, seem to challenge the monolithic categories of role theory. But to what extent do these tours of the world alter the depiction of the homeland? Having paid tribute to the non-West, or to sexualities in former times, the here-and-now turns out to be that rather monotonous stretch constituted as the present. *Autre temps, autre moeurs* are, after all, always somewhere else. Parsonian role theory remains a sufficient characterisation of the post-industrial revolution West. As for the factors of race and class, these remain external modifiers, mere variants on an otherwise invariant depiction of masculinity and femininity and their living socialised representatives, men and women. The sex/gender distinction, for the society it studies, effectively conflates biology and society.

Parsons is often rightly criticised for his presumption that it is men and women respectively who will automatically fulfill the 'non-genderised' social roles. In precisely parallel fashion one could say that, for culturally adapted role theory, biological difference remains, if not the cause, at least a perfectly reliable indicator of uncontested differences between the sexes. The sex/gender distinction does not in practice appear to be a cure-all for the ills of traditional criminology, merely substituting a 'society' quantifier for a biological one. The non-criminal woman continues to be reported as maternal home-maker, passive and obedient, patiently waiting for the fairy godmother of the future to make things different As for the woman involved in crime, she seems to have been almost forgotten. It is not clear that the sociology of gender has any means of conceptualising her at all:

> Attention thus focuses on the informal mechanisms of control, socialisation and the family. The women who do deviate remain anomalies and unworthy of examination.
>
> (Greenwood, 1981, p. 1979)

Subject to such indifference, 'criminal' women remain the mysteries they ever were, pushed aside by those ardent critics of the family and its normalising powers. Clearly such a criticism is pertinent to Heidensohn's re-discovery of social control theory.

These are dilemmas facing the project of a feminist criminology, and any alternative approach to the Woman and Crime question. Indeed that very paradigmatic question which founded the project – that question whose absence from the critiques of the 1970s signalled the marginalisation of women in the discipline and the subordination of women in society – today seems unaskable. The question of female crime has become, for Carlen, 'theoretically unsound and politically ill-judged'. For what kind of link *can* be supposed between women and crime which will not one way or another reproduce the status of women as separate and 'other' than the norm, whether that be the norm of male crime and female non-crime? To accept any grouping of distinctive women's crimes, or a special female criminality, to see all female offenders as conscious or unconscious social bandits rejecting their social role, to glorify in the rare toughness of the professional female villain or, on the contrary, to see women-as-a-group distinctively *disabled* from crime? Each stance seems to perpetuate familiar categorisations of women (and men) in the very moment of challenging the tradition, thereby re-enacting all the past crimes of criminology against the female sex.

Does this mean the end of feminist criminology? Surely, there is an opposite danger for a feminism determined to purge itself of the last vestiges of sexism and essentialism, namely, of implying that sexism has never existed at all, never had any coherent or systematic effects on women's lives? If women are treated differently by the law and society, can these differences not be registered? If mythologies turn out to be more complex in their operation than at first appeared, does this mean they are altogether without significance?

This is to describe an over-arching dilemma which today confronts not just feminist criminology but feminist theory more widely. Nonetheless the particular 'lived' forms of this dilemma within current feminist criminology must be analysed.

Sisters in crime/Brothers in criminology

> the assumptions of some femininst criminologists converge with the traditional and persistent assumptions of most judges and magistrates towards a consensualised view that liberation from female-related domesticity inevitably leads to an increase in female lawbreaking.
>
> (Carlen, p. 6)

> The central hypothesis has been extensively explored and tested, to no finally conclusive results – although it has been refuted to some degree. Its power as a concept is more than just scientific: it has a symbolic value to its proponents, its critics and the public. In a very real sense, then, and in the least helpful way to women offenders or women workers, one branch of feminist criminology has at last made female crime visible.
>
> (Heidensohn, p. 160)

The 'central hypothesis' put forward by 'some feminist criminologists' is the 'sisters in crime' thesis. Initiated in America by Freda Adler and Rita Simon in the 1970s, the debate has had a curious longevity, given its empirical-statistical demolition; it has been hotly contested in Britain for the past ten years by Carol Smart, R. L. Austin, Steven Box and Cynthia Hale. Essentially, 'sisters in crime' congratulates the women's movement for a claimed increase in female crime, marking especially the emergence of a 'new female criminal' engaged in predatory crimes of violence and corporate fraud. Women are, quite literally, breaking into a man's world – the female terrorist and the female executive are its twin heroines. Feminism has allegedly contributed to this phenomenon by removing external obstacles to female access to public life and internal obstacles inhibiting the use of violence and other male skills. What is more, consciousness-raising has fuelled women's awareness of social inequities, urging them to take over male roles and contributing an element of social protest to female criminal motivation. It appears that the work of the Equal Opportunities Commission has not been in vain after all.

This *is* an important debate. Both Carlen and Heidensohn find it vital to address the thesis and discredit its positivities and presumptions. The issues it raises are close to their central concerns; for Carlen, 'sisters in crime' is symptomatic of the failings of feminist theory, and the occasion for her to announce the new project, the abandonment of *any* theories of female crime. For Heidensohn it is a recurrent irritant in a book devoted to demonstrating social factors in female conformity – will she some day, if not now, find herself complicit in a similar thesis about the effects of social change?

'Sisters in crime' is a thesis from which most feminists have dissociated themselves, seeing it as 'misguided', 'unhelpful', a matter of naive Americans, male moral panics, and persistent judicial assumptions. Yet it is not so easily dismissed; it is a proper embarrassment to feminism. This is not because it – the increase in crime or the claim to it – was ever a desired or predicted outcome of the women's movement. The problem is *how* to disavow the connection, how to distinguish oneself from one's close kin. Is the critical vocabulary available? Take the elementary grid for recognising sexist and anti-feminist theories – does 'sisters in crime' malign or ignore the female criminal? No, it speaks of her and her new-found 'freedom' with girlish enthusiasm; meanwhile, as Heidensohn says, it has certainly made female crime visible and made judges take it seriously too. Does it seek to rationalise and justify traditional social relations, to deny their oppressive character? On the contrary, women's past restrictions are emphasised by contrast with the new freedoms while, for those impatient for equalisation to be complete, consciousness of remaining fetters functions as a spur to criminal conduct. Does it rest upon a theory of biological determinism, a view of a fixed pre-social female nature, immutable through the ages? On the contrary, it has even been recommended for its anti-biologism: 'this approach lessens the power of genetic or biological explanation' (Austin, cited in Heidensohn, p. 157). It is quite simple: biological women can become social men.

Other weapons had to be found. For Heidensohn, it is empirical-statistical refutation; for Carlen, a critique of presumptive masculine and feminine categories and classifications. But these new weapons can in fact be recognised as the criticisms of foundational feminism cited in the last section – hence to use them in combating 'sisters in crime' necessarily produces the problem of how to limit their effects. *Can* 'sisters in crime' be cordoned off as a limited area of contagion or must the problems be accepted as epidemic? (Carlen hedges her bets; only 'sisters in crime' is named, but the implications for feminist criminology are drawn at the wider level.)

Heidensohn, reporting the debate, sticks very close to the evidential issues. Nonetheless this itself is important: it is a debate not structured solely around the circulation of images of women but a first blooding in a 'hard-nosed' question of crime. Insofar as 'sisters in crime' has any respectable evidence at all, this evidence falls down in three main ways (simplifying Heidensohn's summary of the debate):

1 Is there in fact any evidence of an increase in the overall female participation rate in crime? The allegedly large leap is produced mainly by

an elementary statistical error of comparing absolute levels of female crime with each other, rather than relative rates as between women and men. In other words, more women may be committing more crime, but so are more men. The ratio has altered little.

2 The 'liberation' thesis would indicate that, since feminists are usually middle-class, so will be the new female criminal. By contrast, in that the ratio between male and female crime has increased at all, it is in fact poor, black women who appear in the statistics, as ever. This supports a marginalisation-and-crime thesis rather and one of expansion-of-egos-and-opportunities. It also corresponds to other deviations in the female crime rate in the past, which has increased in times of decreasing affluence and not just prosperity. Otherwise, the bulk of female crime remains non-occupational petty property offences.

3 Could *any* statistical increase in female crime be simply read as a correct indicator of an actual pattern? Can heavier sentencing be taken as an index of the increasing seriousness of offences? Surely, it is argued, 'sisters in crime' is extremely naive in considering the possible effects of feminism only on criminal behaviour – what of its effects in making female crime more visible in increasing reporting, policing and sentencing of female offenders, all of which may reflect reactions to feminism more than changes in female crime? Such factors in the criminalisation process distort statistical fact-gathering, making official records notoriously unreliable guides to actual patterns of lawbreaking. (Let us not accept yesterday's criminological givens.)

Thus everything seems neatly tidied away. 'Sisters in crime' is a non-debate, more important symbolically than empirically, and a further warning of the virility of 'traditional' assumptions assimilated unwittingly by feminist criminology. Yet, examined more carefully, this empirical refutation is less than impressive as a tribute to the new awareness of criminological pitfalls.

The empirical refutation's first and strongest premise is an impeccable piece of argument, demonstrating statistical incompetence on the part of Adler et al. This is fine, although of course it cannot exactly be claimed as due to an awareness of distinctions between lawbreaking and criminalisation. The second premise refutes the argument that middle-class feminists are the 'new female criminals'; this is hardly the strongest version of the 'emancipation' argument which concerns the nature of social structure and opportunity and by no means predicts that feminists or middle-class women are to be its sole beneficiaries or exemplars. Further, the claim about feminist criminals is refuted by citing the truth of criminal statistics in revealing who the 'real' female criminals are – black, working-class women engaged in petty property offences. This trusting attitude to statistics is, however, abandoned in the last premise which cites the reaction to feminism as a factor in the apparent increase in volume of crime. Clearly the use of criminological scepticism is somewhat selective. One might just as well argue that the new middle-class female criminal would be more likely to go undetected.

Although Carlen too is concerned with criminological scepticisms, criticising 'sisters in crime' for conflating the distinction between lawbreaking and criminalisation, her concern with this thesis lies more at the level of its categories and presumptions than with its empirical refutation. She finds in 'sisters in crime' in effect the two tendencies noted in the last section, a presumption that crime is a necessarily masculine activity and an essentialising view of women. Hence she argues that 'searches for either a global theory of crime (male *or* female) or a special theory of female crime (global or not) are both theoretically unsound and politically ill-judged' (Carlen, p. 6). She distinguishes what could be called objective and subjective versions of these failings, both of which, in her terms, conflate sex and gender as well as lawbreaking and criminalisation.

> as soon as it is assumed that a *special* theory of women's lawbreaking is required, then criminal activities have to be distributed to males and females on the basis of an activity's supposed 'masculine' or 'feminine' characteristics. (In fact what has happened has been much more crude: in circular fashion the crimes most frequently committed by women have been categorised as 'female' crimes, whilst the rest have remained 'male'.)
>
> (Carlen, p. 7)

As examples of the less crude version, one has only to think of studies which seek some general characteristic of feminity, notably non-aggression, and then seek to organise female and male criminality according to such characteristics. Examples of the second version are also familiar, with the female shoplifter a front runner, despite the fact that far more men than women are charged and convicted of this offence. In both cases one finds a form of question-begging – if you set out to find a distinctively male and female crime, you can be guaranteed to find it.

The other perpetuation of the 'gender trap' concerns the subjective motivation ascribed to the female offender, either by the judiciary or by the women themselves. Either way, one must be wary of accounts which 'prove' a male self-definition on the part of the female criminal and award the appropriate male penalty:

> It is easy to see why certain young women may see their own lawbreaking as being a desirable encroachment upon one of the male routes to increased freedom, while their judges (for slightly different reasons) see women's lawbreaking as being both a manifestation of a *lack of femininity* and a justification for increased surveillance and severer punishment.
>
> (Carlen, p. 8)

Clearly, at least 'some' feminist criminologists – the proponents of 'sisters in crime' – can be seen as committing *both* these errors. Their depiction of the 'new female criminal' casts her as biologically female but essentially masculine, 'objectively' so in breaking into traditional areas of male crime and 'subjectively' in her self-perception as emulating men. This masculinity is 'confirmed' by sentencing patterns. The new female criminal turns out to be the old maladjusted masculinist female of traditional criminology, rejecting her proper feminine role. Meanwhile, those other women, engaged in their traditional homely pursuits, non-criminal or marginally so, remain as essentially feminine as ever.

Thus, 'sisters in crime' can be convicted of both varieties of 'reification' discussed earlier (although Carlen continues to use the term sex/gender). Citing Smart, Carlen identifies the sex/gender conflation as the trap of assuming dichotomising categories, distributing all behaviour, crime included onto one or other of two pre-existing, mutually exclusive and self-confirming groupings of sexual differentiation. Citing Cousins, she generalises from this episode to disavow *any* feminist ambition to find an alternative aetiology of female crime:

> *any* explanations of a taken-for-granted 'female criminality' – whether those explanations be styled feminist, radical, marxist, or whatever – *must* by the nature of the project, be as reductionist and essentialising as the much maligned biological ones.
>
> (Carlen, p. 9)

This shift away from the diagnostics of biologism is an important move. Carlen's own glossing of the autobiographies in her book honour this anti-essentialist vow – the crimes documented do not constitute any distinctive group of predictable 'women's crimes' but include post office fraud, burglary, drunk and disorderly offences. The women who speak here may reject the conventional female role but not in order to model themselves on men. Their class and family backgrounds vary considerably. This constitutes a key component of Carlen's 'rationalism: the emphasis is on the *gender-neutral* quality of their wishes and ambitions and the heterogeneity of their routes to criminalisation. 'The essential criminal woman does not exist.' Instead there can only be these diversified and fragmented autobiographies of 'criminal' women whose variety renders ironical the unifying label of criminality. There is, for her, no essential female criminality because there is no essential feminity, no set of special female motives or attitudes to the world, no externally predictable behaviour.

To extend this as a thesis about *criminal* conduct, rather than just female conduct, this rationalist strategy could be seen as a sort of feminist Mertonianism, in which the same goals and aspirations are found to be shared by criminal and non-criminal women, as they are between non-criminal women and men. 'Rationality' here would signify that there is no special pathology distinguishing the (female) criminal being from the rest of society. Rather everyone is seeking 'fun, independence and success' and differences between criminal and non-criminal women, as between men and women, consist largely in differential access and strategies to achieve these goals. The female condition thus consists in oppressive social relations which constitute not so much a feminine nature, biological or social, but in a set of external obstacles to the achievement of such otherwise gender-neutral goals. Some women, in the face of such obstacles, may deliberately choose crime as a means to an otherwise blocked end, but not all women will, nor can all female criminal conduct be understood in this way. This anti-essentialist strand in Carlen's rationalism is also closely linked to anti-determinism: rejected theories of a distinctive female criminality are not just single-factor theories but 'monocausal'; the error of 'sisters in crime' is to presume an 'inevitable' increase in female crime as a consequence of changed social conditions.

Here is the beginning of an approach which can free feminist criminology of its burden of past presumptions. It is not without difficulties and ambivalences, as will be discussed in more detail later. It is slightly hesitant about the extent to which the criticisms will be allowed to characterise feminist criminology at large. In limiting the explicit target of attack to 'sisters in crime' some of the force of these arguments may well be lost. More critically, however, Carlen herself seems unwilling to follow through the implications fully, as manifested in her untroubled retention of familiar items of the foundational critique. Yet the dilemmas and fallacies of 'sisters in crime' can be traced back directly to that critique and its implied alternatives. Thus it is important actually to reconsider what the following familiar item, reproduced by Carlen, might actually imply:

> Explanations of female crime have usually been given in terms of the failure of individual women to adapt themselves to their supposedly natural and/or sociosexual destinies. The implication has been that it is individual women who should change – rather than the social relations which impose restrictive and exploitative roles on all women.
>
> (Carlen, p. 1)

This is, of course, the economy measure which, in the one slogan 'society must change', summons up the two critical traditions of gender sociology and radical criminology. But, in the context of 'sisters in crime' – which insists that society has changed – this familiar rhetoric takes on more sinister connotations – what did it mean? As a formula, we know of course that it is a demand to alter the treatment of the individual offender and reorganise social life as we have known it. But, criticising the usual explanations of crime, suggesting with a 'rather' that some alternative is to be given, we are also back with that allusion to the premised feminist theory which would at last link women's crime somehow to their oppressive social conditions. This of course is an alternative Carlen goes on to repudiate – and one can suddenly see precisely why 'sisters in crime' has caused such a feminist panic. It is the 'proof of the pudding' of that peculiar mixture of gender sociology and radical criminology, a no doubt entirely unintended consequence of the package invocation of social change.

For remember what this phrase connotes in the two genres: Within 'radical' criminology, the reference to exploitative social relations and the assertion that it is society, not the individual offender, which must change is used to counter positivist accounts of the source of crime. It is society, not the individual, which is crimogenic and whose criminalisation procedures actually produce criminals. Within gender sociology, the assertion 'society must change' also makes perfect sense. To recognise the social origin of roles is the first step to changing society and ending widespread female oppression. As invoked here, 'changing society' has nothing to do with crime as such; the address is to the 'normal' constitution of social roles. In this context, 'society must change' is, criminologically, simply empty and meaningless.

However, when put back into the milieu of criminology, the phrase assumes at least the promise of a criminological implication, as being a possible alternative explanation for female crime. Is it to be the same as for the male offender – that social exploitation produces crime and is further expressed in criminalisation? In this case, social change will involve a reduction in female crime. But this parallel is difficult to sustain, given the low level of reported female crime. If the social oppression of women is so widespread, why is there not more female crime? (one logical alternative – perhaps there is . . .) or perhaps social relations are not so oppressive after all. At any rate, the female criminal would certainly be a very untypical female, rejecting her stereotypical social role – like the 'maladjusted 'male' female criminal, or the 'new' female criminal?

Alternatively, one can construct a mirror image case from male crime – oppressive social relations *prevent* female crime, restricting access to public life, controlling female conduct by the variety of mechanisms of formal and informal social controls. 'Sisters in crime' has this alternative covered as well, for these of course are the real feminine women, socially as well as biologically. And if one accepts the mirror image thesis, and still lives with the causal link between society and crime, then of course 'sisters in crime' follows with logical precision. If changing society will reduce male crime then *mutatis mutandis* it will increase female crime. If there is no causal link, why bother to assert that 'society must change'? This is the connection Carlen seeks to ward off by denouncing 'sisters in crime' for positing an 'inevitable' effect. But it is difficult to wriggle out of the implications *and* go on using the slogan.

Behind 'sisters in crime' lurks the even more sinister figure (both metaphoricially and literally) of Otto Pollak, one of the great villains of 'male' criminology, an earlier exponent of the emancipation-and-crime thesis and a notable slanderer of the female character, female deceit being the major item. Nonetheless he is a threat to feminist criminology because his view of female criminality could almost function as a possible 'third alternative' between modelling female criminality on the masculine model or seeing women as imprisoned in social convention. Like 'sisters in crime' his position cannot be simply dismissed as biologistic. Worse, his repertoire includes many elements supposedly distinctive of feminist criminology.

His main thesis is well known, the claim, unique in the criminological view of women, that there exists a vast and undiscovered reservoir of female crime but that it has so far evaded detection through a combination of female cunning, the hidden private sphere in which such crime is committed and the stereotypical blinkers blinding male criminologists:

> In our male-dominated culture, women have always been considered as strange, secretive, and sometimes as dangerous. . . . Suppressing them and needing them at the same time, men have never been completely comfortable in their apparent state of social superiority and have always been apprehensive of the possibility of rebellion or revenge on the part of women. This mood of apprehension exists frequently on the part of oppressors. . . . Basically they have attempted to deny women the ability to do things men do and have either idealised them into sweetness and purity which make them appear docile and harmless, or they have maligned them in order to be able to condemn them. Both types of behaviour help men to feel better about their denial of equality to women. Thus many male attempts to understand women have actually been attempts to rationalise men's treatment of the other sex and have frequently been nothing but self-deceptions. . . . It has been the traditional opinion of criminologists that women commit relatively few crimes and that when they do so they somehow betray their womanhood by venturing out into a reserve of men.
>
> (Pollak, 1961, p. 149)

For Pollak the relations between the sexes must be understood as socially constructed; even such apparently biological givens such as menstruation, he argues, are heavily socially coded, surrounded by taboos and made the subject of shame and secrecy. Female deceitfulness can be traced back to such male reactions to 'difficult' subjects. More generally as well, he regards social gender roles as oppressive and exploitative to women and his account of these conventions is hardly *outré*: 'In our society, the roles of women are still primarily those of homemaker, the preparer of meals, the rearer of children, the nurse of the sick, the shopper and the domestic service worker' (Pollak, p. 152). He catalogues the relations of power involved in these conventional gender roles – the imposition of a double standard of sexual morality for married women, the exploitation of low paid domestic workers, the manipulation of female consumers by advertising techniques. Women clearly have motives for crime and the targets will not surprisingly be their near and dear.

Female crime is thus to be understood in terms of that particular sphere of access given by the female role, combined with the way in which femininity has responded to its oppressive terms, developing the guile originally forced upon them as shame into a form of sex warfare and social protest. Not all women will become criminals since other factors such as family background and differential associations must also be taken into account. But, once formed, the female criminal career is formidable. For the woman, though excluded from the public domain, nonetheless has access to that specialised and lethal preserve of criminal activity, the kitchen and environs. It is here that the oppressed wife, fuelled into a fury of deceptiveness, will meditate upon and eventually carry out her crimes, utilising those familiar items of domestic crime, the poisoned dinner and the electric carver. Or she might turn her attention to other objects, weaker than herself, abusing her children sexually and physically.

All this area of criminality continues to be masked not only by the privacy of the home and the success of female cunning, but by the oafish or, as Heidensohn has it, besotted leniency with which the oppressor continues to regard the oppressed. Pollak sees his brothers in criminology, like all men, as offering rationalisations about female conduct, notably the splitting which insists that women are either totally sweet, pure and docile or entirely evil and unnatural.

Pollak's book should have functioned as an occasion for feminist criminology to specify precisely what kind of alternative would be acceptable. Of course, it is sexist to see women as deceitful and there are many other unacceptable suggestions in the book. But identifying these signs and symptoms is not sufficient in respect to the problems he raises about what a feminist criminology would consist in. His summoning of the reservoir of female crime echoes that equalising wish noted earlier, while he seems to recognise social relations, power and the distortions of criminological presumption. The work falls down on empirical grounds as Heidensohn shows, but the project and terms he sets are never decisively rejected. Nor is his unique relation to criminological tradition ever deemed worthy of comment. How is it that a man with the 'same' sexist views produces the opposite theory of female crime to everyone else? Can the logic of a criminological argument be rendered simply in terms of its 'views' on women?

Thus Pollak's work could even be seen as a parodic version of that third alternative option left by the foundational critique, neither masculinising female crime nor denying its possibility to the little woman. On his account 'society must change' to reduce female crime of the household sort. One might be forgiven (but this is unlikely) for thinking that this could have been seen as a feminist alternative, at least as specified by the critique, the distinctively female criminality 'waiting in the wings' for investigation. Further, in 'discovering' a generically distinct area of female crime on an impressive scale of volume and seriousness, he insists on the social origins of gender roles, views them as exploitative and sees this power relation as a motivation for female revenge (an early version of the social bandit theory?). His use of criminology and sociology may be slightly dotty but is not totally inept, for he draws on theories of differential association and opportunity to refine his position – not all oppressed women will turn into criminals. His claims about the arbitrariness of how acts are criminalised and the masked character of domestic crime have also appeared in feminist discussions. Finally, like all 'emancipation-and-crime' theorists he can hardly be accused of insisting on an eternal and unchanging biologically based femininity. All this a feminist criminology would have to be, in order to be feminist. Is it enough to assert the social origin of gender roles, or to insist on their oppressive quality? *How* would such an insistence illuminate the issue of female crime, as opposed to harping on the need for things to be different? Indeed, how precisely is female crime and criminality posed by the tradition, if this is to function as a scene of avoidance? In what sense is Pollak 'the same' when he says the opposite?

Instead, the critique reiterates a familiar package of the sins of the fathers, a package which blocks thought by reducing all male criminology to a stereotypical sameness. Pollak has been handled in a now familiar set of moves. He is clearly misogynist in his 'views' of women – the theme of female deceitfulness is a calumny as old as Adam and Eve. The undoubted shakiness of his empirical arguments for the existence of this vast reservoir of female crime is to be read primarily as symptomatic of his sexist attitudes, 'more ideological than empirical' (Heidensohn, p. 120). From misogyny, biologism follows as the night the day. His error *must* be seeing women as biologically determined. Thus, for Heidensohn, the main task is to discredit him professionally as a sociologist, to show that his discussion of the social elements in crime and gender is a deceit. He is to be scorned for ignoring major sociological contributions to criminology. Sutherland, for instance, 'rates a passing mention' (Pollak, p. 39) but his theory of differential association is not used' (Heidensohn, p. 119). This despite the fact that Pollak's chapter 'The Social Factors in Crime' begins with a section entitled 'Differential Association', citing Sutherland as the main source. Equally, his account of the social origin of gender characters must be returned to a view of women's 'inherent' deceit; what in one sentence is correctly identified as his linkage of deceptiveness and cultural taboos becomes in the next '*his* negative evaluation of all aspects of the reproductive cylce' (Heidensohn, p. 120, emphasis added). Gradually, he can be transformed back into that one known variety of criminological sexist, whose most secret wish, to link gynaecology and crime, is not to be realised until 1969 when Katherine Dalton announced that great pseudo-medical entity, PMT syndrome.

As Carlen's anti-essentialist move permits, it is no longer necessary to find biological determinism at the heart of every criminological stereotyping. Pollak's error with respect to gender is at the level of presumptive categorisations, assumptions that the categories masculine/feminine will have the same global content and that, correspondingly, men and women all over the world will live them out, as for instance in his presumption of a uniform universal male reaction to menstruation. This presumption can be criticised without trying to find biological determinism as the necessary evil, and contriving all sexists to fit into this mould.

The lessons to be drawn from this are clear and sobering. No wonder the results of the decade have been 'disappointing'. After ten years of work, such misogny-and-biologism critiques should no longer be tolerable as serious work. At the very least they can give the impression that the great undead have never been read. Worse, they give feminist criminology the false assurance that an acceptable 'alternative' will magically emerge simply by asserting society over biology, demonstrating an awareness of power relations and the constructed nature of criminological facts. Pollak does all this and can hardly be called feminist. Yet the critical package has no way of saying why not. The anti-essentialist 'instrument' is an asset, but it is *not* sufficient, for it is necessary to consider seriously what might be at issue not just in questions of women but in questions of women and crime. Here, perverse as it may seem, going back and re-reading such ancient monsters as Lombroso and Ferrero is an important enterprise, as will be argued in the next section.

Taking criminology seriously

One of the main shifts over the past ten years of feminist criminology has been its increasing awareness of criminology as a discipline, a critical consciousness of its methods and resources as well as its limitations, scepticisms and political angsts. This shows up in mundane but useful ways in Heidensohn's book with its conscientious cataloguing of the strengths and weaknesses of available approaches. In Carlen's brief introduction the issues are bigger and more critically posed, for after all she is counselling the abandonment of any special 'women's questions' in relation to crime. In this she can be seen as representative of a wider trend, within and outside specifically feminist criminology, of abandoning 'why' questions in favour of 'how'. Asking 'why' has come to seem too redolent of old presumptions about demarcated classes of beings, criminals, women, women criminals; by contrast, merely asking 'how', especially how individuals are criminalised, has come to seem a less complicit form of investigation.

Thus, one might say that the stance represented by Greenwood and Cousins has had effects even if their writings have not been widely recognised. No one today would naively point to an unresearched area of female criminality crying out for investigation, at least one hopes not. The same would presumably hold for any special question of female *non*-criminality but here, as we shall see, optimism is less justified.

Unfortunately this process of taking criminology seriously is not yet sufficiently installed. The awareness of the discipline and its distinctive categories and concepts, its idiosyncracies even, is still too distant, too much a matter of making external critiques of its hidden agendas and values. Feminist criminology is too laden down with these overly 'wise' pre-packaged critiques from the 1970s which essentially explain criminology by reference to things it is not, notably sociology. Even the 'critiques of the critique' as posed by Greenwood and Cousins are essentially animated by extra-criminological criteria, measures of acceptable theories of sexual differences or the exposure of criminological politics. To make this complaint is not to make a plea for the virtues of criminology-as-a-science, merely a wish that its traditional notions of norm and pathology, crime and criminality be explained, and hence that what it actually says about Women and Crime finally be addressed. We have critiques of the conceptualisation of women as a category; we have critiques of criminology – but they have still not been posed properly to reconstruct traditional criminology's understanding of female criminality. Even Carlen's account is a matter of setting out, in parallel, on one side, the sex/gender conflation and on the other side, the lawbreaking/criminalisation conflation. Paradoxically, for all those endlessly reiterated accounts of Lombroso and Ferrero, their theories have never been understood in their own terms.

Despite the immense influence attributed to such founding texts as *The Female Offender*, there is nonetheless a profound resistance to reading them as criminology. No one has concealed or distorted their statements but nonetheless a set of reading habits dismisses the idea that such obviously misogynist views could have any coherence or logic. Traditional criminology, at least with respect to women, essentially has no content: 'Were the theories of Lombroso, Pollak and others to be rid of their sexism, there would be no theories left which could be treated as plausible' (Smart, 1981, p. 85). Exhausted by their sexism, riddled with revealing contradictions, the only coherence allowed to such texts is as re-presentations of external social relations and prejudices held together by the glue of biologistic pseudo-science. Thus, for Heidensohn, traditional criminology is largely a potpourri of 'views' about women, imported from outside criminology and mindlessly regurgitated in respect to women and crime. For her traditional criminology has two main external sources: for its 'view' of the conventional 'normal' woman it reproduces conventional social roles, while its depiction of the criminal woman is drawn from the murky well of popular myth and folklore with its twisted and archaic images of female monstrosity. There is no question of a 'theory' of female criminality – indeed it would appear that the tradition was not basically asking about women and crime at all, merely reflecting social reality with all its contradictions.

This stubborn indifference to criminology is lodged even more firmly in the heart of the foundational critique, in what amounts to a biologistic fixation. As shown earlier, this one-line depiction of traditional criminology has functioned as a way of identifying and countering 'the' motivated error of the past, at the same time facilitating the appropriation and assimilation of gender sociology and 'radical' criminology. This has been the process of 'negating' past theories by which feminist 'alternatives' have been at least gesturally indicated. If these alternatives have proved less than satisfactory, it is not only because they have been insufficiently thought through, mere negations of past sexism. Rather, as will be argued here, they have been the negation of a phantasm, a creature which is not really the criminological hydra at all. That thesis of biological determinism, countered so neatly by the slogan 'society must change, not the individual', is largely irrelevant. The blame for this mischaracterisation lies precisely in those two useful theoretical resources: from gender sociology traditional criminology is read as if it were a sort of perverted role theory rather than a discipline concerned with crime; radical criminology not only compounds this error but adds its own metaphysical contribution.

Under the heading of 'biological determinism' two main themes of the foundational package of critique-and-alternative may be distinguished: biological v. social origins of gender roles and mechanical v. self-determining individual action. These two themes supposedly capture the erroneous fixities that traditional criminology ascribes to women, a fixity of female character and role, and a fixity of female action. In these two fixities traditional criminology is known and disposed of. First, fixity of role: here biologism and its cognates are seen as asserting an unchanging and unchangeable female nature, a maternal character consisting of a typified bundle of eternal attributes and activities. The allegedly more biological or pre-social or natural origin of this female role is seen as giving it a presumed inevitability. Second, fixity of individual action: here biologism is seen as dictating an iron and mechanical bodily regimentation of individual women's actions as being outside their control, irrational, unintentional, emotional. Female hormones condemn 'normal', and 'criminal' women especially, to a life-time of robotics. These two themes are allied not only in the play on the word 'determinism' but in the depiction of women's treatment at law which combines a sickness model with role-resocialisation.

It has already been shown that this lodestone of biological determinism is unsatisfactory as diagnosis and in the alternatives it summons up. Society could end up as determining and homogenising feminity and females as biology was alleged to be. In any case, it appears that past and present sexist theories have a curious way of neither denying social origins to gender nor the possibility of social change. Pollak and 'sisters in crime' are clear examples here and both even see traditional social roles as exploitative. Here one might add to the list of 'emancipation and crime' theorists Lombroso and Ferrero themselves who also hold that 'criminality increases among women with the march of civilisation'. How they manage to do this at the same time as being biological determinists in the accepted senses is rather difficult to understand – but perhaps this is just another revealing 'contradiction'.

Clearly there is something adrift in the biology/society, determinism/change opposition. Pat Carlen's anti-essentialist move was seen as an attempt to deal with this by shifting the diagnosis of error onto the level of categorisations rather than origins. Yet even she falls back into the old diagnostics of traditional criminology and social mythologies, characterising them as biologistic. This produces a retrograde effect in her, admittedly briefly indicated, new alternative, as can be traced through the multiple connotations of the term 'rational'. As will be shown, this term is put under strain, required to stand for 'anti-essentialist' heterogeneity, but also structured as the alternative to those old sins specified by biological determinism and its pathologisation of the female offender. Consequently, traditional criminology and the criminal justice system remain those unreconstructed old engines of the foundational critique.

Thus we return to that originally sinful text, *The Female Offender* by Lombroso and Ferrero, seeking to identify the logic of its argument. In doing so no attempt is being made to deny the sexism of the views – among the calumnies, one finds that women are not only said to be deceitful, insensitive, unloving and vengeful but actually congratulated for their alleged lack of sexual feeling, and so on. Nor am I making any attempt to reclaim criminal anthropology as a valid science – female atavism is not to be put forward as an 'interesting' proposition. No strikingly new 'discoveries' will be made of new statements in the book – most items will be familiar. What is being insisted upon, however, is that the book cannot be read simply as a self-contradictory jumble of prejudices whose only coherence derives from the society it reflects and the biologism by which it legitimises this society. It will be argued that these propositions are part of a set of questions and answers about Women and Crime, not just a free-floating set of 'views' about women. It is these questions, more than the 'biologism' of the answers, which have shaped the question of female criminality and continue to do so today, even within feminist criminology.

As a preliminary reminder, it is perhaps necessary to record very crudely a few basic aspects of the project of criminological positivism, and its central mission of identifying criminality (see Wolfgang 1960 and Garland 1985). Essentially it was seeking a set of signs by which criminal beings could be identified and distinguished into categories of criminal – the true criminal, the epileptic and lunatic, the occasional criminal, the criminaloid, as broad categories, the murderer, the thief and embezzler as subcategories. The signs it sought were physical anomalies, irregularities and disease. The general thesis was that true criminality arises from a stem of atavism and degeneracy, a regression to an earlier stage of human evolution manifesting itself not only in crime but in other social and individual pathologies such as lunacy and epilepsy. The 'pathology' of this degeneracy consists in the regression itself (more primitive morphological forms) and in the morbidity by which such anomalies deviated from the normal type, ranging from atypical dispositions of the brain inside the skull, to asymmetries of physiognomy to epilepsy and hysteria in men and women. It is in this search for markers of criminality that positivism makes its central displacement from eighteenth century legal concepts of criminal actions and towards the assessment of the criminal beings who commit such acts, the distinction between crime and criminality. Whereas the legal concept seeks to grade acts on a scale of seriousness and award penalties, the burden of positivism was that the treatment of the criminal ought to be by reference to the pathology or non-pathology of the criminal agent. Equal crimes were no longer to be seen as automatically meriting equal treatment. A mere occasional offender should not be regarded in the same way as the true criminal – the same criminal action would not necessarily signify a form of degeneracy, and it was criminological science which could make these distinctions. Indeed, it is part of this approach that the concept of penalty is also displaced along with the concept of gravity of offence, since the objective is to control crime by managing the offender appropriately, not punishing per se. And, by the logic which links criminality to a wider sphere of degeneracy as the object of positive knowledge, it is not only lawbreakers but other degenerate populations which come under scrutiny: hence a dual network for seeking out subjects to measure and identify not only the denizens of the courtroom but the asylum and inebriate hostel as well. While the distinctively physical basis of criminality has been abandoned, many of these distinctions continue to define criminology long after the positivist project was thrown into disrepute.

Crude as this account is, it will be sufficient context to reconsider the framing of the questions of female criminality.

Fixity of character

The Female Offender is concerned to do for female criminals and degenerates what Lombroso had previously done for the male. When he turns his attention to female delinquency he is seeking a parallel set of signifiers of degeneracy among the female population, and here he finds himself confronting the central problem. While such signs can be found among prostitutes they are for the most part absent in female criminals. This 'absence of physical anomalies' is the defining question of the book. Having spent seven chapters presenting all available external measurements of facial angles, armspans, height and weight, internal measurements of brain weight and organ constitution, having pushed further into the preferred area of actual pathology and found few physical deformities, little ugliness or disease, at last in the notorious chapter 8 'The Criminal Type in Women and its Atavistic Origin' it sets itself the task of explaining the 'remarkable rarity of anomalies', the fact that the female criminal is 'of less typical aspect than the male'.

The answer is that she is 'less essentially criminal'; what makes her a woman makes her non-criminal i.e. less degenerate. The reasons are those familiar items: '. . . because in all forms of degeneration she deviates to a less degree, because, being organically conservative, she keeps the characteristics of her type even in her aberrations from it' (pp. 111–12). The woman is closer to her species type than the male and that type is organically more conservative.

This explanation of the lack of signs of female criminality presents two prima facie contradictions identified by Lombroso and Ferrero. First, on their general account, atavistic degeneracy is held to be the stem of criminality – how can it produce the opposite in the female? Second, the true physical anomalies which do show up in the case of the prostitute and the few true female criminals are essentially marks of masculinity, notably a heavy jaw – how can female atavism be towards a fixed feminity for women in general and a masculinity in the case of true female criminals? Seeing how they deal with these contradictions makes the overall argument clearer.

Both male and female are to be understood in terms of an evolutionary schema shaped by the role of reproduction, in a much-quoted phrase, the 'immobility of the ovum compared with the zoosperm' (p. 109). This accounts for the organic conservatism of the female as opposed to the male (political affiliations are cited as confirmation). To this *add* the fact that

> the female, on whom falls the larger share of the duty of bringing up the children, necessarily leads a more sedentary life, and is less exposed than the male to the varying conditions of time and space in her environment.
>
> (p. 109)

It is this *relation* between biology and environment which is the key to their argument that the female is atavistic in the sense of being closer to her species type. The activity of the male leads him into more contact with the world and consequently more adaptations and individual variation. Consequently they have evolved more. By contrast

> the *common* characters of a genus are more evident in the forms of the female. Most naturalists are agreed that for the type of a species one must look to the female rather than the male.
>
> (p. 108)

This account of the relative evolutionary development of male and female is rather like current popular-science accounts of the difference between humans and animals, in which one distinctive feature, e.g. an opposed thumb, leads through greater interaction with the environment to the departure from instinctive behaviour, to individuation over speciation.

Already one can see this is somewhat different from the standard account of Lombroso and Ferrero. It is true that the conservatism of the female species is simply announced, but the ovule is allowed to exist in a world of social duties which add to the insulation from environmental stimulation. (Cesare Lombroso's work was in 1895 'evolving' towards an increasing recognition of social influences.) Further, atavism now has a sense in terms of a logic of evolutionary development understood as the difference between species type and individuation for female and male; it is possible to make generalisations about women in a way one cannot for men.

Consequently women are essentially non-criminal for two reasons, the conservatism of the ovule and the lack of variation in species type. Male degeneracy and hence criminality is explained by variability. The activity and openness to external influence, the range of 'genetic' variation, which makes the male more evolved also makes him more prone to 'transformation and deformation by the influences which determine special and retrogressive variations in the male' (p. 109). This variability also appears in the psychology of the individual criminal, the 'morbid irritation of the psychical centres which find relief in evil action' (p. 158) – internal causes where external causes are absent. Physical deformations are not only signs of degeneracy but initiating causes, the asymmetrical brain, for instance producing unbearable pressures, the insistent irritation which drives the true criminal to otherwise incomprehensible action. If the male had as settled a male constitution as the female has a female one, he would not be criminal.

Let us turn to the second contradiction, the masculine atavism of the prostitute and the true female criminal. To understand this, it must be remembered that women are less evolved, not that they have never changed. By reference to regressive forms, the child and the primitive (racism is a familiar accompaniment to sexism), Lombroso and Ferrero identify an earlier evolutionary stage in which men and women were less differentiated from each other. (Durkheim puts forward a similar view, seeing sexual differentiation of secondary characteristics as yet another instance of the division of labour in society.) This earlier stage is also identified as an era of less sexual restraint, again a familiar piece of 19th-century anthropologising as put forward by Morgan and promulgated by Engels.

What is to be gained by such a return to Lombroso, and Ferrero, apart from the having a slightly more coherent rendering of their position? First, and most generally, it must be recognised that there is a question-and-answer structure to the enterprise, the key *question* which they pose in respect to women and crime is female non-criminality, the absence of physical anomalies or indicators of female criminality and degeneracy. The *answer* to this question is the claim that women are closer to their species type, with the dual consequences of exemplifying its passive-conservatism and possessing a general species homogeneity 'sheltered' from environmental interaction and consequent degenerative (as well as progressive) individuation. This answer is no doubt misogynist, sexist, patriarchal and paternalist; female atavism and inferiority is simply asserted and value-judgments abound; their statements no doubt correspond to 'views' about women circulated in the wider social field and any shifts in that social field induced by civilisation's effect on women are seen as threatening. *But* these are not just 'views' floating in a vacuum, comprehensible only by reference to external social source; they are the raw materials of an answer to what is posed as *the* question of women and crime, namely female non-criminality – why are women not true criminals?

Further, this understanding of female acriminality shapes the understanding of female crime when it does occur. Female crime is, in effect, a paradox, a contradiction in terms, to be explained by saying that females are for the most part only occasional criminals. The non-criminality of their nature, the absence of signs of true criminality, has a discounting effect on the apparent gravity of the act. Hence, the statements about the female maternal nature, their biological proclivities are, for the general run of female crime, used *not* as explanations of crime but of non-crime or, rather, non-criminality. They are explanations of why the female perpetrators are not truly criminal beings. Women are, for the most part, *not* pathological, not 'sick' enough, to count as truely criminal in the positivist scheme; this is why they are, to use Carlen's phrase, 'not real criminals'. Indeed, Lombroso himself later sought to intervene in the 'legal' concepts of seriousness of offence, arguing in *Crime and its Causes* that crimes such as prostitution, abortion and infanticide should not be regarded as crime; these are merely 'legal' crimes.

Hence what Lombroso and Ferrero say about the residual class of true female degenerates and criminals is of little significance. It is their understanding of the typical female criminal as essentially non-criminal that is the more influential and significant part of their claim, for it is this group which constitutes the greatest group of female criminals. What they say about the true female criminal as pathological monster cannot be taken as the essence of their theory of female criminality. On the contrary, it is female non-criminality which is the standard, even for the female criminal; it forms the background against which her apparently criminal action must be shown to be an accident.

Thus, it is possible to see *The Female Offender* as more than just a jumbled and incoherent mass of prejudice, but as text operating with a discernible and connected set of problems and solutions. So far we have only considered the contradictions identified with Lombroso and Ferrero. What of the contradictions which, according to Heidensohn, even a 'superficial examination' will reveal in traditional criminology?

(i) that *only* females are seen as affected by their biology. We have seen how both male and female are understood by Lombroso and Ferrero through their reproductive role; that it is the activity of the male reproductive role which leads to the evolutionary differences between the two.

(ii) that women's biological 'determination' should lead them to experience a much higher crime rate – we have seen that female atavism and the maternal species character are explanations of *non*-criminality for women, that they will be, if anything, mere occasional criminals.

(iii) that true female criminality is, contradictorily, both unnatural and occurring in nature through atavism or hormonal influence – this seems to be partly based just on a misunderstanding of the basic concepts of biology, in which disease or malfunction can develop out of normal functioning, and partly on a misquoting of Lombroso and Ferrero who do not in fact describe the 'monstrous' female criminal as unnatural.

However, there are far more fundamental issues at stake. Lombroso and Ferrero do set the agenda for understanding female crime, not so much through the biologism of their 'views', but in the question-and-answer series. First, as Carlen would argue, they set up female criminality as a *separate* question, seeking a set of markers of female criminality parallel to that of men. Second, and fundamentally, they pose the problem of women's non-criminality as *the* issue to be explained. Third, it is against the backdrop of the equation of femininity and non-criminality that female crime is understood as not really criminal since women are, by and large, not really criminal.

It is these questions and answers which must be interrogated, and they are far from anachronistic. The question of women and crime has been crucially dominated by the single issue of female non-criminality. Why do women, as a group, not commit crime? As Lombroso and Ferrero put it in a less archaic formulation: 'All statistics show that women are much less criminal than men'. (p. 181) Is this a valid question? Heidensohn's answer would presumably be 'yes', since her book is supposed to initiate investigation of the 'previously neglected' area of female conformity, with respect to both criminal and non-criminal conduct. That it is also Lombroso and Ferrero's question might at least give pause for a moment's doubt. Carlen's answer is, in effect, 'no', because any question which starts off from women-as-a-group will end up essentialising women.

However, Lombroso and Ferrero do more than essentialise women. In their answer to the question of female non-criminality, they not only ascribe a homogeneity to women but construe that identity on the map of deviance and non-deviance, and, as has been argued, this has consequences for the understanding of female lawbreakers as well as female law-abiding citizens. This process by which criminology constructs personality by reference to the question of law-breaking has been one of its distinctive features as a discipline. The deviancy-theory critiques of traditional criminology elaborate on the way in which the act/being, crime/criminality displacement has tended to operate. In positivism, it is physical traits, particularly pathological ones, which are linked together as signs of criminality to produce a typology of criminalities under the overall typing of true criminal and non-criminal. Less physicalist criminologies compile other traits, ranging from infractions of school discipline, to IQ measurements, to 'anti-social' habits and hobbies. Out of these traits, a deviant personality is composed, the identity expressed in the outward and inward signs, the linking nature which allows the signs to be referred to each other for mutual intelligibility and confirmation. This is more than a matter of stereotyping individuals or imposing value-judgments since it involves, in addition, an understanding of individual's identities as having a general orientation to rule-breaking, a deviant identity.

In effect, the opposite process happens for women in *The Female Offender*, and the same kinds of fallacies can be identified. An initial phenomenon, the lack of physical anomalies (itself open to question) is then construed in terms of a general disposition (passivity) which is itself used to argue for a general typology of female non-degeneracy. In more modern terms, one could say that a crime/statistical feature (itself dubious given the arbitrariness of which acts are criminalised, and the factors selecting 'who' is caught by the official figures) is then construed in terms of a general characteristic, non-deviance, supposedly covering all conduct and attributed to the entire female species. In both cases aspects of feminity – maternal role, social differentiation of male and female – is not only presumed and moralised but, more significantly, read as a totalised non-deviant personality. This is the kind of answer which seems implicit in posing female non-crime as a valid starting point.

Further, this equation of femaleness with non-criminality has significant effects on the understanding of female crime when it does occur since, as has been argued, female crime is discounted in that it is, for the most part, not committed by true criminals. Hence traditional criminology is misconstrued if it is seen as offering female biology as an explanation of female crime. Such 'explanations' of female crime have not been aimed at explaining female crime at all but at explaining why it is not criminality. The so-called leniency and 'chivalry' of the criminal justice system (if it *can* be directly deduced from criminological theory, which is dubious) presumably follows from this presumption. Hence the difference between male and female criminality; as understood by the tradition, lies in this asymmetrical relationship to criminality. Male criminal conduct, unlike female criminal conduct, is not a contradiction in terms.

This allows the specific differences between male and female criminality to be elaborated. First, there is a different relation presumed between normal and deviant conduct for men and women. For Lombroso and Ferrero, individual variation is the principle of both progress and degeneration. The male degenerative pathological types may be understood on the *same* spectrum as the norm, criminality being a distorted but recognisable version of civilised conduct. The same principle of activity links them. However one puts it, for men, deviance and non-deviance are mutually comprehensible. By contrast, the female norm makes true criminality unintelligible. The monster of the genuine female criminal is not just a creature from the wardrobe of ancient misogyny but a statistical monster and a theoretical monster, since she contradicts the thesis of the female conformist nature. It is not her evil which threatens but her unintelligibility.

Second, men are individuated where women are speciated. For male criminality there is a typology, a range of variation and differentiation and individuation. The female, by contrast, is referred to her species as defined by her reproductive role. By referring female criminality back to the species-type of female non-criminality, female criminality is gendered in a way that male criminality is not.

This, as Heidensohn indicates, has been the norm of the discipline (sub-cultural theories being the only exception). Only female crime is gendered, referred to the femininity of their species for an explanation.

These specific differences are obscured by a rendering of traditional criminology as a doctrine of determination and biology. They are also obscured in that biologism is understood as the underpinning of symmetrical social gender toles, simply extended from the area of 'normal' conduct into the area of crime. Rather the relation of men to women is asymmetrical with respect to crime, *male* conduct or character is on a spectrum from normal to pathological, but for the woman in the tradition this is not true.

Fixity of conduct

In the foundational package, the theme of biologically determined female action is usually seen more or less as a consequence of the view that women have a biologically determined nature or role. However, this theme of mechanical regulation is usually elaborated upon in the context of the treatment of women by the criminal justice system. Here the 'fact', allegedly derived from criminological theory, that women are more at the mercy of their hormones, is seen as determining their image as sick and pathological, as not responsible for their actions. It follows, for the foundational position, that women will tend to be 'treated' rather than punished. Further, the more 'role-deviant' a woman is, the more she will be regarded as abnormal and in need of a psychologised dose of resocialisation.

It is in the area of the criminal justice system that the most successful feminist research has been done over the last ten years. Carlen's *Women's Imprisonment* (1983) is a notable example. Some of this work has thrown the foundational package's image into doubt into various ways. Carlen's introduction to *Criminal Women* complains of the myth that women's prisons 'are not real prisons at all, but hybrids between mental hospitals and some rather saucy St Trinians' (p. 9), although, in line with her earlier diplomacy, she does not identify this as a myth of feminist criminology too. Another anomaly for the package is thrown up by her insistence that 'single women, divorced women and women with children in care being more likely to receive custodial sentences than women who, at the time of their court appearances, are living at home with their husbands and children. (pp. 8–9). This would seem to contradict the claim that the more role-deviant a woman is, the more she is likely to receive non-custodial treatment, as sick. Mary Eaton's work (1985) would allow some development of this theme, in that she offers a reminder of the multiple considerations in sentencing decisions, of which the effects of a custodial sentence on the offender's family is an element.

This applies to both men and women, no doubt in stereotypical ways, the family being seen as deprived of a breadwinner in the one case and a mother's care in the other. She also indicates that being a good parent counts for men as well as for women as a sign of being a normal regular citizen. Thus, in various empirical ways the package image of soft social-control for mechanically driven, sick, women has come into question.

Heidensohn also raises important issues about the 'equalising' logic of the foundational package. As Mark Cousins had argued earlier (1980, p. 30), such a theme, associated with the rhetoric of oppositional discourses, would seem to imply that future justice demands equal incarceration in punitive establishments.

> Imprisoning women does raise some very difficult issues for feminists. Should women be treated exactly as men are? Is it fairer to recognise their lower levels of criminality and their lesser social threat and domestic ties? Should babies be imprisoned with their mothers?
>
> (Heidensohn, p. 83)

Here too, one could add that much of the debate contrasting punitive and treatment models turns not only on criticisms of unrecognised controls of *women*, but in the increasing social and sociological scepticism about 'soft' social control options and the 'widening net' of regulation, surveillance and social management. Simple ironising contrasts between the respective treatment of men and women is clearly no longer sufficient.

Nonetheless, both these books still retain much of the rhetoric and analysis of the old foundational critique, simply juxtaposing it to more critical arguments, or implying that the critical arguments are logical extensions of the basic package. Once again, we find that the foundational critique acts as an obstacle to thinking about issues.

The theme of the mechanical determination of female conduct, and its association with a pathologising, resocialising regime is in fact riddled with contradictions and confusions, some of them deriving not from feminist argument at all but from the borrowed critiques, in this case the criminological critiques of positivism. Applied to female offenders, rather than male, further bewildering developments arise.

For the 'radical' critique of criminology, the image of the criminal fixed inexorably in his conduct is a key way of characterising and dismissing Lombroso's work and its influence on the prison system. Fixity of conduct is associated with the doctrine of the born criminal whose criminality is ineradicable and whose conduct owes nothing to social influences but is prescribed by the forms of degeneracy. Lombroso was also associated (and thereby damned) with the use of medicalising, individualising forms of correction:

> applying special methods of repression and occupation adapted to each individual as a physician does in prescribing dietary rules and special remedies according to the various illness . . .
>
> (*L'uomo delinquente*, quoted in Wolfgang, p. 213)

This criminological 'package' is part of the familiar dismissal of Lombroso's biologism, which, just like the feminist critique, overemphasises the elements of born criminality and the purely physicalist and biologistic basis of his theories. As has been argued earlier, the influence of Lombroso on criminology is far more difficult to eradicate than this easy diagnosis suggests, for physical traits of criminality may easily be replaced with not only psychological but social ones. Equally the development of his views and their real influence on correctionalist institutions simply becomes incomprehensible if he is understood solely through the doctrine of the born criminal. It is not for the born criminal but those others whose criminality is habitual or even occasional that regimes, such as that cited above, are intended.

However, as received by the easy critique, criminological positivism is set up in terms of two basically contradictory themes, mechanicism and treatment, as if they were mutually implicative. To be fair, these themes do correspond to actual debates at different stages of Lombroso's career, but indicating *changes* in his views. They do not make sense if regarded as identities. Thus, the emphasis on mechanically fixed behaviour is part of a basically metaphysical and juristic debate about freedom of the will and responsibility for action. The scientific model of laws of human conduct is essentially based on Newtonian mechanics and even earlier Cartesian themes of the human automaton. Such a view of human action is then pitted against a Christian or legal doctrine of freedom of the will, transparency of motive, responsibility for sin, and a clear differentiation between right and wrong. This is the rationalist model of human conduct, the jurists' 'abstract' focus on the criminal act which Lombroso was indeed to spend his lifetime opposing as a useless premise for understanding criminal action. Clearly, in this juristic debate, the notion of mechanically determined conduct is a key lever for disputing punitive concepts of punishment. There is no point punishing beings who have no control over their actions. It indeed remains the logic of dealing with the born criminal whose conduct is so fixed by his character that only the range of criminative strategies are appropriate, whether by death penalty (a subject of debate among positivists), exile, or lifetime imprisonment: morally blameless, yes, but a permanent social danger – this is a different rationale for incarceration than punishment.

But, quite obviously, the same logic of mechanically fixed preordained conduct cannot be the rationale of treatment, rehabilitation and reform, all those techniques, however eclectically garnered, however pragmatically chosen, by which the individual, not society, is to be *altered*. But this is not for the born criminal, since that would be sheer self-contradiction. The scientific model here is not mechanical laws of motion but the nineteenth-century model of biology, evolution, growth, whether healthy or pathological. It is in this build-up of techniques and in the sciences of identifying and recognising the varieties of criminality that the positivist tradition distinguishes itself.

Nonetheless, this conflation of pathologising with mechanicism has been very influential; the theme of determinism as repudiated in criminology as much as feminism. One of the outcomes of this critique was the 'discovery' that socially based theories of criminality – labelling theory, Marxist accounts of a crimogenic society – were as deterministic as positivism and consequently to be repudiated. Even where labelling theory began its career as an attempt to shift the debate away from causal questions, it nonetheless came to function within the discipline as a sort of alternative aetiology of criminality, ascribing causality to confirmcrs of secondary deviance. The invention of the New Criminological criminal can thus be seen as a further reaction, reasserting the rationality of the human agent as a genuine dignifying recognition of the lived experience of choice and the contribution of the actor to the meaningfulness of their own scripts. Laden down with implicit masculinity or not, the resulting criminal was to be imbued with full eighteenth-century honours, among which it was difficult to exclude culpability and punitive incarceration.

In borrowing this depiction of positivism, including the rationalist final move, the feminist critique of criminology has thus lumbered itself with a rather dismal misunderstanding. Worse than that, it is difficult to see how 'rationality' can be espoused without at the same time requiring the full sway of regimental implications which Heidensohn and Cousins query. Are incarcerating sheriffs to be unsung heroes, at last according the female criminal the full seriousness and intentionality of the real male criminal in his real prison?

However, the construction of this contrast between male and female treatment at law is even more perilous. For, as the above makes clear, this is a contrast essentially between juridical and criminological categories. What does it mean to use this to characterise the *difference* between the treatment of men and women in criminological theory and penal practice? And how can a critique of the pathologising of the individual male offender be, in conscience, borrowed to *deny* male pathologisation? First, consider criminological *theory*. Clearly it does not see real male criminals as rational intentional actors. It is opposing this concept of action and would, crudely speaking, like to pathologise everyone. The most 'pathological', the born criminal, is subject not to alteration but to incarceration on the basis of social defence, not responsibility. Further, as we have seen, the typical female criminal, for positivism, is an occasional criminal and not a true, born criminal. Most female offenders therefore, not regarded as totally determined in their behaviour, are *not pathological enough* to warrant social-defence incarceration, or indeed to be regarded as true criminals at all. Their suitability for medicalising alteration derives from the essentially non-criminal nature of their act. Thus, within criminological theory, it is female non-criminality, their closeness to their species type which occasions the recommended treatment, because women are not as 'sick' as men.

Second, however, criminological theory is not the legal system or prison. The logic of one cannot be substituted for the other; the treatment of men and women at law cannot simply be deduced from criminological theory; the influence of criminology in its attempt to displace legal and juristic concepts and re-model penal institutions was not total. The legal system and sentencing decisions and types of incarcerating institutions are mixed modes, combining concepts which may even seem incompatible, including in sentencing rationales items not even mentioned in this rhetorical contrast between mechanical and free behaviour, considerations such as those mentioned earlier concerning the welfare of the family. Equally, the routes of individuals to prison may be far from intentional outcomes of sentencer's rationales, the large numbers of men and women currently incarcerated for nonpayment of fines being a prime example. Thus male incarceration cannot simply be equated with an ascription of rationality and intentionality by contrast with female irrationality and pathology. Legal concepts of blame, in respect to sentencing, are mixed with criminological assessments of true criminality: however, stereotypically, stealing 'for the children' is regarded as a sign of non-criminality where stealing for pure gain is not. Further, to the (limited) extent that positivism succeeds and male incarcerating institutions are correctionalist, then male incarceration too must be understood in terms of the logic of reformability and 'pathology'. What is actually at stake is not a crude difference between rationality and mechanicism but in different techniques of reform.

Clearly, these are complex histories requiring historical investigation. Yet no such investigation can be undertaken if we are offered such 'background information' on the prison accounts such as the following:

> Imprisonment has historically functioned in three ways, custodially to hold prisoners (and some witnesses awaiting trial), coercively – for example, to resecure payment of a debt – and penally as a punishment.
>
> (Heidensohn, p. 59)

Conclusion

The two books examined here have obviously not been investigated in terms of their own proprieties, but rather as indicators on the map of feminist criminology, its past and future progress. Overall the argument has been that the terms of the foundational critique have had damaging consequences and must be interrogated more carefully. In both these books, even where criticisms are made, or genuine advances made, the retention of the basic terms of reference have been associated with unwanted consequences and obstacles to thinking and empirical analysis. The other theme has been the curious indifference of feminist criminology to criminology itself, its basic lack of interest in the creature it is allegedly anatomising. That it is important to re-read ancient texts has been emphasised, not only to understand the past but in terms of thinking out feminist alternatives.

However, as a final comment, I would also like to suggest that the inseparability of the 'Women and Crime' question from the discipline is true in a more fundamental sense, that the Woman question probes all the weak and idiosyncratic spots of the discipline. The need to situate the incarceration/regulation debate not just in the domain of ironising contrasts but in the broader sphere of debates about hard and soft social control is one example. The treatment of women functions as exemplar of this option in social management and if its regime is unacceptable for women, then lessons over and above those of equalisation can be learned from it.

More classically, the question of woman can be said to pose all those general imponderables of criminology, the question of the 'dark figure' of crime, the existence of illegible motivations, inscrutable sexualities manifesting themselves unpredictably. However, it is in the asymmetrical relation of men and women to norm and pathology that the fortunes of the discipline are most visaged. For men, we saw, positivism sets up a continuum between norm and pathology. The same tendency to variability which produces progress also produces degenerate forms, visible links can be found between more evolved and atavistic types of criminality. Surely we have here, as the 'man' question, the first occurrence of what is to be a recurrent movement in criminology, its endless re-discovery of the link between 'normal' and criminal conduct. This is how the discipline keeps itself so young and fresh. Generation after generation discover that criminal and normal beings share goals and aspirations, cultural norms and identities. Here we find its atavistic form in the heart of positivism.

In respect of this discovery that crime is 'normal', female conduct is the abiding mystery, because, in a sense, non-criminal conduct has become unintelligible. Crime can be known only at the cost of rendering non-deviant social conduct an inexplicable phenomenon. Hence that other movement in criminology, the currently rising star of social control theories which seek to turn the cycle the other way to ask why people do not commit crime.

It is not surprising that the 'new' textbook on Women and Crime is so supportive of such an approach.

References

Carlen, P. (1983) *Women's Imprisonment. A Study in Social Control*, Routledge & Kegan Paul.

Cohen, S. (1974) 'Criminology and the Sociology of Deviance: A recent history and a current report' in P. Rock and M. McIntosh (eds.) *Deviance and Social Control*, Tavistock.

Cousins, M. (1980) '*Men's Rea*: A note on sexual difference, criminology and the law' in P. Carlen and M. Collison (eds.) *Radical Issues in Criminology*, Martin Robertson.

Eaton, M. (1985) 'Documenting the Defendant: placing women in social inquiry reports' in J. Brophy and C. Smart (eds.) *Women-in-Law*, Routledge & Kegan Paul.

Garland, D. (1985) *Punishment and Welfare: A history of penal strategies*, Gower.

Greenwood, V. (1981) 'The Myths of Female Crime' in A. Morris and L. Gelsthorpe (eds.) *Women and Crime*, Cropwood Papers, Cambridge Institute of Criminology.

Lombroso, C. (1911) *Crime, its Causes and Remedies*, Little, Brown.

Lombroso, C. and Ferrero, W. (1980/1895) *The Female Offender*, Fred B. Rothman/T. Fisher Unwin.

McRobbie, A. (1980) 'Settling Accounts with Subcultures: A feminist critique' *Screen Education*, no. 34.

Morgan, F. (1975) *Social Theory and the Family*, Routledge & Kegan Paul.

Pollak, O. (1961) *The Criminality of Women*, Perpetua.

Smart, C. (1977) *Women, Crime and Criminology: A feminist critique*, Routledge & Kegan Paul.

Smart, C. (1981) 'Response to Greenwood' in A. Morris and L. Gelsthorpe (eds.) *Women and Crime*, Cropwood Papers, Cambridge Institute of Criminology.

Wolfgang, M. (1960) 'Caesare Lombroso' in H. Mannheim (ed.) *Pioneers in Criminology*, Stevens and Son.

5

REALIST PHILOSOPHY AND STANDPOINT EPISTEMOLOGIES OR FEMINIST CRIMINOLOGY AS A SUCCESSOR SCIENCE[1]

Maureen Cain

Source: L. Gelsthorpe and A. Morris (eds), *Feminist Perspectives in Criminology*, Milton Keynes: Open University Press, 1990, pp. 124–40.

Neither criminology nor feminism offered the first standpoint epistemology. I believe that Antonio Gramsci (1972: especially 316) did that, although who was first does not matter. In criminology the question of whose side we are on has been around for more than twenty years (Becker, 1967) and, in a discipline which takes processes of societal inclusion and exclusion as its subject matter, decisions about the good and the bad, knowledge that there are at least two sides to every story, constantly threatens to erupt through the well-papered cracks of the discursive surface.

This chapter considers recent feminist standpoint epistemologies and feminist criticisms of them. I then explore the constituent ingredients of successor science: the disjunction between ontology and epistemology and the historicity of knowledge, the reclamation of theory, the new conception of standpoint and the concept of theoretical reflexivity. After that, in an interim section, the critique is reappraised in the light of the new theory. In the conclusion the threads are drawn together so that parts of the outline of a successor science become clear. Here, too, are explored the implications of the project for a feminist criminology.

Feminist standpoint epistemologies

Harding (1986) has ably pulled together and summarized the work of feminist standpoint epistemologists (see also Cain, 1987). In this section, therefore, I will explore only the work of Nancy Hartsock (1983) who stands as an exemplar of the approach.

Bodies, roles, and double vision: the standpoint epistemology of Nancy Hartsock

Like most feminist methodologists Hartsock, in my view, sets up something of a straw man, literally, of the traditional reseacher. But the straw person serves his proper purpose. He establishes for Hartsock what the feminist methodologist is definitely not. The straw man is concerned with establishing absolute truth claims; he achieves this by the monotonic application of a single allowed mode of reasoning; he aims to abstract knowledge formulations which objectify those investigated and which are indifferent to their own understandings of their experiences. He is concerned with separating rather than unifying and prefers dualistic, zero-sum forms for the separations he achieves; he is unemotional and detached, which leaves him in full control of those investigated; this hierarchic relationship is also maintained within the research teams he establishes. We achieve unity as feminists around the fact that we don't like him. For all that he stands for something real.

Hartsock makes the agument that women's bodies and women's life spaces make it easier for them to overcome the dualism between truth and falsity, subject and object, controller and controlled and, she might have added, feeling and detachment. This overcoming is easier for women than for men. It is easier because their subordinate position gives them access to two worlds. In living they are forced to participate both in their own life world *and* in that of the dominant group. This is an essential survival strategy. Thus women become aware of the complexity of social life and of the socially constructed nature of the world. Men do not have occasion to achieve this double vision in the course of their daily routines.

Secondly, and more concretely, Hartsock argues that in the course of domestic life, in cooking, cleaning and child rearing, women are routinely engaged in the production of use values. This applies whether or not they are also engaged in waged labour. So women are pulled away from the abstractions and objectifications of capital and they have more choice and control over whether they use concrete or abstracted modes of thought. (I am slightly distorting Hartsock here because I do not believe she disapproves of all abstract thought.)

Thirdly, women's bodily boundaries are continually being invaded or blurred. The particular examples of this which Hartsock gives are childbirth, pregnancy, coitus and menstrual flow. This, too, means that they are less concerned with separation and with dualistic thinking than are men.

Lastly, Hartsock argues, women are typically involved in processes of change and growth, in voluntarily reducing their control so that others may grow. Their success is measured in terms of how well others – their children – manage without them. This means that women's everyday thinking cannot be hierarchic, although it must be responsible. The dualistic choice is daily revealed as a nonsense so that it is easier for women to be anti-hierarchic.

Women are not only better situated to overcome dualistic thinking and hierarchic patterns of relationships than men: they need to develop these alternatives in order to give expression to their experiences. So the standpoint of women is epistemologically privileged: it is a standpoint from which it is easier to understand more and better. Even so, Hartsock is aware that working from the standpoint of women demands a political choice. The life space is facilitative; the standpoint is chosen. Hers is not a determinism. If women simply could not help knowing better we would have a dual knowledge system not a dominant and subjugated one.

Standpoint epistemologies: a critique

Hartsock's sophisticated analysis had the advantage of building on the work of earlier standpoint epistemologists such as Smith (1980) and Jaggar (1983a; 1983b). In the same way, I had the opportunity of assessing her contribution before developing my own (Cain, 1986a) discussion of what a feminist standpoint might entail for criminologists. In this section, therefore, I add my appraisal of Hartsock's work to the assessments of Harding (1986; 1987) and Smart (this volume), before arguing for a particular approach to standpoint epistemologies.

Because it so explicitly seeks to avoid determinism, Hartsock's argument is a very strong one. There are, however, two difficulties with it. In the first place, a lurking essentialism can be identified in her third argument. While accepting Midgley's (1988) point that more philosophical work needs to be done on 'natural' sex differences, I jib at Hartsock's argument here – even on biological grounds. Does semen not leave men's bodies as menstrual blood leaves women's bodies? Does not coitus involve a *mutual* 'blurring' of bodily boundaries? To see only the woman's bodily boundary as blurred is to accept, perhaps, men's definition of the difference between penetration and reception. But it is as easy to see the relation as a joining – a concept which gives primacy to neither of the bodies involved but rather sees both as equally 'blurred'.

Hartsock's other three points are concerned with the social position of women and I find them both plausible and closely fitting my own experience. But there are risks inherent in the first of these arguments too, for one corollary might be that if women stopped being subordinate they would lose their double vision. Their philosophy and their research work might become worse as a result. The points about involvement in production of use values and child rearing have more encouraging corollaries carrying a clear political message. If women abandon their involvement in these two kinds of activities in order to become more like untransformed men then their research will become worse. If, however, people of both sexes become involved in child rearing and the production of use values then women's research will stay the same and that of men will improve.

Harding makes the important point (1987: 187) that all the feminist epistemologies we have should be regarded as 'transitional epistemologies'. They should not be construed as finished products but as efforts which inform an ongoing practical struggle. This shapes our practice of criticism: the object of it is now to see what can be learned from the efforts of others. Scoring points off each other would at the least imply that we were competing for position in an already finished world. Not so.

Her critical discussion of standpoint epistemologies is, therefore, undertaken in this pedagogical spirit. Their value, she says (1986: 162), is that they question the argument that the social identity of the observer is irrelevant to the results, the belief that bias can be eliminated by the ritualistic application of technique, and the idea that political commitment reduces objectivity. On the other hand, some important issues are exposed and left unresolved:

1 A focus on women's world view supports men's notion that women are all the same. Women are different from one another and each woman also has multiple (or fractured) identities, any one of which might arguably provide a 'standpoint' for knowledge.
2 Harding argues that 'women's different reality . . . is also less than the reality we want, is not the only alternative reality, and is disappearing' (1986: 176). Even if women's reality were unitary, would we want it to be the only basis for knowledge production?
3 Comparative analysis suggests that purported women's and men's world views are ethno- and culturo-centric constructs. African men, Harding argues, have many similarities in their thinking to European women.
4 Harding also asks whether or not we really mean that if we can find the most repressed group of all their way of seeing is potentially the most true (1986: 191).

None the less Harding remains open minded. Successor science projects may be the best weapon women have in their engagement with men's knowledge; moreover, she argues (1986: 247) that at this stage in the struggle successor science projects and postmodernist deconstructive efforts require each other's success. As I have argued elsewhere (Cain, 1989; 1990), a strategy for reconstruction is also necessary for a transgressive feminist criminology.

Smart (this volume) points out an additional problem with standpoint feminism, namely, that it has ignored masculinity. Whatever the theoretical arguments, in focusing on women's experiences of oppression standpoint feminists have tended to write of an essential woman, not one in a reciprocally constructive relationship with 'maleness', a concept including both men and men's powers and talk. Not all standpoint epistemologists have done this (see, for example, Stanley and Wise, 1983; Cain, 1986a), but the point is well taken that within criminology those who have studied women's experiences have (with notable exceptions such as Kersten, 1989) tended not to problematize masculinity.

For a successor science

Ingredients of an argument

In this section I argue that it is indeed possible to develop a successor science, although it may be helpful to escape the connotations of the term science and the clouds of meaning which it trails. In an earlier attempt to construct some guidelines for a successor science I referred to that which we aim to produce quite simply as 'good quality knowledge' (Cain, 1987). This preferred term connotes a discerning consumer and announces the fact that, however it is authenticated, the knowledge produced should not be accepted uncritically.

Key ingredients of this are, first, the Bhaskarian notion of the disjunction between ontology and epistemology, from which I elaborate a particular account of the historicity of knowledge (see Cain, 1986a; 1986b; 1987). A second crucial ingredient is an alternative meaning and justification for theory. I spend rather longer on this because I have not written about it before. Thirdly, I elaborate a conception of standpoint which is not vulnerable to the Harding–Smart critique. I re-present the concept as I developed it in 1986 (Cain, 1986a), elaborating it where necessary to take account of the way the debate has developed. I leave to a later section two major questions of the relevance of all this for criminological work and of how good quality knowledge can be recognized or distinguished from knowledge of a poorer quality.

The disjunction between ontology and epistemology

Bhaskar (1971/89) makes the fundamental point that the construction of an ontology in which the reality of objects is independent of knowledge and in which objects can therefore impact directly upon people in no way amounts to a claim that objects in the world can be directly apprehended. Death, floods and relationships of class and gender might be such objects. Similarly, while the realist position must leave open the possibility of correct understanding, there is no way at all that people can ever be sure that they have got things right. Death, floods and relationships of class and gender might be figments of our imagination, false constructions with which we constitute and make sense of our existences. To say that there are realities which exist whether we think about them or not is not to say that we can ever be sure that our knowledges correspond to any or all of them. We do have to make some kind of sense of our bumps up against unthought about reality, though.

Bhaskar borrows the grammatical term 'intransitive' to describe these realities. Once people think about them, however, the realities may become transitive, changed by the ways in which people are thinking about them and relating to them. Patterns of relationships between people are realities which are particularly sensitive to this process, though it seems to be the case that 'nature' has also been changed as a result of being conceived as a passive state for men (*sic*) to 'master' or work upon (Gross and Averill, 1983).

The postulated existence of intransitive, unthought about realities demands a methodology appropriate to their 'discovery', as Bhaskar calls it. Criminologists as well as other social scientists are constrained by these methodological requirements (Cain, 1987). However, there are a number of reasons why knowledge, with whatever care we treat it, can never be certain. I choose to characterize this uncertainty as the *historicity* of knowledge (Cain, 1986a; 1987). Knowledge is historically specific rather than tunelessly true because the relationships and human understandings which the sociologist investigates are themselves historical, that is, constantly changing. The larger the scope of the configuration of relationships that we are describing the slower, by and large, will be the rate of change. Thus we can still usefully 'identify' a configuration of relationships called 'class', although particular class relationships have been changing dramatically throughout the twentieth century. But even our most general concepts are liable to become totally obsolete given time.

Apart from the fact that we study shifting objects, we simply cannot find a non-historical or a non-social place from which to do our knowing. There are two reasons for this. In the first place we can only 'know' with discourses historically and culturally available to us: see E. H. Carr (1961) on this issue. Secondly, and here we reconnect with the feminist standpoint epistemologists, we are all located within a (changing) web or configuration of relationships. We all have relationships with other people and we speak each from our own unique site in a complex configuration of interrelated people. In this sense, there are as many knowledges as there are people. And it is to deal with precisely this point that the standpoint epistemologies have been developed. Before returning to them, however, and to criminology, we have the other key ingredients of my version of the realist alternative to consider.

Theorization and humility

Feminists have become increasingly hostile to theory. In the first place, women have been 'misthought' so often, told how they ought to think and feel and be in order to be women, and all this psychic oppression has been justified in the name of theory. More recently, women have discovered that they were also oppressing each other by trying to encapsulate all the rich variety of womanhood in one theory, with one alternative set of needs and feelings and one political direction. A triumph of the 1980s has been that women have concerned themselves with differences from each other and with fractured identities, while maintaining a still recognizable women's movement. The identification of differences has led to sophistication, not schism. We should be proud. But all this has led women to see theory as a weapon of the opposition. I disagree.

Theory is a discursive means for constituting, distinguishing and explaining phenomena. As such, it is culture bound. So when a realist, or this realist, talks about theory she is knowingly speaking from within the historical epistemology described above. She is making a set of culture-bound statements which cannot be proved right in the short term and which are doomed to inevitable obsolescence. She is making them from her own unique site in a configuration of relationships. So let us take all that for granted and enquire briefly what is the difference between theory and any old set of explanatory remarks.

Following Gramsci again I argue that theory is a special kind of knowledge because of the self-consciousness with which it is formulated. Theoretical knowledge is made up of concepts, the relationships between which are logical and therefore public. Because of this, theoretical knowledge is easier to share than other knowledges. Logic too may be culturally specific but the self-conscious awareness of its character by its proponents, the fact that they have a theory of how they are theorizing, makes it easier to transmit it with a confidence that it will be received in a way which is near enough the same for all practical purposes. Knowledge with such a form can therefore be called objective. For the same reasons, theoretical knowledges are easier to defend than less elaborated or common-sense knowledge. Thirdly, and again for the same reasons, theoretical knowledges are more persuasive than other forms of knowledge.

In a movement with strong political objectives, like feminism, these are convincing arguments for giving one's knowledge a theoretical, that is to say an 'objective', form. It is politically important to be able to hold one's knowledge product up to view, to assess it, to communicate it beyond the boundaries of an immediate empathetic group. The pitfall here is to forget that the objectivized knowledge was created for a purpose, from a site and so on. Feminist thought, however, is sufficiently sophisticated to contain both objectivized knowledge and knowledge scepticism and so, for the time being, to attain the best of both worlds.

Apart from the form of theory, there is the question of what theory does. A major plank of realism, starting from Keat and Urry (1975), has been to substitute the notion of mechanism for the empiricist concern with constant conjunction when considering causality. In this view the job of theory is to indicate how underlying realities make surface realities happen. A social mechanism, however, leads to just those 'one way only' kinds of explanations with which women have been policed for so long and which feminists have come to abhor. But acceptance of the fundamental realist ontological claim that there are intransitive realities does not commit one to a mechanical conception of cause any more than it commits one to a naive epistemology.

The theory of such a humble realist in sociology maps relationships, constructing concepts which constitute and specify patterns of articulation (many and diverse) and dis-connection between the relationships observed, identified and explored. The humble realist, while never forgetting the limits of her vision and her enterprise, is free to map the articulations between configurations of relationships of various scopes. She may relate observed teenage mating customs to any or all of domestic structures and ideologies, labour markets, religious beliefs, patriarchy or social class. She will do this without arguing that a segmented labour market causes young girls to flirt and mature women to cook. The concept of underlying mechanism does not give her enough precision to deal with her deviant cases or enough space for cross-cultural manoeuvre. She will need a subtler and gentler concept than either mechanism or constant conjunction, with much more room for fall out (Marsh, 1982).

Because she has not yet thought of a concept of cause that will do this work she will be content, for now, to constitute and record the signs, the characteristics of the connections, until in tranquillity she finds a philosophic name for what she has been almost doing all the while. The new concept will not be one like cause, in which one relationship is deemed to dominate another. Whatever the name for the explanatory device, there will be more room for interchange and resistance within it.

These are explorations in reconstruction: for a theory of openings rather than closure. And in the meantime they raise questions of the observer's transitive understandings and of the relationships between these and the transitive understandings – the world views if you will – of those observed.

Standpoints, theories, fractured identities and difference

There can be no getting away from the fact (*sic*) that we all think (speak, write, create and distribute knowledge) from somewhere in our society, from some site or other. Putting it another way, we all have relationships. The particular intersection of these relationships in us is the site from which we produce knowledge and in that sense each site is unique, historical and changing. Some of these relationships form part of our identity, others are part of the way we think about the world but are not conscious of at all. I was not really aware of my ethnic identity until I lived in a country where virtually everyone else was African or Indian (Afro- or Indo-Caribbean). Before then being white was like being male (I assume). I knew that I was white but I regarded that as the normal thing to be. It was always other people who had something non-normal called ethnicity.

But as a realist I have to accept that I am certainly also involved in relationships of which I have no knowledge at all and which no one else knows anything about either (yet or maybe ever). Harding (1983a) has argued that the sex–gender structure used to be like that, but now it usually causes a laugh when men talk about themselves as if they were everybody. That laughter (which succeeds rage) means that one is in the presence of both politics and theory. Both are essential to the generation of standpoint-specific knowledges, as standpoint specific knowledges are reciprocally necessary for both theory and successful politics.

A standpoint, then, is a site which its creator and occupier has agreed to occupy in order to produce a special kind of knowledge and practice and of which he or she is aware in a special, theoretical way. If knowledge is site specific then changing what it is possible to know involves changing your site. This is why agreement, the decision to change or not, is fundamental to the concept of standpoint. Changing one site for another involves changing relationships. If you want to know *for* women, say, you must connect yourself 'organically' (Gramsci, 1972) *with* women, move to an appropriate site from which to generate this knowledge. Both men and women can and have to do this. Goodwill is not enough. Being a woman does not mean that one can automatically speak for women from a feminist standpoint. This is because 'being' a woman means, precisely, being caught up in 'womanish' relationships, in multiple ways. We are not talking about biological givens. So too women have to agree or choose to speak as feminists and this agreement often means that they have to make an effortful choice to align themselves with other women or change their relationships.

The implication of this is that the production of subversive knowledge is an activity *constitutive* of a feminist standpoint. It is in this sense that standpoint-specific knowledges are integrally knowledges for women. But this sense of the pronoun *for* also makes it clear that we are not speaking of knowledge which is guaranteed to be right or, sadly, even successful. The successor science remains a science of uncertainties.

This brings me to the last point of the definition, the question of awareness. In presenting our field work we have to be *personally reflexive*, that is, present a description of our changing relationship with the researched population based on feminist common (or co woman) sense. But in order to decide which site to speak from or to understand a pre-given site we have to engage in *theoretical reflexivity*, based on the new kind of theories we are constructing. Theoretical reflexivity is a key concept and a key practice in the identification of standpoints and in the production of knowledge from a feminist standpoint. Theoretical reflexivity means thinking about oneself in terms of a theory and undertanding theoretically the site one finds oneself in. For us this means understanding theoretically how being a professional criminologist articulates both with personal and particular relationships, as well as with relationships of more general scope such as class, race, age and gender.

Such theoretical knowledge about oneself is what makes it possible to say that if I want to work from a feminist standpoint I must make connections with feminist struggle – join a women's group or get involved in feminist teaching, lobbying, advocacy, cooperative marketing or child minding. Theoretical reflexivity makes it possible to continue working on one's standpoint in order to improve the fit between its constitutive relationships and one's ideological claim to speak *for*. Theoretical reflexivity tells you whether anything in your personal site must be changed in order for a standpoint claim to be made for it. It is simultaneously structural and personal, more than a site and more than an opinion. (See Val Kerruish (forthcoming) for an elaboration of the distinction between standpoint and opinion.) People who share standpoints have differing views. The standpoint does not cause one to have a thought but it does both discursively and structurally shape the thoughts, whether creative or established, that one is likely to have.

In defence of standpoints

To what extent does this realist elaboration of the concept of standpoint make it possible to defend it against the new feminist critics? It is necessary to deal with this defensive question, to make sure that we can now hold our ground, before moving on to examine the considerable advantage for social science generally and for criminology in particular which is represented by realist epistemology, including the concept of standpoint.

The main criticisms can be reduced to three: standpoint epistemologies are essentialist; standpoints cannot be identified because of differences between women and across cultures; and finally there are problems of linking knowledges to presently existing theoretical sites.

Both in this paper and previously (1986a) I have argued that standpoint is a relational concept which, so far from being essentialist, uniquely explains how a man can work from a feminist standpoint. A standpoint is constituted by politics, theory, theoretical reflexivity and choice (of site), not biology.

This elaborated concept of standpoint also addresses directly the second criticism. First it must be reiterated that occupancy of a standpoint does not foreclose debate. Standpoints do not 'cause' knowledge so much as reshape possibilities for the imagination. Opinions between those generating/occupying a standpoint can, do and should differ. Secondly, what about fractured identities? Is a woman's class, femaleness or colour to shape her vision? Black women in Africa see differently from black women in the USA, the West Indies and Australia, as well as from white Americans, white Europeans, Polynesians and Asiatic women. Where on earth can a standpoint be found in all of this? If one thinks about it, however, it is this criticism which is essentialist not the concept of standpoint. The presumption is that identities are fixed and that sites may not be chosen or changed. This criticism also denies the role of theory in 'recognizing' fractured identities and in identifying unities of which occupants of sites may be unaware. Theory, or theoretical work by us, is an essential ingredient of the identification of standpoints. It enables us to abstract from the myriad differences between us without denying them, and to reunite around important samenesses. In that complex process our theory changes, we refine it and it gets better. It is only when we try to think more theoretically that we can work out where the fractures that matter are and why and when they matter. It is hard work. But the alternative is to base our alliances on essentialist (common-sense, ideological) identifications of sameness and difference or on a political whimsy.

There is also a positive aspect to diversity. Rather than succumbing to impossibilism we should, perhaps, begin to see our divisions as evidence of the potential richness of women's contributions to knowing and to welcome the challenges, both intellectual and political, posed by our wondrous variety. I am left with the criticism that standpoint-specific knowledges are linked to presently existing historical sites. What seems important here is that standpoints are not just given sites in an intersection of relationships: they are agreed to or chosen and that choice involves a politics, a theory and theoretical self-reflection, all of which are brought to bear on an only partially transitive site. The people constituting standpoints may, therefore, be aware of their own historicity, not trapped by it, and of the historicity and temporality of the knowledge they generate.

Why bother with standpoint epistemologies?

We can now address some of the things the standpoint epistemologist can do. She can evade dominant knowledges. She can share the knowledges she produces with others in the standpoint and also with others who share the site (recruitment) or who are sympathetic (alliance). She can generate new knowledge from repressed common senses. She can make shareable decisions about how to treat those she investigates. (This is discussed more fully by Loraine Gelsthorpe and Liz Kelly in this volume and in Cain, 1986a.) She can change things. She is strong. But there are three particular things that I wish to dwell on, from among all that the standpoint epistemologist can do: she can make alliances; she can be accountable; and she can be scholarly in a way denied to all other theorists so far. There are particular advantages for the criminologist in all of this.

Standpoint epistemologies and alliances

In an earlier paper (1986a) I argued that it is not possible to work from two standpoints at once. I received several letters from people saying they agreed with all the rest of the argument but not that. Now I am not sure about the answer in logic: it is a bit like asking whether three or only two angels can dance upon the point of a needle. If a person fully occupies two standpoints then it must be that she will be aware of the contradictions between them and try to theorize and make sense of these in order to achieve an improvement in the position of both groups, say women as a whole and black people or the working class or children too. For my part, I can usually only direct my energies, whether intellectual or political, to one thing at a time. And I, therefore, prefer the concept of an alliance to describe my relations with the full range of groups whose causes I may from time to time espouse. I do not think my problem is unique. Black women in the West Indies are more aware of four centuries of denigration and oppression of blackness than they are of the problems of white women in Europe. What is important is to reflect upon a uniquely fractured site, reclaim it as a standpoint for knowledge production and political work and use this theoretical reflection to understand the relationships with other's sites and standpoints.

What is also important is to allow this continuing process of theoretical reflection to determine not only who shares the standpoint and who does not, but also to shape the decision about which groups we should be *in alliance* with at any point in time and the nature of that alliance. We have not got an adequate understanding of the fractures and contradictions yet. But I suggest that feminist standpoint epistemologists, in the wake of those who are already engaged with the issue at a practical level, are in a strong position to produce one. Moreover, because standpoints are relational as well as theoretically reflective, we can understand that the sites and standpoints of both individuals and groups change as people go their own ways or work together.

This way of thinking resolves some dilemmas for feminist criminologists who, for example, may find that their work with incarcerated girls leads to alliances with decarceration movements generally or with children's rights movements or with black or radical social workers. They will have to decide with whom they share a standpoint in order to devise an appropriate research strategy. But they must be prepared – theoretically and politically – to decide which alliances will be fruitful, which carry dangers of co-option and how to deal with these risks, and which alliances could be diverting or damaging for those whose standpoints they share. This brings me to the issue of accountability.

Standpoint epistemologies and accountability

Once we have admitted the historical specificity of knowledges we cannot rely on truth or discovery procedures and their professional guardian to deal with the problems of accountability for us (Feyerabend, 1978). For the person working from a standpoint the objective is to produce knowledge from a site that one has identified theoretically and agreed or chosen to occupy *for* those people whose standpoint one shares. Standpoint epistemologists take that inevitability one stage further arguing that it can be made positive use of if brought to a theoretical consciousness which enables the criminologist to understand and control or choose the site from which she produces knowledge. This means that she can theoretically determine, and choose, for whom the knowledge she produces will be most useful. As I have argued, it is in this sense that all knowledge is produced for those whose standpoint (or site) you share.

That preamble leads me to a rather simple point about accountability. Accountability is to those whose standpoint you share, based on a full understanding of the configuration of relationships which constitutes the standpoint. The knowledge is for them. And because they make use of this knowledge, it is to them that the feminist criminologist, say, is answerable for the quality of the knowledge she produces. This is why polemic, cooking the books or inadequate or insufficiently public evidence cannot be accepted. Those whose standpoint you share will be more likely to make mistakes if the knowledge they have to work with is not of a high quality. They are the ones who stand to lose, so it is to them that the feminist criminologist is accountable (see also Cain and Finch, 1981). Just think of the suffering that has been caused to women by mistheorizations of their atypical behaviours, by the rending of families by practices of 'care' (Carrington, 1989) and you will know to whom you are accountable for the quality of the knowledge you produce.

For good quality knowledge: feminist criminology as a successor science

Those who argue that all knowledge is historical and site specific have two big problems about science and scholarship. They have the problem as to whether or not their knowledge is determined by the site. (Did being a middle-class white female sociologist in the West Indies with a particular career and personal biography 'make' me write this paper the way I have?) They also have the problem as to whether any criteria for assessing knowledge exist at all, other than temporary conventional agreements within various scientific and other communities which have achieved enough power to establish the conventions. In one sense or another, and coming from totally opposed directions, both these arguments boil down to the view that knowledge is *only* politics. I profoundly disagree.

The first argument has, I think, already been dispensed with adequately. A realist ontology which views the social world as configurations of *relationships*, some intransitive, others transitive, creates a space in which human agency can change the sites people speak from. It can then be argued that people can have some degree of choice about the sites they occupy. One aspect of a standpoint theory of knowledge stems from this. Add this to the non-causal theory of explanation which I have argued for in these pages and the first problem is simultaneously acknowledged and dispensed with by realist historicism.

The second problem is the one that has more recently been vexing feminist philosophers and social scientists, because the relativism which had seemed the only alternative to essentialism and empiricism left no possibility of guidance for those setting out to do research. The concluding sections of this essay address this issue.

Guidelines for the conduct of social research

In 1987 I presented a long account of the guidelines for social research which might be developed from an elaboration of realist ontology and epistemology (Cain, 1987). I present them here in an abbreviated form.

Guidelines derived from realist ontology

1 Intransitive relationships require: (a) open techniques (to allow for the hitherto unthought about to impinge or impact upon knowledge production) and technical inventions (the most recent example is probably the videoed group interview (Lees, 1986)); (b) theory (the practice which enables the constitution and reconstitution of new experiences and relationships); (c) open-mindedness about thought processes leading to theory building (see Keat and Urry, 1975); and (d) technical outreach (if the multidimensional mapping which constitutes explanation is to conclude only when the multiple and contradictory connections with configurations of relationships of the most general scope have been discerned, then *empirical* routes out from the unit of observation must be identified. This is why technical outreach is required rather than mental abstraction).

2 Transitive relationships require: hermeneutic techniques, so that the discursive worlds of those investigated can be included in the investigation.

Guidelines derived from realist epistemology

1 *Constant change in the relationships observed requires*: building duration into the investigation. This could take the form of a historical analysis of an institution studied, follow up studies, biographical data on those investigated, or just staying in the field a long time.

2 *The site specificity of knowledges produced requires*: theoretical reflexivity, choice of site, a politics (each working from a standpoint) and acknowledgements of accountability to those whose standpoint you work for, your scholarship and your ethics.

If all this begins to sound even more stringent than positivism, well, it is. Oppositional knowledges will always be under attack and it would be stupid to leave ourselves vulnerable to criticisms on avoidable technical grounds. But realism is nothing if not realistic. This realist methodology is able to allow for, say, access problems or dispersed populations which rule out observations or budgets which rule out follow up studies or relationships which are only investigable by survey techniques. These real-life occurrences are dealt with by means of a final guideline: *theoretical pragmatism*. This means quite simply that with an elaborated and emerging theory of method, and elaborated and emerging theory of what you are investigating, you are in a position to assess the loss resulting from non-adherence to the guidelines and to take account of this assessment in your analysis.

What is good quality knowledge?

The argument has reached its denouement. For a successor science to achieve credibility it (we) must be able to distinguish between good and poor quality knowledge. Just as the guidelines are not rules, because they can be broken without total loss, so the distinction between good and poor quality knowledges is not an absolute one. We are not so much interested in damning knowledges as in finding out how much is in them for us. To do this we do need criteria which we can justify and which are not simply *ad hoc*. The theory of knowledge outlined here offers the following criteria:

1 Good quality knowledge is knowledge produced according to the guidelines just discussed.
2 Good quality knowledge is integrally political. This is the way in which we reclaim the inevitably value-full (site-specific) character of all knowledge. We embrace the fact that we are creating knowledge for a collectivity, from their standpoint. If this is so then the knowledge can be evaluated in terms of how well it works for those from whose standpoint it was produced. To 'work' is to explain relationships in a way that enables the occupants of the standpoint to assess their situation and to act upon those assessments in ways they find useful. This second criterion, then, is a *retrospective heuristic*, an academic way of saying that only time will tell.
3 If knowledge is to be useful then it must be capable of being very thoroughly assessed by those for whose use it was intended. This third criterion, therefore, is *publicity* (see also Cain and Finch, 1981). Publicity has three elements: (a) The knowledge must be *theoretical*, in the sense that the relationships between concepts and terms deployed must be clear. In other words, the knowledge itself must be public or 'objective' in its form. (b) The mode of production of the knowledge must be public. This is where *personal reflexivity* is relevant. We need to know the researcher's standpoint (that is taken care of by adherence to the guidelines) but we also need to know the particular circumstances of the knowledge's making. (c) The mode of production of the knowledge is made public by *displaying techniques*. It is here that incidence statements and quantification of observation categories can be helpful. Within criminology, Mary Eaton's work (1986) on the deployment of familial discourse in magistrates' courts is exemplary here.
4 Lastly, the theory we produce should account for our own knowledge as well as for that of those we investigate. I call this *theoretical inclusion*, deliberately choosing a term which does not imply a smooth or continuous theoretical totalization but which allows for contradictions

and discontinuities. As in the case of the subject–object relation (Cain, 1986a), if we accept that our input to the knowledge we make is inevitably considerable, then we need one theory to explain both ourselves and those whom we investigate. Otherwise we have two discrete theories purporting to explain the same result: one of us and one of them. Instead we should ensure that we push our knowledge outward until we identify a configuration of relationships of sufficient scope to include both us and them. If we can do this to identify our standpoint relations then we can do it, too, in order to explain our knowledge. The process also encourages a healthy scepticism about our own expertise.

If these four criteria of conformity with the guidelines are met then we have knowledge of a very high quality indeed. And they are not impossible criteria. They are relatively often met by feminist scholars.

Feminist criminology?

This has been a long theoretical journey. As each word has been developed into a concept, page by page I have had the reader, the feminist criminological reader, very much in mind. For it is feminism that has insisted that we get away from silly dichotomies like science/unscience and silly exam questions like 'is history, sociology, criminology a science or not?' It depends how good the history, sociology, criminology is, if we want to keep the term science at all. The questions we should be asking now, using the new criteria, are does this particular work meet the realist standard for good quality knowledge? And how can we evaluate theoretically the extent of any fall from perfection?

It is criminology, uniquely within sociology, which has insisted that there are at least two sides to every knowledge: that of the authorities and that of the defendant, that of the victim, that of the police(man) and that of the culprit, that of the non-conforming girl and that of her tormentors. So this is a theory for feminists and criminologists which accepts those glorious uncertainties and opens a way to live with and create uncertainties while still retaining a great pride in our craft as knowledge makers. This essay, like all knowledges, now has to wait a retrospective heuristic.

Note

1 I am indebted to Sandra Harding (1986) for this term as, indeed, for much else.

References

Becker, H. (1967). 'Whose side are we on?' in H. Becker (ed.), *Sociological Work*. London: Allen Lane.

Bhaskar, R. (1971/1989). *The Possibility of Naturalism*. Brighton: Harvester.
Cain, M. (1986a). 'Realism, feminism, methodology and law', *International Journal of the Sociology of Law*, **14**, 3/4, 255–67.
Cain, M. (1986b). 'Socio-legal studies and social justice for women', *Australian Law and Sociology Association Conference*. Brisbane: 1986 mimeo.
Cain, M. (1987). 'Realist philosophy, social policy and feminism: on the reclamation of value full knowledge.' Paper presented to the British Sociological Association Annual Conference, Leeds: 1988 mimeo.
Cain, M. (1989). 'Introduction: feminists transgress criminology', in M. Cain (ed.), *Growing Up Good. Policing the Behaviour of Girls in Europe*. London: Sage.
Cain, M. (1990). 'Towards transgression: new directions in feminist criminology', *International Journal of the Sociology of Law*, **18**, 1, 1–18.
Cain, M. and Finch, J. (1981). 'Towards a rehabilitation of data', in P. Abrams (ed.), *Practice and Progress: British Sociology 1950–1980*. London: Allen and Unwin.
Carr, E. H. (1961). *What Is History*? Harmondsworth: Penguin.
Carrington, M. (1989). *Manufacturing Female Delinquency: A Study of Juvenile Justice*. PhD thesis, School of Behavioural Sciences, Macquarie University, Australia.
Eaton, M. (1986). *Justice for Women? Family, Court and Social Control*. Milton Keynes: Open University Press.
Feyerabend, P. (1978). *Science in a Free Society*. London: New Left Books.
Gramsci, A. (1972). *Selections from the Prison Notebooks*. London: Lawrence and Wishart.
Gross, M. and Averill, M. (1983). 'Evolution and patriarchal myths of scarcity and competition', in S. Harding and M. Hintikka (eds), *Discovering Reality*. Dordrecht: D. Reidel.
Harding, S. (1983a). 'Why has the sex–gender structure become visible only now?', in S. Harding and M. Hintikka (eds), *Discovering Reality*. Dordrecht: D. Reidel.
Harding, S. (ed.) (1986). *The Science Question In Feminism*. Milton Keynes: Open University Press.
Harding, S. (ed.) (1987). *Feminism and Methodology*. Milton Keynes: Open University Press.
Hartsock, N. (1983). 'The feminist standpoint: developing the ground for a specifically feminist historical materialism', in S. Harding and M. Hintikka (eds), *Discovering Reality*. Boston: D. Reidel.
Jaggar, A. (1983a). 'Feminist politics and epistemology: justifying feminist theory', in A. Jaggar (ed.), *Feminist Politics and Human Nature*. Brighton: Harvester.
Jaggar, A. (ed.) (1983b). *Feminist Politics and Human Nature*. Brighton: Harvester.
Keat, R. and Urry, J. (1975). *Social Theory as Science*. London: Routledge and Kegan Paul.
Kerruish, V. (forthcoming). *Jurisprudence as Ideology*. London: Routledge.
Kersten, J. (1989). 'The institutional control of girls and boys: toward a gender specific approach', in M. Cain (ed.), *Growing Up Good*. London: Sage.
Lees, S. (1986). *Losing Out: Sexuality and Adolescent Girls*. London: Hutchinson.
Marsh, C. (1982). *The Survey Method*. London: Allen and Unwin.
Midgley, M. (1988). 'On not being afraid of natural sex differences', in M. Griffiths and M. Whitford (eds), *Feminist Perspectives in Philosophy*. London: Macmillan.
Smith, D. (1980). 'A sociology for women', in J. Sherman and E. Beck (eds), *The Prism of Sex*. Madison, Wisconsin: University of Wisconsin Press.
Stanley, L. and Wise, S. (1983). *Breaking Out: Feminist Consciousness and Feminist Research*. London: Routledge and Kegan Paul.

6

FEMINIST APPROACHES TO CRIMINOLOGY OR POSTMODERN WOMAN MEETS ATAVISTIC MAN

Carol Smart

Source: L. Gelsthorpe and A. Morris (eds), *Feminist Perspectives in Criminology*, Milton Keynes: Open University Press, 1990, pp. 70–84.

Some ten years ago it was *de rigueur* to start any paper on this topic with a reference to the dearth of material in the field. Now it is difficult to keep up with the production of papers and books. On the face of it this might seem a good thing but on closer inspection we might begin to have some doubts since it is usually quality rather than quantity that counts. This is not to imply that there has not been a substantial amount of good work; rather it might be that valuable energies have been misdirected. In this chapter, I want to explore schematically how feminist work in this field has developed and some of the problems that have been encountered. But first it is necessary to give some consideration to criminology – the atavistic man of my title. I shall argue that the core enterprise of criminology is problematic, that feminists' attempts to alter criminology have only succeeded in revitalizing a problematic enterprise, and that, as feminist theory is increasingly engaging with and generating postmodern ideas, the relevance of criminology to feminist thought diminishes.

It should be stressed of course that this is not exactly a novel exercise. Criminology seems to be *the* enterprise that many scholars desert or reject (Hirst, 1975; Bankowski *et al.*, 1977). However, these notable rejections of criminology were based on a particular reading of Marx which led to the conclusion that Marxism and criminology were fundamentally incompatible. I am not interested in treating a text as a means of focusing and restricting thought and so I shall not be appealing to a feminist orthodoxy with which criminology is incompatible. Rather I shall draw attention to the rich variety of feminist scholarship at large when compared to the limited horizons of feminist criminology. I see criminology as something of a siding for feminist thought, with feminist criminologists risking something of a marginalized existence – marginal to criminology and to feminism.

The problem of criminology

The appliance of science

It is a story that has been told many times (although most effectively in *The New Criminology* (Taylor *et al.*, 1973)) that criminology is an applied discipline which searches for the causes of crime in order to eradicate the problem. Admittedly, criminology as a subject embraces much more than this. For example, it tends to focus also on the operations of the criminal justice system, the relationship between the police and communities or systems of punishment. However, such topics fit just as easily under the rubric of the sociology of law or even philosophy. What is unique about criminology, indeed its defining characteristic, is the central question of the *causes* of crime and the ultimate focus of the 'offender' rather than on mechanisms of discipline and regulation which go beyond the limits of the field of crime. It is this defining characteristic with which I wish to take issue here. Arguably, it is this which creates a kind of vortex in this area of intellectual endeavour. It is the ultimate question against which criminology is judged. Can the causes of crime be identified and explained? Moreover, once identified, can they be modified?

Criminologies of the traditional schools have been unashamedly interventionist in aim if not always in practice. This goal was criticized by the radical criminologists of the 1970s for being oppressive, conservative and narrowly partisan (that is, on the side of the state and/or powerful). Moreover, the radicals argued that the traditional criminologists had, in any case, got their theories wrong. Crime, it was argued, could not be explained by chromosomal imbalance, hereditary factors, working-class membership, racial difference, intelligence and so on. So, among the many errors of traditional criminology, the two main ones to be identified were an inherent conservatism and inadequate theorization. The repudiation of these errors was condensed into the most critically damning term of abuse – positivist. To be positivist embodied everything that was bad. Positivism, like functionalism, had to be sought out, exposed and eliminated. Now, in some respects I would agree with this; but the problem we face is whether critical criminologies or the more recent left realist criminologies have transcended the problem of positivism or whether they have merely projected it on to their political opponents while assuming that they themselves are untainted.

I would argue that positivism is misconstrued if its main problem is seen as its connection to a conservative politics or a biological determinism. The problem of positivism is arguably less transparent than this and lies in the basic presumption that we can establish a verifiable knowledge or truth about events: in particular, that we can establish a causal explanation which will in turn provide us with objective methods for intervening in the events defined as problematic. Given this formulation, positivism may be, at the level of political orientation, either socialist or reactionary. The problem of positivism is, therefore, not redeemed by the espousal of left politics. Positivism poses an epistemological problem; it is not a simple problem of party membership.

It is this problem of epistemology which has begun to attract the attention of feminist scholarship (the postmodern woman of my title). Feminism is now raising significant questions about the status and power of knowledge (Weedon, 1987; Harding, 1986) and formulating challenges to modes of totalizing or grand theorizing which impose a uniformity of perspective and ignore the immense diversity of subjectivities of women and men. This has in turn led to a questioning of whether 'scientific' work can ever provide a basis for intervention as positivism would presuppose. This is not to argue that intervention is inevitably undesirable or impossible, but rather to challenge the modernist assumption that, once we have the theory ('master' narrative (Kellner, 1988)) which will explain all forms of social behaviour, we will also know what to do and that the rightness of this 'doing' will be verifiable and transparent.

The continuing search for the theory, the cause and the solution

It is useful to concentrate on the work of Jock Young as a main exponent of left realism in criminology. His work is particularly significant because, unlike many other left thinkers, he has remained inside criminology and, while acknowledging many of the problems of his earlier stance in critical criminology, has sustained a commitment to the core element of the subject. That is to say he addresses the question of the causes of crime and the associated problems of attempting to devise policies to reduce crime. For example, he states:

> It is time for us to *compete* in policy terms . . . the major task of radical criminology is to seek a solution to the problem of crime and that of a socialist policy is to substantially reduce the crime rate.
>
> (1986: 28, emphasis in the original)

This is compelling stuff but it is precisely what I want to argue is problematic about the new forms of radical criminology for feminism. It might be useful initially to outline Young's position before highlighting some of the problems it poses.

As part of his call for a left realist criminology, Young (1986) constructs a version of the recent history of post-war criminology. He sees it as a series of crises and failures (and in this respect we are at one). He points to the positivist heritage of post-war criminology in Britain which, in his account, amounts to a faith in medicine and cure and/or a reliance on biologically determinist explanations of crime. He sees the influence of North American criminology in a positive light (for example, Cohen, 1955; Cloward and Ohlin, 1961; Matza, 1969) and then turns to the work of the 'new criminologists' in Britain who constructed a political paradigm in which to reappraise criminal behaviour. He is, however, critical of the idealism of this work and interprets it as the 'seedbed' of more radical work to come rather than a real challenge to mainstream orthodoxy or an adequate account in and of itself.

The failures of the criminological enterprise overall which Young identifies are twofold. The first is the failure 'really' to explain criminal behaviour. The theories are always flawed either ontologically or politically. The second is the failure to solve the problem of crime or even to stem its rise. These are not two separate failures, however, as the failure to stop crime is 'proof' of the failure of the theories to explain the causes of crime. Young argues:

> All of the factors which should have led to a drop in delinquency if mainstream criminology were even half-correct, were being ameliorated and yet precisely the opposite effect was occurring.
>
> (1986: 5–6)

It is through this linkage between theory and policy that the positivism of the left realists comes to light. The problem is not that there is a commitment to reducing the misery to which crime is often wedded, nor is the problem that socialists (and feminists) want policies which are less punitive and oppressive. The problem is that science is held to have the answer if only it is scientific enough. Here is revealed the faith in the totalizing theory, the 'master' narrative which will eventually – when sufficient scales have fallen from our eyes or sufficient connections have been made – allow us to see things for what they really are.

To return to Young's story, we pick up the unfolding of criminology at the point of intervention by the new criminologists. Young points out that while this intervention may have excited the academic criminologists there was simultaneously another revolution in mainstream criminology. This revolution was the transformation of traditional criminology from a discipline concerned with causes and cures to one concerned with administrative efficiency and methods of containment. Young argues that mainstream criminology has given up the search for causes, the goal of the meta-narrative of criminal causation. It has gone wholeheartedly over to the state and merely provides techniques of control and manipulation. Again it is important to highlight the linkages in Young's argument. On the one hand, he is critical of what he calls administrative criminology because it has become (even more transparently?) an extension of the state (or a disciplinary mechanism). But the reason for this is identified as the abandonment of the search for the causes (a search which was, according to Young, in any case misdirected). The thesis, therefore, is that to abandon the search for the causes is to become prey to reactionary forces. This, it seems to me, is to ignore completely the debates which have been going on within sociology and cultural theory about the problems of grand and totalizing theories. And such ideas are coming not from the right but precisely from the subjects which such theoretical enterprises have subjugated, that is, lesbians and gays, black women and men, Asian women and men, feminists and so on. I shall briefly consider aspects of this debate before returning to the specific problem of feminism in criminology.

The debate over postmodernism

There is now a considerable literature on postmodernism and a number of scholars are particularly concerned to explore the consequences of this development for sociology (Bauman, 1988; Smart, 1988; Kellner, 1988) and for feminism (Fraser and Nicholson, 1988; Weedon, 1987; Harding, 1986). The concept of postmodernism derives from outside the social sciences, from the fields of architecture and art (Rose, 1988). Bauman (1988) argues that we should not assume that postmodernism is simply another word for post-industrialism or post-capitalism. It has a specific meaning and a specific significance, especially for a discipline like sociology (and by extension criminology), one which challenges the very existence of such an enterprise. Postmodernism refers to a mode of thinking which threatens to overturn the basic premises of modernism within which sociology has been nurtured.

Briefly, the modern age has been identified by Foucault (1973) as beginning at the start of the nineteenth century. The rise of modernity marks the eclipsing of Classical thought and, most importantly, heralds the centring of the conception of 'man' as the knowing actor who is author of his own actions and knowledge (that is, the liberal subject) and who simultaneously becomes the object of (human) scientific enquiry. Modernism is, however, more than the moment in which the human subject is constituted and transformed. It is a world view, a way of seeing and interpreting, a science which holds the promise that it can reveal the truth about human behaviour. The human sciences, at the moment of constituting the human subject, make her knowable – a site of investigation. What secrets there are will succumb to better knowledge, more rigorous methodologies, or more accurate typologizing. Implicit in the modernist paradigm is the idea that there is progress. What we do not know now, we will know tomorrow. It presumes that it is only a matter of time before science can explain all from the broad sweep of societal change to the motiviations of the child molester. And because progress is presumed to be good and inevitable, science inevitably serves progress. Knowledge becomes nothing if it is not knowledge for something. Knowledge must be applied or applicable – even if we do not know how to apply it now, there is the hope that one day we will find a use for it (space travel did after all justify itself for we do now have non-stick frying pans).

Modernity has now become associated with some of the most deep-seated intellectual problems of the end of the twentieth century. It is seen as synonymous with racism, sexism, Euro-centredness and the attempt to reduce cultural and sexual differences to one dominant set of values and knowledge. Modernism is the intellectual mode of Western thought which has been identified as male or phallogocentric (for example, by Gilligan, 1982 and Duchen, 1986) and as white or Eurocentric (for example, by Dixon, 1976 and Harding, 1987). It is also seen as an exhausted mode, one which has failed to live up to its promise and which is losing credibility. As Bauman argues:

> Nobody but the most rabid of the diehards believes today that the western mode of life, either the actual one or one idealized ('utopianized') in the intellectual mode has more than a sporting chance of ever becoming universal . . . The search for the universal standards has suddenly become gratuitous . . . Impracticality erodes interest. The task of establishing universal standards of truth, morality, taste does not seem that much important.
>
> (1988: 220–1)

Clinging to modernist thought, in this account, is not only antediluvian; it is also politically suspect. It presumes that sociology (which for brevity's sake I shall take to include criminology in this section) as a way of knowing the world is superior, more objective, more truthful than other knowledges. However, it is easier said than done to shake off the grip of a way of knowing which is almost all one knows. In turn, this reflects a dilemma which has always plagued sociology. If we say we do not know (in the modernist sense) then we seem to be succumbing to the forces of the right who have always said we knew nothing – or, at least, that we were good for nothing.

The irony is, as Bauman (1988) points out, that we are damned if we do and also if we do not. He points to the way in which sociology has little choice but to recognize the failure of its originating paradigm. On the one hand, doubts cannot be wished away and we cannot pretend that sociology produces the goods that the post-war welfare state required of it. On the other hand, governments already know this. We cannot keep it a secret. State funding of sociological research is already much reduced and what will be funded is narrowly restricted to meet governmental aims. It may have been possible in the past to claim that more money was necessary or that a larger study was imperative before conclusions could be drawn but now we know (and they know) that conclusions, in the sense of final definitive statements, cannot be drawn. The point is whether we argue that all the studies that have been carried out to date have been inadequate or whether we reappraise the very idea that we will find solutions. Young, for example, is scathing about a major study carried out on 400 schoolboys by West (1969). He points out that this was one of the largest and most expensive pieces of criminological work to be carried out in Britain. Yet, he argues disparagingly, it could only come up with a link between delinquency and poverty and no real causes. For Young the problem is the intellectual bankruptcy of the positivist paradigm. From where I stand he is right, but, as I shall argue below, the problem is that he locates himself inside exactly the same paradigm.

The vortex that is criminology

It is, then, interesting that Young acknowledges many of the problems outlined above, although he does not do so from a postmodern stance. Rather he is situated inside the modernist problematic itself. He acknowledges that mainstream criminology has given up the search for causes and the 'master' narrative. He also recognizes the power of governments to diminish an academic enterprise which they no longer have use for. Hence, to keep their jobs, criminologists have had to give up promising the solutions and knuckle down to oiling the wheels. He is rightly critical of this, but, rather than seeing the broad implications of this development, these criminolog*ists* are depicted as capitalist lackeys while criminology as an enterprise can be saved from such political impurity by a reassertion of a modernist faith. While applauding Young's resistance to the logic of the market which has infected much of criminology (and sociology), I am doubtful that a backward looking, almost nostalgic, *cri de coeur* for the theory that will answer everything is very convincing. Yet Young can see nothing positive in challenging the modernist mode of thought; he only sees capitulation. The way to resist is apparently to proclaim that suffering is real and that we still need a 'scientific' solution for it.

In so doing Young claims the moral high ground for the realists, since to contradict the intellectual content of the argument appears to be a denial of misery and a negation of the very constituencies for whom he now speaks. So, let me make it plain that the challenge to modernist thought, with its positivist overtones which are apparent in criminology, does not entail a denial of poverty, inequality, repression, racism, sexual violence and so on. Rather it denies that the intellectual can divine the answer to these through the demand for more scientific activity and bigger and better theories.

The problem which faces criminology is not insignificant, however, and, arguably, its dilemma is even more fundamental than that facing sociology. The whole *raison d'être* of criminology is that it addresses crime. It categorizes a vast range of activities and treats them as if they were all subject to the same laws – whether laws of human behaviour, genetic inheritance, economic rationality, development or the like. The argument within criminology has always been between those who give primacy to one form of explanation rather than another. The thing that criminology cannot do is deconstruct crime. It cannot locate rape or child sexual abuse in the domain of sexuality or theft in the domain of economic activity or drug use in the domain of health. To do so would be to abandon criminology to sociology; but more importantly it would involve abandoning the idea of a unified problem which requires a unified response – at least, at the theoretical level. However, left realist criminology does not seem prepared for this: see, for example, Young, 1986: 27–8.

Feminist intervention into criminology

I have argued that the core enterprise of criminology is profoundly problematic. However, it is important to acknowledge that it is not just criminology which is inevitably challenged by the more general reappraisal of modernist thinking. My argument is not that criminology alone is vulnerable to the question of whether or not such a knowledge project is tenable. But criminology does occupy a particularly significant position in this debate because both traditional and realist criminological thinking are especially wedded to the positivist paradigm of modernism. This makes it particularly important for feminist work to challenge the core of criminology and to avoid isolation from some of the major theoretical and political questions which are engaging feminist scholarship elsewhere. It might, therefore, be useful to consider schematically a range of feminist contributions to criminology to see the extent to which feminism has resisted or succumbed to the vortex.

Feminist empiricism

Sandra Harding (1986 and 1987) has provided a useful conceptual framework for mapping the development of feminist thought in the social sciences. She refers to feminist empiricism, standpoint feminism and postmodern feminism. By feminist empiricism she means that work which has criticized the claims to objectivity made by mainstream social science. Feminist empiricism points out that what has passed for science is in fact the world perceived from the perspective of men, what looks like objectivity is really sexism and that the kinds of questions social science has traditionally asked have systematically excluded women and the interests of women. Feminist empiricism, therefore, claims that a truly objective science would not be androcentric but would take account of both genders. What is required under this model is that social scientists live up to their proclaimed codes of objectivity. Under this schema, empirical practice is critiqued but empiricism remains intact. Such a perspective is not particularly threatening to the established order. It facilitates the study of female offenders to fill the gaps in existing knowledge;

men can go on studying men and the relevances of men as long as they acknowledge that it is men and not humanity they are addressing.

In criminology there has been a growth in the study of female offenders (for example, Carlen, 1988; Heidensohn, 1985; Eaton, 1986). It would be unjust to suggest that these have merely followed the basic tenets of mainstream empirical work, but a motivating element in all of these has been to do studies on women. But, as Dorothy Smith pointed out in 1973, to direct research at women without revising traditional assumptions about methodology and epistemology can result in making women a mere addendum to the main project of studying men. It also leaves unchallenged the way men are studied.

Harding sees a radical potential in feminist empiricism, however. She argues that the fact that feminists identify different areas for study (for example, wife abuse rather than delinquency) has brought a whole range of new issues on to the agenda. It is also the case that feminists who subscribe to empiricism have challenged the way we arrive at the goal of objective knowledge. Hence different kinds of methods are espoused, note is taken of the power relationship between researcher and researched and so on (Stanley and Wise, 1983). The move towards ethnographic research is an example of this (although this is not, of course, peculiar to feminist work).

It is perhaps important at this stage to differentiate between empiricism and empirical work. Harding's categories refer to epistemological stances rather than practices (although the two are not unrelated). Empiricism is a stance which proclaims the possibility of objective and true knowledge which can be arrived at and tested against clearly identified procedures. Mainstream criminology, having followed these tenets, claimed to have discovered valid truths about women's criminal behaviour (and, of course, men's). The initial reaction of feminism to this claim was to reinterpret this truth as a patriarchal lie. It was argued that the methods used had been tainted with bias and so the outcome was inevitably faulty (Smart, 1986). This left open the presumption that the methods could be retained if the biases were removed because the ideal of a true or real science was posited as the alternative to the biased one.

Empirical research does not have to be attached to empiricism, however. To engage with women, to interview them, to document their oral histories, to participate with them, does not automatically mean that one upholds the ideal of empiricism. To be critical of empiricism is not to reject empirical work *per se*. However, some of the empirical studies, generated under the goal of collecting more knowledge about women, which feminist empiricism engendered presented a different sort of problem for the project of a feminist criminology.

This problem was the thorny question of discrimination. The early feminist contributions did not only challenge the objectivity of criminological thought; they challenged the idea of an objective judiciary and criminal justice system. Hence there grew up a major preoccupation with revealing the truth or otherwise of equality before the law in a range of empirical studies. Some studies seemed to find that the police or courts treated women and girls more leniently than men and boys. Others found the opposite. Then there were discoveries that much depended on the nature of the offence or the length of previous record or whether the offender was married or not (see, for example, Farrington and Morris, 1983). As Gelsthorpe (1986) has pointed out, the search for straightforward sexism was more difficult than anyone imagined at first. It was, of course, a false trail in as much as it was anticipated that forms of oppression (whether sexual or racial or other) could be identified in a few simple criteria which could then be established (or not) in following a ritual procedure. So in this respect the (with the benefit of hindsight) overly simplistic approach of early feminist work in this field has created an obstacle to further developments.

The other drawback to this type of research is the one which has been highlighted by MacKinnon (1987). She argues that any approach which focuses on equality and inequality always presumes that the norm is men. Hence studies of the criminal justice system always compare the treatment of women with men and men remain the standard against which all are judged. This has led to two problems. The first arouses a facile, yet widespread, reaction that if one has the audacity to compare women to men in circumstances where men are more favourably treated, then in those instances where they are treated less favourably one must, *ipso facto*, also be requiring the standard of treatment for women to be reduced. Hence, in comparing how the courts treat men and women, the response is inevitably the threat that if women want equality they must have it in full and so some feminists want women to be sent in their droves to dirty, violent and overcrowded prisons for long periods of time. This is what Lahey (1985) has called 'equality with a vengeance'.[1]

The second problem goes beyond the transparent difficulties of treating women as if they were men to the level of the symbolic. Basically the equality paradigm always reaffirms the centrality of men. Men continue to constitute the norm, the unproblematic, the natural social actor. Women are thus always seen as interlopers into a world already organized by others. This has been well established in areas like employment law where the equality argument has been seen unintentionally to reproduce men as the ideal employees, with women struggling to make the grade (Kenney, 1986). Underlying such an approach in any case is the presumption that law is fundamentally a neutral object inside a liberal regime, thus wholly misconstruing the nature of power and the power of law (Smart, 1989). Law does not stand outside gender relations and adjudicate upon them. Law is part of these relations and is always already gendered in its principles and practices. We cannot separate out one practice – called discrimination – and ask for it to cease to be gendered as it would be a meaningless request. This is not to say we cannot object to certain principles and practices but we need to think carefully before we continue to sustain a conceptual framework which either prioritizes men as the norm, or assumes that genderlessness (or gender-blindness) is either possible or desirable.

Standpoint feminism

The second category identified by Harding is standpoint feminism. The epistemological basis of this form of feminist knowledge is experience. However, not just any experience is deemed to be equally valuable or valid. *Feminist* experience is achieved through a struggle against oppression; it is, therefore, argued to be more complete and less distorted than the perspective of the ruling group of men. A feminist standpoint then is not just the experience of women, but of women *reflexively* engaged in struggle (intellectual and political). In this process it is argued that a more accurate or fuller version of reality is achieved. This stance does not divide knowledge from values and politics but sees knowledge arising from engagement.

Arguably, standpoint feminism does not feature strongly in feminist criminology except in quite specific areas of concern like rape, sexual assault and wife abuse. It is undoubtedly the influence of feminists engaged at a political level with these forms of oppression that has begun to transform some areas of criminological thinking. Hence the work of Rape Crisis Centres (for example, London Rape Crisis Centre, 1984) has been vital in proffering an alternative 'truth' about rape and women's experience of the criminal justice system. However, as far as mainstream criminology is concerned we should perhaps not be too optimistic about this since the accounts provided by such organizations have only been partially accepted and, even then, as a consequence of substantiation by more orthodox accounts (Blair, 1985; Chambers and Millar, 1983).

Taking experience as a starting point and testing ground has only made a partial entry into criminology and, interestingly, where it has entered has been in the domain of left realism. It is here we find the resort to experience (that is, women's experience of crime) a constant referent and justification. Women's fear of rape and violence is used in this context to argue that rape and violence must be treated as serious problems. The question that this poses is whether we now have a feminist realist criminology or whether left realism (and consequently criminology as a whole) has been revitalized by the energies and concerns of a politically active women's movement. If we consider texts like *Well Founded Fear* (Hanmer and Saunders, 1984) or *Leaving Violent Men* (Binney *et al.*, 1981), we find that the motivating drive is the desire to let women's experiences be told. These experiences are not meant to stand alongside the experiences of the police or violent men; they represent the expression of subjugation which will replace the dominant account. Hanmer and Saunders outline methodological procedures for tapping into this experience and produce what Harding has referred to as a 'successor science'. As she argues, 'the adoption of this standpoint is fundamentally a moral and political act of commitment to understanding the world from the perspective of the socially subjugated' (1986:149). In fact, it goes beyond this as the researchers, as feminists, also inhabit the world of the socially subjugated. It is not an act of empathy as such but a shared knowledge.

The real issue remains unresolved, however. For while feminist work is generating another sort of knowledge (for example, other ways of accounting for violence), feminist work which fits under the umbrella of left realist criminology does not embrace the full scope of what Young has called for (see, for example, Gregory, 1986).[2] This is because standpoint feminism has not taken masculinity as a focus of investigation. Precisely because standpoint feminism in this area has arisen from a grassroots concern to protect women and to reveal the victimization of women, it has not been sympathetic to the study of masculinity(ies). Indeed, it would argue that we have heard enough from that quarter and that any attempt by feminists to turn their attention away from women is to neglect the very real problems that women still face. So the feminist realists (if we can use this term for the sake of argument) are on quite a different trajectory from the left realists. It may be convenient to the left to support the work of feminists in this area but it is unclear to me where this unholy 'alliance' is going analytically. Like the protracted debate about the marriage of Marxism and feminism, we may find that this alliance ends in annulment.

Feminist postmodernism

It would be a mistake to depict feminist postmodernism as the third stage or synthesis of feminist empiricism and standpoint feminism. Feminist postmodernism does not try to resolve the problems of other positions; rather it starts from a different place and proceeds in other directions. Much postmodern analysis is rooted in philosophy and aesthetics (Rorty, 1985; Lyotard, 1986; Fekete, 1988) but in the case of feminism it started in political practice. It began with the separate demises of sisterhood and of Marxism.

By the demise of sisterhood, I mean the realization that women were not all white, middle class and of Anglo-Saxon, Protestant extract. Feminism resisted this realization by invoking notions of womanhood as a core essence to unite women (under the leadership of the said white, middle-class and Protestant women). However, black feminists, lesbian feminists, Third World feminists, aboriginal feminists and many others simply refused to swallow the story. To put it simply, they knew power when they saw it exercised. Feminism had to abandon its early framework and to start to look for other ways of thinking which did not subjugate other subjectivities. But at the same time, feminism came to recognize that individual women did not have unitary selves. Debates over sexuality, pornography and desire began to undo the idea of the true self and gave way to notions of fractured subjectivities. These developments were much influenced by the work of Foucault and psychoanalytic theory but they cannot be dismissed simply as a 'fad' because the recognition of the inadequacy of the feminist paradigm was not imposed by the intellectuals but arose out of a series of painful struggles for understanding combined with a progressive political stance.

The other key element in this development was the demise of Marxism as a rigorously policed grid of analysis, adherence to which had meant the promise of the total explanation or master narrative. Again, feminist practice revealed the inadequacy of the grand theoretical project of Marxism quite early in the second wave. But the struggle to retain the paradigm lasted much longer. None the less it is now realized that we cannot keep adding bits of Marxist orthodoxy to try to explain all the awkward silences. While many Marxian values may be retained, the idea and the promise of the totalizing theory have gradually loosened their grip.

The core element of feminist postmodernism is the rejection of the one reality which arises from 'the falsely universalizing perspective of the master' (Harding, 1987: 188). But unlike standpoint feminism it does not seek to impose a different unitary reality. Rather it refers to subjugated knowledges, which tell different stories and have different specificities. Thus the aim of feminism ceases to be the establishment of the feminist truth and becomes the deconstruction of truth and analysis of the power effects which claims to truth entail. So there is a shift away from treating knowledge as ultimately objective or, at least, the final standard and hence able to reveal the concealed truth, towards recognizing that knowledge is part of power and that power is ubiquitous. Feminist knowledge, therefore, becomes part of a multiplicity of resistances. Take, for example, feminist interventions in the area of rape. This is an area which I have explored in detail elsewhere (Smart, 1989) but for the sake of this discussion I wish to rely on the work of Woodhull (1988). Woodhull, in an article on sexuality and Foucault, argues against a traditional feminist mode of explanation for rape. She concentrates on Brownmiller's (1975) approach which seeks to explain rape in terms of the physiological differences between men and women. Woodhull's argument is that in explaining rape in this way, Brownmiller puts sex and biology outside the social, as preceding all power relations. What is missing is an understanding of how sexual difference and the meanings of different bits of bodies are constructed. Woodhull argues:

> If we are seriously to come to terms with rape, we must explain how the vagina comes to be coded – and experienced – as a place of emptiness and vulnerability, the penis as a weapon, and intercourse as violation, rather than naturalize these processes through references to 'basic' physiology.
>
> (1988: 171)

So it becomes a concern of feminism to explore how women's bodies have become saturated with (hetero)sex, how codes of sexualized meaning are reproduced and sustained and to begin (or continue) the deconstruction of these meanings.

This is just one example of how postmodernism is influencing feminist practice (for others, see Diamond and Quinby, 1988; Jardine, 1985; Weedon, 1987; Fraser and Nicholson, 1988) and it is clear that the ramifications of the epistemological crisis of modernism are far from being fully mapped or exhaustively considered as yet. We are in no position to judge what shapes feminism will take in the next decade or so. However, it might be interesting to consider, albeit prematurely, what all this means for criminology.

Concluding remarks

It is a feature of postmodernism that questions posed within a modernist frame are turned about. So, for a long time, we have been asking 'what does feminism have to contribute to criminology (or sociology)?'. Feminism has been knocking at the door of established disciplines hoping to be let in on equal terms. These established disciplines have largely looked down their noses (metaphorically speaking) and found feminism wanting. Feminism has been required to become more objective, more substantive, more scientific, more anything before a grudging entry could be granted. But now the established disciplines are themselves looking rather insecure (Bauman, 1988) and, as the door is opening, we must ask whether feminism really does want to enter.

Perhaps it is now apt to rephrase the traditional question to read 'what has criminology got to offer feminism?' Feminism is now a broadly based scholarship and political practice. Its concerns range from questions of philosophy to representations to engagement; it is, therefore, no longer in the supplicant position of an Olivia Twist. On the contrary, we have already seen that a lot of feminist work has revitalized radical criminology. It might be that criminology needs feminism more than the converse. Of course, many criminologists, especially the traditional variety, will find this preposterous; but perhaps they had better look to who their students are and who their students are reading.

It is clear that if mainstream criminology remains unchanged it will follow the path that Young has outlined into greater and greater complicity with mechanisms of discipline. However, the path of radical criminology seems wedded to the modernist enterprise and is, as yet, unaffected by the epistemological sea changes which have touched feminism and other discourses. Under such circumstances, it is very hard to see what criminology has to offer to feminism.

Notes

1 I have argued against equality feminism elsewhere (Smart, 1989). However, my criticism is that equality feminism misunderstands the nature of the law and the

state and naively asks for equal treatment on the assumption that it will improve things. Evidence indicates that equality legislation only improves things for men (MacKinnon, 1987; Fudge, 1989).

2 Jeanne Gregory's paper in the Matthews and Young (1986) collection is an interesting example of what I mean here. Located alongside Young's call for a re-emphasis on criminology and deviance is Gregory's paper which starts within a criminological perspective but moves rapidly outside this field as she progresses on to a discussion of the future direction of feminist work.

References

Bankowski, Z., Mungham, G. and Young, P. (1977). 'Radical criminology or radical criminologist?' *Contemporary Crises*, **1**, 1, 37–52.

Bauman, Z. (1988). 'Is there a postmodern sociology?', *Theory, Culture and Society*, **5**, 2/3, 217–38.

Binney, V., Harknell, G. and Nixon, J. (1981). *Leaving Violent Men: A Study of Refuges and Housing for Battered Women*. Leeds: Women's Aid Federation.

Blair, I. (1985). *Investigating Rape: A New Approach for the Police*. London: Croom Helm.

Brownmiller, S. (1975). *Against Our Will: Men, Women and Rape*. London: Secker and Warburg.

Carlen, P. (1988). *Women, Crime and Poverty*. Milton Keynes: Open University Press.

Chambers, G. and Millar, A. (1983). *Investigating Sexual Assault*. Edinburgh: HMSO, Scottish Office Social Research Study.

Cloward, R. and Ohlin, L. (1961). *Delinquency and Opportunity: A Theory of Delinquent Gangs*. London: Routledge and Kegan Paul.

Cohen, A. K. (1955). *Delinquent Boys: The Culture of the Gang*. New York: Free Press.

Diamond, I. and Quinby, L. (eds) (1988). *Feminism and Foucault*. Boston: Northeastern University Press.

Dixon, V. (1976). 'World views and research methodology', in L. King, V. Dixon and W. Nobles (eds), *African Philosophy: Assumptions and Paradigms for Research on Black Persons*. Los Angeles: Fanon Centre.

Duchen, C. (1986). *Feminism in France*. London: Routledge and Kegan Paul.

Eaton, M. (1986). *Justice for Women? Family, Court and Social Control*. Milton Keynes: Open University Press.

Farrington, D. and Morris, A. (1983). 'Sex, sentencing and reconviction', *British Journal of Criminology*, **23**, 3, 229–48.

Fekete, J. (1988). *Life after Postmodernism: Essays on Value and Culture*. London: Macmillan.

Foucault, M. (1973). *The Order of Things*. New York: Vintage Books.

Fraser, N. and Nicholson, L. (1988). 'Social criticism without philosophy: an encounter between feminism and postmodernism'. *Theory, Culture and Society*, **5**, 2/3, 373–94.

Fudge, J. (1989). 'The effect of entrenching a Bill of Rights upon political discourse: feminist demands and sexual violence in Canada', *International Journal of the Sociology of Law*, **17**, 4, 445–463.

Gelsthorpe, L. (1986). 'Towards a sceptical look at sexism', *International Journal of the Sociology of Law*, **14**, 2, 125–52.

Gilligan, C. (1982). *In a Different Voice*. London: Harvard University Press.
Gregory, J. (1986). 'Sex, class and crime: towards a non-sexist criminology', in R. Matthews and J. Young (eds), *Confronting Crime*. London: Sage.
Hanmer, J. and Saunders, S. (1984). *Well Founded Fear: A Community Study of Violence to Women*. London: Hutchinson in association with the Explorations in Feminism Collective.
Harding, S. (ed.) (1986). *The Science Question In Feminism*. Milton Keynes: Open University Press.
Harding, S. (ed.) (1987). *Feminism and Methodology*. Milton Keynes: Open University Press.
Heidensohn, F. (1985). *Women and Crime*. Basingstoke: Macmillan.
Hirst, P. (1975). 'Marx and Engels on law, crime and morality', in I. Taylor *et al.* (eds), *Critical Criminology*. London: Routledge and Kegan Paul.
Jardine, A. (1985). *Gynesis*. London: Cornell University Press.
Kellner, D. (1988). 'Postmodernism as social theory: some challenges and problems', *Theory, Culture and Society*, **5**, 2/3, 239–70.
Kenney, S. J. (1986). 'Reproductive hazards in the workplace: the law and sexual difference', *International Journal of the Sociology of Law*, **14**, 3/4, 393–44.
Lahey, K. (1985). '. . . until women themselves have told all that they have to tell . . .' *Osgoode Hall Law Journal*, **23**, 3, 519–41.
London Rape Crisis Centre (1984). *Sexual Violence: The Reality For Women*. London: The Women's Press.
Lyotard, J. (1986). *The Postmodern Condition*. Manchester: Manchester University Press.
MacKinnon, C. (1987). *Feminism Unmodified: Discourses on Life and Law*. Cambridge, MA: Harvard University Press.
Matthews, R. and Young, J. (eds) (1986). *Confronting Crime*. London: Sage.
Matza, D. (1969). *Becoming Deviant*. Englewood Cliffs, NJ: Prentice Hall.
Rorty B. (1985). 'Habermas and Lyotard on postmodernity', in R. Bernstein (ed.), *Habermas and Modernity*. Cambridge: Polity Press.
Rose, G. (1988). 'Architecture to philosophy – the postmodern complicity', *Theory, Culture and Society*, **5**, 2/3, 357–72.
Smart, C. (1986). 'Feminism and law: some problems of analysis and strategy', *International Journal of the Sociology of Law*, **14**, 1, 109–23.
Smart, C. (1989). *Feminism and the Power of Law*. London: Routledge.
Smith, D. (1973). 'Women's perspective as a radical critique of sociology', *Sociological Inquiry*, **44**, 1, 7–13.
Stanley, L. and Wise, S. (1983). *Breaking Out: Feminist Consciousness and Feminist Research*. London: Routledge and Kegan Paul.
Taylor, I., Walton, P. and Young, J. (1973). *The New Criminology*. London: Routledge and Kegan Paul.
Weedon, C. (1987). *Feminist Practice and Poststructuralist Theory*. Oxford: Basil Blackwell.
West, D. (1969). *Present Conduct and Future Delinquency*. London: Heinemann.
Woodhull, W. (1988). 'Sexuality, power and the question of rape, in I. Diamond and L. Quinby (eds), *Feminism and Foucault*. Boston: Northeastern University Press.
Young, J. (1986). 'The failure of criminology: the need for a radical realism', in R. Matthews and J. Young (eds), *Confronting Crime*. London: Sage.

7

FEMINISM IN CRIMINOLOGY

Engendering the outlaw

Dana M. Britton

Source: *The Annals of the American Academy of Political and Social Science*, 571 (September 2000), 57–76.

Abstract

This article assesses the progress of and prospects for feminism in criminology. The focus is on the last 25 years of feminist research and theorizing about women offenders, victims, and workers in the criminal justice system. A general overview is provided of the directions of this scholarship, and key debates between mainstream and feminist perspectives are reviewed. The article also examines the contributions of feminist activists both within and outside the discipline to concrete social change for women victims and offenders. The article closes with a discussion of emerging trends in feminist criminology. New research and theorizing about women's experiences with crime challenge and subvert the traditional divisions and domains of mainstream criminology.

Criminology remains one of the most thoroughly masculinized of all social science fields; certainly, it is one of the last academic bastions in which scholars regularly restrict their studies to the activities and habits of men without feeling compelled to account for this (Rafter and Heidensohn 1995). The reason lies, at least in part, in the fact that criminology is in possession of one of the most consistently demonstrated findings in all of the social sciences: as long as statistics have been collected, they have revealed that men are considerably more likely than women to engage in activities defined as criminal. Students are thus attracted to criminology courses by the promise of studying dangerous men; so, too, have scholars been fascinated for decades by the allure of the male outlaw, "hoping perhaps that some of the romance and fascination of this role will rub off" (Chesney-Lind 1995, xii).

In this context, the phrase "feminist criminology" may well seem something of an oxymoron. However, while the vast overrepresentation of men as criminals has served some as a rationale for ignoring women, for others, it has been a point of departure for considering them. The founding of feminist criminology can be somewhat arbitrarily fixed at 1976, with the publication of Carol Smart's *Women, Crime and Criminology: A Feminist Critique*. Though a handful of earlier works had addressed some of the general themes she raised, Smart's book brought them together in a systematic critique of the treatment (or lack thereof) of women offenders in mainstream criminology and the neglect of women's experiences as victims in an attempt to set out some directions for the new field of feminist inquiry.

Almost 25 years later, a substantial body of research has accumulated in the areas specified in Smart's pioneering work, and the field has moved considerably beyond these boundaries. As has been the case for many disciplines, however, the feminist revolution in criminology is still incomplete. Some universities do now routinely offer courses like "Women and Crime," and the Division on Women and Crime has taken its place among other specialty sections in the American Society of Criminology. Even so, these labels bespeak the marginalization of feminist criminology, which is still regarded, by and large, as something outside the mainstream. Feminist criminologists have made great strides in terms of adding women in at the margins of the discipline, but they have, as yet, been less successful in deconstructing its central frames of reference and theoretical and methodological assumptions (Morris and Gelsthorpe 1991).

As is the case in most areas of academic feminism, there is ongoing debate over what the aims of feminist inquiry in criminology should be and over what counts as work that can carry the name. I will not attempt to resolve this debate here. The emerging subject divisions in the field are easier to discern. Feminist criminology may be divided into work that focuses on women as criminal offenders, women as victims of crime, and women as workers in the criminal justice system. Reviews of the field generally do not include the third category, which is something of a hybrid, attracting scholars from both criminology and the sociology of work. I will focus here, however, on all three areas, attempting to give readers a very brief sense of what we know, a review of some key work and important debates, and a sense of the directions in which the field seems to be moving. I will conclude with a discussion of some of the central challenges that remain for feminist criminology.

Before moving on, a caveat is necessary. Although I have referred to the discipline thus far as if it existed as a unified set of frameworks and assumptions, this is not really the case. There are a wide variety of theoretical and methodological perspectives in criminology, and some (for example, critical, interactionist, and Marxist approaches) have been more receptive to feminism than others. My focus here, however, will be on the mainstream in criminology, which I take to be a set of theoretical and methodological frameworks and empirical studies aimed at understanding the etiology of crime (a category taken to be a given) and proposing, implementing, and evaluating methods of crime control. This kind of criminology has historically been very closely allied with state mechanisms of social control, and it is the state that provides the lion's share of research funding in these areas. Therefore, while one might accurately say that there are a variety of criminologies currently extant, mainstream criminology is clearly hegemonic and has most thoroughly marginalized feminist research and theory. It will be my focus in the analysis to follow.

Women as offenders

Women are vastly underrepresented as criminal offenders. Of course, any data claiming to represent the facts about crime are always the end product of an interaction between the responses of social control authorities and the behaviors of the individuals involved. Even so, there is no serious dispute among criminologists that the extant data substantially misrepresent the actual sex ratio of criminal offending. The primary source of such data, the Uniform Crime Reports (UCR) program of the Federal Bureau of Investigation (FBI), reports detailed information on eight index crimes (these are homicide, forcible rape, robbery, aggravated assault, burglary, larceny-theft, motor vehicle theft, and arson). Women composed 26 percent of those arrested for these offenses in 1997. The UCR also reports statistics for less serious offenses, which constitute the bulk of all arrests. For men and women, these offenses are consistently similar, with larceny-theft (a category largely of petty theft, including shoplifting), simple (nonaggravated) assault, drug offenses, and driving under the influence of alcohol (DUI) topping the list for women in 1997, accounting for 45 percent of women's arrests. For men, the top four offenses were drug crimes, DUI, simple assault, and larceny-theft, composing 38 percent of men's arrests (Maguire and Pastore 1999).

These data indicate that men and women are actually quite similar in terms of the offenses for which they are most often arrested and that the majority are crimes that most would view as petty, for example, larceny-theft. The most striking difference is the absolute level of men's and women's offending. Although larceny-theft accounts for 16 percent of arrests of women, men's arrest rate for this crime is almost 2.5 times higher. Data for violent offenses illustrate this pattern in much clearer detail. In 1997, women were only 16 percent of those arrested for the index offenses of homicide, forcible rape, robbery, and aggravated assault (known collectively as the index of violent crime). Men's arrest rate for homicide was 9 times higher than women's; for rape, 83 times higher; for robbery (defined as the taking or attempted taking of property by force or fear), 10 times higher; and for aggravated assault, 5 times higher. The only offenses for which women's arrests exceed men's are prostitution, for which women are 60 percent of those arrested, and running away from home (a juvenile offense), for which girls were 58 percent of those arrested in 1997.

Arrest rates vary by race as well. In 1997, whites were 63 percent of those arrested for all index offenses; African Americans were 35 percent. For violent index offenses, whites accounted for 57 percent of arrests, versus 41 percent for African Americans. The FBI does not publish arrest statistics by sex and race. We do know, however, that African American men and women are over-represented among those arrested. Studies of unpublished UCR data and self-reports show that African American women have higher rates of arrest and participation in homicide, aggravated assault, and other index offenses than white women (Simpson and Elis 1995). For some offenses, such as larceny-theft, arrest rates for African American women most closely match those for white men (Chilton and Datesman 1987); black men's arrest rates are the highest; white women generally rank at the bottom, regardless of the offense.

This statistical picture illustrates some of the challenges facing feminist criminology. The sex ratio of offending is remarkably constant, which seems to indicate the need for theory that would account for why it is that women are so much less likely than men to offend. Indeed, this was the place that criminology, when it considered women at all, often began. Paradoxically, however, rather than being viewed as successes, women have been seen by mainstream theorists as aberrant because they do not commit crime. Newer feminist work in this vein has viewed women's conformity in a somewhat more positive light, relying, for example, on Carol Gilligan's theories of moral development to suggest that women's "ethic of care" makes them less likely to offend (Steffensmeier and Allan 1996). Even a cursory examination of the statistics on sex and race, however, reveals the dangers that can come from viewing women as a unitary category. Differences in arrest rates between African American and white women are often dramatic, and feminist criminology has only just begun to grapple with the implications of these differences (Daly and Maher 1998). Even more problematic is the almost complete lack of data about criminal offending among other racial groups, such as Asian or Hispanic women.

The first studies of women and offending that fell, at least putatively, in the realm of feminist criminology appeared in 1975, with the publication of Freda Adler's *Sisters in Crime* and Rita James Simon's *Women and Crime*. Though these books differ slightly in focus, both make the same general theoretical argument, which has come to be known as emancipation theory. Adler and Simon both contended that women's lower rates of participation in criminal activity could be explained by their confinement to domestic roles and by discrimination that limited their aspirations and opportunities (Daly and Chesney-Lind 1988). With the advent of the women's movement, the situation could be expected to change, however. Adler saw increasing participation in violent crime as inevitable as women became more like men as a result of their social and political emancipation. Simon believed that opportunities created by women's higher levels of formal labor market activity would lead to higher arrest rates for property and occupational crimes, such as fraud, larceny, and embezzlement. Adler did consider race, arguing that black women's higher rates of participation in crime could be explained by their more liberated status: "If one looks at where Black women are as criminals today, one can appreciate where white women are headed as liberated criminals in the coming years" (154).

This argument has obvious appeal for opponents of the feminist movement, but empirically, the theory has received very little support. While women's rates of violent crime have increased, in absolute terms, their rates relative to men's have not changed substantially since 1960 (Steffensmeier 1995). Contrary to popular mythology, there is simply no evidence of the large-scale existence of a new, more violent female offender (Maher 1997). Women's rates of property offending relative to men's have increased since the 1960s, but almost all of the increase has come from higher rates of arrest for larceny-theft, mostly shoplifting (Chilton and Datesman 1987). Rather than reflecting expanding opportunities, however, this increase is more likely due to women's increasing economic marginalization and changing views of women by social control authorities (Morris 1987). There is also no evidence that women with more feminist attitudes are more likely to be criminal; in fact, the opposite is true (Simpson 1989). Although there is now fairly broad consensus that Adler's and Simon's work would not fall within the purview of feminist criminology (Morris and Gelsthorpe 1991; cf. Brown 1986), these books did put women's crime on the empirical agenda for the discipline, and they were groundbreaking in their attempts to build a theory that would explain men's as well as women's crime.

In addition to documenting the levels of women's criminal offending, feminist criminologists have drawn attention to women's (and men's) treatment by police, the courts, and the prison system. Contradicting popular stereotype, studies of women's experiences with the criminal justice system have revealed that women do not benefit, at least not uniformly, from chivalry at the hands of police, prosecutors, and judges. In some instances, such as juvenile status offenses, girls are subject to much harsher treatment than boys (Chesney-Lind 1989). Some research reveals that African American women receive more negative treatment by police, are more likely to be sentenced to prison, and receive longer sentences than white women (Mann 1995), although there is still considerable debate around this issue. A series of studies (for example, Daly 1987) has shown that women who are married and have children do sometimes receive more leniency than other defendants. This effect is double edged, however; women who do not conform to traditional stereotypes of wives and mothers or who are perceived to shirk their responsibilities may be dealt with especially severely (Morris and Wilczynski 1994).

The kinds of quantitative studies reviewed here have provided some answers to the question of how women's rates of offending and treatment by the system compare to men's and, as such, are a crucial first step. This equity approach (Cain 1990) has been guided largely by liberal feminist precepts, conceptualizing gender as an independent variable and seeing men and women as essentially equal and therefore deserving of equal treatment (Daly and Maher 1998). The fundamental limitation of such a strategy is put best by Cain (1990):

> Equity studies do not enable us to pose the question whether or not even absolutely equal sentences might be unjust . . . too high or too low in themselves, or [whether] behaviour . . . should not, from some standpoints at least, be subject to penalty. A concern with equity leaves the substance of what is being equalised un-analysed. (2–3)

This kind of liberal feminist approach poses men as the criminal yardstick and equates justice with equality. Larger questions about the processes of criminalization of some acts, rather than others, and the inherent justice or injustice of the system are left unanswered. Such studies also fail to question the meanings and active construction of the categories of sex, race, and class, taking them simply as givens.

More recently, a substantial body of ethnographic and interview research has appeared that takes as its central focus the construction and meaning of such categories. This work has substantially deepened our understanding of the lives of women involved in crime. Mirroring overall trends in feminist theory, the best of this work is moving toward a nuanced and contingent conception of women's agency, one that sees women neither exclusively as victims nor as unfettered actors. Lisa Maher's richly textured ethnographic study of women involved in street-level sex and drug markets (1997) is a particularly good example. Maher convincingly demonstrates that the women she studies are not liberated drug kingpins, but nor are they mindless slaves, willing to sink to any depth of depravity to serve their addictions. Rather, they actively work within the constraints of the male-dominated informal economy, rarely controlling significant resources; they perform a range of gender-typed tasks, such as "copping" (buying) drugs for customers fearful of being arrested. While women do sometimes initiate violence, they are more likely to be the targets of victimization by police, male partners, and "tricks."

Feminist research and theorizing on women's offending has also been closely connected with activism. This has been the case on a number of fronts but has perhaps been most visible in the area of women's imprisonment. America is in the throes of an imprisonment binge—since 1990, our prison population has grown by about 6.5 percent per year. Women constitute only about 7 percent of those incarcerated, but their rates of imprisonment have been rising much faster than men's. Between 1988 and 1997, arrests for men increased by only 11 percent, and the number of men incarcerated increased by 96 percent. For women, the situation was much starker: arrests increased by 40 percent, and women's prison population increased 146 percent. This increase fell particularly heavily on Hispanic and African American women, whose rates of incarceration, respectively, are 3.5 and 8.0 times those of white women (Maguire and Pastore 1999).

Advocates for women in prison have been instrumental in bringing these facts to light and in generating public concern over women's rising rates of imprisonment. They have also brought about practical changes that have improved the lives of women inmates, including the elimination of some laws that imposed harsher (indeterminate) sentences on women, the expansion of medical services, improvements in job training and educational opportunities, and even some in-prison nurseries, such as the pioneering program at New York's Bedford Hills (Price and Sokoloff 1995). This work has also generated serious policy alternatives that take into account men's and women's different life histories (for example, women in prison are six times more likely to report prior sexual abuse than their male counterparts), the context of their offending (women are much more likely than men to be first-time offenders or to have committed only nonviolent offenses previously), and women's much lower rates of recidivism compared to men (Chesney-Lind 1996; Davis 1997).

Women as victims

As in the case of offending, women are underrepresented as victims of crime, at least as victimization is measured by the statistics most widely used by criminologists. The primary source of data derives from the National Crime Victimization Survey (NCVS), conducted annually since 1973 by Census Bureau personnel for the Bureau of Justice Statistics. The NCVS is administered to approximately 101,000 individuals, who are asked questions about their crime victimization. NCVS data consistently show that men are more likely to be victimized by all kinds of violent crime than are women, except rape and sexual assault. Men's overall rate of violent crime victimization in 1997 was 45.8 (per 1,000 population aged 12 years or older); women's was 33.0. Data on homicide, collected by the FBI, show that men are three times as likely to be victims.

NCVS data also indicate that African Americans and Hispanics are more likely to be victims of violent crime than whites and that the young and those with lower incomes also have higher rates of victimization. Unlike the UCR, the NCVS does publish victimization statistics that are disaggregated by sex and race combined, and the dramatic differences they reveal again demonstrate the danger of treating women (or men) as a unitary category. For homicide, white women have the lowest rates of victimization; African American women's rates are about four times higher, and African American women are more likely even than white men to be victims. African American men's rates of homicide victimization—eight times higher than those of white men—starkly testify to an epidemic level of violence, as does the persistent finding that for violent crimes other than homicide, African American men are about one and a half times as likely to be victims as white men. Among women, African Americans are generally much more likely than whites to be victims of all kinds of violent crime; generally, their rates of victimization most closely match white men's rather than white women's.

Feminist criminology has perhaps made its greatest impact on mainstream criminology in the area of women's victimization. The realm in which this has happened, however, has been somewhat limited, as the literature has generally focused on the kinds of offenses of which women are most likely to be victims. As the foregoing data suggest, rape has been a central concern and so, too, has intimate violence. NCVS data indicate that, although women's levels of violent victimization are lower than men's overall, their victimization is much more likely to be personal; from 1992 to 1996, women were five to eight times more likely than men to be victimized by intimates (Maguire and Pastore 1999). Though there is little question that women face specifically gendered violence of this kind, concentrating only on these offenses has had the effect of highlighting the differences between men and women as victims and excludes an analysis of the ways in which other kinds of victimization (which account for far more incidents overall) may be gendered (Chesney-Lind 1995). Even so, feminist research in these areas has clearly been influential; mainstream criminology texts now invariably include sections on rape and intimate violence, and many discuss feminist empirical work and theory.

Unlike studies of female offenders, which did exist before feminist criminology drew attention to them in the 1970s, there simply was no comparable research in mainstream criminology on women's experiences of victimization or on the crimes that disproportionately affect women. A rare exception is Menachem Amir's *Patterns in Forcible Rape* (1971). Although this was one of the first attempts to untangle the dimensions along which rape offending varies (for example, sex, race, class, circumstances), the study paid no attention to the experiences of the victims themselves. The effect of this omission becomes particularly clear in Amir's introduction (or perhaps official legitimation) of the concept of "victim-precipitated" rape, which he claimed accounted for about 19 percent of the cases in his study:

> [Victim-precipitated rape occurs in] those rape situations in which the victim actually, or so it was deemed, agreed to sexual relations but retracted before the actual act or did not react strongly enough

> when the suggestion was made by the offenders). The term applies also to cases in risky situations marred with sexuality, especially when she uses what could be interpreted as indecency of language and gestures, or constitutes what could be taken as an invitation to sexual relations. (266)

Feminist critics, both within and outside criminology, quickly charged that this notion clearly placed criminology in collusion with the rapist, who can apparently claim sexual access whenever he deems that his victim has aroused him (Schwendinger and Schwendinger 1983).

The first influential feminist studies of women's victimization appeared during the 1970s and focused on wife battering and rape. Susan Brownmiller's work (1975), in particular, is a deft synthesis of mainstream criminological research on rape offenders (including Amir's study) with a radical feminist perspective that views rape as the sine qua non of men's control of women under patriarchy. Both in content and in timing, these early feminist accounts posed a powerful challenge even to radical criminology, which was rising to prominence during the 1970s. At the heart of the radical perspective was a view of crime as resistance to class and race domination (Taylor, Walton, and Young 1973) and a conceptualization of the offender as the "rogue male" using the only resources available to him in fighting an unjust system. Radical criminologists were caught off guard by the rising tide of radical feminist research on the experiences of women who disproportionately suffered at the hands of such outlaws (Gelsthorpe and Morris 1988). Roger Matthews and Jock Young, two leading British radical criminologists, have admitted that feminist research convinced them of "the limits of the romantic conception of crime and the criminal" (Matthews and Young 1986, 2). Subsequently, radical criminology has taken a more "realist" turn, attempting to come to terms with women's victimization as well as the fact that the poor and working classes are disproportionately the victims of crime (DeKeseredy 1996).

Unlike research on women's offending, which has been guided largely by liberal feminist ideas and methodologies, women's victimization has been a central issue for radical feminists. The relationship with mainstream criminology has been an awkward one, complicated both by radical feminism's antipositivist assumptions and by its advocacy of social change. Modern mainstream criminology, born at the turn of the twentieth century, is also called the positivist school. To oversimplify, this means that most traditional criminologists have used the tools of the scientific method, such as the social survey and statistical methodology, to document what has been conceptualized as a universe of preexisting social categories. Such inquiry has been framed as value neutral, and it posits the discovery of facts about the social world as an eventual goal. In criminology, scholars have gone about measuring crime and victimization as if these behaviors were readily apparent, uncontested, and invariant in their meaning across social groups. The equity studies discussed previously are examples of this approach, and some of its limitations have already been noted.

Radical feminists take this critique one step further. Radical feminist accounts, like Brownmiller's, have argued that violence against women cannot simply be equated with the victimization of men but, rather, that it takes on a different meaning in the context of a social system in which men are dominant over women. Thus women's violence against men is not the same as men's violence against women. Radical feminists have also pointed to the role of social institutions (such as the criminal justice system and the family) and social norms around sexuality and violence in working together to erase and normalize women's victimization. As a result, victims of rape and battery are often persuaded that such things are either normal or justified, and their victimization may not be apparent, even to themselves. This stance clearly renders any mere quantification of experiences of victimization necessarily incomplete. In addition, radical feminists have argued for the use of research as a tool for social change, a position also at odds with mainstream criminology.

Fault lines have formed around a number of issues, but the ongoing debate over statistics on women's victimization is a particularly apposite case. As noted earlier, the NCVS serves as the primary source of victimization data used by criminologists. Yet before 1992, this instrument did not query sample respondents specifically about rape or sexual assault, asking instead only whether they had been "beaten up" or attacked in other ways. Nor did the survey specifically attempt to measure victimization in the home, inquiring only whether "anyone" had committed violence against the respondent. An extensive redesign process, prompted in part by criticisms from feminist advocacy groups (although general methodological criticisms had also been raised by others), led to the inclusion of questions specifically about rape as well as an item addressing victimization in the home. After the redesign, overall estimates of personal victimization increased by 44 percent, but rape and sexual assault victimization rates increased by 157 percent. The new instrument also produced a 72 percent increase in women's reporting that they had been victimized by intimates, and a 155 percent increase in reports of victimization by other relatives (Bachman and Saltzman 1995). There is little doubt that the statistical picture has become a more accurate one.

Even so, criminology has remained resistant to the implications of radical feminism's assumption that women may not see violence against them in terms of standard legal categories, such as those used in the NCVS. Much feminist empirical work on women's victimization has employed substantive definitions of these acts, asking respondents in general terms if they, for example, have had sex against their will due to force, threat of force, or incapacity to consent. Such studies typically yield higher prevalence estimates than those reflected in official statistics. For example, while 14.0 percent of the ever-married women in Russell's sample (1982) reported incidents of victimization by their husbands that fit the legal definition of rape, only

0.9 percent of these women mentioned these experiences when asked directly if they had ever been the victim of a rape or an attempted rape. Such research has been the subject of a considerable backlash from critics, however, who typically rely on official statistics, such as the UCR and NCVS, to assert that feminists have vastly inflated the extent of women's victimization.

A second area of dispute has arisen around the radical feminist assumption that any analysis of victimization is incomplete without an understanding of the patriarchal context that shapes the meaning of these acts (Hanmer and Maynard 1987). The implication of this critique is that any simple count of events, no matter how accurate, will necessarily fail to tell the whole story. Perhaps the best example of this controversy is the debate over statistics on rates of partner or spousal violence, which has crystallized recently around the mutual combat hypothesis. Briefly, this notion arose from research employing an instrument (the Conflict Tactics Scale) that directs respondents to count instances of their own use of a wide spectrum of physically aggressive techniques against their partners during marital or relationship conflicts (Straus, Gelles, and Steinmetz 1980). Surprisingly, studies using this instrument indicate that women are just as likely to use physical violence as men. This result has been offered as a fundamental challenge to feminist constructions of marital violence as a problem experienced primarily by women in the patriarchal context of marriage. Calls for attention to the problem of battered husbands have followed, and the mutual combat hypothesis has achieved wide cultural and disciplinary currency. Criminology texts now largely refer to "partner" or "spousal" violence; I recently reviewed a criminology textbook-in-development that began the section on violence in marriage by framing the problem as one of mutual combat.

Feminist critics have responded that the context in which violence is experienced is crucial. Women are much more likely than men to use violence in self-defense, more likely to be injured by acts of intimate violence directed against them, more likely to feel seriously threatened by it, less likely to be able to effectively defend themselves, and less likely to have the resources to leave violent relationships (Nazroo 1995; for a review, see Gelles and Loeske 1993). Again, this controversy illustrates the uneasy relationship between criminology's positivist tradition and the antipositivist implications of the assumptions that undergird radical feminist research and theorizing on women's experiences of violence. A similar controversy exists in research on fear of crime, an area in which women's much higher rates of expressed fear are seemingly unaccounted for by their lower rates of victimization. Pioneering work by Elizabeth Stanko (1990) and others, however, has revealed that much of women's victimization is hidden (that is, not accounted for by official statistics), routine, and socially legitimated (Madriz 1997) and that women have ample reason to express high levels of fear.

As in the case of women offenders, activism both within and outside the discipline has been instrumental in framing women's victimization as a legitimate social problem and in making concrete changes in the criminal justice system. Presumptive arrest policies regarding domestic violence incidents, now in place in the majority of U.S. jurisdictions, were prompted in large part by empirical research conducted by criminologists (Sherman and Berk 1984). While such a strategy represents an important symbolic step, indicating that such violence is finally being taken more seriously by the system, subsequent research (Sherman 1992) indicates that such policies are not working as well as their proponents had hoped, and in some cases, they appear to increase the chances of repeat violence. Debate and research within criminology continue to be influential in shaping policy in this area. Other significant legal and political changes include revisions in laws defining rape or sexual assault; the passage of "rape shield" laws, which do not allow the discussion of victims' sexual histories in court; and the recent passage of the Violence Against Women Act, which defines gender-based victimization as a hate crime and allocates increased funds for battered women's shelters, rape crisis centers, and policing and research efforts directed to reducing the number of crimes against women.

Women as workers

During the last 25 years, increasing numbers of women have entered criminal justice occupations. Most research to date has addressed women's experiences in policing, prison work, and law, and these will be my focus here. Before the 1970s, few women were employed in any of these jobs. A variety of factors eased women's entry. As has been the case with most male-dominated occupations, legislative change and legal pressure have been most influential; Title VII and the Equal Employment Opportunity Act formally opened all of these occupations to women. Title IX was also important for women in law, as it struck down policies that had either barred them from law schools entirely or kept their numbers to a minimum. Even so, administrators, coworkers, and clients did not immediately welcome women. Lawsuits challenging recruitment and promotion practices, among other things, were necessary to fully open the doors for women's entry (Martin and Jurik 1996).

Women have also benefited from demographic changes. The sheer number of people employed in all of these jobs has increased dramatically over the last two decades, and women have filled the gap as the supply of male workers has not been adequate to meet the rising demand. This effect has been particularly dramatic in prison work. Between 1983 and 1995, the number of staff in prisons and jails increased 187 percent, but the number of female staff almost quadrupled, increasing by 372 percent (American Correctional Association 1984; Maguire and Pastore 1999). Additional factors, specific to law, policing, and prison work, have also contributed to women's increasing representation in these fields. By 1998, women constituted 12 percent of all police officers, 24 percent of all prison officers, and 34 percent of all attorneys (Bureau of Labor Statistics 1999).

Increasing access has not necessarily meant equal rewards. There is a considerable wage gap in each occupation; women's incomes in policing are only 86 percent of those of their male counterparts; in prison work, 89 percent; and in law, 70 percent. The relatively smaller gaps in policing and prison work are undoubtedly due to the fact that the employer in these cases is the government, a labor market sector in which recruiting and promotion practices are at least somewhat formalized. Law, on the other hand, is practiced in highly diverse settings, each with its own set of employment practices and its own reward structure. Regardless, women in all three occupations are likely to be found at the lowest rungs of their respective occupational ladders. In policing, for example, women are 16 percent of municipal officers but only 7 percent of state police (National Center for Women in Policing 1999). Women in prison work continue to face blocked access to supervisory positions (Britton 1997), and women in law are concentrated in the least prestigious specialties (for example, family law and public defense) and work in the lowest-paid settings (Pierce 1995).

While there have always been women criminals and women victims, until a quarter-century ago, there was a paucity of women working in criminal justice occupations. What this means is that, although mainstream criminological research existed on police, prison workers, and attorneys prior to 1975, these studies essentially focused on "the men and their work" and lacked an analysis of gender. Subsequently, a considerable volume of literature on women in criminal justice occupations has appeared. I will not attempt to cover the literature on each occupation here (for a review, see Martin and Jurik 1996). Two clear, though sometimes overlapping, areas of research have emerged in studies of women's experiences in all three occupations, however. The first has involved a focus on difference, asking questions about how or whether women perform their jobs differently from men and about the unique gendered characteristics women bring to their work. The second line of research has contended that these jobs and the organizations in which they are performed are themselves gendered and has looked at the ways in which gendered organizational structures, ideologies, policies and practices, interactions, and worker identities assume and reinforce inequality.

Theoretical and empirical work in the first vein is in some ways a response to critics who have long argued that women, on account of their gender, do not possess the characteristics necessary for success in these heavily masculinized and male-dominated occupations. As a male attorney interviewed by Pierce (1995) put it, "I think Clarence Darrow once said women are too nice to be lawyers. I think he was right. It's not that I don't think women are bright or competent—they just don't have that *killer* instinct" (26). Similar, and usually less charitable, sentiments can be found in both popular and academic discussions of the role of women in prison work and in policing.

Research from the difference perspective has attempted to turn this critique on its head, arguing that women are not the same as their male counterparts but that the gendered qualities that they bring with them are actually assets.

In some ways, this line of argument represents a return to the discourse employed by women criminal justice system reformers of the nineteenth century. Claims that women were simply inherently better able to deal with women victims, suspects, clients, and prisoners were largely successful in persuading state and local governments to hire policewomen, whose main responsibility was to deal with delinquent women and girls and to build reformatories, staffed exclusively by women, to hold women inmates (Appier 1998; Freedman 1981). The principal change is that such rhetoric is now being used to argue for the integration of women into male-dominated occupations, rather than the establishment of separate, sex-segregated jobs and institutions. Menkel-Meadow (1987), for example, argues that women bring a "different voice" to the practice of law and that women, by virtue of their socialization and experiences, will be less adversarial, more interested in substantive justice (rather than strict procedural fairness), and will ultimately seek to empower their clients, rather than themselves. Advocates for women in policing have long contended that women's supposedly superior communication skills will make them better at resolving conflicts through dialogue, rather than force, and that they will be more empathetic and effective in working with victims and suspects (Appier 1998; Martin 1997). A similar argument has been made for increasing the number of women officers in men's prisons, where their presence is held to "normalize" and "soften" the work environment (Britton 1997).

On balance, however, empirical research and experience have not been supportive of these kinds of claims. Neither policing, nor prison work, nor law have been radically transformed or even become much kinder and gentler as women have increasingly moved into these occupations. The reason lies, in part, in a factor left out of the difference equation, the gendered structure of occupations and organizations themselves. This has been the focus of the second line of research. Pierce (1995), for example, finds that the adversarial structure of the legal profession, and litigation work in particular, leaves women few options; to succeed, they must adopt the tactics of their successful male peers, developing qualities such as aggression, intimidation, and impersonality. This creates a double bind for women, as those who take on this role are usually perceived more negatively than their male counterparts. Some women do resist, but most do so at the cost of success, at least as it has been defined by others. The gendered structure of the practice of litigation leaves little room for the meaningful assertion of difference, even if women lawyers were so inclined. Further, the masculinization of these occupations and of the organizations in which they are performed means that the rewards that accrue to difference vary dramatically by sex. Britton (1997) finds that male officers in men's and women's prisons benefit from asserting their unique abilities to use physical force. Women's purportedly unique gendered abilities, such as higher levels of empathy, emotionality, and communication skills, are often seen by administrators and coworkers, particularly in men's prisons, as either dangerous or extraneous.

These kinds of findings should not be taken to mean, however, that difference is immaterial. Women in these occupations do often differ from their male counterparts, particularly in relationship to issues like balancing work and family. Research also demonstrates that many do see themselves as different, both in terms of work styles and personality. It is also clear that we can meaningfully speak of characteristics that have been more or less associated with masculinity and femininity. Whether they display these characteristics or not, research and experience tell us that individual workers will be held accountable for them. An emerging trend in research on women in criminal justice occupations (and research on women and work more generally) recognizes this but at the same time argues that organizational and occupational structures are also important. This approach is in some ways a synthesis of the two perspectives outlined earlier and contends that the crucial issue is context; some work settings are more amenable to, or at least less penalizing of, gendered characteristics associated with women workers (Britton 2000). Miller (1999), for example, finds that community policing draws on traits like empathy, a service orientation, and communication skills and that women are often drawn to the work for this reason. Ely (1995) finds that women in law firms with a higher proportion of women in positions of power are less likely to see feminine-stereotyped characteristics as impediments to success and are more flexible in their ideas about gender overall. Anleu's research (1992) indicates that women have greater career opportunities in corporate legal departments than in private law firms, at least partly because occupational demands and domestic responsibilities are not as incompatible. Taken together, these findings suggest that while increasing the number of women in these occupations is an important step, structural changes in policing, prison, and legal organizations are also necessary to produce significant change in the direction of equality for women.

Emerging issues

Kathleen Daly and Lisa Maher (1998) divide feminist criminology into two periods. The first phase, into which much of the work previously described falls, has focused on the tasks of filling in gaps, comparison, and critique. With little knowledge about women offenders, victims, and workers in the criminal justice system available, the first chore of feminist criminology was to provide this information. Though a substantial beginning has been made, it is likely that research in these areas will continue.

The second phase is characterized by work that disrupts the existing frameworks of criminology in more fundamental ways, resulting in the growth of a body of research and theory that Maureen Cain (1990) has called "transgressive criminology." For example, some feminist criminologists have crossed the traditional division between offending and victimization. As research on women offenders accumulated, it became clear that they were usually also victims, having experienced substantial physical and verbal abuse at the hands of intimates. The "blurred boundaries" thesis argues that women's offending is intimately linked to their previous victimization; a central task for feminist criminology in the years to come will be filling in the black box (Daly 1992) that connects the two. Undoubtedly, this will require a new, more nuanced conception of women offenders that disrupts the dichotomy in which they have been seen only either as innocent victims or as hardened criminals. Some work in this vein has already appeared; Lisa Maher's research (1997), described earlier, is but one example.

This dichotomy is deeply racialized, and this presents yet another challenge for feminist criminology. There is little doubt that the face of the much-mythologized new, more dangerous, female offender is that of a woman of color and that the most innocent victims have always been white. Feminist criminology is just beginning to come to terms with this. Whatever the difficulties posed by official statistics, research and theorizing must continue to reject the essentialism inherent in treating women as a unitary category (Simpson 1989). We already know much about the ways in which race, class, and sexual inequality interweave with women's experiences as victims, offenders, and workers. The challenge for feminist criminology in the years to come will lie in formulating theory and carrying out empirical studies that prioritize all of these dimensions, rather than relegating one or more of them to the background for the sake of methodological convenience.

Given men's overrepresentation as offenders and victims, the screaming silence in criminology around the connection between masculinity and crime has always been something of a paradox. Feminist criminology has recently begun to draw attention to this issue. Messerschmidt's (1993) was one of the first significant theoretical contributions in this area; it argues that, for men who lack access to other resources, crime can serve as an alternate means of doing masculinity. More recent accounts (see Newburn and Stanko 1994 for a review) have begun to untangle the contexts in which this use of crime is more or less likely and to explore the kinds of masculinities that result. A similar line of research has very recently begun to inquire into the social construction and reproduction of gendered identities among women involved in crime. On a parallel track, studies of work in criminal justice occupations are drawing attention to the individual and organizational construction of gender among both men and women workers (Britton 1997; Miller 1999; Pierce 1995). This research represents a promising direction for the field, both because it finally acknowledges men as men and because it moves us beyond dichotomized, static, individualistic notions about gender.

Finally, one of the most important issues facing activists in the discipline during the coming years will undoubtedly lie in rethinking feminist criminology's relationship with the state. Those working on issues connected to women offenders have already recognized the perils of the liberal strategy of strict legal equality. Such policies, when imposed in an already unequal and gendered context, have almost invariably disadvantaged women. Victimization activists have been more enthusiastic about the criminal justice system as a force for change but find that even well-intentioned policies, such as presumptive arrest for domestic violence offenders, have had unanticipated negative consequences. Women in policing, prison work, and law have also found that obtaining the legal right of access to these jobs is not enough to ensure equality.

Simply creating new laws to enforce, providing more offenders to incarcerate, and allowing women to work in the system have done little to disrupt its underlying structure, which is deeply gendered and racialized. As Carol Smart (1998) notes, the turning point for feminist criminology will come in realizing that "law is not simply . . . a set of tools or rules that we can bend into a more favourable shape" (31). Smart herself, arguably one of the founding mothers of feminist criminology, has recently disavowed the project entirely, arguing instead for a deconstructionist approach that disrupts and subverts criminology's traditional categories and frames of reference (Smart 1995). Rethinking feminist criminology's relationship to the state and to the criminal justice system does not necessarily mean that feminists in the discipline (or elsewhere) should reject efforts directed toward legal change. What this critique does suggest is that in feminism's continuing encounter with criminology, conceptions of justice, rather than law, should occupy a much more central place in our thinking (Klein 1995).

References

Adler, Freda. 1975. *Sisters in Crime: The Rise of the New Female Criminal.* New York: McGraw-Hill.

American Correctional Association. 1984. *Juvenile and Adult Correctional Departments, Institutions, Agencies and Paroling Authorities, United States and Canada.* College Park, MD: American Correctional Association.

Amir, Menachem. 1971. *Patterns in Forcible Rape.* Chicago: University of Chicago Press.

Anleu, Sharon Roach. 1992. Women in Law: Theory, Research and Practice. *Australian and New Zealand Journal of Sociology* 28(3):391–410.

Appier, Janis. 1998. *Policing Women: The Sexual Politics of Law Enforcement and the LAPD.* Philadelphia: Temple University Press.

Bachman, Ronet and Linda E. Saltzman. 1995. *Violence Against Women.* Washington, DC: Bureau of Justice Statistics.

Britton, Dana M. 1997. Gendered Organizational Logic: Policy and Practice in Men's and Women's Prisons. *Gender & Society* 11:796–818.

——. 2000. The Epistemology of the Gendered Organization. *Gender & Society* 14(3):418–435.

Brown, Beverley. 1986. Women and Crime: The Dark Figures of Criminology. *Economy and Society* 15(3):355–402.

Brownmiller, Susan. 1975. *Against Our Will: Men, Women, and Rape*. New York: Simon & Schuster.

Bureau of Labor Statistics. 1999. *Highlights of Women's Earnings in 1998*. Washington, DC: Government Printing Office.

Cain, Maureen. 1990. Towards Transgression: New Directions in Feminist Criminology. *International Journal of the Sociology of Law* 18:1–18.

Chesney-Lind, Meda. 1989. Girls' Crime and Women's Place: Toward a Feminist Model of Female Delinquency. *Crime and Delinquency* 35(1):5–29.

——. 1995. Preface. In *International Feminist Perspectives in Criminology: Engendering a Discipline*, ed. Nicole Hahn Rafter and Frances Heidensohn. Philadelphia: Open University Press.

——. 1996. Sentencing Women to Prison: Equality Without Justice. In *Race, Gender, and Class in Criminology: The Intersection*, ed. M. D. Schwartz and D. Milovanovic. New York: Garland.

Chilton, Roland and Susan K. Datesman. 1987. Gender, Race, and Crime: An Analysis of Urban Arrest Trends, 1960–1980. *Gender & Society* 1(2):152–71.

Daly, Kathleen. 1987. Discrimination in the Criminal Courts: Family, Gender, and the Problem of Equal Treatment. *Social Forces* 66(1):152–75.

——. 1992. Women's Pathways to Felony Court: Feminist Theories of Lawbreaking and Problems of Representation. *Southern California Review of Law and Women's Studies* 2:11–52.

Daly, Kathleen and Meda Chesney-Lind. 1988. Feminism and Criminology. *Justice Quarterly* 5:497–538.

Daly, Kathleen and Lisa Maher. 1998. Crossroads and Intersections: Building from Feminist Critique. In *Criminology at the Crossroads*, ed. Kathleen Daly and Lisa Maher. New York: Oxford University Press.

Davis, Angela Y. 1997. Race and Criminalization: Black Americans and the Punishment Industry. In *The House That Race Built*, ed. Wahneema Lubiano. New York: Pantheon.

DeKeseredy, Walter S. 1996. The Left-Realist Perspective on Race, Class, and Gender. In *Race, Gender, and Class in Criminology*, ed. M. D. Schwartz and D. Milovanovic. New York: Garland.

Ely, Robin J. 1995. The Power in Demography: Women's Social Constructions of Gender Identity at Work. *Academy of Management Journal* 38(3):589–634.

Freedman, Estelle. 1981. *Their Sister's Keepers: Women's Prison Reform in America, 1830–1930*. Ann Arbor: University of Michigan Press.

Gelles, Richard and Donileen Loeske, eds. 1993. *Current Controversies on Family Violence*. London: Sage.

Gelsthorpe, Loraine and Allison Morris. 1988. Feminism and Criminology in Britain. *British Journal of Criminology* 28(2):93–110.

Hanmer, J. and M. Maynard. 1987. *Women, Violence, and Social Control*. London: Macmillan.

Klein, Dorie. 1995. Crime Through Gender's Prism: Feminist Criminology in the United States. In *International Feminist Perspectives in Criminology: Engendering a Discipline*, ed. Nicole Hahn Rafter and Frances Heidensohn. Philadelphia: Open University Press.

Madriz, Esther. 1997. *Nothing Bad Happens to Good Girls: Fear of Crime in Women's Lives*. Berkeley: University of California Press.

Maguire, Kathleen and Ann L. Pastore. 1999. *Sourcebook of Criminal Justice Statistics*. Washington, DC: Government Printing Office. Available at http://www.albany.edu/sourcebook.

Maher, Lisa. 1997. *Sexed Work: Gender, Race, and Resistance in a Brooklyn Drug Market*. New York: Oxford University Press.

Mann, Coramae Richey. 1995. Women of Color and the Criminal Justice System. In *The Criminal Justice System and Women: Offenders, Victims, and Workers*, ed. Barbara Raffel Price and Natalie J. Sokoloff. New York: McGraw-Hill.

Martin, Patricia Y. 1997. Gender, Accounts, and Rape Processing Work. *Social Problems* 44(4):464–82.

Martin, Susan E. and Nancy C. Jurik. 1996. *Doing Justice, Doing Gender: Women in Law and Criminal Justice Occupations*. Thousand Oaks, CA: Sage.

Matthews, Roger and Jock Young. 1986. *Confronting Crime*. London: Sage.

Menkel-Meadow, Carrie. 1987. Portia in a Different Voice: Speculating on a Women's Lawyering Process. *Berkeley Women's Law Journal* 1(1):39–63.

Messerschmidt, James W. 1993. *Masculinities and Crime*. Boston: Rowman & Littlefield.

Miller, Susan L. 1999. *Gender and Community Policing*. Boston: Northeastern University Press.

Morris, Allison. 1987. *Women, Crime, and Criminal Justice*. New York: Basil Blackwell.

Morris, Allison and Loraine Gelsthorpe. 1991. Feminist Perspectives in Criminology: Transforming and Transgressing. *Women & Criminal Justice* 2(2):3–26.

Morris, Allison and Ania Wilczynski. 1994. Rocking the Cradle: Mothers Who Kill Their Children. In *Moving Targets: Women, Murder, and Representation*, ed. Helen Birch. Berkeley: University of California Press.

National Center for Women in Policing. 1999. *Equality Denied: The Status of Women in Policing, 1998*. Arlington, VA: Feminist Majority Foundation.

Nazroo, James. 1995. Uncovering Gender Differences in the Use of Marital Violence: The Effect of Methodology. *Sociology* 29(3):475–94.

Newburn, Tim and Elizabeth A. Stanko, eds. 1994. *Just Boys Doing Business? Men, Masculinities and Crime*. New York: Routledge.

Pierce, Jennifer. 1995. *Gender Trials: Emotional Lives in Contemporary Law Firms*. Berkeley: University of California Press.

Price, Barbara Raffel and Natalie J. Sokoloff, eds. 1995. *The Criminal Justice System and Women: Offenders, Victims, and Workers*. New York: McGraw-Hill.

Rafter, Nicole Hahn and Frances Heidensohn. 1995. Introduction: The Development of Feminist Perspectives on Crime. In *International Feminist Perspectives in Criminology: Engendering a Discipline*, ed. Nicole Hahn Rafter and Frances Heidensohn. Philadelphia: Open University Press.

Russell, Diana E. H. 1982. *Rape in Marriage*. New York: Macmillan.

Schwendinger, Julia R. and Herman Schwendinger. 1983. *Rape and Inequality*. Newbury Park, CA: Sage.

Sherman, Lawrence A. 1992. *Policing Domestic Violence*. New York: Free Press.

Sherman, Lawrence A. and Richard A. Berk. 1984. The Specific Deterrent Effects of Arrest for Domestic Violence. *American Sociological Review* 49(2):261–92.

Simon, Rita James. 1975. *Women and Crime*. Lexington, MA: Lexington Books.

Simpson, Sally S. 1989. Feminist Theory, Crime, and Justice. *Criminology* 27: 605–31.
Simpson, Sally S. and Lori Elis. 1995. Doing Gender: Sorting out the Caste and Crime Conundrum. *Criminology* 33(1):47–81.
Smart, Carol. 1976. *Women, Crime and Criminology: A Feminist Critique*. Boston: Routledge & Kegan Paul.
——. 1995. *Law, Crime and Sexuality: Essays in Feminism*. London: Sage.
——. 1998. The Woman of Legal Discourse. In *Criminology at the Crossroads*, ed. Kathleen Daly and Lisa Maher. New York: Oxford University Press.
Stanko, Elizabeth. 1990. *Everyday Violence*. London: Pandora.
Steffensmeier, Darrell. 1995. Trends in Female Crime: It's Still a Man's World. In *The Criminal Justice System and Women*, ed. Barbara R. Price and Natalie J. Sokoloff. New York: McGraw-Hill.
Steffensmeier, Darrell and Emilie Allan. 1996. Gender and Crime: Toward a Gendered Theory of Female Offending. *Annual Review of Sociology* 22:459–88.
Straus, Murray A., Richard J. Gelles, and Suzanne Steinmetz. 1980. *Behind Closed Doors*. New York: Doubleday.
Taylor, Ian, Paul Walton, and Jock Young. 1973. *The New Criminology*. London: Routledge & Kegan Paul.

Part 2

THE CRIMINOLOGICAL RESPONSE: PROBLEMATISING MEN AND MASCULINITY

8

MUSCLE, 'HARD MEN' AND 'IRON' MIKE TYSON

Reflections on desire, anxiety and the embodiment of masculinity

Tony Jefferson

Source: *Body and Society*, 4:1 (1998), 77–98.

Let me start with two memories. Both have to do with my relation to my body. Since both of them are vividly remembered, I take them to possess emotional significance and hence relevance for the set of investments underpinning my sense of (masculine) identity. The first goes back to my college days when I had a vacation job, labouring on a site constructing cooling towers. Cooling towers are built by constructing a double circle of wooden shutters to accommodate the thickness of the wall. These shutters are bolted together. Cement is then poured in. This sets overnight and the next day the shutters are unbolted and moved up a level. Then the whole process is repeated. My job was to loosen the bolts securing the shutters around the set concrete. I was a PE student – young, fit and strong. I took pride in my physical abilities. But at first, try as I might, I could not loosen the bolts. On this particular occasion, the foreman, an older man of few words and unmemorable physique, saw me struggling, came over, took the spanner from me, loosened the bolt effortlessly, smiled silently, returned me my spanner, and left me – smiling weakly, but feeling horribly crushed.

The second memory involves a couple of photos of me around the age of 18, executing two standard 'muscle man' poses in my parents' back-garden. I had been weight-training for a short while and these photos were intended as some kind of visual record of my efforts. The point of the story (and the pain of the memory) is that despite my obvious investment in my developing body, I felt (and still feel) embarrassed in my pride in its public display, and have never since shown them to anybody until recently, when I got them out (in the interests of 'science'!) for a friend similarly interested in questions of masculinity. Even then it was an anxious moment.

Two stories. Each about my investment in my body; each addressing the strong body; but each doing so in importantly different ways. The first contains an image of strength, and perhaps mental resolve, as I failed to live up to the 'strong arm' standard set by the foreman. The second contains a more complex image. The strengthening of muscle in pursuit of an idea of the 'body beautiful' embraces strength and beauty – and begins to account for my more mixed feelings: pride in the strength exhibited, embarrassment at the vain uselessness of such a 'preening' (feminine?) pursuit of 'beauty'. Both attest in different ways to my acute awareness of my male body, its centrality to my sense of who I am as a person – which is to say, to my identification as a man. This bodily awareness (and its sometimes tragic cost) is movingly attested to also in David Jackson's critical autobiography, *Unmasking Masculinity*. In it he talks of learning to identify himself as a 'he-man', of learning to 'embody force' by 'tautening your muscles, holding yourself firm and upright, striding with a cocky strut, throwing out your chest and walking from your shoulders' (1990: 54). I have countless photos of my father (and some of me, unfortunately) surreptitiously 'tautening muscles' for the camera.

All this is a far cry, apparently, from Ros Coward's view that the defining feature of the male body is its neglect.[1] Because men are the subjects and not the objects of the gaze, they exempt themselves from some of the repercussions such as the extensive attention to the body that women can hardly avoid, thereby retaining control: 'controlling the look, men have left themselves out of the picture because a body defined is a body controlled' (Coward, 1984: 229). Perhaps the two viewpoints can be reconciled, however, when we bear in mind that one aspect of 'hardness' is a certain indifference to the body, a theme to which I return later.

So, this is an article about the embodiment of masculine identity; of how particular discourses about male bodies become emotionally invested – suffused with desire or anxiety[2] – and hence provide materials for the construction of masculine identities. It is thus about representations of the masculine body *and* their psychic underpinnings; for without the latter it is impossible to comprehend how masculine body imagery has sufficient affect to be reproduced across the generations. Specifically, since the case study chosen to exemplify this is that of the boxer Mike Tyson, my focus will be on the strong or hard body – though 'hardness' connotes mental as well as physical toughness, a point I shall develop further.

Dutton (1995), in his exploration of the origins of contemporary interest in the muscular body, has recently reminded us that the heroic, muscular figure of a Grecian God or a statue by Leonardo is a specifically Western ideal of physical development, and a far cry from the contemplative, soft-bellied look of Eastern deities. In tracing the various historical manifestations of the muscular or 'developed' body, from its origins in classical Greek sculpture to its Renaissance revival and the modern cult of the body-builder, Dutton attests to the longevity of this particular iconic embodiment of masculinity. But he traces also both strands identified already – the body as pure strength, and the body beautiful. He shows, for example, that the Greek tradition moved from portraying the typical athlete as 'the strong man, the boxer or wrestler, depicted as a vigorous and heroic male without any suggestion of sexual attraction . . . the personification of power and endurance' to portraying him as an 'athletic youth . . . as remarkable for his physical beauty as for his bodily strength' (1995: 357). Dutton interprets this dual nature of the muscular body, through its various manifestations, according to his fundamental theme, namely:

> . . . that the symbolism of muscularity in western societies has been developed within the context of two principal metaphors: the muscular body as power-symbol, and as pleasure-symbol. The pleasure element may take the form of aesthetic or erotic pleasure, or it may gravitate ambiguously between the two.
>
> (1995:16)

Since this connects nicely with my opening stories, it is a useful starting point for my purposes too.

The masculine body and gender

One thing missing from Dutton's engaging narrative is quite what questions of bodily strength and beauty have to do specifically with gender development.[3] I have said these have played a part in my development of a masculine self; but quite why this should be the case has been taken for granted so far.[4] As is well-known, Freud's answer to the riddle of gender difference centred on the presence or absence of a particular bodily organ, the penis, and the castration anxiety that for little boys leads to a shift in emotional allegiance from the mother to identification with the father. But if the actual penis seems now too reductive a basis upon which to found a whole theory of masculine embodiment, its currently fashionable replacement by a symbol, the Lacanian phallus, does not seem to alter things much. This is not just because of the difficulty of conceptualizing the phallus disconnected from its anatomical referent, as Frosh (1995: 176) has recently argued (see also Butler, 1993: 84), but also because its symbolic significance has been 'vastly exaggerated' (Connell, 1983:27). Thus, I am not much persuaded by Dyer's argument that 'the excessive, even hysterical quality of so much male imagery . . . clenched fists, the bulging muscles, the hardened jaws, the proliferation of phallic symbols . . . are all straining after what can hardly ever be achieved, the embodiment of phallic mystique' (1989: 206).[5] Of course, that still leaves open the question of quite what all the 'bulging muscles', etc. do signify. Dutton's response is that the striving after a developed body should be read symbolically as a 'metaphor of perfection' – a notion which puts me in mind of the constant unattainability which is central to Lacan's paradoxical notion of desire as lack, or 'the phallus as mastery' (Frosh, 1995: 175). But this only pushes the question back a stage: why muscular strength as a symbol of perfection; why not something else?

In suggesting that 'there is a whole range of ways in which the body can be defined, perceived, cathected and symbolised as masculine', Connell (1983: 27) would appear to be offering an opening towards a less reductionist, more pluralistic, answer; one more in keeping with contemporary sensibilities. Yet he goes on in effect to suggest that this 'range of ways' reduces to the embodiment of 'force' and 'competence':

> In linking the construction of masculinity with the social power structure of patriarchy, I think we have to take much more seriously the combination that comes up repeatedly in schoolboy sport, in physical labour, in the cult fantasies of bodily perfection: the combination of strength and skill. It is important here that these are attributes of the body as a whole; they are not focused, even symbolically, on a particular part of it. What it means to be masculine is, quite literally, to embody force, to embody competence.
>
> (1983: 27)

So Dutton's strength and beauty become Connell's strength and skill (or competence). The term common to both authors is strength. One could go further. It seems to me that Dutton's notion of strength derived from the Greek tradition presumed an athlete, thereby subsuming, effectively, both strength and skill. Perhaps, then, we should focus on strength, and how this is connected to gender development? Here Connell's answer that 'force and competence are, obviously enough, translations into the language of the body of the social relations which define men as holders of power, women as subordinate' (1983: 28) still assumes – in that 'obviously enough' – what to me is far from obvious, namely, why strength is 'chosen' (so often) to carry, and reproduce, patriarchal power? In attempting to answer this question, we shall need to take the question of strength, with its connotations of hardness, more seriously and, in line with object relations and Kleinian theory generally, shift our focus from the Oedipal to the pre-Oedipal moment in thinking of the 'origins' of gender development. First, we need a firmer grasp on the meaning of hardness.

Hard men, physical toughness and courage

In talking about the historical origins of the Belfast 'hard men' in local, neighbourhood-based, bare-fisted street-fighters, Feldman situates them firmly, if somewhat reductively, within industrial capitalism:

> [The] era of the hardman coincided with the cultural dominance of industrial capitalism in Belfast. The hardman fight and its locales and characters were central to the iconograpy of industrial working class culture. The hardman ethic was a revaluation of the body confronted with the power of the machine.
>
> (1991: 56)

Bathrick similarly links the emergent iconic status of the boxer in avant-garde writings of Weimar Germany to the 'profound cultural and political transformations within post-Wilhelminian modernity' (1990: 114), though for him the 'hardness of the boxer's body' (1990: 134) is emblematic of the new, brutal, machine-driven reality, not its antithesis:

> If sport, along with Jazz, dancing revues, Josephine Baker, or the pragmatic Henry Ford came to symbolize American toughness and the up-to-date, then the figure of the boxer served as its corporeal representation *par excellence*.
>
> (1990: 118)

Whatever their differences, both statements assume a cultural revalorization of 'hardness' as a consequence of industrialism. However, we need also to attend to what precisely hardness *means*. Feldman's definition that 'hardness is an interiorized quality extracted from risking the body in performance' (1991: 53) is a succinct starting point.

A willingness to risk the body in performance connotes at least two things in addition to the physical strength obviously required in street-fighting or boxing. First, an indifference to the body's (often painful) fate, an attitude quite opposed to the displayed 'body beautiful' of the muscular body-builder.[6] Second, courage or bravery, qualities of *mental* toughness which have nothing necessarily to do with muscle. Many sports, like motor racing, though physically demanding, do not require hard muscles. But indifference to pain and mental toughness are *de rigueur*.[7] Over and above physical aptitude, talent, ability, judgement, vision and all the other qualities drawn upon to discuss the undisputed male 'giants' of sport, hardness, this willingness to risk the body in performance, is what, for me, is the perennial sub-textual answer to the sports journalists' insistent question: how are these men different?[8]

In trying to articulate why Juan Fangio, the most successful racing driver of all time, so often managed 'to rise above unhelpful conditions, superior opposition, or faulty equipment . . . sometimes, being Fangio, all three at once', Williams (1995a: 12) never surpasses his headline writer: 'Best and bravest racer of them all'. Perhaps, 'best *because* bravest' would have made the point more explicitly. Peter Nichols introduces thus his article on Mick Doohan, world motorcycling champion in 1994 despite badly shattering his leg in 1992, an accident that required major surgery:

> People bandy the word courage in sport as part of the common vocabulary – like disaster, humiliation and despair. They do not talk about courage in motorcycling; it is part of the equipment, like leathers and a helmet. If you do not have it, you would not race.
> (1995)

Doohan's airy disclaimer ('I don't see it as brave. It's all calculation out there.')[9] only heightens the aura: this man is hardness personified – a reading which gets endorsed later when Nichols reports Doohan's remarks that winning the world championship 'doesn't make me pull back'. Nichols, apparently, can see the proof of this in Doohan's eyes: 'his eyes, almost intimidating in their directness, say that he would not ever'.

When Miguel Indurain achieved, uniquely, his fifth *successive* victory in, what is by common consent, cycling's toughest race, the Tour de France, he not only joined the ranks of the 'superhuman', he became, arguably 'the world's greatest living athlete' – given the Tour's reputation as 'perhaps the most demanding sporting event of all' (all according to Stephen Bierley, 1995). What marks him out from more ordinary riders[10] is surely not his extraordinary ability to 'draw eight litres of air into his lungs at a single gasp' (Williams, 1995b: 16), much less his 'perfectly sculpted barrel thighs' (Fotheringham, 1995b: 21), important though these physical attributes are to a professional cyclist. What thrills (and chills) the heart in reading about the Tour (as I do each year from the comfort of my armchair), and what underscores Indurain's claim to the title of 'the world's greatest living athlete' and the notion of the Tour as the 'most demanding sporting event' are the twin demands of 'hardness': the unique combination of pain-endurance and courage required for success. During the mountain stages, riders must not only endure the excruciatingly painful physical demands of the ascents – 'when climbing some mountains, Tour riders' heart-rates can reach 200 beats per minute – enough to cause a heart attack in a sedentary person' (Fotheringham, 1995a) – but also prepare themselves mentally for the courage demanded during the high-speed and dangerous descents ('[a]fter the lung-bursting, leg-breaking hour to the Roseland summit came the 60mph descent on single-track roads with bumps where the tarmac had melted and moved in the sun, and potholes where it had been cracked by frost', Fotheringham, 1995a). Any child can ride a bike; but it is the willingness 'to risk the body in performance' that ensures that 'every rider who finishes the Tour de France receives a medal' (Bierley, 1995).[11]

The idea that hardness is as much a mental as a physical quality finds support in the ethnographically based work of Westwood (1990) and Mac an Ghaill (1994) on black British youth. In both studies, though physical toughness is important, being able to 'handle yourself' is a broader, more mentally based attribute:

> What is called up in relation to being streetwise is the ability to handle the dangers of street life, and this links masculinity, defence, and manly behaviour. Contrary to popular views, however, that being streetwise privileges physical prowess and fighting acumen, it is essentially an intellectual, cerebral attribute. What is required as a context for being streetwise and being able to operate safely on the streets is an intimate knowledge of locality which all the men shared. . . . Faced with the power of the police the men would say that it was vital 'to know how to handle yourself' and this meant everything but a physical response. As Dev commented, 'You have to stay cool and let them heat up'. Staying cool is essentially about maintaining dignity and control in a situation which very often denies both.
>
> (Westwood, 1990: 64)

Here, the ability to risk the body in performance is directed towards achieving a non-confrontational outcome, *without* losing face. The other side of the coin, of course, is that the body may have to be risked in confrontation, if face is otherwise going to be lost.

Likewise with one of Mac an Ghaill's interviewees:

> *MM*: Does a black guy have to be tough?
>
> *Kevin*: It depends. You gotta act kinda tough. I mean there's two kinds of toughness. You can talk right and you can be physical. If you're just physical, I wouldn't mix with that somebody. I want somebody who can talk and is physical right. I don't want to mix with a stupid head-case. He will cause unnecessary trouble.
>
> (1994:188)

Arguably, boxing provides the ultimate arena for the display of hardness. The willingness to risk the body in performance is extreme, as two men enter a small ring, each with the sole intention of inflicting pain directly on the body of the other and, if possible, knocking the other senseless (with all the attendant risks of injury and worse entailed) in the shortest possible time. The mental demands are equally, if not more, severe; in addition to the courage to overcome the fear that stops most of us from ever stepping in a boxing ring in the first place, a boxer – if he wants to be respected as a fighter – needs the mental resolve to fight on regardless of pain, discomfort and possible injury, even though the body be broken. Wacquant, who spent much time with boxers in Southside Chicago, regards the willingness to do this as the unique core of a boxer's 'honour': "The *specific honour* of the pugilist, like that of the gladiator, consists in refusing to concede and kneel down' (1995b: 496; emphasis in original).

A boxer may be admired and respected for his wonderful talent, extraordinary skills and sheer artistry, as was, for example, the young 'float like a butterfly, sting like a bee' Muhammad Ali (then Cassius Clay). But it was not until he demonstrated that he also had 'heart', that he could soak up punishment as well as dish it out, as he had to in his punishing battles with Joe Frazier as an older, slower, less skilful boxer, that his true greatness as a fighter was secured (even as it probably cost him his health). It was as if the blessedly talented but immaturely 'lippy' young Clay had finally come of age as a 'man's man'. Similarly with the middleweight Sugar Ray Robinson, who, even the great Ali conceded, was quite probably the greatest ever exponent of the art of boxing, pound for pound. But, like Ali (whose quick-footed, dancing style and lightning reflexes were so reminiscent of the young Sugar Ray), Robinson's enormous reputation in boxing requires both the lengthy, punishing come-back battles of his later years, when he was clearly past his best, as well as the incandescent skills of his youth.

Given that boxing requires all that hardness connotes – a strong, physically developed body, mental toughness, courage and 'guts' – it is perhaps not surprising that the boxer remains the supreme emblem of the hard man, thus explaining boxing's macho status in the sports hierarchy, and why the heavyweight boxing champion of the world remains the highest (best paid) prize in sport. Lighter boxers, or men from other sports like Fangio and Indurain, may have more heart, gymnasts more developed bodies, dancers more skill or weight-lifters more strength, but a wannabe heavyweight champion must combine all these attributes – courage, developed muscle, skill and strength – in one, preferably large, frame. Small wonder that as a 10-year-old I wanted to be the heavyweight champion of the world, despite my conscious knowledge (born of my one try out with boxing gloves) that I had no 'heart' (or stomach) for it (though it has to be said that it was a below-the-belt punch that did for me!).

This exploration of hardness through both its mental and physical connotations of toughness has reconnected us, via the example of boxing and some of its legendary figures, to our starting point: the idea that strength in the service of displayed beauty (the bodybuilder's muscles) is suspect because latently feminine; whereas beauty in the service of strength or courage (the boxing of Ali or Sugar Ray) is, by contrast, solidly masculine. In both cases, it took the decline of their 'beautiful' skills to secure the point. In the case of the young Tyson, however, there was never any doubt that whatever boxing skills he had (a much contested point), these were but an almost superfluous adjunct to his indisputable hardness – a combination of extraordinary ferocity in the ring, a physique of teak-like solidity, and a killer punch – attributes that quickly earned him the ultimate soubriquet, namely, 'Iron' Mike, and a fast-track route into boxing's all-time Hall of Fame. The time has come to see how focusing on Tyson might help us understand better the relationship between desire and the embodiment of masculinity.

The embodiment of black masculinity: Toms, Coons and Bucks

Before coming to the psychic dimension, I need to render the story of the male body more specific and, in particular, say something about the images of embodied black masculinity available to the young Tyson, growing up in the 1970s and reaching maturity in the 1980s. The stereotypical images of the black man as more natural, spontaneous, fun-loving, child-like, expressive, rhythmic, sexual, violent and lazy than the white – as altogether more 'primitive' and physical – undoubtedly owe much to a whole series of racist projections: the socially unacceptable, hence repressed, characteristics of dominant, white, 'civilized' males unconsciously projected on to the black, male body. It is the sort of relational dynamic, as Hoch illuminatingly reminds us, upon which social hierarchy, and the accompanying repression, always depend:

> Social hierarchy would be impossible without such beasts. If they did not exist – and perhaps they exist only as a *consequence* of social and psychological repression – the law and order forces would have to invent them. In this sense, the bestial criminal, foreign barbarian, subversive, devil or brutish member of a subordinate race or class represents an *externalisation* of a beast within who is, in another sense, an *internalisation* of the repression without.
>
> (1979: 56; emphases in original)

These stereotypical images, according to Wallace's review of Donald Bogle's extensive look at characterizations of blacks in American film, cohere into a few basic stereotypes: on the male side into 'Toms, Coons and Bucks':

> We are all familiar with Uncle Tom. He is devoted to whites, religious, hardworking, loyal, trustworthy, patient, and restrained. The Coon is happy-go-lucky, a clown, a buffoon, a child, clever and witty but unable to perform the most simple task without guidance. He's a trickster, cunning and resourceful. . . . The Buck is the only black stereotype that is sexual. He is brutal, violent, virile, tough, strong – and finds white women especially appealing. . . . He is the personification of the black threat to womanhood and, more importantly, to white male authority and dominance.
>
> (Wallace, 1990: 25)

Of course, stereotypes, fuelled as they are by projected, sometimes exotic, fantasies, can never capture the complexities and contradictoriness of lived experience: its richly textured if mundane daily round; its finely grained amalgam of excitements and frustrations, dignity and disappointment, courage and resignation, successes and failures. On the other hand, the stereotypes offered us are not simply divorced from our 'real lives' either, existing 'out there'. Even as they represent our experienced realities in the form of stereotypical fantasies, such fantasies constitute, also, sources of 'information' about how we might be. In other words, 'Toms', 'Coons' and 'Bucks' are both stereotypes *and* reference points for potential survival strategies in a hostile world: the compliant Uncle Tom 'house nigger', the devious Coon hiding his cunning behind a grinning mask, the bad-assed Buck 'nigga with attitude', are, potentially anyway, types as well as stereotypes, even if particular individuals are complex (and contradictory) mixtures beyond any simple stereotype.

The point of this reminder, to put it very schematically, is threefold:

1 post-slavery, a whole host of racist practices, from discriminatory hiring to mob lynching, served to keep black males, economically, politically, socially and juridically, in their 'place' (the low-waged ghetto, the gaolhouse or the graveyard). These restricted opportunities served to amplify the salience of the stereotypes, partly because ghetto escape routes, such as they were, were confined to areas – entertainment, sports – requiring the 'natural' physical talents of the clowning Coons and strong Bucks, and partly because restricted opportunities applied also to the white-dominated image-making process;
2 these restricted opportunities began to channel black aspirations into the 'physical' areas of sports and entertainment, a fact which also demonstrates the success with which blacks had themselves introjected the stereotypes. This, in turn, helped produce the formidable rise of the Afro-American athlete, musician, performer, which then further demonstrated the success of the equation between black males and sensuality;
3 by the time of the multiple challenges to the manifold iniquities of this system of racism during the 1960s – the Civil Rights Movement, the riots and Black Power: the effects of both restricted opportunities and internalization (what Wallace calls the 'Americanization' of the black experience, 1990: 25) – the only model of black manhood available to galvanize young, black men, in effect, was that of the 'Buck'. If 'Stokely [Carmichael] was the nightmare America had been dreading – the black man seizing his manhood, the black man as sexual, virile, strong, tough, and dangerous' (Wallace, 1990: 36), it was a stereotype that the Black Movement embraced and fostered, enthusiastically (and which, according to Wallace, 1990, was to prove its undoing).[12]

However one judges the rise and fall of Black Power, and the undoubtedly complex nature of the legacy, certain outcomes seem indisputable. First, a combination of processes, including economic recession, capitalist restructuring, government cutbacks and 'law and order' politics, has produced 'a sharp deterioration' in the black ghettos, and 'has effected an institutional transformation that effectively dooms ever-larger numbers of inner-city residents to prolonged social marginality and economic redundancy' (Wacquant, 1995c: 418, 419). Second, the image of 'Black Macho' lives massively on (cf. Singh, 1995), but now divorced completely from a political context save that of internecine gang warfare, the informal economy of drugs, and crime and battles with 'the law', yet buttressed continually by movies riddled with Buck imagery, by rap music, and by black sporting super-heroes – what Singh calls the growth of the 'black-aesthetic commodity' (1995:46). This was the legacy, these the images, bequeathed the young Tyson, born in the poor Brownsville district of New York City in 1966, the year Malcolm X was assassinated, and one year before the formation of the Black Panthers in Oakland.[13]

Mike Tyson and hardness

Mike Tyson was not always 'Iron Mike'. As all the biographies reveal (see Heller, 1989; Illingworth, 1992), for a while he was a passive, podgy, lisping, apparently ill-adjusted child of the ghetto who was the butt of local bullies, and was known as 'little fairy boy'. At this point in time, we can surmise, he felt neither 'hard', nor happy, in his body. Indeed, it is arguable that his large, but muscularly undeveloped body, combined with his high-pitched lisping voice and general passivity (in short, his 'feminine' softness), were what attracted the bullies in the first place, if we subscribe to the view (and I do) that male bullying has a lot to do with projecting one's despised weaknesses on to apparently weaker others precisely in order to feel stronger, more powerful and more masculine. Homophobia, and the 'hate' crimes that can result from such feelings, are a particular, developed version of this misanthropy. But, at a certain point in time, the young Tyson was pushed too far (allegedly after a local bully had cruelly decapitated one of his beloved pigeons) and fought back, successfully, from which point on his status in the neighbourhood changed and he became a local gang member, bully boy and thief. The psychological transformation involved in making the shift from bullied to bully I have detailed elsewhere (Jefferson, 1996). For the moment, I wish to focus on what this signifies in terms of hardness. Since, at this stage of his life, his body remained untransformed, it seems reasonable to suggest that the initial shift was a mental one. In other words, the shift from passivity to (successful) activity is accompanied by/made possible because of a new mental 'hardness': a new willingness to risk the body in performance.

Thereafter, the young Tyson gets into sufficient trouble to find himself locked up in a reformatory for young 'hard-core' delinquents. Whether he was actually a tough 'incorrigible' is a moot point, since the man who first taught him to box in the reformatory described him then as 'scared of his own shadow' (quoted in Illingworth, 1992: 8). Be that as it may, what I think is significant is that much later on, as a successful boxing champion, Tyson appeared to revel in this image of his younger self; in brief, he appeared to identify with the connotations of hardness inscribed in the idea of the incorrigible delinquent, someone whose tough persona is impervious to the appeals and punishments of 'carers' and 'controllers' alike.

While in the reformatory, he begged to be taught to box, and quickly discovered he had both talent and appetite for 'the noble art'. As I have already argued earlier, the successful boxer requires both mental and physical toughness. If by then Tyson had already made certain mental transformations, it remained to discipline his body through boxing's many physical training routines – running, skipping, sparring, shadow-boxing, bag-punching, weight-watching, etc. – and thereby literally harden it. Progress was rapid on all fronts. His appetite for fitness training was unquenchable: 'frightening', in the words of his trainer, describing how Tyson would continue shadow-boxing late into the night in his reformatory cell. In the ring, his ferocity was such that seasoned sparring partners cried off rather than risk being knocked out by a fearsome teenager with a potentially lethal punch. Mentally speaking, the art of boxing is all about learning how to overcome your own fear and instill it into (or project it on to) your opponent, a point his beloved manager Cus D'Amato constantly stressed. Though there is some evidence that Tyson's fearlessness could occasionally desert him if the quick knock-out (his speciality) was not forthcoming, Tyson's aptitude for the mental tasks of boxing seemed to develop as naturally as his extraordinary punching ability. If sparring partners cried off in training, even nationally ranked juniors would sometimes cry off rather than face the prospect of three rounds with Tyson (Illingworth, 1992: 58). Once again, however ferocious and fearsome the real Tyson, the significant point is that Tyson revelled in this hard, brutal self-image, sometimes detailing his 'bad intentions' in after-fight interviews with sadistic glee, much to the embarrassment of his management team (Berger, 1990: 125).

Quicker than anyone else had ever done so, at the youthful age of 20, Tyson fulfilled D'Amato's early predictions and became the heavyweight boxing champion of the world. By now, his frightening mental toughness was matched by an awesomely developed physical presence. In ten short years, the 'little fairy boy' had become 'Iron' Mike, the 'baddest' man on the planet (Sen, 1992: 31): truly 'tougher than the rest' (to borrow a line from a Springsteen song); the ultimate 'hard man'. Physically developed as he was/is, it seems important to reiterate that the notion of hardness resides less in the body as such, and more in the body's capacity in action, when risked in performance: the capacity to give and take physical punishment, rather than as passive exhibit in a body-building competition, or the body as spectacle as in a wrestling match.

Three pictures I collected for the purpose of this article nicely demonstrate these differences. In the first, Arnold Schwarzenegger, the bodybuilder, reclines passively in a deck-chair holding a towel behind him in a way that exhibits his body to good effect (*Observer Magazine*, 10 November 1991). He is looking away from the camera, as if (like us) admiring one of his own huge biceps. The title to the photo is simply 'Mr Big'. In the second, an unnamed wrestler bedecked with a Union Jack cape and wearing white tights torn to reveal a second pair of tights which match the cape, and Union Jack wristbands, is standing astride the ring ropes with arms aloft and fists clenched, baring a highly developed, bronzed torso, glistening with oil (*Observer Magazine*, 29 March 1992). The superman connotations are inescapable, even as the extravagant dress performance emphasizes the image as spectacle – a point underscored by the headline 'Back With A Bang'.[14] The final image is a photo of Tyson at a pre-fight weigh-in (source unknown). He stands in nothing but his Calvin Klein underwear, arms held in classic bodybuilder pose to reveal his highly developed biceps, winking at the camera. The difference between his pose and the Schwarzenegger one is all in the wink; it is a play on the image of the bodybuilder for the benefit of the spectators, subtly undercutting the passivity of the muscle man both in actively returning the gaze and in sending up the pose. It is an unconscious recognition of the paradox of using his masculine musculature for the purpose of feminine display, a symbolic message to all and sundry that the real business takes place in the ring when the muscles will get used for real; posing is just the 'fun' preliminary.

In similar fashion it is worth reflecting on the difference between the muscle man contest and the boxers' weigh-in. Whereas bodies in the former invite the spectator to gaze admiringly at the purely aesthetic display of muscle bulk and definition, the scene at the weigh-in is quite different. Here well-developed bodies are similarly on display, but the narcissism and aesthetics of the body beautiful are both subordinate to the display of menace. Whatever the practical purpose of the weigh-in, namely, to ensure each boxer is inside the weight limit (a totally unnecessary exercise for heavyweights, of course, since there is no upper weight limit), the psychological purpose for the fighters themselves is to 'psych out' each other. This may take many forms, from the notorious 'eye-balling', to ritual insults and threats, to exuding a serene but focused inner strength and confidence: a detached fearlessness. In this sense, Tyson winking at the camera in muscle man pose is unusual; more usual is another photo of him at the weigh-in prior to his return fight after four years in gaol (*Daily Telegraph*, 19 August 1995). In this he stands looking at a spot straight in front of him, arms at his side; in repose, but ready for action. The caption, 'Weighing in . . . there were gasps when Mike Tyson disrobed to reveal muscles like teak', crystallizes the important distinction; this is a body displayed, but without affecting display – a body whose true power will only be unleashed later. The gasps are an awe-full premonition of the 'yet-to-be-actively-displayed' power of the body in action. The 'winner' at the weigh-in is not the man with the most developed body, but he who exudes the most menace and potential power;

which is why at the Bruno/Tyson fight Tyson was also the pre-fight winner, despite Bruno's more classically beautiful/sculpted physique. It remains to unravel just how we might make sense of this, Tyson's 'hardness'.

Hardness, opportunity, practice and identification

I have already talked about how restricted opportunities for Afro-American males, combined with the effective reduction of discourses about embodied black masculinity to that of the 'Buck', constituted the habitus of the young, growing Tyson. Thus, one simple way to think about Tyson's early biographical 'choices' – delinquent gang member, then boxer – is in terms of this depleted opportunity structure at both the practical and the discursive level. However, to rest here, within the realm of the social, is to tell only part of the story. It is an important starting point, but cannot be our endpoint since opportunities constitute a field of possibilities only (however narrow) until Tyson (or anyone) somehow turns possibility into actuality. The Sartrean thrust of the previous sentence was deliberate, since one way of thinking how subjects 'interiorize' some part of the social is via the notion of practice. That is to say, lives are practical accomplishments, constituted through the ongoing choices, made self-consciously or unreflexively through habit, that render actual particular actions from the 'field of the possible'. With Sartre, however, practice is conceptualized within a traditional understanding of the mind/body split wherein the existentialist credo charges the 'sleeping' mind to become consciously responsible for the choices that, collectively, constitute one's life project.

More recently, Wacquant has taken up this practice-based approach, but inflected by Merleau-Ponty's efforts to overcome this mind/body dualism, in his efforts to understand boxers' 'willing embrace and submission' to the physical pains and rigours of their calling (Wacquant, 1995d: 88); their willingness to 'choose' the boxing option from the 'field of the possible'. Translated into my terms, he is attempting to explain their investment in boxing. He quite rightly dismisses rational/utilitarian/voluntaristic explanations (boxers don't simply misperceive the dangers, nor are they simply in it for the money) and the culturally determinist alternative which sees boxing as an example of 'normative compliance to some external cultural dictate' (Wacquant, 1995d: 88). In my terms, he too rejects the over-socialized accounts of the 'willing embrace'. Rather, he suggests, the boxer is one for whom there is an:

> . . . *unconscious fit between his (pugilistic) habitus and the very field which has produced it*. . . . The boxer's *desire* to fight flows from a *practical belief* constituted in and by the immediate copresence of, and mutual understanding between, his (re)socialized lived body and the game.
>
> (1995d: 88; emphases in original)

This he regards as the same conclusion drawn by Merleau-Ponty:

> The 'lived body' is not in the first instance an *object* of consciousness but the pre-objective medium of consciousness, indeed the veritable *subject* of human social practice if there is ever to be one . . . boxing suggests the need to place the *socialized lived body*, and the incorporating practices that shape its structures, at the center of the analysis of social action.
>
> (Wacquant, 1992: 249; emphases in original)

In moving beyond the mind/body dualism he would appear to be laying to rest all dualisms (voluntarism/determinism and, following Bourdieu, agency/structure), a move that others interested in understanding the 'socialized lived body' have also made (see Crossley, 1995a, 1995b, 1996; Young, 1980). This also constitutes a serious challenge to the other well-trodden route in the study of the body, namely, the Foucauldian one in which the body is the site of discursive inscriptions. Indeed, this would now seem to be the new dualism in the field: the body as always already embodied ('lived') versus the body as always already inscripted. I find I have problems with both positions. Let me approach the basis of my difficulties using Wacquant's review article: 'Why Men Desire Muscles' (1995a).

This article is an extended review of Sam Fussell's (1991) book on his involvement in body-building. Interestingly for my purposes, it represents the other side of the muscular body, the body beautiful as opposed to the hard, strong body exemplifed by the boxer. Perhaps it is this shift of focus that delivers my problem with Wacquant's 'the body as lived' formulations. At one point, Wacquant talks of Fussell's book being a treatise on 'hidden anxiety' (1995a: 170) and 'an unusually perceptive exploration of the constitutive predicament of masculinity' (1995a: 171). Later, he uses the language of embodiment as he did with the argument about boxers:

> Yet another invaluable contribution of *Muscle* is to supply a dense and convincing 'thick description' of the active *embodiment* of a particular manhood complex, of the multisided process through which the masculine *illusio* – i.e., the shared belief in, and collectively manufactured illusion of the value of the games (real) men play – becomes progressively instilled and inscribed in a particular biological individual.
>
> (1995a: 173; emphases in original)

My difficulty is captured in the disjunction I perceive between these two discourses: the psychoanalytically derived discourse of anxiety, and the Merleau-Ponty derived one of embodiment. In other words, the text subsumes two contrasting discourses: that of insecurities, albeit with multiple origins (gender-, class- and ontologically-based), which *precede* (or motivate or somehow underlie) the desire to build muscle; and that of the 'lived body', the 'pre-objective medium of consciousness' to requote Wacquant (1992: 249), a notion which precludes preceding motives since the presence of such, however conceived, returns us to a mind/body distinction. The failure to resolve this issue – the meaning of why Fussell desired muscle in the first place – returns to haunt Wacquant's perplexed endpoint: how to understand Fussell's loss of desire to build muscles; his quitting the bodybuilding world.

So, with the help of Wacquant's (brilliantly perceptive) confusion, we return, I believe, to an untranscended problematic: the question of the motivational, *psychic investments* underpinning Fussell's commitment to bodybuilding, Tyson's to the 'hard' world of boxing (and mine to the masculine body generally). In thinking about this within a psychoanalytic frame, I have already expressed my dissatisfaction with Dyer's notion that 'bulging muscles' and the like are attempts to embody 'phallic mystique'. This seems altogether too general and abstract an approach. In this regard, Wacquant's use of Chodorow (1978), with her emphasis on the importance of early, pre-Oedipal object relations to the development 'of men . . . endowed with fragile self boundaries and a deep ambivalence toward intimacy' (Wacquant, 1995a: 172), is for me a step in the right direction, not least because it feels more experientially recognizable. The problem, as Chodorow (1989, 1994) herself came to see, the idea of men and women pursuing different developmental paths on account of their differential experiences of mothering, risked becoming too general (and sociological) an account of gender formation (women have separation problems, men have difficulties relating), albeit using psychoanalytic terminology. Thus, when Wacquant suggests a close fit between 'the manic building of ramparts of muscles' and men's 'fragile self boundaries and deep ambivalence toward intimacy' (Wacquant, 1995a: 172), I don't disagree with the emphasis on fragility; but in its generalizing thrust, it begins to feel a bit like Dyer's 'phallic mystique'.

Can we begin to render this notion less purely sociological while hanging on to its undoubted insight about insecurity (and remembering that Wacquant did not wish to reduce insecurity to gender-based insecurity)? The first step in doing so would seem to be to return to Connell's point that the value of psychoanalysis lies in the detail of the case study (Connell, 1994, 1995). In my chosen example, the case of Tyson, we are not addressing body-building but 'hardness', the 'interiorized quality extracted from risking the body in performance'. How can we account for Tyson's 'willing embrace' of this? Moreover, though all boxers necessarily risk the body in performance, not all are equally 'hard' in the sense of having 'interiorized' the 'extracted quality'. In other words, there are degrees of hardness, even among the hard men of boxing; and Tyson would seem to belong at the extreme end of this continuum. This is not just because Tyson's style of boxing places him with the slugger/fighters (Dempsey/Marciano) rather than the stylish boxers (Louis/Ali); rather, it has to do with his commitment to boxing as licensed aggression, a legitimate arena for the display of 'bad intentions'. It is perhaps easier to make the point in relation to boxing's unofficial equivalent, the streetfighter. As Mac an Ghaill's informant put it (see earlier), he'd not want to hang out with a 'stupid head-case' because 'he will cause unnecessary trouble'. In other words, the 'head-case', or 'nutter', is the extreme example of hardness because his willingness to risk the body in performance is apparently unfettered by any of the normal constraints, fears and calculations.

If this is the case, I feel we need to be more specific about the 'insecurities' or anxiety entailed here. Klein's work on anxiety is helpful (Hinshelwood, 1991; Elliott, 1994: 75–80), especially her distinction between depressive anxiety (which is reality-based) and persecutory or paranoid anxiety (which is so threatening to one's sense of self that it is defended against by denying or distorting reality). One of the commonest forms of defence against persecutory anxiety is that of splitting/projection. This entails dealing with that which is threatening or anxiety-invoking by splitting it off, disowning it as a too uncomfortable part of the self, and projecting it on to another where it can be safely attacked. The extreme homophobe, psycho-dynamically speaking, would appear to fit this pattern of someone unable to tolerate any mixed feelings about homosexuality, and the threatening possibilities about the 'truth' of the self this might reveal. Ambivalent feelings about sexuality and desire are safely purified by splitting off the unwanted, threatening ones and violently projecting them on to 'poofters', 'queers' and 'faggots', anywhere and everywhere. The extreme hard man would also seem to fit this pattern: unable to tolerate any hint of weakness or softness, because it is too threatening to his sense of selfhood, he must split off this unwanted part (and the reservoir of hate), project it on to others, and then mercilessly attack it there.

Now all of us are more or less anxious: none of us escape anxiety's grip entirely. And, we can exhibit peculiar mixtures of anxiety, being depressively anxious about some things and persecutorily anxious about other things. At different times of our lives, circumstances can cause a shift in our current pattern of anxieties. Having said all that, there is no doubt that we all tend to exhibit a characteristic pattern of anxiety; which brings us back to the source of anxiety. Developmentally speaking, persecutory anxiety is more primitive than the depressive variety, the latter indicating a greater capacity to face reality and tolerate uncomfortable feelings, even if the anxiety experienced is still high or 'excessive' in relation to the threat. However incomplete and however contingent the achievement of acknowledging reality, it remains the case that some never move beyond the primitive, persecutory phase in their dealings with at least part of their 'reality', and hence are especially prone to resort to the defence of splitting/projection. Why is this?

One contending explanation focuses on gender. If it is true, as Chodorow (1978) suggests, that men have to sharply differentiate themselves from the mother and the (threat of) dependency she represents in the interests of securing their masculinity, this would seem to create at least some of the preconditions for mobilizing primitive 'distorting' defences such as splitting/projection and denial. Craib (1987) has argued that the defence of denial is more characteristic of men than women. However, as Wacquant reminds us, there are other non-gender-related bases of insecurity. He talks of socially based sources, like class and 'dilemmas generic to the modern human condition', citing both Heidegger and Giddens in aid (Wacquant, 1995a: 172). I believe, though, there is more to be said about psychic sources, especially early life experiences of trust. When these have never enabled the build up of trust, when love is withheld, withdrawn, abused or somehow distorted, the resulting threats to the self can be so severe as to frustrate the level of security necessary for the achievement of integration (bringing together of, or not splitting, the good and the bad, or the hard and the soft). In such situations, primitive defences may become characteristic. Winnicott talked wisely of 'good enough' mothering (Elliott, 1994: 68–9), a reference to the minimum preconditions of loving care necessary for the build up of trust and feelings of security in the developing infant.

If we return now to Tyson and think about his childhood, there are signs of emotional malnourishment, both in the stories of a mother too pressured and care-worn to cope,[15] and, more directly, in Tyson's failure to thrive: his passivity, withdrawnness and fear ('scared of his own shadow'). These all seem symptomatic of an unhealthy level of anxiety for a young child. Then came the transformations, first to violent bully, then to aggressive boxer: from 'little fairy boy' to the 'compleat destroyer', a story I have detailed at greater length elsewhere (Jefferson, 1996). What interests me, and what provides the article's motivation and focus, is the apparent relish with which he 'willingly embraced' his new-found identity as hard man. Even as I agree intellectually with Mac an Ghaill's interviewee, with his reference to 'stupid head-case', I remain emotionally drawn in, fascinated, by that degree of hardness – perhaps because it remains utterly beyond me to be the 'nutter'. Similarly, I remain fascinated by Tyson's ring aggression, even as I could never summon up that willingness to inflict pain. In that, I am probably like many men: drawn in by the discourse of hardness; utterly incapable of living it.[16] Tyson, by contrast, can somehow both identify with and embody the hard man. To do so, I am suggesting, there has to be a set of social and psychic congruences, which add up to a compelling satisfaction in or desire to inflict punishment and thereby triumph over the threat of having it inflicted, that are neither wholly specific to him, nor are they shared with every man. The social legacy of being a poor, ghetto-born Afro-American with few options or images beyond the tough, sexual, 'badass' athlete-performer, combined with a painful psychic legacy of emotional neglect and the resulting pattern of anxiety in which, I believe, primitive defences would be characteristic, produced the sort of ability to split off or deny parts of himself, for example, that provided his particular route to being able to embody, or 'live', hardness. That is not to say it is the only route; but to make sense of any route, I contend, we will need to be sensitive to both dimensions, the social and the psychic, in all their myriad complexities, privileging neither.

Notes

Earlier versions of this paper were presented at the 2nd *Theory, Culture & Society* Conference on 'Culture and Identity: City/Nation/World', Berlin, 10–14 August 1995 and to the Men and Masculinity group, University of California at Berkeley, December 1996. Thanks to all the discussants on those occasions, and to Yaba Badoe for her comments. Special thanks, as always, to Wendy Hollway for her interest, care and judicious insights.

1 This is not borne out by empirical research. Ninety-five percent of college-age men surveyed by Mishkind et al. in the USA 'expressed dissatisfaction with some aspect of their bodies', and 'more than 70 per cent of undergraduate men saw a discrepancy between their own body and their ideal body type' (1987: 38). Similar evidence can be found also in Glassner (1989: 310–12). See also Wacquant (1995a: 171).
2 For a theoretical elaboration of my understanding of the relationship between desire and anxiety, see Jefferson (1994).
3 There is, for example, no Index entry for either 'gender' or 'masculinity'.
4 Glassner's statement that 'muscles are *the* sign of masculinity' (1989: 311) endorses the broader significance of my question, but does not answer it.
5 Even if I were persuaded, still it would leave unanswered the question of differential investment: how it is that some, but not all, men succumb to the appeal of muscularity?
6 On the centrality of pain to manliness and sport, see, for example, Sabo (1989: 184–6).
7 Whether such mental toughness is a product of thought, or an absence of thought (since if you thought about it first you would never do it), remains an important but open question in the study of masculinity. I am indebted to Wendy Hollway for this insight.
8 I am talking deliberately about men here. Outstanding women athletes, it seems to me, still get discussed, largely, in terms of how they manage to fit it all in: training, babies, childcare, domestic responsibilities.
9 This would seem to suggest that mental toughness is not a product of thought. See footnote 7.
10 Like the Italian who, when asked whether 'he was within the time-limit for the stage' replied, 'I hope not' (reported by Fotheringham, 1995a).
11 These three examples of sporting heroes – Fangio, Doohan and Indurain – were taken pretty much at random from the *Guardian* during a week or two's reading in July 1995. Frank Keating's (1995: 12) *Guardian* obituary of the fast bowler, Harold Larwood, member of the infamous 'body-line' tour team of 1932–33, during the same period supplied another good example of writing about a sporting 'great' replete with a subtext about Larwood's 'hardness'. Open any paper on any day and you are likely to find an example of the discourse somewhere in the sports columns.
12 For an alternative assessment, see Singh (1995).
13 This is not to deny the contemporary expansion of available images for Afro-American youth. George, for example, talks convincingly of the emergence of

'four new African American character types . . . that began germinating in the 70s and blossomed in the '80s . . . the Buppie, ambitious and acquisitive, determined to savor the fruits of integration by any means necessary; the B-boy, molded by hip hop aesthetics and the tragedies of underclass life; the Black American Princess or Prince a/k/a Bap, who, whether by family heritage or personal will, enjoys an expectation of mainstream success and acceptance that borders on arrogance; and the Boho, a thoughtful, self-conscious figure . . . whose range of interest and taste challenges both black and white stereotypes of African American behavior' (1994: 2). For my purposes though, given Tyson's highly disadvantaged social position, only the B-boy 'type', in my terms a contemporary manifestation of the 'Buck', is likely to have had much salience to the young Tyson.

14 On wrestling as spectacle, see Barthes (1973: 15–25).

15 'Not once during Tyson's nine-month stay [in Tryon School for Boys, a New York State Reformatory] did Lorna [his mother] visit the facility, send any Christmas presents, or write a letter' (Illingworth, 1992: 9).

16 One of my most vivid (and painful) memories as a teacher of physical education is of how I felt after using a slipper, for the first time, to punish a young man who had driven me to this extreme measure. Afterwards, I felt physically sick and never again resorted to physical punishment. Though this was also a 'politically' driven position on punishment, the truth is that I was emotionally incapable of administering physical pain as punishment, and sometimes secretly envied those who could, especially when it 'appeared' to produce the desired results.

References

Barthes, R. (1973) *Mythologies*. St Albans, Herts.: Paladin.

Bathrick, D. (1990) 'Max Schmeling on the Canvas: Boxing as an Icon of Weimar Culture', *New German Critique* 51: 113–36.

Berger, P. (1990) *Blood Season*. London: Queen Anne Press.

Bierley, S. (1995) 'A Man on His Own and His Bike', *Guardian* 22 July.

Butler, J. (1993) *Bodies that Matter: On the Discursive Limits of Sex*. London: Routledge.

Chodorow, N. J. (1978) *The Reproduction of Mothering: Psychoanalysis and the Sociology of Gender*. Berkeley: University of California Press.

Chodorow, N. J. (1989) *Feminism and Psychoanalytic Theory*. London: Yale University Press.

Chodorow, N. J. (1994) *Feminities, Masculinities, Sexualities: Freud and Beyond*. Lexington: The University Press of Kentucky.

Connell, R. W. (1983) 'Men's Bodies', pp. 17–32 in R. W. Connell *Which Way is Up? Essays on Sex, Class and Culture*. London: Allen & Unwin.

Connell, R. W. (1994) 'Psychoanalysis on Masculinity', pp. 11–38 in H. Brod and M. Kaufman (eds) *Theorizing Masculinities*. London: Sage.

Connell, R. W. (1995) *Masculinities*. Cambridge: Polity.

Coward, R. (1984) *Female Desire: Women's Sexuality Today*. London: Paladin.

Craib, I. (1987) 'Masculinity and Male Dominance', *Sociological Review* 34(4): 721–43.

Crossley, N. (1995a) 'Merleau-Ponty, the Elusive Body and Carnal Sociology', *Body & Society* 1(1): 1–21.

Crossley, N. (1995b) 'Body Techniques, Agency and Intercorporeality: On Goffman's *Relations in Public*', *Sociology* 29(1): 133–49.

Crossley, N. (1996) 'Body-Subject/Body-Power: Agency, Inscription and Control in Foucault and Merleau-Ponty', *Body & Society* 2(2): 99–116.

Dutton, K. R. (1995) *The Perfectible Body: The Western Ideal of Physical Development*. London: Cassell.

Dyer, R. (1989) 'Don't Look Now', pp. 198–207 in A. McRobbie (ed.) *Zoot Suits and Second Hand Dresses*. London: Macmillan.

Elliott, A. (1994) *Psychoanalytic Theory: An Introduction*. Oxford: Blackwell.

Feldman, A. (1991) *Formations of Violence*. London: University of Chicago Press.

Fotheringham, W. (1995a) 'Indurain the Indestructible', *Guardian* 12 July.

Fotheringham, W. (1995b) 'Pantini Fizzes into Flight', *Guardian* 13 July: 21.

Frosh, S. (1995) 'Masculine Mastery and Fantasy, or the Meaning of the Phallus', pp. 166–87 in A. Elliott and S. Frosh (eds) *Psychoanalysis in Contexts: Paths Between Theory and Modern Culture*. London: Routledge.

Fussell, S. W. (1991) *Muscle: Confessions of an Unlikely Bodybuilder*. New York: Poseidon.

George, N. (1994) *Buppies, B-Boys, Baps and Bohos: Notes on Post-Soul Black Culture*. New York: HarperPerennial.

Glassner, B. (1988) *Bodies: Why We Look The Way We Do (And How We Feel About It)*. New York: Putnam.

Glassner, B. (1989) 'Men and Muscles', pp. 310–20 in M. S. Kimmel and M. A. Messner (eds) *Men's Lives*. New York: Macmillan. (Reprinted from Glassner, 1988.)

Heller, P. (1989) *Tyson: In and Out of The Ring*. London: Robson.

Hinshelwood, R. D. A. (1991) *A Dictionary of Kleinian Thought*, 2nd edn. London: Free Association Books.

Hoch, P. (1979) *White Hero Black Beast: Racism, Sexism and the Mask of Masculinity*. London: Pluto.

Illingworth, M. (1992) *Mike Tyson: Money, Myth and Betrayal*. London: Grafton.

Jackson, D. (1990) *Unmasking Masculinity: A Critical Autobiography*. London: Unwin Hyman.

Jefferson, T. (1994) 'Theorizing Masculine Subjectivity', pp. 10–31 in T. Newburn and E. Stanko (eds) *Just Boys Doing Business? Men, Masculinities and Crime*. London: Routledge.

Jefferson, T. (1996) 'From "Little Fairy Boy" to "The Compleat Destroyer": Subjectivity and Transformation in the Biography of Mike Tyson', pp. 153–67 in M. Mac an Ghaill (ed.) *Understanding Masculinities: Social Relations and Cultural Arenas*. Milton Keynes: Open University Press.

Keating, F. (1995) 'Harold Larwood: Ashes and Sackcloth', *Guardian* 24 July: 12.

Mac an Ghaill, M. (1994) 'The Making of Black English Masculinities', pp. 183–99 in H. Brod and M. Kaufman (eds) *Theorizing Masculinities*. London: Sage.

Mishkind, M. E., J. Rodin, L. R. Silberstein and R. H. Striegel-Moore (1987) 'The Embodiment of Masculinity: Cultural, Psychological and Behavioural Dimensions', pp. 37–52 in M. S. Kimmel (ed.) *Changing Men: New Directions in Research on Men and Masculinity*. Newbury Park, CA: Sage.

Nichols, P. (1995) 'Doohan the High Speed Calculator', *Guardian* 22 July.

Sabo, D. (1989) 'Pigskin, Patriarchy and Pain', pp. 184–6 in M. S. Kimmel and M. A. Messner (eds) *Men's Lives*. New York: Macmillan. (Reprinted from *Changing Men*, Summer 1986.)

Sen, S. (1992) 'Few Could Tame the Brutality of the Animal', *The Times* 12 February: 31.

Singh, N. P. (1995) 'Black Liberation – The Theatre of Nationality: The Black Panthers and "Undeveloped Country" of the Left', in C. E. Jones (ed.) *The Black Panther Party Reconsidered: Reflections and Scholarship*. Baltimore, MD: Black Classic Press.

Wacquant, L. J. D. (1992) 'The Social Logic of Boxing in Black Chicago: Toward a Sociology of Pugilism', *Sociology of Sport Journal* 9(3): 221–54.

Wacquant, L. J. D. (1995a) 'Why Men Desire Muscles', *Body & Society* 1(1): 163–79.

Wacquant, L. J. D. (1995b) 'The Pugilistic Point of View: How Boxers Think and Feel about Their Trade', *Theory and Society* 24(4): 489–535.

Wacquant, L. J. D. (1995c) 'The Ghetto, the State and the New Capitalist Economy', pp. 418–49 in P. Kasinitz (ed.) *Metropolis: Centre and Symbol of Our Times*. London: Macmillan.

Wacquant, L. J. D. (1995d) 'Pugs at Work: Bodily Capital and Bodily Labor among Professional Boxers', *Body & Society* 1(1): 65–93.

Wallace, M. (1990) *Black Macho and the Myth of the Superwoman*. London: Verso.

Westwood, S. (1990) 'Racism, Black Masculinity and the Politics of Space', pp. 55–71 in J. Hearn and D. Morgan (eds) *Men, Masculinities & Social Theory*. London: Unwin Hyman.

Williams, R. (1995a) 'Best and Bravest Racer of Them All', *Guardian* 18 July: 12.

Williams, R. (1995b) 'The Giant Who Does as He Likes', *Guardian* 24 July: 16.

Young, I. M. (1980) 'Throwing Like a Girl: A Phenomenology of Feminine Body Comportment, Motility and Spatiality', *Human Studies* 3: 137–56.

9

VARIETIES OF 'REAL MEN'

James Messerschmidt

Source: J. Messerschmidt, *Masculinities and Crime*, Maryland: Rowman and Littlefield, 1993, pp. 119–53.

It was a theoretical breakthrough in social theory when the family came to be recognized generally as both gendered and political. Feminist work has now begun to reveal theoretically what we have known for some time in practice—that other social milieux, such as the street and workplace, are not only political but also gendered (Acker, 1990; Connell, 1987; Cockburn, 1983). Chapter 5 extends this theoretical insight through an analysis of how the social structures of labor, power, and sexuality constrain and enable social action within three specific social settings: the street, the workplace, and the family. I focus on how some men, within particular social situations, can make use of certain crimes to construct various public and private adult masculinities.

Research reveals that men construct masculinities in accord with their position in social structures and, therefore, their access to power and resources. Because men situationally accomplish masculinity in response to their socially structured circumstances, various forms of crime can serve as suitable resources for doing masculinity within the specific social contexts of the street, the workplace, and the family. Consequently, as in Chapter 4, I emphasize the significant differences among men and how men utilize different types of crimes to situationally construct distinct forms of masculinities. We begin with the street and an examination of pimping.

The street

In Chapter 4, we examined how middle-class, working-class, and lower-working-class young men exhibit unique types of public masculinities that are situationally accomplished by drawing on different forms of youth crime. Moreover, class and race structure the age-specific form of resources employed to construct the cultural ideals of hegemonic masculinity. Such public arenas as the school and street are lush with gendered meanings and signals that evoke various styles of masculinity and femininity. Another type of public masculinity found in the social setting of the street is that of the adult pimp. This particularized form of masculinity is examined here within the context of "deviant street networks."

The pimp and his network

Eleanor Miller's (1986: 35–43) respected work *Street Woman* reports that in Milwaukee, Wisconsin, African American men in their mid to late twenties and early thirties dominate what she calls "deviant street networks." Deviant street networks are groups of men and women assembled to conduct such illegal profit-making ventures as prostitution, check and credit-card fraud, drug trafficking, burglary, and robbery. Although both men and women engage in various aspects of these "hustling activities," gender relations are unequal, reflecting the social structures of labor, power, and normative heterosexuality. Miller (p. 37) found that a major source of continuous income in these networks "derives from the hustling activity of women who turn their earnings over to the men in exchange for affection, an allowance, the status of their company, and some measure of protection." Commonly referred to as "pimps," the men act as agents and/or companions of these women, substantially profiting from their labor. Miller found that to work as street hustlers, it is essential that women have a "male" sponsor and protector. However, this "essential" has not always existed in the history of prostitution.

Throughout the 1800s, U.S. prostitution was condemned but not classified as a criminal offense, and was conducted primarily under the direction of a "madam" in brothels located in specific red-light districts (Rosen, 1982: 27–30). In an attempt to halt prostitution, state legislatures enacted laws in the early 1900s in order to close down these red-light districts and, contemporaneously, women-controlled brothels. Predictably, rather than halting prostitution, new forms of prostitution emerged from this attempt at legislating morality. As Rosen (p. 32) shows in *The Lost Sisterhood*, the closing of the brothels simply increased streetwalking for women; because prostitutes could no longer receive "johns" "in the semiprotected environment of the brothel or district, . . . they had to search for business in public places—hotels, restaurants, cabarets, or on the street." This search for customers in public places exposed prostitutes to violent clients and police harassment. Consequently, these women turned to men for help in warding off dangers, providing legal assistance, and offering some emotional support. Eventually, the overall prostitution business came to be dominated by individual pimp entrepreneurs or masculine-dominated syndicated crime.

In today's deviant street network, the pimp usually controls two to three women (labeled "wives-in-law") on the street (Miller, 1986: 37–38). The women turn over their earnings to the pimp and he decides how it will be spent. The disciplinarian of the network, the pimp also "decides upon and metes out the punishment" (Romenesko and Miller, 1989: 120). Indeed, as Romenesko and Miller (p. 117) show in their interviews with street hustlers, the pimp demands unquestioned respect:

> Showing respect for "men" means total obedience and complete dedication to them. Mary reports that in the company of "men" she had to "talk mainly to the women—try not to look at the men if possible at all—try not to have conversations with them." Rita, when asked about the rules of the street, said, "Just basic, obey. Do what he wants to do. Don't disrespect him. . . . I could not disrespect him in any verbal or physical way. I never attempted to hit him back. Never." And, in the same vein, Tina said that when her "man" had others over to socialize, the women of the family were relegated to the role of servant. "We couldn't speak to them when we wasn't spoken to, and we could not foul up on orders. And you cannot disrespect them."

This authority and control exercised by pimps over women is also clearly exemplified in biographies of pimp life (Malcolm X, 1965; Slim, 1967). Christina Milner and Richard Milner (1972: 52–53) reported a similar form of gendered power in their study of African American pimps in San Francisco:

> First and foremost, the pimp must be in complete control of his women; this control is made conspicuous to others by a series of little rituals which express symbolically his woman's attitude. When in the company of others she must take special pains to treat him with absolute deference and respect. She must light his cigarettes, respond to his every whim immediately, and never, never, contradict him. In fact, a ho [prostitute] is strictly not supposed to speak in the company of pimps unless spoken to.

Gender is a situated accomplishment in which we produce forms of behavior seen by others in the same immediate situation as masculine or feminine (see discussion in Chapter 3). Within the confines and social setting of the street, economically marginal men and women create street networks for economic survival, yet simultaneously "do gender" in the process of surviving. In this manner, deviant street networks become the condition that produces material survival as well as the social setting that reaffirms one's gender. The result is a gendered, deviant street network in which men and women do masculinity and femininity, albeit in a distinct manner.

In short, the division of street network labor is concerned both with rationally assigning specific tasks to network members and with the symbolic affirmation and assertion of specific forms of masculinity and femininity (discussed further below). Consequently, pimps simultaneously do pimping and masculinity. As marginalized men, street pimps choose pimping in preference to unemployment and routine labor for "the man." Lacking other avenues and opportunities for accomplishing gender, the pimp life-style is a survival strategy that is exciting and rewarding for them as men. The deviant street network provides the context within which to construct one's "essential nature" as a man and to survive as a human being.

The cool pose of the badass

African American street pimps engage in specific practices (constrained by class and race) intended to construct a specific "cool pose" as an important aspect of their specific type of masculinity (Majors, 1986; Majors and Billson, 1992). In the absence of resources that signify other types of masculinity, sex category is held more accountable and physical presence, personal style, and expressiveness take on an increased importance (Messner, 1989: 82). Consequently, as Richard Majors (1986: 5) argues, many "black males have learned to make great use of 'poses' and 'postures' that connote control, toughness and detachment," adopting a specific carriage, that exemplifies an expressive and distinct assertion of masculinity.

The often flamboyant, loud, and ostentatious style of African American pimps signifies aspects of this cool pose. The exaggerated display of luxury (for example, in the form of flashy clothing) is also a specific aspect of the cool pose distinctively associated with African American pimps. Majors and Billson (1992: 81–84) argue that the "sharp" and "clean" look of pimps is intended to upstage other men in the highly competitive arena of the street where they earn street applause for their style, providing an "antidote to invisibility." Pimps literally prance above their immediate position in the class and race divisions of labor and power, thereby constructing a specific masculine street upper-crust demeanor.

Notwithstanding, this cool presence complements an intermittent and brutal comportment to construct masculinity and, in the process, show that the pimp means business. In other words, the African American pimp must always be prepared to employ violence both for utilitarian reasons and for constructing and maintaining a formidable, portentious profile (Katz, 1988: 97). The following account by Milner and Milner (1972: 232) illustrates this unpredictable use of violence:

> One ho known as Birthday Cake said she worked for a pimp for four years, gave him a new Cadillac every year, and one night came home from work with her money "funny" and got the beating of her life. She walked in and handed over the money; he counted it and said, "That's all right, honey," drew her a bath, laid her down afterwards on the bed, went to the closet and got a tire iron and

> beat her senseless with it. She showed us the long scars which required hundreds of stitches and demonstrated her permanent slight limp.

This "badass" form of masculinity (Katz, 1988: 80–113) is also publicly displayed for, and supported by, other pimps. Milner and Milner (1972: 56) discuss how a pimp took one of "his" prostitutes (who was also a dancer) into the dancer's dressing room and "began to shout at her and slap her around" loud enough for everyone in the bar to hear. "The six pimps sitting at the back of the bar near the dressing room began to clap and whistle loudly," seemingly for the current dancer, "but in reality to cover the noise of the beating from the ears of the straight customers" (p. 56). Emerging from the dressing room and joining the others, the pimp exclaimed, "Well, I took care of that bitch." Then they all began to "joke around." In contrast, when the prostitute emerged, not "one of them (pimps) felt it proper to comfort her in any way" (p. 56). Such violence, neither out-of-control nor ungovernable, is situationally determined and regulated. Thus, pimp violence becomes a means of disciphning the prostitute and of constructing a badass public masculinity.

The combined cool pose and badass identity of African American pimps clearly represent a specialized means with which to transcend class and race domination. Yet, it also demonstrates the socially constrained nature of social action, and how African American pimps rework the ideals of hegemonic masculinity as a vehicle for achieving that transcendence. Pimping, then, is a resource for surmounting oppressive class and race conditions and for reasserting the social dominance of men. Moreover, like other men, pimps associate masculinity with work, with authority and control, and with explicit heterosexuality.

Within deviant street networks, the prostitute/pimp relationship represents a reworking of these hegemonic masculine ideals under specifically structured social possibilities/constraints. Through their authority and control within deviant street networks, pimps create a class- and race-specific type of masculine meaning and configuration, resulting in a remodeling of heterosexual monogamy in which the pimp provides love, money, and an accompanying sense of security for his "wives-in-law" (Romenesko and Miller, 1989: 123).

Normative heterosexuality is the major focus of activities: wives-in-law are expected to be sexually seductive to men, receptive to the sexual "drives" and special "needs" of men (including the pimp), and to work for men who "protect" them and negotiate the "rough spots."[1] Pimping, as a resource for demonstrating that one is a "real man," distinguishes pimps from prostitutes in a specific way. Within the social context of the deviant street network, this pimp type of masculinity is sustained by means of collective and gendered practices that subordinate women, manage the expression of violence against women, and exploit women's labor and sexuality. Indeed, the individual style of the pimp is somewhat meaningless outside the group (Connell, 1991: 157);

it is the deviant street network that provides meaning and currency for this type of masculinity.[2] Pimping, in short, is a practice that facilitates a particular gender strategy.

In spite of the above, in attempting to transcend oppressive social structures, African American pimps ultimately reproduce them. Their masculine style is at once repugnant to "conventionality"—their source of wealth anathema to traditional morality (Katz, 1988: 97)—yet simultaneously reactionary and reproductive of the gendered social order. In other words, African American pimps respond in a gender-specific manner to race and class oppression, which in turn locks them into the very structured constraints they attempt to overcome. Thus, pimping becomes a form of social action that ultimately results in the reproduction of the gender divisions of labor and power as well as normative heterosexuality.

The following section examines two distinct types of masculinity constructed in the workplace.

The workplace

The gender divisions of labor and power and normative heterosexuality structure gender relations in the workplace. The workplace not only produces goods and provides services but is the site of gendered control and authority. Because women historically have been excluded from paid work or segregated within it, today the gender division in the workplace is both horizontally and vertically segregated (Walby, 1986; Reskin and Roos, 1987; Game and Pringle, 1984).[3] The result is that women are concentrated overwhelmingly at the lower levels of the occupational hierarchy in terms of wages and salary, status, and authority. Indeed, a recent study of nearly four hundred firms revealed that the vast majority of women were either completely or nearly completely segregated by gender (Bielby and Baron, 1986). Consequently, gender relations throughout much of the paid-labor market—like gender relations in schools, youth groups, and deviant street networks—embody relations of power: the domination of men and the subordination of women. Moreover, the creation of "male" and "female" jobs helps to maintain and reproduce this power relationship. Accordingly, gender differences are maintained through gender segregation, and occupational segregation is born of practices ultimately based on conceptions of what constitutes the "essential" natures of men and women.

In addition, the concepts "worker" and "a job" are themselves gendered. As Joan Acker (1990) recently demonstrated, these concepts embody the gender divisions of labor and power. Historically, the idea of a job and who works it has assumed a specific gendered organization of public and private life: a man's life centers on full-time work at a job outside the household; a woman's life focuses on taking care of all his other needs. Consequently, as the abstract worker is masculinized (p. 152):

> it is the man's body, his sexuality, minimal responsibility in procreation, and conventional control of emotions that pervades work and organizational processes. Women's bodies—female sexuality, their ability to procreate and their pregnancy, breast feeding, childcare, menstruation, and mythic "emotionality"—are suspect, stigmatized, and used as grounds for control and exclusion.

Because organization and sexuality occur simultaneously, the workplace is sexualized and normative heterosexuality actually conditions work activities (Hearn and Parkin, 1987). As Rosemary Pringle (1989: 162) recently reported, heterosexuality in the workplace is actively perpetuated in a range of practices and interactions exemplified in "dress and self-presentation, in jokes and gossip, looks and flirtations, secret affairs and dalliances, in fantasy and in the range of coercive behaviors that we now call sexual harassment."

Within the social situation of gendered segregation, power, and normative heterosexuality, men and women in the paid-labor market actively construct specific types of masculinity and femininity, depending upon their position in the workplace. In other words, social action is patterned in the workplace in terms of a distinction between masculine and feminine. Regarding men specifically, a power hierarchy exists in the workplace among men and, not surprisingly, different forms of masculinity correspond to particular positions in this hierarchy.

Let us now look at two differing forms of masculinity in the workplace: (1) workers and their relation to shop-floor theft and a specific type of sexual harassment and (2) corporate executives and their involvement in corporate crime and a variant form of sexual harassment. In each case, I demonstrate how specific crimes are a resource for constructing particularized representations of private masculinity—those that are occluded from the vision, company, or intervention of outsiders.

Workers and shop-floor theft

In Chapter 4, I discussed how white, working-class boys (the lads) associate manual labor with the social superiority of masculinity and mental labor with the social inferiority of femininity. These youths regard mental work as effeminate, "sissy-stuff," a type of work performed only by "wimps." Thus, work that is traditionally repetitive, unhealthy, demeaning, and mind numbing is turned into a virtue, because "real men" do it (Donaldson, 1987: 167).[4] A growing amount of research reveals that the meaningless work environment of the shop floor is given significance by associating manual work with a physically strong and active type of masculinity. After examining a good portion of this research, Paul Willis (1979: 196) concluded:

> The working situation is partially reinterpreted into a heroic exercise of manly confrontation with "the task." Difficult, uncomfortable, or dangerous conditions are seen, not for themselves, but for their appropriateness to a masculine readiness and hardness. They are understood more through the toughness required to survive them, than through the nature of the imposition which asks them to be faced in the first place.

Other evidence likewise indicates that masculinity on the shop floor stresses the presentation and celebration of physical prowess (Lippert, 1977; Cockburn, 1983; Clatterbaugh, 1990).

Furthermore, manual laborers construct this specific kind of masculinity in direct contrast to that of management. For manual laborers, the rough and tough masculinity of the shop floor is differentiated and superior to the politeness, cleanliness, and more restrained demeanor of management: the "true self" is expressed on the shop floor, not in an office (Collinson and Collinson, 1989: 97). Indeed, managers are dubbed "paper pushers" and "yes men," and consistently ridiculed on the shop floor as effeminate. In this way, within the social setting of the shop floor, manual laborers construct a specific type of collective masculinity that reflects a desire to deny their subordinate position within the hierarchical power relations among men in the firm.

Nevertheless, although the shop floor masculinizes, the workplace (like the school discussed in Chapter 4) simultaneously denies certain hegemonic masculine ideals: independence, control, and dominance. And the employer-employee implied contract sets the conditions for this masculine denial. Under contractual relations, workers exchange labor power for specified wages and fringe benefits. Management then translates their labor into productive ability by setting workplace standards, goals, rules, and regulations to which workers must adhere. In most cases, these commands are extremely inflexible, predictably despised, and thus opposed by a large proportion of workers.

Mike Donaldson (1987: 168), for example, demonstrates how workers experience the workplace as both masculinizing and "infantalizing." According to Donaldson, authoritarian workplace policies are perceived by men on the shop floor as "childish." Accordingly, the contradictory nature in the construction of shop-floor masculinity should be clear: masculinity is very much connected to the world of manual labor; yet, for working-class men this work experience is humiliating. They are subjected to work relations that threaten their conception of hegemonic masculinity (Game and Pringle, 1984: 22).

Thus, because of this authoritarian relationship between men, which is inherent in the job itself, contentious issues in the workplace focus on job control and enhancing autonomy. In short, a sense of independence develops on the shop floor that is expressed in thoughts and feelings of brotherhood.

What is at stake is a fight for masculine status: "a dignity which is at least partially defined against the company and within a collective solidarity and brotherhood" (Donaldson, 1987: 171). Workers consistently attempt to wield control over shop-floor practices and in so doing, fashion a united masculine autonomy.

Because manual labor is collective labor, it is inexorably organized around the group. A collective masculinity arises that consists of a particular style—a way of asserting, within the constraints of the "contract," collective control of the shop floor. The manual workers' experiences at work, expressed through interaction with the group, create a compensating solidarity—shared masculinity that enables the manual worker to bond with his peers and to resist management authority (Clatterbaugh, 1990: 111). Tolson (1977: 59) describes this vividly:

> Manual labour is collective labour: it is necessarily organized around the work-group. In part, this is simply because conditions of work are made more manageable by keeping a "happy medium" with your mates. The individual contributes to a collective effort and the rhythms of working are reaffirmed by a collective culture—an "occupational culture" (of jokes, gestures, the exchange of favours) on the job itself. To be "one of the lads" is to be placed inside a group's informal boundary, to be a party to the symbolic play.

Major aspects of this solidarity and resistance to authority include the variety of practices employed to gain informal control of the work process. One such traditional practice is for workers to control the speed of production, thus limiting output. Another such practice is resource control, such as time at work and who performs what job (Mars, 1983: 93). This informal attempt at group control should not be minimized, however, inasmuch as it is here that "strategies for wresting control of symbolic and real space from official authority" emerge (Willis, 1979: 192). In addition, it is within the work group that extensive "fiddling" and shop-floor theft occurs. Because manual labor is often organized on the basis of informal masculine practices, workers either steal as a group or their individual theft is controlled by the group.

As Willis (p. 192) points out, theft of materials is widespread in working-class jobs and is "endorsed by implicit informal criteria. Ostracism is the punishment for not maintaining the integrity of this world against the persistent intrusions of the formal."[5] Shop-floor theft permits the worker to "symbolically liberate himself from the 'bullshit' by 'beating the system' " (Altheide, Adler, Adler, and Altheide, 1978: 105), and is thus symbolic of personal and collective control. Altheide et al. (pp. 106–107) provide numerous examples of shop-floor theft as a means of demonstrating "control of the situation." Shop-floor theft is not purely utilitarian in the economic sense; workers also steal on the job because of what it means to do so. In other words, men on the shop-floor simultaneously resist class oppression and construct a specific masculinity through the same ongoing practice of shop-floor theft. Shop-floor theft is a social practice that facilitates a particularized worker gender strategy.

In *Cheats at Work*, Gerald Mars's (1983) discussion of "Wolfpack Jobs" shows clearly that this type of employee theft cannot exist outside the context of the group. Indeed, survival of employee theft is linked to survival of the group. As Mars (1983: 96) emphasizes, "individual group members *must* cooperate" in such situations. On the shop floor, there exists a particular working-class sensibility and it is the ability to share this sensibility that admits the "insider" to an all-male work group (Tolson, 1977: 59). Moreover, group acceptance requires that the manual worker must also recognize and support group definitions of hierarchies based on such criteria as age and seniority. Mars (1983: 98–99) found that such hierarchies themselves structure shop-floor theft—for example, older men and men with more seniority have greater access to the "fiddles." Senior men always get the best "pickings" and newcomers get what remains. Mars (p. 102) states further that the group ranks and thus allocates jobs, which is crucial because "it gives both overall control of resources and specifically control of fiddles" to the group. Coworkers collectively determine, within a masculine power hierarchy, how and what to steal, and establish limits beyond which one must not go (Altheide et al., 1978: 111). Other research, as well, confirms that the shop-floor group determines what is acceptable and unacceptable behavior in employee theft (Henry, 1978; Ditton, 1977).

The presence of this informal group organization most clearly distinguishes shop-floor masculinity from corporate-executive masculinity. Moreover, this specific masculine articulation enables the group to control the shop floor. Accordingly, to be one of "the guys" at work—to avoid ostracism—most manual workers choose to participate in its functions. The group and its collective format are seductive, promising to fulfill the worker's search for strategic actions that permit him to accomplish gender in ways that capitalist relations deny. Nevertheless, the worker may engage in resistance only as part of the group. To enjoy solidarity with other workers, then, he participates in group activity and he does gender—he constructs his "essential nature" in a specific way and within specific socially structured constraints. For to engage in group activities, including employee theft, is to draw on and exhibit one's "essential nature" as a man. Consequently, what is produced and reproduced is manual labor, theft, and a specific type of "maleness" that is sustained as a particular collective practice in a specific workplace milieu. By participating in this collective effort, the manual worker simultaneously does gender (and class) while he "does shop-floor theft." Indeed, shop-floor theft is a principal resource for maintaining group solidarity and for constructing a specific type of masculinity that resolves the problem of masculine accountability at work.[6]

It is within the social setting of the shop floor that men experience their daily lives from a particular position in society. In this specific social setting, hegemonic masculinity is both reworked and constructed in a unique way.

In other words, certain shop-floor practices define and sustain specific conceptions of masculinity. And one such practice is shop-floor theft that in the collective social situation of manual labor, provides working-class men with an available resource for "doing gender." For these men, their taken-for-granted "essential nature" is undermined and threatened within the confines of the contract. Thus, faced with this predicament, one's sex category is particularly salient and masculinity is held more accountable. By joining the work group and participating in shop-floor theft, working-class men resolve the gender accountability problem and exhibit to others that they are "real men." Participation in this group theft validates a man's "essential nature" and is specifically chosen not only for "the goods," but the capacity to impress other men. Shop-floor theft helps workers shape a valued masculine identity by exhibiting those hegemonic masculine ideals the capitalist workplace denies—independence, dominance, daring, and control.[7]

Workers and sexual harassment

Studies also highlight the persistence and dominance of normative heterosexuality on the shop floor—such practices as exhibiting men's sexuality as biologically driven and perpetually incontinent, whereas women are the objects of a sexuality that precipitates men's "natural urges" (Willis, 1979; Cockburn, 1983; Hearn, 1985; Gray, 1987). This macho sexual prowess, mediated through bravado and sexist joking, is constructed and encouraged on the shop floor (Collinson and Collinson, 1989: 95–98). Moreover, failure to participate in this specific interaction raises serious questions about one's masculinity. In this way, situationally specific notions of heterosexuality are reproduced through the construction of shop-floor masculinity and center on men's insistence on exercising power over women.

Under such conditions, when women enter the shop floor as coworkers, a threatening situation (for the men, that is), results. In this situation, some shop-floor men are likely to engage in forms of interaction quite different from their interaction with women outside the workplace. Not surprising, sexual harassment is more prevalent in this type of social setting. For example, one study of a manufacturing firm (in which the vast majority of manual laborers were men) found (DiTomaso, 1989: 81):

> the men in the plant acted differently than they would if they interacted with these women in any other context. Their behavior, in other words, was very much related to the work context itself. It appeared to provide a license for offensive behavior and an occasion for attempting to take advantage of many of the women in the plant.

In DiTomaso's study, the younger women on the shop floor were perceived by the men as the most threatening because they were competing directly for the same kinds of jobs as were the men. Consequently, these women were more likely than other women to be subjected to demeaning forms of social interaction: the men's behavior was more likely to exceed simple flirtation and to involve specific forms of sexual harassment. The following are comments from several women in the plant (pp. 80–81):

> "The men are different here than on the street. It's like they have been locked up for years."
>
> "It's like a field day."
>
> "A majority of the men here go out of their way to make you feel uneasy about being inside the plant and being a female; nice guys are a minority."

Research reveals that sexual harassment occurs at all levels in the workplace—from shop floor to management. However, sexual harassment by men on the shop floor generally is twice as serious and persistent, and is different from sexual harassment by managers (Hearn, 1985: 121). In the shop-floor setting (where men are the majority), sexual harassment is "a powerful form of economic protection and exclusion from men's territory. Women workers are perceived as a threat to solidarity between men" (pp. 121–122). Studies of shop-floor sexual harassment suggest that 36 to 53 percent of women workers report some type of sexual harassment (Gruber and Bjorn, 1982); furthermore, a recent study of workplace sexual assault suggests that manual workers (as opposed to other men in the firm) committed the overwhelming majority of both attempted and completed assaults within the entire firm (Schneider, 1991: 539).

Notwithstanding, the most common types of sexual harassment on the shop floor involve such demeaning acts as sexual slurs, pinches or grabs, and public displays of derogatory images of women (Schneider, 1991: 539; Carothers and Crull, 1984: 222). Perceptively, women shop-floor coworkers are more likely than women coworkers in other occupational settings to describe this sexual harassment as designed to label them as "outsiders." The "invasion" of women on the shop floor poses a threat to men's monopoly over these jobs, and one way to discourage women from attempting to compete in this domain is to remind them, through remarks and behavior, of their "female fragility" (Carothers and Crull, 1984: 224). In this way, then, shop-floor men attempt to secure the "maleness" of the job by emphasizing the "femaleness" of women coworkers (DiTomaso, 1989: 88).

Although most shop-floor workers clearly do not engage in sexual harassment, the unique social setting of the shop floor increases the likelihood that this particular type of sexual harassment will occur. Indeed, this specific shop-floor sexual harassment must be seen as a practice communicating anger against women for invading a "male" bastion and for threatening the economic and social status of men (Carothers and Crull, 1984: 224). In addition, however, the shop floor is an ideal arena for differentiating between masculinity and femininity—performing manual labor demonstrates to others that such workers are "real men." The presence of women on the shop floor dilutes this gender distinction: if women can do what "real men" do, the value of the practice for accomplishing masculinity is effectively challenged. Because "doing gender" means creating differences between men and women, by maintaining and emphasizing the "femaleness" of women coworkers, shop-floor men are attempting to distinquish clearly between women and men manual laborers, thus preserving the peculiar masculinity of the shop floor. This type of sexual harassment serves as an effective (albeit primitive) resource for solidifying, strengthening, and validating a specific type of heterosexual shop-floor masculinity, while simultaneously excluding, disparaging, and ridiculing women (Segal, 1990: 211).[8]

Moving from shop floor to boardroom, we will next consider how corporate crime and a different type of sexual harassment provide certain white corporate executives with resources for constructing a specific form of private masculinity.

White corporate executives and corporate crime

White corporate executives have major decision-making power in corporations. In terms of gender, it is critical to understand who become executives and how they obtain such positions. Concomitantly, the fact that men control the activities of management likewise is critical to understanding corporate crime.[9] As more and more women enter the paid-labor market, they find it organized not only for purposes of producing goods, services, and profits, but also for gender. In other words, the gender divisions of labor and power continue to operate within the labor market. This is especially so in the corporate setting.

Corporations are organized to ensure that men receive the greatest share of material benefits. Moreover, although women hold approximately 38 percent of all management, executive, and administrative positions in the United States, they are relegated to lower-status positions within these occupations (Blau and Winkler, 1989). In fact, women are relegated to such areas as personnel, research, affirmative action, and equal employment—management areas that do not lead to major decision-making positions within the corporation (Kaufman, 1989). Also, these "patronizing" positions are where women do the work to discern what is needed, make recommendations, and "then *men decide* what is to be done with regard to these recommendations" (Sokoloff, 1980: 243). This gendered segregation of corporate managerial positions perpetuates the gendered divisions of labor and power because women usually work for men (p. 243):

> at lower wages, with fewer resources, and with less power than male managers, thus allowing men the benefits of money, status, power,

resources, and specialization in decision-making control and order—without directly competing with other male managers for their privileged positions.

In short, the gender (and race) division of labor, reproduced within the corporation today, ensures white men positions of power, where corporate crimes orginate.[10] Indeed, no more than 2 percent of top executive positions are held by women and there are no women who hold the position of chief executive officer in any *Fortune 500* U.S. corporation (Powell, 1988: 13; L. Brown, 1988: 267).

The old-boy network is crucial to maintaining the gender divisions of labor and power and for understanding corporate crime. The old-boy network basically is a sponsorship system that recruits junior executives to upper echelons of corporate managerial sectors. In other words, men recruit men who share similar norms, attitudes, values, and standards of behavior. Accordingly, junior executives who make decisions in the corporate interest are guaranteed career promotion. The hierarchy of senior and junior executives establishes "the allegiance of the former to the latter" (Sokoloff, 1980: 240). In other words, if junior executives do what they are expected to do, they are rewarded with wealth, authority, and corporate control. Maintaining business as usual—making profits—these men eventually are rewarded not only financially but also with power over men and women. Indeed, white-executive masculinity is constructed partially around competition with other men for status and prestige: junior executives must maneuver for position and negotiate their rank relative to other men (Cockburn, 1985: 178).

Men who are junior executives, hoping to make it to the top, learn quickly what is right and what is wrong from their sponsor: they learn to conduct themselves and perform practices in ways that exemplify executive conceptions of masculinity. Foremost among these is the ability to compromise personal principles in order to move up the ladder. In fact, junior executives frequently must sacrifice personal ethics for the "good" of the company simply to remain in business. A recent survey by the Columbia University Business School reports that 40 percent of a sample of 1,070 businessmen had been rewarded for engaging in conduct they considered "ethically troubling"; 31 percent of men who refused to commit an ethically troubling act had been penalized (*Wall Street Journal*, 1990: B1).

A study by Edward Gross (1978) sheds some light on this situation. Gross analyzed a substantial body of research on corporate mobility to discern what qualities corporate positions demand and what sort of junior executives are most likely to be promoted. He found that men who are promoted to top corporate positions are ambitious, shrewd, and nearly amoral. Their ambition, however, is not merely personal—they soon discover their personal goals are best attained by assisting the corporation in attaining its goal—profit. As Gross (p. 71) states, these men "believe in the organization, they want it to attain its goals, they profit personally from such goal attainment. So they will try hard to help the organization attain those goals."

The gendered promotion system within the corporation, however, promotes not exclusively men who strongly identify with the goals of the corporation, but also (as Gross found) men who possess the personal characteristics necessary to commit, if needed, corporate crime. Given that the corporation "must engage in illegal activities to attain its goals, men with a nondemanding moral code have the least compunctions about engaging in such behavior" (p. 71). Men with non-demanding moral codes are more likely to be promoted to the top, a characteristic that frees them to engage (when necessary) in corporate crime. For corporate executives face both "pressure for profits" and "pressure for promotion." Most often remedied by legal means, when legitimate approaches fail, corporate executives are positioned to engage in specific illegitimate practices that seek to ensure not only their own, but corporate success as well. For example, executives involved in the production of the exploding Pintos operated under an ideology that "safety doesn't sell." As Cullen, Maakestad, and Cavender (1987: 161) point out, "When asked whether anyone had gone to Lee Iacocca and informed him of the Pinto's problems, a high-ranking company engineer responded, 'Hell no. That person would have been fired.'"

Another executive who worked at Ford for thirty years exemplified the nondemanding moral code of many Ford engineers by stating (p. 166): "Engineers who spoke out about safety didn't 'get that promotion' or 'salary increase.'" In short, "safety doesn't sell" became a defining feature of corporate executive masculinity and social practice. This type of masculinity was sustained as a collective practice within the context of the corporate boardroom.

Essentially, corporate crime simply assists the corporation and young upwardly mobile men reach their goals. In other words, corporate crime is a practice with which men gain corporate power through maintaining profit margins. Moreover, as corporate executives do corporate crime, they simultaneously do masculinity—construct a masculinity specific to their position in the gender, race, and occupational divisions of labor and power.

Tolson (1977: 81–82) points out that this type of masculinity differs from that found on the shop floor in two important ways. First, the corporate executive "does not do a 'job,' he pursues a 'career,' he is paid not a 'wage,' but a 'salary'; he works not by the 'clock,' but by 'appointment.' His career is a long-term investment, a ladder of individual achievement, finally rewarded by the 'golden handshake'" (p. 81). Highly committed to the future, the corporate executive cultivates a strategic expertise and fuels an inner desire to achieve. Second, because career is a long-term commitment, a man's undivided identification and a sense of duty are required. The discipline of corporate executive effort "is not the impersonal discipline of factory production, but *self*-discipline, an internalized desire to work" (p. 82). This desire is sustained by one's faith in a higher authority, the corporation. Corporate-executive masculinity, then, entails calculation and rationality as well as struggle for success, reward, and corporate recognition. The corporate executive perceives work as "a series of stages, leading finally to recognition by the community of individual achievement" (p. 83). Such men struggle with other men and measure masculinity by their success in the corporate world. Corporate crime is a practice that facilitates this particular gendered strategy of action.

Nevertheless, this type of white masculinity—devotion to achievement and success measured by promotion and profit making—can be threatened by certain obstacles that interfere with executive ability to realize profitmaking easily and without violating regulations. Stuart Hills (1987: 190) notes the following:

> In a capitalist economy, profit-seeking firms must often compete in an uncertain and unpredictable environment. Competitive market pressures, fluctuating sales, increasing costs for safety and health measures, consumer and environmental concerns, government regulations, and other constraints may limit the ability of the business firm to achieve its profit goals through legitimate opportunities. Thus, some corporations may evade and violate the law or engage in practices that many Americans would consider unethical, endangering the well-being of workers, consumers, and citizens.

Because threats to profitmaking are threats concurrently to masculine accomplishment, corporate crime is a means of overcoming both problems: corporate crime is a resource for accomplishing profit and gender. If profitmaking is undermined, an important resource for corporate executive masculinity is threatened. In such a predicament, sex category is particularly salient and doing masculinity necessitates extra effort. Thus, corporate crime may be invoked as a practice when corporate executives lack other resources for profitmaking and, therefore, to accomplish gender.

Moreover, social action is often designed with an eye to one's gender accountability both situationally and in the future (see discussion in Chapter 3). Crime can provide a resource for doing masculinity in specific social settings, such as the corporate boardroom, as well as for some future time when gender accountability may be at risk. The following statement by a B.F. Goodrich executive who conspired with others to cover up falsified test data on aircraft braking systems shows his concern for maintaining a "good provider" masculinity then, and in the future (Vandivier, 1987: 155):

> At forty-two, with seven children, I had decided that the Goodrich Company would probably be my "home" for the rest of my working life. The job paid well, it was pleasant and challenging, and the future looked reasonably bright. My wife and I had bought a home and were ready to settle down into a comfortable, middle-age, middle-class

> rut. If I refused to take part in the fraud, I would have to either resign or be fired. . . . But bills aren't paid with personal satisfaction, nor house payments with ethical principles.

The fraud was viewed by this executive as contributing not only to corporate profits, but also maintaining an income with which he could continue to provide for his family. Thus, in this case, corporate crime is a resource for being both a successful executive and an effective father/husband. Corporate crime helped solve the "male" accountability problem at work and home.

Consequently, within the corporation a specific masculinity is created among men at the top. This masculinity centers on practices reflecting not only the nondemanding moral code identified by Gross and the struggle for success, reward, and recognition identified by Tolson, but also "a tough-minded approach to problems" and "a capacity to set aside personal, emotional considerations in the interests of task accomplishments" (Kanter, 1977: 22). By setting aside such emotional reflections, white corporate executives are better prepared to handle the problems of profitmaking and are less inclined to question the corporate theft and violence they may generate. "Tough decisions" often involve making people suffer; not everyone can make the "necessary" decisions that simultaneously inflict pain upon others. It is the gendered corporate process that ensures that those who reach the top are sufficiently unemotional to make the tough decisions. Indeed, John McMullan (1992: 77) reviewed several studies on gender and the corporation, concluding that the studies "strongly suggest that the hallmark of modern corporate bureaucratic organization is a type of heartless masculinist rationality that undervalues collective nurturance and responsibility." For McMullan (pp. 77–78), it is a cold and abstract masculine calculus that underlies corporate crime.[11]

White corporate executives construct an accommodating corporate masculinity that reflects their wholehearted obligation to the corporation and its overall enterprise. Thus, because masculinity is a behavioral response to the particular conditions and situations in which men participate, corporate executives do masculinity when they do corporate crime. Moreover, their corporate position both constrains and enables certain forms of social action, and they monitor their actions accordingly. And when profitmaking is threatened through environmental uncertainties, sex category is particularly salient, and therefore, doing masculinity necessitates extra effort.

Corporate crime serves as a resource, then, for masculine accomplishment and facilitates profitmaking. Consequently, executives who reach the top of the corporate ladder enjoy positions of nonaccountable and unconstrained power, and are "in a high state of preparedness to commit corporate crime should they perceive it as being necessary 'for the good of the company'" (Box, 1983: 41).

Choosing corporate profit over people is made easier by gender relations that demand emotional insensitivity in executive men. In short, the desire to "get to the top" and to maintain profit margins often entails illegal and socially harmful behavior. Doing promotion, doing profitmaking, and doing masculinity involve essentially the same ongoing practices—and corporate crime is a resource for accomphshing all three. As McMullan (1992: 78) points out, this callous and insensitive masculinity of the corporate boardroom silences opposition and discourages "all but the most aggressive and competitive from engaging in business." Moreover, (p. 78):

> It lends support to law evasion, law avoidance and law-breaking. Against a backdrop of instrumental rationality and a dichotomized social world, corporate men stride and stumble into their illegal and criminal enterprises, loudly proclaiming their virtue and respectability from the bureaucratic shadows in the name of profits.

Corporate crime, then, can be understood as a practice for maintaining or reestablishing a masculine identity that has, or is about to be, damaged. Corporate executive masculinity—accountable to other executives in identical situations and accomplishing gender by engaging in corporate crime—provides a masculine resolution to the spectacle of environmental uncertainties.[12]

White corporate executives and sexual harassment

Sexual harassment is yet another resource available to corporate executives for constructing a specific type of masculinity. Because of their subordinate position in the corporation, women "are vulnerable to the whim and fancy of male employers or organizational superiors, who are in a position to reward or punish their female subordinate economically" (Box, 1983: 152). In other words, corporate-executive men are in a unique position to sexually exploit, if they desire, women subordinates. Executive exploitation of sexuality is often a means of reinforcing men's power at the same time as making profits. For example, secretaries frequently are treated as conspicuous "possessions"; therefore, by hiring the "best looking" instead of the most competent secretary, managers exploit secretarial sexuality to "excite the envy of collegues, disarm the opposition and obtain favors from other departments" (Hearn, 1985: 118). Thus, as Jeff Hearn (p. 118) points out, exploitation of secretarial sexuality is not only a matter of directly objectifying women but also of using their sexuality for the eyes of other men. Economic and gender relations are produced simultaneously through the same ongoing sexual practices.

In addition to this direct exploitation of secretarial sexuality, corporate executives sometimes engage in specific types of sexual harassment. While shop-floor men who engage in sexual harassment are more likely to undertake practices that create a sexually demeaning work environment characterized by slurs, pictures, pinches, and grabs, white corporate-executive men are more likely to threaten women workers and lower-level managers who refuse to comply with demands for sexual favors with the loss of their jobs (Carothers and Crull, 1984: 222). One secretary described this type of sexual harassment from a corporate executive as follows (cited in Carothers and Crull, 1984: 222):

> He always complimented me on what I wore. I thought he was just being nice. It got to the place that every time he buzzed for me to come into his office for dictation, my stomach turned. He had a way of looking at me as if he were undressing me. This time as his eyes searched up and down my body and landed on my breast, he said, "Why should your boyfriend have all the fun. You could have fun with me *and* it could pay off for you. *Good* jobs are really scarce these days."

The harassment of women in subordinate positions by an executive man more likely involves hints and requests for dates or sexual favors, which, when rejected, are likely followed by work retaliation (p. 224). Essentially, this particular type of sexual harassment involves economic threats by white, corporate-executive men such that if a woman employee or would-be employee refuses to submit, she will, on the one hand, not be hired, retained, or promoted or, on the other hand, will be fired, demoted, or transferred to a less-pleasant work assignment. Assuming that the woman employee or potential employee does not desire a sexual relationship with the executive, such threats are extremely coercive. Given the economic position of many of these women, termination, demotion, or not being hired is economically devastating. When women depend on men for their economic well-being, some men take advantage of their economic vulnerability and engage in this particular practice of sexual harassment.

Although the imbalance of corporate gender power can be exercised coercively, sexual harassment is by no means automatic. Women often enter into genuine and humane relationships with men in the workplace, notwithstanding the fact that these men may be in supervisory positions vis-à-vis the woman.[13] Nevertheless, the general power imbalance within the corporation often creates conditions such that men in supervisory positions may exercise economic coercion to gain sexual access without genuine overt consent. Indeed, the corporate structural position of white executive men ensures that such exploitation will more likely be manipulative than violent.

One recent study of workplace assaults found that shop-floor workers utilized physical force more often than other forms of coercion because they lack the institutionalized economic means with which to force compliance. Corporate executives are much more likely to use economic coercion than physical force as a means with which to obtain sexual access to women subordinates (Schneider, 1991). Two women who experienced this type of sexual assault stated in part (cited in MacKinnon, 1979: 32):

> "If I wasn't going to sleep with him, I wasn't going to get my promotion."
>
> "I was fired because I refused to give at the office."

When women refuse to "give at the office," some corporate executives retaliate by exercising their power over women's careers. In one case, an executive, "following rejection of his elaborate sexual advances, barraged the woman with unwarranted reprimands about her job performance, refused routine supervision or task direction, which made it impossible for her to do her job, and then fired her for poor work performance" (MacKinnon, 1979: 35).

The social construction of masculinity/femininity in the executive/secretary relationship shows clearly how this specific type of sexual harassment comes about. A secretary is often expected to nurture the executive by stroking his ego, making his coffee, cleaning the office, and ensuring he is presentable (Sokoloff, 1980: 220). Secretaries are often symbolically hired as "office wives." In one case, an executive had his secretary do all his grocery shopping and even go to his home and take his washing off the line! (Pringle, 1989: 169–170).

Rosabeth Moss Kanter (1977: 88) noted some time ago that a "tone of emotional intensity" pervades the relationship between secretary and executive. The secretary comes to "feel for" the executive, "to care deeply about what happens to him and to do his feeling for him." In fact, according to Kanter (p. 88), secretaries are rewarded for their willingness "to take care of bosses' personal needs." In other words, women subordinates construct a specific type of femininity by performing an extensive nurturing service for the executive.[14] Women do in the workplace what they traditionally have done in the home. It should come as no surprise that some executives come to expect such nurturance from women subordinates, just as they do from their wives, and that some take this nurturance further to include sexual nuturing. The result is that some women are coerced to exchange sexual services for material survival. As Carothers and Crull (1984: 223) observe in their important study of sexual harassment:

> The male boss can use his power over women within the organizational structure to impose sexual attentions on a woman, just as he can coerce her into getting his coffee. They both know that if she does not go along, she is the one who will lose in terms of job benefits.

Corporate-executive harassment and sexual coercion are practices that simultaneously construct a specific form of masculinity. This type of sexual harassment arrogantly celebrates hegemonic masculinity, its presumed heterosexual urgency, and the "normality" of pursuing women aggressively.

In an attempt to "score" with his secretary, the corporate-executive sexual harasser strengthens gender hierarchy, thereby "affirming in men a shared sense of themselves as the dominant, assertive and active sex" (Segal, 1990: 244). The corporate executive enjoys an immediate sensation of power derived from this practice, power that strengthens his masculine self-esteem.

In this way, in addition to normative heterosexuality, white, corporate-executive sexual harassers attempt to reproduce their gender power. Through the practice of corporate sexual harassment, executives exhibit, as MacKinnon (1979: 162) argues, "that they can go this far any time they wish and get away with it." White, corporate-executive sexual harassment, constructed differently than by shop-floor men, provides a resource for constructing this specific type of heterosexual masculinity that centers on the "driven" nature of "male" sexuality and "male" power.

Although clearly most corporate executives do not engage in sexual harassment, the social setting of the executive/secretary relationship increases the probability that this specific form of sexual harassment will occur. Corporate executives engage in sexual harassment to reinforce their power by sexualizing women subordinates, creating "essential" differences between women and men by constructing this particular type of masculinity.

The family

In addition to the street and the workplace, the divisions of labor and power frame social interactions and practices in the contemporary nuclear family where, for example, women remain responsible primarily for unpaid housework and child care while men remain responsible primarily for paid labor. Indeed, the gender division of household labor defines not only who does most of the unpaid household labor but also the kind of household labor assigned to men and women. Moreover, the sociological evidence indicates clearly that in Western industrialized societies gender asymmetry in the performance of household labor continues to exist (Andersen, 1988: 141–145; Messerschmidt, 1986: 74; Hartmann, 1981; Berk, 1985; Hochschild, 1989, 1992) and women share less in the consumption of household goods (from food to leisure time) than do men (Walby, 1989: 221).

It is true that barely 10 percent of all U.S. heterosexual households consist of a husband and wife with two children living at home, where the husband is the sole breadwinner (Messerschmidt, 1986: 74). Further, as fertility is delayed or declines, and with more and more women working during pregnancy and child-rearing years, active motherhood is shrinking as a component of most women's lives (Petchesky, 1984: 246). Nevertheless, evidence indicates that women continue to perform most of the household labor, even as these demographic changes occur and women's participation in the paid-labor market increases dramatically. Indeed, Arlie Hochschild (1992: 512) concluded in her study of fifty-two heterosexual couples over an eight-year period that just as "there is a wage gap between men and women in the work place, there is a 'leisure gap' between them in the home. Most women work one shift at the office or factory and a 'second shift' at home."

This gender division of labor embodies the husband's power to define the household setting in his terms. While conscious efforts are being made in many households to dismantle familial power relations (Connell, 1987: 124), especially in the middle class (Ehrenreich, 1983), for most couples the capacity of each spouse to determine the course of their shared life is unequal: men alone make the "very important" decisions in the household; women alone make few "important" decisions (Komter, 1989). In many dual-career families, men's power is deemed authentic and an acceptable part of social relations. This legitimized power in the family provides men with considerably greater authority (Kompter, 1989; Pahl, 1992; Bernard, 1982). Concomitantly, the marital sexual relationship, as with other aspects of marriage, likely embodies power, unless consciously dismantled, and "in most cases it is the husband who holds the initiative in defining sexual practice" (Connell, 1987: 123).

Chapter 2 argued that the concept of patriarchy has lost its strength and usefulness as a theoretical starting point for comprehending gender inequality in Western industrialized societies. Nevertheless, the concept is helpful to describe a certain type of masculinity that persists today: some men are simply *patriarchs* in the traditional sense. Patriarchs fashion configurations of behavior and pursue a gender strategy within the family setting that control women's labor and/or sexuality. Moreover, these men will most likely use violence against women in the family. In this final section of Chapter 5, the discussion focuses on two forms of violence against women in the family—wife beating and wife rape—and analyzes how these crimes serve as a resource for the construction of specific types of patriarchal masculinities.

Wife beating and battering rape

Victimization surveys indicate that in the home, wives are assaulted much more often by their husbands than husbands are by their wives (less than 5 percent of domestic violence involves attacks on husbands by their wives) and women are much more likely than men to suffer injury from these assaults (Dobash, Dobash, Wilson, and Daly, 1992).[15] Wife beating also develops within a setting of prolonged and persistent intimidation, domination, and control over women (Dobash et al., 1992; Dobash and Dobash, 1984; Pagelow, 1984). Accordingly, wife beating is the "chronic battering of a person of inferior power who for that reason cannot effectively resist" (Gordon, 1988: 251).

Violence by men in the household derives from the domestic authority of men and is intimately linked to the traditional patriarchal expectation (1) that men are the credible figures within monogamous relationships and (2) that men possess the inherent right to control those relationships. As

Susan Schechter (1982: 222) argues, "a man beats to remind a woman that the relationship will proceed in the way he wants or that ultimately he holds the power."

Katz's (1988: 18–31) discussion of "righteous slaughter"—killing among family members, friends, and acquaintances—by men aids in understanding how this focus on household authority and control results in wife beating as a resource for masculine construction. Katz argues that for the typical killer, murder achieves *Good* by obliterating *Bad*. Moreover, the killer has no capacity to "ignore a fundamental challenge" to his self-worth and identity. From the killer's perspective, the victim teases, dares, defies, or pursues the killer. Accordingly, the killer sees himself as simply "defending his rights." In other words, the killer's identity and self-worth have been taken away—by an insult, losing an argument, an act of infidelity—and such events attack an "eternal human value" that calls for a "last stand in defense of his basic worth." The "eternally humiliating situation" is transformed into a blinding rage and the compulsion to wipe away the stigmatizing stain through the act of murder. And the rage is not random and chaotic but, rather, "coherent, disciplined action, cunning in its moral structure" (p. 30). The killer "does not kill until and unless he can fashion violence to convey the situational meaning of defending his rights" (p. 31).

Investigations of wife beating indicate further the application of the notion "defending his rights." Violence is regarded by the husband as achieving *Good* by pulverizing *Bad*; such men engage in a coherent and disciplined rage to defend what they consider to be their rights. According to interviews with wife beaters, their wife is perceived as not "performing well," not accomplishing what her "essential nature" enjoins and stipulates. Women are beaten for not cooking "up to standards," for not being obeisant and deferential, and for not completing or performing housework sufficiently—for not being a "good wife" (Ptacek, 1988: 147). According to the offender, the "privileges of male entitlement have been unjustly denied" because the wife is not submissive and, therefore, not conforming to his standards of "essential femininity" (p. 148). Irene Frieze's (1983: 553) interviews with wife beaters found that they believe "it is their right as men to batter wives who disobey them."

Dobash and Dobash (1984: 274) similarly found that most wife beating is precipitated by verbal confrontations centering on possessiveness and jealousy on the part of the husband and a husband's demand concerning domestic labor and services. During an argument over such issues, "the men were most likely to become physically violent at the point when the woman could be perceived to be questioning his authority or challenging the legitimacy of his behavior or at points when she asserted herself in some way" (p. 274). In other words, wife beating arises not solely from gendered subordination but also from women actively contesting that subordination (Gordon, 1988: 286). In such situations, the wife beater is punishing "his wife" for her failure to fulfill adequately her "essential" obligations in the gender division of labor and power and for her challenge to his dominance. The wife beater perceives that he has an inherent patriarchal right to punish "his woman" for her alleged wrongdoing.

Wife beaters are piously sure of their righteousness, and thus fashion their violence to communicate the situational meaning of defending their patriarchal rights. Indeed, the more traditional the gender division of labor (regardless of class and race position) the greater the likelihood of wife beating (Edleson, Eisikovits, and Guttman, 1986; Messerschmidt, 1986; Smith, 1990). In such traditional patriarchal households, both husband and wife tend to perceive the lopsided gender division of labor and power as "fair" (Berk, 1985). Linda Gordon's (1988: 260–261) historical study of family violence found that in households where wife beating is prevalent:

> Women as well as men professed allegiance to male-supremacist understandings of what relations between the sexes should be like. These shared assumptions, however, by no means prevented conflict. Women's assumptions of male dominance did not mean that they quit trying to improve their situations.

The wife beater attempts to resolve in *his* way what he regards as a conflict over this "fair" arrangement, even when the wife is not actively or consciously contesting that "fair" household organization.[16] Accordingly, as West and Zimmerman (1987: 144) argue, "It is not simply that household labor is designated as 'women's work,' but that a woman to engage in it and a man not to engage in it is to draw on and exhibit the 'essential nature' of each." By engaging in practices that maintain gender divisions of labor and power, husbands and wives do not simply produce household goods and services, but also produce gender. Indeed, husbands and wives develop gendered rationalizations and justifications for this asymmetrical household labor. What follows are selected but representative examples (Komter, 1989: 209):

> *By wives*:
> "He has no feeling for it."
> "He is not born to it."
> "It does not fit his character."
>
> *By husbands*:
> "She has more talent for it."
> "It is a woman's natural duty."

When this asymmetry is questioned (whether consciously or not), the wife beater assumes that his "essential rights" are being denied—an injustice has occurred, a violation of the "natural" order of things. The "essential nature" of wife beaters is that they control familial decision making and thus dominate the family division of labor and power. When wives "question" this decision making, through words or actions, they threaten their husband's control of the gender division of labor and power. In other words, the husband interprets such behavior as a threat to his "essential nature"—control and domination of the household. Because spousal domestic labor is a symbolic affirmation of a patriarch's masculinity and his wife's femininity, such men are extremely vulnerable to disappointment when that labor is not performed as they expect (Gordon, 1988: 268).

According to the wife beater, it is his duty to determine, for example, what constitutes a satisfactory meal, how children are cared for, when and how often sexual relations occur, and the nature of leisure activities (Ferraro, 1988: 134). Women are beaten for some of the most insignificant conduct imaginable: for example, preparing a casserole instead of a meat dish for dinner, wearing their hair in a ponytail, or remarking that they do not like the pattern on the wallpaper. Kathleen Ferraro (p. 135) discusses a case in which even the issue of wearing a particular piece of clothing was perceived by the husband as a threat to his control:

> On her birthday, she received a blouse from her mother that she put on to wear to a meeting she was attending without Steven. He told her she could not wear the blouse, and after insisting that she would, Steven beat her. It was not only her insistence on wearing the blouse that evening that triggered Steven's abuse. It was the history of his symbolic control, through determining her appearance that was questioned by wearing the new blouse.

Wife beaters (regardless of class and race position) presume they have the patriarchal right—because it is part of their "essential nature"—to dominate and control their wives, and wife beating serves both to ensure continued compliance with their commands and as a resource for constructing a "damaged" patriarchal masculinity. Thus, wife beating increases (or is intended to do so) their control over women and, therefore, over housework, child care, and sexual activity.

Yet wife beating is related not only to the husband's control over familial decision making, but also develops from another form of control, possessiveness. For some wife beaters, spousal demonstration of loyalty is a focal concern and is closely monitored. For instance, time spent with friends may be interpreted by a wife beater simply as disloyalty. Indeed, sexual jealousy of friends is a common theme in the literature on wife beating (Dobash and Dobash, 1979, 1984; Ferraro, 1988; Frieze, 1983), and indicates the importance of the social structure of normative heterosexuality to understanding wife beating. The wife's uncommitted wrong is the potential to be unfaithful, which to her husband is not only a serious challenge to his patriarchal ideology, but his very real fear that his wife will choose another man and, thereby, judge him less "manly" than his "competitor." Thus, because time spent with friends endangers his ongoing interest in heterosexual performance, wife beating reassures him that his wife is his to possess sexually.

Moreover, not only potential sexual competitors can threaten a patriarchal husband, but relatives may also pose threats to a wife's loyalty. Pregnancy, for example, is closely associated with wife beating, and reflects the husband's resentment of the fetal intruder (Ferraro, 1988). Walker (1979: 83–84) offers an example of a husband and wife who planned to spend the day together, but the wife broke off the plans, choosing instead to baby-sit her three-year-old granddaughter. Her husband (Ed) seems to have interpreted this choice as disloyal behavior and a challenge to his ultimate control:

> Ed became enraged. He began to scream and yell that I didn't love him, that I only loved my children and grandchildren. I protested and said, "Maybe you would like to come with me," thinking that if he came, he might feel more a part of the family. He just became further enraged. I couldn't understand it. . . . He began to scream and yell and pound me with his fists. He threw me against the wall and shouted that he would never let me leave, that I had to stay with him and could not go. I became hysterical and told him that I would do as I saw fit. . . . Ed then became even further enraged and began beating me even harder.

Thus, under conditions where labor services are "lacking" and possesiveness is "challenged," a wife beater's masculinity is threatened. In such a scenario, predictably, the wife beater attempts to reestablish control by reconstructing his patriarchal masculinity through the practice of wife beating.

Approximately 30 to 40 percent of battered women are also victims of wife rape (Walker, 1979; Russell, 1982; Frieze, 1983). These "battering rapes," as Finkelhor and Yllö (1985) describe them, do not result from marital conflicts over sex; rather, the rape is an extension of other violence perpetrated on the victim. The wife beating/rape represents punishment and degradation for challenging his authority and, thus, the traditional division of labor and power. In fact, although wife beating and battering rapes extend across all classes and races (for the reasons discussed above), they occur most frequently in working-class and lower–working-class households wherein the traditional patriarchal gender division of labor and power—husband decision maker and wife caretaker—is strongest (Straus, Gelles, and Steinmetz, 1980; Finkelhor and Yllö, 1985; Smith, 1990a; Walker, 1977–78; Messerschmidt, 1986: 144). Research consistently shows that class conditions are associated with wife beating: for example, low-income (Straus et al., 1980; DeKeseredy and Hinch, 1991) and working-class wives are approximately twice as likely as middle-class wives to experience wife beating (Smith, 1990; Stets and Straus, 1989).

Moreover, among couples in which the husband is unemployed or employed part-time, the level of husband-to-wife violence is three times as high as the level among couples in which the husband is fully employed (Straus et al., 1980; DeKeseredy and Hinch, 1991).

Finally, Michael Smith's (1990a: 49) study of risk factors in wife beating found that "the lower the income, the higher the probability of abuse." This same study went on to report that the chances of a low-income woman being severely battered during marriage exceed those of a middle-class woman by a factor of ten. Smith's (1990: 267) data reveals that "men with relatively low incomes, less educated men, and men in low-status jobs were significantly more likely than their more privileged counterparts to subscribe to an ideology of familial patriarchy. These men were also more likely to have beaten their wives."

Although at work he is individually powerless, at home the working-class battering rapist is a patriarch endowed with individual authority. His ability to earn money (if available) "authorizes" his patriarchal power as husband/father. But his masculine identity depends on the demarcation of public and private responsibility; consequently, any challenge to the status quo in the home is taken personally as a confrontation (Tolson, 1977: 70). In seeking to sustain this specific type of patriarchal masculinity, working-class men develop an intense emotional dependency on the family/household (Donaldson, 1987), demanding nurturance, services, and comfort on their terms when at home. As Lynne Segal (1990: 28) points out, "the sole site of authority" for such men is in the home. And when their power and authority are threatened or perceived to be threatened at home, working-class men are more likely than other men to employ battering rapes to accomplish gender and reestablish their control. As Harris and Bologh (1985: 246) point out in their examination of "blue collar battering," "If he can establish an aura of aggression and violence, then he may be able to pass as a 'real man,' for surely it is admirable to use violence in the service of one's honor."

Battering in this sense is a resource for affirming "maleness." Because of their structural position in the class division of labor, working-class men—in particular, lower–working-class men—lack traditional resources for constructing their masculinity and, as a result, are more likely than are middle-class men to forge a particular type of masculinity that centers on ultimate control of the domestic setting through the use of violence. Moreover, unemployment and low occupational status undermine the patriarchal breadwinner/good provider masculinity: he cannot provide for his wife and children. Such men are more likely than are economically advantaged husbands to engage in wife beating and battering rapes to reestablish their masculinity. As Kathleen Ferraro (1988: 127) puts it, "for men who lack any control in the civil realm, dominance within the private realm of the home becomes their sole avenue for establishing a sense of self in control of others."[17]

In sum, most working- and lower–working-class husbands do not abuse their wives, nor is this particular type of abuse limited to this class of men.

Nevertheless, the peculiar social conditions prevalent in working- and lower–working-class families increase the incidence of this type of abuse. For these men, power is exercised in the home in ways that hegemonic masculinity approves: men are allowed to be aggressive and sexual. Lacking dominance over others at work or the ability to act out a breadwinner (or even economic contributor) masculinity, sex category is particularly important, and working- and lower–working-class men are more likely to express their masculinity as patriarchs, attempting to control the labor and sexuality of "their women." Consequently, when patriarchal relations are "challenged," their taken-for-granted "essential nature" is undermined and, accordingly, doing masculinity requires extra effort. Wife beating/rape is a specific practice designed with an eye to one's accountability as a "real man" and, therefore, serves as a suitable resource for simultaneously accomplishing gender and affirming patriarchal masculinity.

Force-only rape

However, wife rape is not limited to the victims of wife beating. Indeed, in Finkelhor and Yllö's (1985) study, 40 percent of their sample were "force-only rapes"—situations in which husbands use only the force necessary to coerce their wives into submission. The perpetrators and victims of force-only rapes were significantly more educated than those of battering rapes, more often middle-class, and almost half held business- or professional-level jobs.[18] Moreover, the perpetrators and victims of force-only rapes were much less likely to have been in a relationship based on the traditional gender divisions of labor and power. Sex was usually the issue in force-only rapes, and the offenders were "acting on some specifically sexual complaint," such as how often to have sex or what were acceptable sexual activities (p. 46).

In some sectors of the "progressive" middle class, there have been serious attempts to become truly equal marriage partners, where the wife has a career and where the husband participates equally in child care and housework. However, the greater the income differential between husbands and wives, the less involved some husbands are in parenting and housework, and there exists greater equality in dual-career families than in dual-income families (Segal, 1990: 38). Consequently, as Barbara Ehrenreich (1989: 218–220; see also 1983, 1984) argues, a new heterosexual masculinity on the part of certain progressive, middle-class men has emerged, consisting of choosing a mate who can "pull her own weight" economically and who is truly committed to sharing household labor equally.

Notwithstanding, this progressive "dual-career" relationship is not supplemented, in many cases, by a progressive sexual relationship. As Andrew Tolson (1977: 121) argued as early as 1977, for many progressive, middle-class men, sexual passion is "still acted out in familial terms of masculine 'conquest'—to which women could only 'respond.'" Although many progressive, middle-class men seriously seek "free women" who live for themselves and their careers (Ehrenreich, 1984), in bed they continue to demand submission and the affirmation of masculinity through heterosexual performance (Tolson, 1977: 121). That is, many progressive, middle-class men continue to adhere to the hegemonic masculine ideology that "entitles" them to sex with their wives whenever they want it. For example, Finkelhor and Yllö (1985: 62–70) discuss the case of Ross, a middle-class businessman who somewhat represents this progressive middle class, yet who frequently raped his wife. Ross describes below how one such rape occurred during an argument over sex that his wife was winning (p. 66):

> She was standing there in her nightie. The whole thing got me somewhat sexually stimulated, and I guess subconsciously I felt she was getting the better of me. It dawned on me to just throw her down and have at her . . . which I did. I must have reached out and grabbed at her breast. She slapped my hand away. So I said, "Lay down. You're going to get it." She replied, "Oh, no, you don't," so I grabbed her by the arms and she put up resistance for literally fifteen seconds and then just resigned herself to it. There were no blows or anything like that. It was weird. I felt very animalistic, and I felt very powerful. I had the best erection I'd had in years. It was very stimulating. . . . I walked around with a smile on my face for three days.

Ross believed his wife not only controlled the sexuality in their lives, but that she had "completely and totally emasculated" him (p. 68). The rape was both a way to overcome that loss of power in his life and a means to construct a specific type of patriarchal masculinity centering on heterosexual performance and the domination and control of women's sexuality.

Another businessman, Jack, stated to Finkelhor and Yllö (p. 72), "When she would not give it freely, I would take it." He felt that his wife did not have the right to deny sex, he had the right to sex when he pleased, and it was her duty to satisfy his sexual needs. Similarly, in Irene Frieze's (1983: 544, 553) study of wife rape, the vast majority of wife rapists engaged in this form of violence in order to prove their "manhood," believing "that their wives were obligated to service them sexually in whatever ways they desired."

Thus, in force-only rapes, the assaults are practices of masculine control based on expectations that sex is a right. Both battering and force-only rapists consciously choose such violent action to facilitate a patriarchal gender strategy and to protect what they view as their "essential" privileges. The resulting masculine construction is not only an exhibition of their "essential nature," but also illustrates the seductive quality of violence for displaying that "essential nature." For these men, masculine authority is quite simply expressed through the violent control of women.

Nevertheless, such personal choices become enigmatic when detached from social structures. In battering rapes, because the traditional division of labor and power is prevalent and the struggle is over authority and control of that division, these men construct a patriarchal form of masculinity that punishes and degrades the wife for deviating from her "essential" duties. In force-only rapes, however, the gender division of labor is not the issue: this is the classic, middle-class, dual-career family in which both partners participate in decision making and household tasks, and in which the husband accepts, in a general way, his wife's autonomous right to develop her own interests. However, the force-only rapist feels specifically wronged, cheated, and deprived in the sexual realm. Some progressive, middle-class men simply adhere to the hegemonic masculine ideology that entitles them to sex whenever they want it. Sex is considered a marriage right by which gender is accomplished through effective performance in the sexual realm. Like sexual harassment, a similar type of crime, wife rape can be a resource for accomplishing masculinity differently. And as the social setting within the nuclear family changes, so does the conceptualization of what is normative masculine behavior. Different social settings generate different masculinities, even when the particular resource (crime) is similar.

In sum, the structure of the gender division of labor and power and normative heterosexuality impinges on the construction of masculinity. These structural features both preclude and permit certain forms of crime as resources that men may use to pursue a gender strategy and construct their masculinity. Although both battering and force-only rapists try to control their wives, they do so in qualitatively different ways. The social relations extant within their respective gender divisions of labor and power are different, and different options exist for maintaining their control. The choices made by each type of rapist, and the resources available to carry out those choices, develop in response to the specific social circumstances in which they live. For these reasons, then, these men employ different forms of violence to construct different types of private masculinities.

This chapter has attempted to demonstrate that men produce specific configurations of behavior that can be seen by others within the same immediate social setting as "essentially male." These different masculinities emerge from practices that utilize different resources, and class and race relations structure the resources available to construct specific masculinities. Pimps, workers, executives, and patriarchs generate situationally accomplished, unique masculinities by drawing on different types of crime indigenous to their distinct positions within the structural divisions of labor and power. Because men experience their everyday world from a uniquely individualistic position in society, they construct the cultural ideals of hegemonic masculinity in different ways.

Social structures are framed through social action and, in turn, provide resources for constructing masculinity. As one such resource, specific types of crime ultimately are based on these social structures. Thus, social structures both enable and constrain social action and, therefore, masculinities and crime. In Chapter 6, we address the question of how the social construction of masculinities shapes the state and gender politics.

Notes

1 Prostitutes, or "wives-in-law," are constructing a femininity that both confirms and violates stereotypical "female" behavior. In addition to the conventional aspects of femininity just mentioned, prostitute femininity also ridicules conventional morality by advocating sex outside of marriage, sex for pleasure, anonymous sex, and sex that is not limited to reproduction and the domesticated couple. This construction of a specific type of femininity clearly challenges, in certain respects, stereotypical femininity. Nevertheless, the vast majority of prostitutes do not consider themselves feminists: they know very little about the feminist movement, do not share its assumptions, and believe men and women are "naturally" suited for different types of work (Miller, 1986: 160).

2 The masculinity constructed by African American pimps is fittingly comparable to the masculinity associated with men (usually from working-class backgrounds) who are members of white motorcycle gangs. The men in such groups act extremely racist and similarly exploit the sexuality and labor of "biker women." However, biker men do not display a "cool pose" with an accompanying show of luxury in the form of flashy clothing and exotic hairstyles. On the contrary, a biker usually has long unkempt hair, a "rough" beard, and his "colors" consist of black motorcycle boots, soiled jeans, and a simple sleeveless denim jacket with attached insignia (see Hopper and Moore, 1990 and Willis, 1978).

3 Horizontal segregation allocates men and women to different types of jobs; vertical segregation concentrates men and women in different occupations at different steps in an occupational hierarchy.

4 Approximately 45 percent of all men in the active labor force hold these types of proletarian jobs (Harris, 1992: 221). Moreover, although the proportion of African American men holding these jobs is almost twice as high as that of white men (Farley, 1989), because the research utilized here does not distinguish by race, my discussion concentrates solely on class and masculinity.

5 This is not to say that employee theft is insignificant at the managerial level; on the contrary, it is quite widespread (Beirne and Messerschmidt, 1991: 174–175).

6 Dock pilferage by longshoremen provides a good example of this type of theft. In dock work, cargo is winched from the ship onto the dock, stacked, and checked. A work group of twelve to twenty men "work a boat" with the group deciding who will have which responsibilities. Thus it allocates available jobs to its members (Mars, 1983: 101). Moreover, the group orchestrates employee theft. As Mars (p. 104) points out, to steal cargo, "holdsmen need the support of the winchman and signaller, while stowers need the support of the forklift truck drivers and acquiescence of the hatch-checker." Group members are judged as "men" by how well they work within the group and by how consistently, not to what extent, they steal goods.

7 This specific masculine meaning attached to group employee theft most likely explains women's lesser involvement in this type of occupational crime. Moreover, Box (1983: 181–182) adds that employment is not as criminogenic for women as it is for men because "the aggregation of male workers and their collectivist responses has a longer history and a greater impact" for men than women. The result is, as Kathleen Daly (1989: 772) points out, "that work place social bonds are stronger for men than for women, and thus occupational crime as a group activity is more likely for men."

8 Nevertheless, it should be pointed out that increasing numbers of men are attempting to counter sexism on the shop floor and, therefore, reconstruct shop-floor masculinity. For an excellent example see Gray, 1987.

9 Corporate crime is defined as "illegal and/or socially injurious acts of intent or indifference, that occur for the purpose of furthering the goals of a corporation, and that physically and/or economically abuse individuals in the U.S. and/or abroad" (Beirne and Messerschmidt, 1991: 184; see pp. 185–198 of this work for a wide range of examples).

10 It has been determined that 5.2 percent of executive, administrative, and managerial positions and 6.7 percent of professional positions are held by African Americans (Beirne and Messerschmidt, 1991: 566). As Anthony R. Harris (1991: 118) concludes after examining the relationship among class, race, and corporate crime: "the advantages of race exist *over and above* those of class. The opportunity to commit suite crime is still greater for a class-advantaged white than for a class-advantaged black."

11 The deregulation policies of the Reagan administration in the 1980s ushered in a new form of corporate crime, what Calavita and Pontell (1990: 321) call, "collective embezzlement," or "the siphoning off of funds from savings and loan institutions for personal gain at the expense of the institution itself *and with the implicit or explicit sanction of its management*." This type of corporate crime is quite different from manufacturing and industrial corporate crime. In the latter, corporate crime helps the corporation reach its goal of profit maximization and continued financial stability. Indeed, corporate executives have an individual and gendered interest in the continued survival of the corporation. In contrast, perpetrators of collective embezzlement in the savings and loan industry "have little to lose by their reckless behavior" and their "main concern is to get in and out of the 'house' with as much of the pot as possible" (p. 336). This crime against the corporation by those who run it clearly represents not only a new crime, but a new type of white corporate masculinity as well.

12 Kathleen Daly's (1989: 788) important study, "Gender and Varieties of White-Collar Crime," found that women's involvement in corporate crime was negligible, and this rare presence of women who are corporate criminals can be explained in the sense that women "may be more averse than men to abusing positions of organizational power, or they may be excluded from men's corporate crime groups, or perhaps both." The latter explanation is clearly the most plausible. Yet a woman who does engage in corporate crime is not simply doing masculinity. Although her very position is a protest against conventional femininity, she is still gender accountable and under pressure to show that she is an "essentially" feminine being, despite appearances to the contrary (West and Zimmerman, 1987: 140). In other avenues of everyday life, she most likely engages in stereotypical femininity. Thus, as with girls in street gangs who engage in violence, women who participate in corporate crime are constructing a specific type of femininity that consists of a combination of conventional and unorthodox gendered practices.

13 Indeed, office romances seem to be flourishing because women more routinely work beside men in professional and occupational jobs (Ehrenreich, 1989: 219).

14 This particular type of femininity has been explored by Pringle (1988).

15 Despite devastating criticisms of the Conflict Tactics Scale as a methodological tool (Dobash, Dobash, Wilson, and Daly, 1992), some researchers (remarkably) continue to use it to guide their work, concluding that women are about as violent as men in the home (Straus and Gelles, 1990), or even in some cases, that more men are victimized in the home than are women (McNeely and Mann, 1990).

16 Unfortunately, there is scant research on wife beating in racial-minority households. Nevertheless, what evidence there is on African American households suggests that when violence does occur, both husband and wife are likely to accept the traditional patriarchal division of labor and power as natural and that complete

responsibility for the battering, when questioned, "lies with white society" (Richie, 1985: 42; see also Asbury, 1987). Consequently, I am forced to concentrate solely on class and wife beating.

17 This is not to deny that many middle-class men engage in wife beating for the reasons discussed earlier in this section. What I suggest, following Segal (1990: 255) and others, is that it is clearly less common in middle-class households because such men have access to other resources, possibly more effective resources, through which they exert control over women without employing violence.

18 Because Finkelhor and Yllö (1985: 9) found no significantly higher rate of marital rape among African Americans than among whites, I do not distinguish by race.

References

Acker, Joan. (1990). "Hierarchies, Jobs, Bodies: A Theory of Gendered Organization." *Gender and Society* 4 (2): 139–58.

Altheide, David L., Patricia A. Adler, Peter Adler, and Duane A. Altheide. (1978). "The Social Meanings of Employee Theft." In *Crime at the Top*, ed. John Johnson and Jack Douglas, 90–124. New York: Lippincott.

Andersen, Margaret. (1988). *Thinking About Women*. New York: Macmillan.

Asbury, Jo-Ellen. (1987). "African American Women in Violent Relationships: An Exploration of Cultural Differences." In *Violence in the Black Family*, ed. Robert L. Hampton, 89–105. Lexington, MA: Lexington Books.

Beirne, Piers, and James W. Messerschmidt. (1991). *Criminology*. San Diego, CA: Harcourt Brace Jovanovich.

Berk, Sarah Fenstermaker. (1985). *The Gender Factory: The Apportionment of Work in American Households*. New York: Plenum Press.

Bernard, Jessie. (1982). *The Future of Marriage*. New Haven, CT: Yale University Press.

Bielby, William, and James N. Baron. (1986). "A Woman's Place Is with Other Women: Sex Segregation within Organizations." In *Sex Segregation in the Workplace: Trends, Explanations, Remedies*, ed. Barbara Reskin, 27–55. Washington, DC: National Academy Press.

Blau, Francine D., and Anne E. Winkler. (1989). "Women in the Labor Force: An Overview." In *Women: A Feminist Perspective*, ed. Jo Freeman, 265–86. Palo Alto, CA: Mayfield.

Box, Steven. (1983). *Power, Crime and Mystification*. New York: Tavistock.

Brown, Linda Keller. (1988). "Female Managers in the U.S. and in Europe." In *Women in Management Worldwide*, ed. Nancy J. Adler and Dafna N. Izraeli, 265–74. Armonk, NY: M.E. Sharpe.

Carothers, Suzanne C., and Peggy Crull. (1984). "Contrasting Sexual Harassment in Female- and Male-Dominated Occupations." In *My Troubles Are Going to Have Trouble with Me*, ed. Karen Brodkin Sacks and Dorothy Remy, 219–28. New Brunswick, NJ: Rutgers University Press.

Clatterbaugh, Kenneth. (1990). *Contemporary Perspectives on Masculinity*. Boulder: Westview Press.

Cockburn, Cynthia. (1985). *Machinery of Dominance: Women, Men and Technical Know-How*. London: Pluto Press.

Cockburn, Cynthia. (1983). *Brothers: Male Dominance and Technological Change*. London: Pluto Press.

Collinson, David L., and Margaret Collinson. (1989). "Sexuality in the Workplace: The Domination of Men's Sexuality." In *The Sexuality of Organization*, ed. Jeff Hearn, Deborah L. Sheppard, Peta Tancred-Sheriff, and Gibson Burrell, 91–109. Newbury Park, CA: Sage.

Connell, R. W. (1991). "Live Fast and Die Young: The Construction of Masculinity among Young Working-Class Men on the Margin of the Labour Market." *Australian and New Zealand Journal of Sociology* 27 (2): 141–71.
Connell, R. W. (1989). "Cool Guys, Swots and Wimps: The Interplay of Masculinity and Education." *Oxford Review of Education* 15 (3): 291–303.
Connell, R. W. (1987). *Gender and Power.* Stanford, CA: Stanford University Press.
Cullen, Francis, William J. Maakestad, and Gray Cavender. (1987). *Corporate Crime Under Attack.* Cincinnati: Anderson.
Daly, Kathleen. (1989). "Gender and Varieties of White Collar Crime." *Criminology* 27 (4): 769–93.
DeKeseredy, Walter, and Ronald Hinch. (1991). *Woman Abuse: Sociological Perspectives.* Lewiston, NY: Thompson Educational Pub., Inc.
DiTomaso, Nancy. (1989). "Sexuality in the Workplace: Discrimination and Harassment." In *The Sexuality of Organization*, eds. Jeff Hearn, Deborah L. Sheppard, Peta Tancred-Sheriff, and Gibson Burrell, 71–90. Newbury Park, CA: Sage.
Ditton, Jason. (1977). *Part-Time Crime.* New York: Macmillan.
Dobash, R. Emerson, and Russell P. Dobash. (1984). "The Nature and Antecedents of Violent Events." *British Journal of Criminology* 24 (3): 269–88.
Dobash, R. Emerson, and Russell P. Dobash. (1979). *Violence Against Wives.* New York: Free Press.
Dobash, Russell P., R. Emerson Dobash, Margo Wilson, and Martin Daly. (1992). "The Myth of Sexual Symmetry in Marital Violence." *Social Problems* 39 (1): 71–91.
Donaldson, Mike. (1987). "Labouring Men: Love, Sex and Strife." *Australian and New Zealand Journal of Sociology* 23 (2): 165–84.
Edleson, Jeffrey L., Zvi Eisikovits, and Edna Guttman. (1986). "Men Who Batter Women: A Critical Review of the Evidence." *Journal of Family Issues* 6 (2): 229–47.
Ehrenreich, Barbara. (1989). *Fear of Falling.* New York: Pantheon.
Ehrenreich, Barbara. (1984). "A Feminist's View of the New Man." *New York Times Magazine*, May 20, 1984: 36–48.
Ehrenreich, Barbara. (1983). *The Hearts of Men.* New York: Doubleday.
Farley, Reynolds. (1989). "Three Steps Forward and Two Back? Recent Changes in the Social and Economic Status of Blacks." In *Ethnicity and Race in the USA: Toward the Twenty-first Century*, ed. Richard D. Alba, 4–28. New York: Methuen.
Ferraro, Kathleen J. (1988). "An Existential Approach to Battering." In *Family Abuse and its Consequences*, ed. Gerald T. Hotaling, David Finkelhor, John T. Kirkpatrick, and Murray Straus, 126–38. Newbury Park, CA: Sage.
Finkelhor, David, and Kristi Yllö. (1985). *License to Rape: Sexual Abuse of Wives.* New York: Holt, Rinehart and Winston.
Frieze, Irene H. (1983). "Investigating the Causes and Consequences of Marital Rape." *Signs* 8 (3): 532–53.
Game, Ann, and Rosemary Pringle. (1984). *Gender at Work.* Boston: Allen and Unwin.
Gordon, Linda. (1988). *Heroes of Their Own Lives.* New York: Viking.
Gray, Stan. (1987). "Sharing the Shop Floor." In *Beyond Patriarchy*, ed. Michael Kaufman, 216–34. New York: Oxford University Press.
Gross, Edward. (1978). "Organizational Sources of Crime: A Theoretical Perspective." In *Studies in Symbolic Interaction*, ed. Norman K. Densin, 55–85. Greenwich, CT: JAI Press.
Gruber, James, and Lars Bjorn. (1982). "Blue Collar Blues: The Sexual Harassment of Women Autoworkers." *Work and Occupations* 9 (3): 271–98.
Harris, Ian. (1992). "Media Myths and the Reality of Men's Work." In *Men's Lives*, ed. Michael S. Kimmel and Michael A. Messner, 225–31. New York: Macmillan.

Harris, Richard N., and Roslyn Wallach Bologh. (1985). "The Dark Side of Love: Blue and White Collar Wife Abuse." *Victimology* 10 (1–4): 242–52.
Hartmann, Heidi. (1981). "The Unhappy Marriage of Marxism and Feminism: Towards a More Progressive Union." In *Women and Revolution*, ed. Lydia Sargent, 1–41. Boston: South End Press.
Hearn, Jeff. (1985). "Men's Sexuality at Work." In *The Sexuality of Men*, ed. Andy Metcalf and Martin Humphries, 110–28. London: Pluto Press.
Hearn, Jeff, and Wendy Parkin. (1987). *"Sex" at "Work"*. New York: St. Martin's Press.
Henry, Stuart. (1978). *The Hidden Economy*. London: Martin Robertson.
Hills, Stuart L. (1987). *Corporate Violence*. Totowa, NJ: Rowman and Littlefield.
Hochschild, Arlie. (1992). "The Second Shift: Employed Women are Putting in Another Day of Work at Home." In *Men's Lives*, ed. Michael S. Kimmel and Michael A. Messner, 511–15. New York: Macmillan.
Hochschild, Arlie. (1989). *The Second Shift*. New York: Viking.
Hopper, Columbus, and Johnny Moore. (1990). "Women in Outlaw Motorcycle Gangs." *Journal of Contemporary Ethnography* 18 (4): 363–87.
Kanter, Rosabeth Moss. (1977). *Men and Women of the Corporation*. New York: Basic Books.
Katz, Jack. (1988). *Seductions of Crime: Moral and Sensual Attractions in Doing Evil*. New York: Basic Books.
Komter, Aafke. (1989). "Hidden Power in Marriage." *Gender and Society* 3 (2): 187–216.
Lippert, John. (1977). "Sexuality as Consumption." In *For Men Against Sexism*, ed. Jon Snodgrass, 207–13. Albion, CA: Times Change Press.
MacKinnon, Catherine A. (1979). *Sexual Harassment of Working Women*. New Haven, CT: Yale University Press.
McMullan, John L. (1992). *Beyond the Limits of the Law: Corporate Crime and Law and Order*. Halifax: Fernwood Publishers.
McNeely, R. L., and CoraMae Richey Mann. (1990). "Domestic Violence Is a Human Issue." *Journal of Interpersonal Violence* 5 (1): 129–32.
Majors, Richard. (1986). "Cool Pose: The Proud Signature of Black Survival." *Changing Men* 17: 5–6.
Majors, Richard, and Janet Mancini Billson. (1992). *Cool Pose: The Dilemma's of Black Manhood in America*. New York: Macmillan.
Malcolm X. (1965). *The Autobiography of Malcolm X*. New York: Grove Press.
Mars, Gerald. (1983). *Cheats at Work*. Boston: Unwin.
Messerschmidt, James W. (1986). *Capitalism, Patriarchy and Crime: Toward a Socialist Feminist Criminology*. Totowa, NJ: Rowman and Littlefield.
Messner, Michael. (1989). "Masculinities and Athletic Careers." *Gender and Society* 3 (1): 71–88.
Miller, Eleanor. (1986). *Street Woman*. Philadelphia: Temple University Press.
Milner, Christina, and Richard Milner. (1972). *Black Players: The Secret World of Black Pimps*. Boston: Little, Brown.
Pagelow, Mildred D. (1984). *Family Violence*. New York: Praeger.
Pahl, Jan. (1992). "Money and Power in Marriage." In *Gender, Power and Sexuality*, ed. Pamela Abbott and Claire Wallace, 41–57. London: Macmillan.
Petchesky, Rosalind. (1984). *Abortion and Woman's Choice*. New York: Longman.
Powell, Gary N. (1988). *Women and Men in Management*. Newbury Park, CA: Sage.
Pringle, Rosemary. (1988). *Secretaries Talk: Sexuality, Power and Work*. New York: Verso.
Pringle, Rosemary. (1989). "Bureaucracy, Rationality and Sexuality: The Case of Secretaries." In *The Sexuality of Organization*, ed. Jeff Hearn, Deborah L. Sheppard, Peta Tancred-Sheriff, and Gibson Burell, 158–77. Newbury Park, CA: Sage.

Ptacek, James. (1988). "Why Do Men Batter Their Wives?" In *Feminist Perspectives on Wife Abuse*, ed. Kersti Yllö and Michele Bogard, 133–57. Newbury Park, CA: Sage.

Reskin, Barbara, and Patricia Roos. (1987). "Status Hierarchies and Sex Segregation." In *Ingredients for Women's Employment Policy*, ed. Christine Bose and Glenna Spitze, 3–21. Albany: State University of New York Press.

Richie, Beth. (1985). "Battered Black Women: A Challenge for the Black Community." *The Black Scholar* 16 (2): 40–44.

Romenesko, Kim, and Eleanor M. Miller. (1989). "The Second Step in Double Jeopardy: Appropriating the Labor of Female Street Hustlers." *Crime and Delinquency* 35 (1): 109–35.

Rosen, Ruth. (1982). *The Lost Sisterhood: Prostitution in America: 1900–1918*. Baltimore: John Hopkins University Press.

Russell, Diana E. H. (1982). *Rape in Marriage*. New York: Macmillan.

Schechter, Susan. (1982). *Women and Male Violence*. Boston: South End Press.

Schneider, Beth E. (1991). "Put up and Shut Up: Workplace Sexual Assaults." *Gender and Society* 5 (4): 533–48.

Segal, Lynne. (1990). *Slow Motion: Changing Masculinities, Changing Men*. New Brunswick, NJ: Rutgers University Press.

Slim, Iceberg. (1967). *Pimp: The Story of My Life*. Los Angeles: Holloway House.

Smith, Michael D. (1990). "Patriarchal Ideology and Wife Beating: A Test of a Feminist Hypothesis." *Violence and Victims* 5 (4): 257–73.

Smith, Michael D. (1990a). "Sociodemographic Risk Factors in Wife Abuse: Results from a Survey of Toronto Women." *Canadian Journal of Sociology* 15 (1): 39–58.

Sokoloff, Natalie J. (1980). *Between Money and Love*. New York: Praeger.

Stets, Jan E., and Murray A. Straus. (1989). "The Marriage License as a Hitting License: A Comparison of Assaults in Dating, Cohabitating and Married Couples." In *Violence in Dating Relationships*, ed. Maureen A. Pirog-Good and Jan E. Stets, 38–52. New York: Praeger.

Straus, Murray A., and Richard J. Gelles. (1990). "How Violent Are American Families? Estimates from the National Family Violence Survey and Other Studies." In *Physical Violence in American Families*, ed. Murray A. Straus and Richard J. Gelles, 95–112. New Brunswick, NJ: Transaction.

Straus, Murray A., Richard J. Gelles, and Susan Steinmetz. (1980). *Behind Closed Doors*. New York: Doubleday.

Tolson, Andrew. (1977). *The Limits of Masculinity*. New York: Harper and Row.

Vandivier, Kermit. (1987). "Why Should My Conscience Bother Me." In *Corporate Violence*, ed. Stuart L. Hills, 145–62. Totowa, NJ: Powman and Littlefield.

Walby, Sylvia. (1989). "Theorizing Patriarchy." *Sociology* 23 (2): 213–34.

Walby, Sylvia. (1986). *Patriarchy at Work: Patriarchal and Capitalist Relations in Employment*. Minneapolis: University of Minnesota Press.

Walker, Lenore E. (1979). *The Battered Woman*. New York: Harper and Row.

Walker, Lenore E. (1977–78). "Battered Women and Learned Helplessness." *Victimology* 2 (4): 525–34.

Wall Street Journal. (1990). "Doing the 'Right' Thing Has its Repercussions," B1.

West, Candace, and Don H. Zimmerman. (1987). "Doing Gender." *Gender and Society* 1 (2): 125–51.

Willis, Paul E. (1978). *Profane Culture*. London: Routledge & Kegan Paul.

Willis, Paul E. (1979). "Shop Floor Culture, Masculinity and the Wage Form." In *Working Class Culture*, ed. John Clarke, Chas Critcher, and Richard Johnson, 185–98. London: Hutchinson.

10

CULTURE, MASCULINITIES AND VIOLENCE AGAINST WOMEN

Joachim Kersten

Source: T. Jefferson and P. Carlen (eds), *Masculinities, Social Relations and Crime, Special Issue of the British Journal of Criminology*, 36:3 (1996), 381–95.

Abstract

The visibility of male-dominated criminal violence differs substantially from culture to culture. Accordingly, a perception of masculinity and male dominated violence as monolithic categories is misleading. Australian, German, and Japanese data display significant variations in the visibility of violence against women. In the light of this, standard gender neutral explanations of comparative criminology will be reviewed. In a conceptualization of 'hegemonic masculinity' in the context of sexual assault the visibility of the rapist in Australia is interpreted as a consequence of economic and cultural crises of gender relations causing a transformation of hegemonic masculinity. At present, historical and political constellations in Germany and Japan result in the visibility of different features of male dominated violence.

Theoretical considerations: crime, masculinities, and sexual assault

In recent social science research 'relational and, hence, fluid conceptions of masculinity' have been employed to examine '(re)presentations of gender' in the media, in film, and in television programmes (Saco 1992: 25). An interesting case in question is the analysis of an icon of American masculinity: Clint Eastwood (Smith 1994). Such studies start to deconstruct masculinities like Dirty Harry and his enemies in the streets and in the police force. The criminological mainstream, however, is still reluctant to ponder obvious traits of the gendered reality of crime, victimization, and crime control although, across cultures and (modern) times, lawbreaking is an activity related to 15–23 years old unmarried urban males (Braithwaite 1989; Renzetti and

Curran 1992; Gibbons 1993). Correspondingly, crime control is a domain of males, and as such crime and crime control constitute a 'state of play' between hegemonic masculinity and subordinated masculinities (Connell 1987; Messerschmidt 1993; Kersten 1993*a*, 1995*a*, *b*).

Criminology has a record of ignoring gender. When gender was raised in theorizing, the fact that women commit fewer crimes of a violent nature than men has resulted in binary and/or essentialist notions of male and female. The criminalization of females, although an area in definite need of research (Gibbons 1993), is in logical terms not exactly a good starting point for an analysis of male over-representation. Sex ratio variations in reported crime data across cultures or time are indicative of differential treatment against females (Gibbons 1992; historically informed, Feeley and Little 1991) and no suitable basis for a theory of masculinity and crime (Cain 1989, 1990).

In mainstream criminology and sociology, antisocial or criminal practices of masculinities are traditionally located in subcultural life worlds and neglected elsewhere. When, in the realm of male-dominated power and control such as management, politics, military, police, justice, law, medicine, and academia, crime became a subject, gender was rarely taken into consideration. 'Hyper-masculinity' and a vague notion of 'machismo' became synonyms for ethnic and lower-class masculinitises. In summary, criminology tends to employ masculinity as a taken for granted, essential category that needs no further deconstruction. As recent work demonstrates, masculinity is neither a monolithic entity (Gilmore 1990; Newburn and Stanko 1994; Polk 1994), nor part of the male 'sex role' (for a criticism of the 'role' paradigm in gender studies see Edwards 1983; Connell 1987, 1990, 1995; Saco 1992; Messerschmidt 1993). Masculinity as an abstract configuration of social orientations and practices, and masculinities as acting agents of power, domination, and the use of force have, without any doubt, ties to deviance *and* social control. This holds, particularly, in regard to violent crime *and* to violence as a result of 'protection' and punishment. In most cultures and historical times only very few of these connections between masculinity and violence can be grasped with one-dimensional assumptions about the 'annihilation of women' being 'the source of meaning and identity for men'/'all men are rapists' and the like. The 'violent heterosexual male' has served as the protagonist for substantial parts of theorizing (for a detailed critique see Messerschmidt 1993: 39–45), but to use Messerschmidt's metaphor, as the one and only *angstgestalt* he is as practical for research into variations of male-dominated crime across cultures and times as a bulldozer.

Consequently, a social science focus on gender and male over-representation means more than to 'simply . . . add another variable and stir—the variable itself needs to be studied and understood' (Menkel-Meadow and Diamond 1991: 223). The binary conceptualization of gender has led to flaws in the conceptualization of male-dominated interpersonal crime and also of female victimization. Messerschmidt (1993) conceives of specific forms of crime and violence, including robbery and sexual violence, as public representations of masculinity and as displays of particular hegemonic masculinity. Hence, constructs of masculinity are dependent on interactions in which control of the situation is paramount. In the case of street crime such control can be achieved by means of dehumanizing 'others' as victims of robbery, assault, and sexual assault. In these confrontations structural subordination of masculinities, mainly along the categories of class and race, can be momentarily reversed.

In historical studies, though without an explicit reference to gender, John Dower (1986) and Christopher Browning (1991) have described the mechanisms that lead 'ordinary men', not underclass males, into committing atrocious crimes. Masculinity then, becomes a key issue in the dehumanization of 'others', and in the actual commitment of murderous work and rape on a mass-scale level during the times of war and ethnic fighting.[1]

In more general terms, hegemonic masculinity is: '. . . a social ascendancy achieved in a play of social forces that extends beyond contests of brute power into the organization of private life and cultural processes'. In a connection to crime and violence ' "hegemony" does not refer to ascendancy based on force', but it is not irreconcilable with the use of violence (Connell 1987: 184).

In recent studies of cultural anthropology, concepts and practices of 'good' masculinity are associated with three areas of social action. These have been claimed as essential properties of 'maleness' and as such they constitute the core of hegemonic masculinity in patriarchal societies:

- 'procreation' as normative heterosexuality and as a domain of sexual domination over women;
- 'protection' as practices of physical control of men as enemies and women as property of men;
- and 'provision' of goods and food for families and communities which legitimate the exclusion of women from high status areas of paid work and decision making (Gilmore 1990; see also Badinter 1992 and Connell's 1995: 32f criticism of Gilmore's comparative study).

In a context of crime, such constructs of 'good' or 'real' masculinities are subject to both the self definition of deviant 'outlaw' masculinities and to the construction of the criminal offender, and (even more pronouncedly) to the image of the 'gang' as the collective 'other'. Constructs of 'evil' masculinities make up the control discourse of hegemonic masculinity, particularly in the media, and in the institutionalized practices of the criminal justice system. There, the gestalt of the offender figures as the antithesis of legitimate, male-dominated social action and as a threat to those practices of procreation (normative heterosexuality), protection (police/military/state), and provision (breadwinning) that produce and reproduce hegemonic masculinity in a given culture at a given time.[2] Although the crime control discourse focuses on the control of lower class males with whom a display of gender as particular hegemonic masculinity may serve as the last resort to status, the above functions relate to constructs of masculinity across the borderlines of class, race, and even age. The male fixation with procreation as normative heterosexuality, with domination through control over weaker persons, mostly women and children, forms the decisive nexus to practices of sexual assault. Such practices and their control may differ due to historical, cultural, and situational causes. However:

- perpetrators of hetero- and homosexual rape are nearly always male;
- across historical times and different cultures hetero- and homosexual rape has been identified as a domain where proof of masculinity and male domination are at stake;
- rape or seduction of females (as male properties) is a traditional origin of male feuds;
- sexual assault is situated at the borderline of state control of crime and gender policies;
- forcible rape of females occurs as a collective male practice at times of war and ethnic fighting, in police stations, or in criminal subcultures (e.g. bikers, organized crime). Collective practices of sexual abuse/assault perpetrated by white (also Japanese) males of upper- and middle-class origin can be seen in sex tourism.

These traits of sexual assault demonstrate that rape is a practice linked to specific frameworks of gender relations in which issues of hegemonic masculinity are transformed, or at stake. Rape has to do with male power but in more varied and complicated ways than the radical view has put it in early theorizing. Visibility of rape is highly selective and promotes a 'stranger-danger' perception of the crime (Kersten 1993*a*: 465f). Besides, the 'stranger-danger' rapist as an image of fear of crime is a preferred protagonist of popular culture coverage of crime. This portrayal of rape is resistant to changes in the known facts about rape. It has a powerful impact on law and order debates (Soothill 1991; Kersten 1994). Media coverage of rape is influenced by factors independent of the empirical reality of rape. The visibility of the 'stranger' as the perpetrator of rape in the media appertains to the cultural fascination/apprehension of the most fearful image of evil masculinity a society can muster in any given time and culture (Kersten 1993*a*: 466f). The following is the exploratory investigation of a proposition:

> The image of the rapist as a stranger, as a public enemy and as the antithesis of hegemonic masculinity is an artifact that corresponds to specific cultural crisis of gender relations due to changes

in the social and economical framework of male work, male dominated protection, and a change in gender relations of a given society.

Cross-cultural variation in the visibility of sexual assault

In this comparison the term 'visibility of sexual assault' appertains to official crime statistics, victim survey data, and media coverage of rape in three countries during the last years. Australia, Germany, and Japan as industrialized countries display substantial differences in the visibility of male-dominated assaultive crimes (see Kersten 1993*a*: 466ff; 1995*b*). Among other reasons, Australia has been selected for this comparison because of the country's high incidence of assault victimization. The situation has similarities to that of the US, but bears no link to racial discrimination or inner-city neighbourhood social disintegration.

The reported crime data demonstrate suggestive differences in all areas of violent crime, but they are most pronounced in the categories of serious assault and sexual assault. In other publications (Kersten 1991, 1993*a*, 1995*b*) the comparative data are presented in detail. In this paper a summary of the main characteristics of assault visibility in the three countries will have to suffice:

- At the end of the 1980s/early 1990s rates of reported sexual assault in the Australian states exceeded the Japanese rates of reported rape by a factor of more than 20. German rates were at about one third of the Australian rates (Dörmann in Kühne and Miyazawa 1991; Chappell 1993; Kersten 1993*a*).
- As much as a comparison of reported rates across nations is a fault-ridden (but routinely used) exercise in criminology, and does not allow for far-ranging conclusions, the long-term steady rise of the Australian rates from 5.3 reported incidents per 100,000 population in 1976/77 to more than 20 in 1991/92 is an indication of the visibility of rape in that country (National Committee 1991: 24). Rates in all areas of reported interpersonal crime have shown a substantial increase in the Australian jurisdictions, but the longitudinal growth of reported rape is steeper than that of robbery and serious assault (Mukherjee and Dagger 1992).
- In Germany the case load of reported rape has decreased by 30 per cent in the last decade. Since reunification, rates of rape have shown an increase (BKA 1994: 121). In Japan during the same time period rates of reported rape per 100,000 population have been reduced by 50 per cent. There, between 1960 and 1990 rates of reported rape have altogether decreased by 78 per cent (Dörmann in Kühne and Miyazawa 1991: 40; Research and Training Institute Ministry of Justice Japan 1993: 59; Kersten 1993*a*: 469). A decline of such size can hardly be explained by

> factors like 'shame culture' or 'inferiority of Japanese women'. As a result of rapid modernization, an active Japanese women's movement has, among other things, achieved a public debate about rape and *sekuhara* (sexual harassment). Why should there be a drop in the willingness to report violent crime victimization?

A substantially higher visibility of interpersonal crime in Australia is supported by the findings of recent international crime survey data (Japan Urban Security Research Institute 1990; Kühne and Miyazawa 1991; Chappell 1993). The most comprehensive survey included 16 industrialized countries. Again, serious doubts about the validity of the findings have been raised. Still, the German, Japanese, and Australian rates of sexual assault victimization data exhibit proportionate variations similar to those in the official statistics. The Australian sample displays a victimization rate in the category 'sexual attack, sexual molestation' of 7.3 per cent, the German 2.8 per cent, and the Japanese 1.4 per cent of respondents. Australia's victimization rate under the heading 'sexual incident' is the highest of all 16 participating nations.

During 1991, in the Australian press, rape and child abductions with a sexual background were much more visible than in German or Japanese papers. The influential Melbourne newspaper *The Age* had 209 reports and articles on sexual assault. These relate to cases in the state of Victoria (4 million population). Nearly ten reports were full-page features on topics of sexual abuse of children/incest, and date rape. About 50 per cent were longer than 50–100 words. During 1991, the Tokyo edition of *Asahi Shimbun* had 60 news items covering sexual assault in the Tokyo Metropolitan district (population: 14 million) and in other prefectures. Nearly all of these reports were short. In the same year *Süddeutsche Zeitung* (Munich) had 86 reports covering sexual assault, mainly cases in Munich and Bavaria (population: 11 million). This included more than ten reports about rape cases in other countries. Twenty-four articles exceeded the length of short news items.

In the late 1980s, visibility of violent attacks, among them a number of massacres where Australian amok shootists killed innocent bystanders, including many women and children, resulted in the inauguration of a National Committee on Violence.[3] During the second National Conference on Violence, the (then) director of the Australian Institute of Criminology summarized the findings of the committee's research groups:

> These . . . observations about the state of violence in the nation confirm . . . that Australia remains a society afflicted by intolerable levels of violence. Our society is also one which has long condoned this violence as a means of resolving disputes across a wide range of activities and setting.
>
> (Chappell 1993: 12)

While at first the debate about violence remained at a fairly general level of gender neutral 'interpersonal' crime, the prevalence of male-dominated violence against women and children shifted the focus to domestic violence, rape, and incest. In 1991 in Australia, concerns about stranger-rape were widespread and were reported to influence the everyday life behaviour of citizens (Westbury 1991: 82). Women were quoted to be afraid to use public transport or to use taxis after a series of rapes committed by taxi drivers, or to go out after dark or without male protection. A media campaign 'Violence is ugly', financed by the state government of Victoria addressed everyday life features of physical and sexual violence against women. In 1992 ABC aired a television documentary on sexual assault ('Without Consent') which caused an enormous riposte. This led to a conference of the Australian Institute of Criminology where further details of the size of the Australian rape problem were revealed[4] (Easteal 1993).

In a new edition of the first study of the history of women in Australia and the Australian women's movement (Summers 1994), the author names aspects of the culture of Australia[5] which support a notion of 'aggressive masculinism' as a cultural trait. Historical studies have seen this at the basis of Australian gender relations since the days of transportation (Saunders and Evans 1992: 101; Carmichael 1992: 107; Hughes 1987; Kersten 1995*b*).

In the light of these data, it seems appropriate to conclude that sexual assault of the type that is most likely to be reported to police or to victimization survey interviewers is much more visible in Australia than in Japan and Germany. Furthermore, despite increased awareness of rape victimization, feminist campaigns, refuge and rape crisis centre policies in all three countries, a significant increase in figures of reported rape is only visible in Australia while in the other countries under comparison rates have been stable or decreased substantially.

Overall, the percentage of Australian victims who report crimes to police is roughly the same as that of other nations (Walker 1990: 4). Given the results of recent self-report victimization data, less than 20 per cent of Australian rape victims reported the rapes they suffered. Rapes by strangers (43.5 per cent) and estranged husbands (29.2 per cent) were far more likely to be reported than those which had acquaintances and family members as perpetrators (Easteal 1993: 81). However, in official Australian data stranger-rapists figure as a minority (between 22 per cent and 40 per cent). Most reported rape crimes have perpetrators whom the victim did know before the rape occurred (Moran 1993: 45). It follows that in official data strangers are proportionally 'over-reported' and acquaintances are under-reported. It also follows that victimization in Australia occurs mostly during date, acquaintance, and intra-family rapes. In official and victimization data children and young persons constitute half of the victim population (ibid. 48; Easteal 1993: 76) with family members as the most likely offenders of sexual assault against children under age 11.

Variations in the visibility of sexual assault: examples of gender-neutral explanations

In other work the 'routine' theories of comparative criminology have been criticized for their lack of capacity when it comes to the low crime rates in Japan (Hamilton and Sanders 1992; Braithwaite 1989; Kersten 1993*b*). For lack of space these arguments have to be summarized. With respect to Japan's internationally accredited low crime rates, in Western writing most credit goes to the effectiveness of formal crime control, i.e. policing (Bayley 1976). Japanese criminologists have raised some serious arguments against such claims by pointing out that Japanese police given their number and powers are less efficient than their American or European counterparts (Araki 1988; S. Miyazawa, 1992). Other Western studies emphasize the efficiency of informal control or a unique cultural propensity towards 'shaming' which would make crime prevention in Japan such a successful collective effort (Braithwaite 1989; see Kersten 1993*b*). They generally refer to Ruth Benedict's work (1946) about Japanese shame culture,[6] without providing further evidence to substantiate the link between the 'national character' and fewer crimes. Other authors point at the alleged co-operation between the Japanese police force and organized crime, *Yakuza* (night-time policing), and the alleged fact that at times the police turn a blind eye to underworld crime are seen as explanations for the low crime rates in Japan (van Wolferen 1989: 103).

However, in the realm of crimes with masculinity as a primary or background motivation, to a substantial degree gangsters themselves are seen to commit the crimes in question. Large proportions of the homicide rate and the rates of sexual assault and serious assault are attributed to *yakuza* members (Hoshino 1988: 35; Tamura 1992; Kersten 1993*a*). Rapes and murders of foreign sex workers appertain to 'control' practices in the underworld dominated sex industry, and are not the acts of outsiders.

Japan and Germany are generally perceived as countries with an enduring historical and political tradition of authoritarianism, i.e. a strong shared belief in authority, discipline, and order. If such assumptions would result in a higher willingness to report rape, assaults ought to be reported at a higher rate in these countries than in Australia. The German and the Japanese penal codes share a common heritage to the extent that the German 'Strafgesetzbuch' was imported into Japanese law after the Meiji modernization. Both penal laws are characterized by a high degree of codification and inquisitorial procedures. Furthermore, police numbers (in proportion to the population) are higher in Japan and Germany than in the Australian states. Police powers of investigation in Japan and Germany greatly exceed those of their Australian counterparts, while in Australia (and in Germany) defence lawyers certainly have more rights than in Japan. Police/rape victim relations are problematic in all three societies, and cannot be the single reason for a lower willingness to report rape to the authorities in Japan and Germany. Germany and Japan have compulsory registration laws which—in both countries—are even more strictly policed for foreign residents. This makes it fairly easy for police to locate citizens when criminal investigations are carried out against suspects. Japan has an additional family register which increases the number of available strategies for surveillance and identification. Germany and Japan have compulsory ID card systems. In contrast, Australian states have no address registration system for their citizenry. Australian residents have no ID cards; they need a passport only if they intend to travel to overseas countries. Before the statutes were changed only a few years ago, police in Victoria had no right to take fingerprints[7] or forensic samples, if suspects did not consent.

In spite of the lower rate of police presence and with limited powers of investigation, Australian police 'clear' between 70 and 80 per cent of sexual assault, i.e. equivalent proportions of the crime are cleared in all three countries. It follows that different structural determinants of formal control in the countries under comparison are not a satisfactory explanatory device for the variations in rape visibility.

Similarly, on a routine basis variations in population density, urbanization, and climate are pointed at to explain differences in crime visibility. The urbanization of Australia, supposedly one of the highest of all industrialized countries, is routinely used as an explanation for high rates of victimization (Walker 1990: 5; Chappell 1993).[8] Compared to cities in Japan and Germany, most of the suburbs of Australian cities display a parkland scenario. Urbanized areas of Japan (e.g. Kanto or Kyoto-Osaka) or urban conglomerates in Germany (Main or Ruhrgebiet) are definitely more crowded than any of Australia's cities. Another approach sees climate (i.e. the geographical latitude of countries) as the main variable predicting the occurrence of victimization: Australians would spend less time indoors than people elsewhere (Walker 1990). However, most reported and unreported sexual assaults in Australia occur in the homes of victims or perpetrators. With most of its densely populated region having extremely hot and humid temperatures in the summer months, Japan's crime rates should at least exceed those of Germany.

Cultural coherency/'racial harmony' assumptions tend to link rising rates of violent crime with the growing number of foreign residents in each country. Given the characteristics of rape reporting, one can assume that non-nationals are over-represented in the statistics of reported sexual assault. However, in all three countries, rape is a domain of home grown, male-dominated crime. Despite an increase in crime in Australia, with regard to crimes committed by non-Australians, it has been established quite clearly that the crime rates in these sectors of the population are generally lower than those of the Australian-born population (Hazlehurst 1987). In conclusion, it seems that none of the standard macro-explanations of comparative criminology sits very comfortably with the differences in the visibility of sexual assault victimization that can be observed in the three countries.

Variations in the visibility of sexual assault: explanations that include gender

In all three societies hegemonic masculinity is established as a hierarchy of genders, classes, and majority/minority relations; as a gender and race specific division of labour in public and private spheres; as a domination of women by men, and younger men by older men; of workers by men with status and access to power; of males, females, and children with minority status by mainstream culture, by the state and its institutions. While in all countries under comparison majority and minority women can be the subjects of sexist discrimination, both cultural majority men and women in Japan, Germany, and Australia draw substantial advantage from practices of social and racial discrimination against minority men and women.

Standard assumptions of Western sociology about the link between reported rape (as visible sexual assault) and notions of gender 'equality', ubiquity of pornography, etc. do not fit well with the variation of visibility discussed in this research. Consider findings by Baron and Straus (1990) about the impact of such factors as 'gender inequality', 'pornographic readership', 'cultural spillover', and 'social disorganization' on cross-national rape rates in the US. This comparison of cross-cultural rates of rape, although based on much more heterogeneous sets of data than the US study, comes to different conclusions. Gender equality measured in terms of job equality resulted in lower rates of rape victimization in Baron and Straus's work; the opposite is the case here: job equality (in the mechanical definition of Baron and Straus) is lowest in Japan and highest in Australia. Pornographic readership was positively linked to rape in the US; in Japan the low visibility of rape corresponds with widespread fictitious accounts of blatant sexism and pornography including rape (e.g. in *manga*), with very high distribution. Japan has a tradition of erotic illustrations (perceived as pornography in the West) and public displays of oversized genitalia during religious festivities (Bornoff 1991; Shimada 1994). Moral censorship and a Victorian tradition of prudishness is most commonplace in Australia (Dysart 1992: 52f), where rape is extremely apparent. To untangle the variation in the visibility of rape as a powerful symbol of male domination/normative heterosexuality, socio-economic and cultural factors in gender relations and in the 'state of play' between hegemonic and subordinated masculinities need to be considered. None of these issues bears any significance in the rape research by Baron and Straus.

Low rape visibility in Japan

Unsubstantiated claims about the ubiquity of rape and rapists in Japan need to be taken with care. Indeed, the most explicit critics agree that Japan's streets are safer for women than those in Western countries (Horsley and

Buckley 1991: 236; Taylor 1983: 193; Condon 1991: 83; van Wolferen 1989: 194). Instead of fear of crime, these authors claim, there is a more pronounced feeling of being safe from attacks of assaulters. This may be the case for attacks originating from non-acquaintances, but is it also valid for rape and incest in the context of intimate relationships like the family, and for date rape? The official data display a significant over-representation of 'strangers': of 1,335 reported rapes (1991) only 11 had family members and 288 acquaintances as perpetrators. All other offenders were listed as strangers. Although it seems safe to conclude that acquaintance rape is dramatically under-reported, a number of factors may lead to a lower incidence of date rape and sexual assault in the family or against intimate partners. In contrast to the record of Japanese soldiers in China, Korea, and other occupied countries during the war (Buruma 1993; Dower 1986), a tradition of non-confrontational behaviour within the boundaries of the culture and within the individual's reference group is certainly a factor that contributes to a lower degree of visible physical assault in public. In spite of remarkable drinking customs among *salariimen*, public fights are rare. This may also result in fewer violent assaults on females in public. The architecture of Japanese cities and suburbs (although changing to a less favourable design—Miyazawa 1990: 229f), and the organizational set up of school, workplace, and family life seems less conducive to both forms of sexual violence, to assault in 'the dark alley', and to the indoor variety of sexual attacks that spread fear in many Western societies. It is commonplace knowledge in the West that school and work schedules for the Japanese population are demanding. Additionally, the group relatedness of most male and female social activity in educational institutions, at work and in the (scarce) leisure periods serves as a safeguard against attacks. First dates often involve pairs of young males and females. Because of the lack of privacy in the home, or the availability of other spaces, dating (and even married) couples use 'love hotels' for more intimate exchanges. Generally, seduction, which by definition borders on force, plays a less pronounced role in Japan. This may result in lower rates of date rape.

The contractual bases of the majority of marriages involve their own family and the in-laws as a control agency for assaultive behaviour. Neighbourhood control and other forms of surveillance (e.g. in parks) are more intense than in the West. The co-sleeping patterns (Lebra 1976: 140) may protect married women from unwanted sexual pursuits by a husband during the few hours he is at home at night. As the popular saying goes, the most important fact about husbands is their health and that they are *not* at home. *Salariiman* fathers tend to have only guest status in the family. Unemployment is low, and alcohol is normally consumed with workmates in pubs, not at home where there is rarely enough space to have parties. All this may protect family members from attacks which figure exceptionally high in Australian rape statistics.

Consider the different understanding of sexuality in the Japanese culture. There, sexual practices are not so much located in paradigms of love, romance, exclusive intimacy, and normative heterosexuality[9] but rather in a paradigm of health. Sexuality is conceived of as a bodily function, and there are rules for communication about sexual desires, e.g. when a room in a 'love hotel' is required. The status of Japanese women as the head of the family in all decisive areas of family finances (husbands have to hand their salaries to their wives) leads to a situation of economic autonomy which does not exist in Western countries. Such phenomena of women's financial independence and domination in everyday life affairs are rarely acknowledged when the construct of the 'miserable' and oppressed Japanese woman has to serve as the 'other' of the 'liberated' Western model of femininity (for an informed debate see Cherry 1987). In contrast, domestic violence and rape of intimates have obvious links to the economic dependency that marks the situation of most victimized (and non-victimized) women in Western countries.

Messerschmidt's (1993) conceptualization of 'tough' masculinity as a public situational display and reflection of male gender, in the context of male-dominated violence, often in connection with otherwise low status and lack of resources, fits the image of members of *yakuza* underworld groupings (Buruma 1984; Gilmore 1990; Kersten 1993*b*) but not that of the average salaried member of the work force. In the life worlds of *salariimen* public displays of toughness, independence, and potency as indicators of masculinity defined as social and physical achievement are rather frowned upon. The group of males in the workplace and in the pub after work exhibits patterns of 'maternal' values: understanding, an emphasis on caring for others and on reliability, displays of emotions etc. *Karoshi*, i.e. 'death from working too much' is not so much a consequence of 'hyper competitive' orientations but rather a result of 'hyper devotion' to the firm or the boss. The Japanese cultural mainstream concept of masculinity is, in a way, another transformation of the *samurai* ethos. This makes it entirely different from the masculine 'bushman and digger' ethos of Australian nationalism. Japanese constructs of masculinity are much less homophobic and 'machismo' focused than the masculinities of frontier societies like Australia or the US, and their perpetual emphasis on 'real' manhood (for examples of frontier and gun lobby masculinities in these countries see Connell 1995). Despite their aggressive business tactics in the West, in Japan's *salariiman* culture, group acceptance and membership in successful groups are ranked much higher than a display of the individually successful tough guy (Kersten 1994*b*). If rape is correlated to feelings of power and domination over weaker objects (female or male), such individual or group orientations are more pronounced in cultures where male power in traditional domains of protection and provision are dwindling. In that regard, present day corporate Japanese members of the dominant *salariiman* culture invest much less in displays and proofs of such specific masculinity than their Australian counterparts. Japan's hegemonic status in business and finance, and the fact that provision in Japan is male-controlled, may produce less demand for displays of masculinity that subdue weaker subjects by sexually assaulting them. Japanese men are clients of the 'water trade' with its 'ejaculation' branch (prostitution). They purchase emotional and/or sexual services by women to boost their masculinity on a mass scale. The 'water trade' exploits women from Asian and other poor countries. Bornoff calls sex tourism the 'rape your neighbour' version of Japanese men's sexuality. All this may result in a lower visibility of certain rapes, namely the ones that are most likely to be reported in Australia and elsewhere in the West in Japan herself.

As the recent 'comfort women' affair (forced prostitution of women in occupied territories) and the 'sekuhara' (sexual harassment) debate have demonstrated, suspicions about official and private strategies of denial of shameful aspects of Japanese past and present are quite appropriate. It may well be that sexual assault is seriously under-reported in Japan, but there is, at the same time, clear evidence that the visibility of certain types of rape as a public threat to women play no significant role in contemporary Japan. The opposite is true for Australia.

High rape visibility in Australia

The extreme visibility of Australia's 'uncontrollable and dangerous' men has to be deciphered against a background of a deep social, cultural, and economic crisis on the fifth continent which has repercussions for gender relations. The seemingly self-evident construct of an Australian 'national masculinity' with an emphasis on physical prowess and independence[10] is crumbling (Kersten 1993*a*, 1995*b*). The loss of masculine identity through the loss of traditional functions that provide legitimacy for male cultural domination produces dire needs, especially on the part of marginalized men. Among them self-hate and a need to compensate for the loss of legitimate avenues to a male status are related to crime rates. A practice that proves the remnants of strength in the male person when a weaker and despised object (female, childish, homosexual, of other ethnic or racial origin) is dehumanized and victimized can be interpreted as one of the outcomes of masculinities under pressure (Messerschmidt 1993). The rape in the dark alley (and not the one in the victim's house or car) figures as the 'other' of hegemonic masculinity on the fifth continent, and as such it becomes the focus of widespread fear and apprehension. With physical and sexual assaults as a fact of daily life, the protection of females and children can compensate for the loss in other realms of hegemonic masculinity. In Japanese culture, the physical man *as an individual* was never a model of masculinity. This relates to (rural) traditions of collective work shared by men and women, young and old. In contrast to the individual image of the boss as a 'real man' in Australia and Germany, the 'mothering' aspects of Japanese work masculinity require much less physical masculine presence. Germany and Japan no longer have large-scale farming. Farmers are part of a historical tradition of agriculture where the primary groups of the family and the village community have traditionally been more important than the physical strength of the individual farm worker. Farming, a heavily subsidized enterprise in both Germany and Japan, is not seen in masculine terms, nor is both countries' postwar advancement in high-tech electronics or automobile production in the secondary sector conceived as 'masculine'. Accordingly, there is less need to legitimize physical masculinity in both other countries. Again, in Australia the visibility of assault with force may serve the purpose of demonstrating the need for 'good' physical men who are otherwise useless in a society increasingly dependent upon the tertiary sector and tourism.

Crime and masculinities in a cross-cultural perspective

This collection of evidence for cultural and economical determinants in the construction of culture-specific gender relations and masculinities has tried to find causes for the lower visibility of sexual assaultive behaviour in Japan. The argument is of a speculative nature and needs further theoretical scrutiny and empirical testing. Whatever the flaws of this approach, it looks at gender, economic, social, and cultural factors as the basis of variations in the visibility of certain male-dominated violence. Almost all gender-neutral routine theorizing of the criminological 'malestream' is hopeless when it comes to such variations of phenomena as rape, assault, and the like (Gibbons 1993). As far as this blind spot of criminology is concerned, an exploratory gender theory approach is a more promising track than the continuation of gender-blind 'business as usual'.

In other work by the author the visibility of Germany's skinheads (Kersten 1994*c*) and Japanese gangsterism (Kersten 1993*b*) are interpreted as indications of a different type of crisis related to each culture's problems in politics, the work sector, and other domains of masculinity. These appertain to both nations' postwar and, particularly, Germany's post-reunification record of *verdrängung* of the responsibility of each country's military and 'elders' as hegemonic masculinity, not just the *Führer* and the *Tenno*, for the atrocities during the war and during the occupation of neighbouring countries. In such analyses, the description of the variations 'in the . . . forms of race, class and sexual orientation . . .' (Menkel-Meadow and Diamond 1991: 225) leads to insights into the cultural and historical construction of masculinities. As far as violence and masculinities are concerned, the study of variations is more promising than the continued use of a monolithic understanding of masculinity in the tradition of binary concepts of 'male' and 'female'.

Notes

1 Ex-Yugoslavia provides terrible support for Dower's and Browning's theorizing.

2 Although this discussion is concerned primarily with masculinities, it is appropriate to note that historical analyses have identified images of 'evil women' as the basis of penal practices against 'witches'. Such constructs are equally linked to the domains of hegemonic masculinity. Witches and their powers were seen as the cause of impotence in husbands (procreation); or were held responsible for the poisoning or mothers and infants (protection); or as causing the failure of mothers to breastfeed their children (provision); or as being responsible for bad harvests or weather.

3 In the late 1980s in Germany a similar committee on violence ('Gewaltkommission') started work after the killing of a police officer by violent demonstrators. Sexual assault played no significant part in the report.

4 Although comparative survey data are not available, it is questionable whether the findings of an Australian survey on women's perception of men as rapists would find a similar response in Japan or Germany In the Australian data more than two thirds of female respondents (n=5,303) agree (35 per cent 'strongly') to the statement 'All kinds of men, many of them normal and respectable in other ways, are rapists' (Easteal 1993: 23).

5 '. . . when most Australian men say to a girl they have just met at a party "Do you want a ride home?" or if they ring her and say "Do you want to go to a drive-in?" what they generally mean is "Do you want a fuck?", and any girl who takes the invitation at face value is likely to find herself landed on a lonely road and forced to walk home or else spend the evening fighting off a genuinely amazed male who refuses to believe that she did not realize the contract she had entered into' (Summers 1994: 253).

6 For a critical discussion of Benedict and Japanese "shame culture' cf. Geertz (1988: 115–26). In a thorough study of Germany's and Japan's postwar strategies of denial and acceptance of responsibility for the atrocities of World War II, Ian Buruma (1993) firmly rejects Benedict's notion of a unique Japanese shame culture as a 'mechanical' concept, and in his book on the Western perception of Japan Shimada (1994) comes to similar conclusions.

7 In contrast, expatriates who reside in Japan or citizens or Korean descent who live in Japan in the third generation were (at the time of writing) still being fingerprinted as a matter of routine.

8 Australian criminologists, although discussing the very same survey data, use a definition of urbanization which appears to be in complete contradiction to that underlying the international victims' survey ranking. There Australia ranks at the bottom of the scale (JUSRI 1990: 101).

9 To the author's best knowledge attacks on homosexuals are not known in Japan. Buruma's (1984) work indicates a wider variety of gender displays in Japan, and a cultural acceptance of intermediate forms, e.g. *onnagata* actors in *kabuki*.

10 A construct constantly celebrated in the ANZAC legend and in "true blue' Australianness in the advertising, for example for such heterogeneous commodities as Victorian beer, federal financial institutions, and (ironically) Australian-made Toyota automobiles.

References

Araki, N. (1988), 'The Role of Police in Japanese Society', *Law and Society Review*, 22/5: 1033–6.

BADINTER, E. (1992), *XY: De l'Identité Masculine*. Paris: Odile Jacob.

BARON, L., and STRAUS, M. (1990), *Four Theories of Rape in American Society*. New Haven: Yale University Press.

BAYLEY, D. H. (1976), *Forces of Order—Police Behavior in Japan and the United States*. Berkeley: University of California Press.

BENEDICT, R. (1946), *The Chrysanthemum and the Sword*. Tokyo: Charles E. Tuttle.

BORNOFF (1991), *Pink Samurai—The Pursuit and Politics of Sex in Japan*. London: Grafton.

BRAITHWAITE, J. (1989), *Crime, Shame and Reintegration*. Cambridge: Cambridge University Press.

BROWNING, C. (1991), *Ordinary Men—Reserve Police Battalion 101 and the Final Solution in Poland*. New York: Harper Collins.

BUNDESKRIMINALAMT (1994), *Polizeiliche Kriminalstatistik*. Wiesbaden: BKA.

BURUMA, I. (1984), *A Japanese Mirror*. London: Jonathan Cape.

—— (1994), *The Wages of Guilt. Memories of War in Germany and Japan*. New York: Farrar Straus Giroux.

CAIN, M. (1989), *Growing up Good—Policing the Behaviour of Girls in Europe*. London: Sage.

—— (1990), 'Towards Transgression: New Directions in Feminist Criminology', *International Journal of the Sociology of Law*, 18: 1–12.

CARMICHAEL, G. (1992), 'So Many Children. Colonial and Post-Colonial Demographic Patterns', in K. Saunders and R. Evans, eds., *Gender Relations in Australia. Domination and Negotiation*, 103–43. Marricksville: Harcourt Brace Jovanovich.

CHAPPELL, D. (1993), 'How Violent is Australian Society?' Address given at the Second National Conference on Violence, Canberra 15 June.

CHERRY, K. (1987), *Womansword. What Japanese Words say about Women*. Tokyo: Kodansha.

CONDON, J. (1991), *A Half Step Behind—Japanese Women Today*, newly expanded edn. Tokyo: Charles E. Tuttle.

CONNELL, R. W. (1987), *Gender and Power*. Sydney: George Allen and Unwin.

—— (1990), 'The State, Gender, and Sexual Polities', *Theory and Society*, 19/5: 507–44.

—— (1994), 'The Making and Remaking of Masculinities in Contemporary Societies', paper presented at the Conference: 'Reproduktion und Wandel von Männlichkeit', Munich, 27–8 September.

—— (1995), *Masculinities*. Cambridge: Polity Press.

CRAIG, S. (1992), *Men, Masculinity, and the Media*. Newbury Park: Sage.

DOWER, J. (1986), *War without Mercy—Race and Power in the Pacific War*. New York: Pantheon.

DYSART, D. (1992), 'Eroticism and Sexual Imagery in Australian Art', *Art and Australia*, 30/1: 50–3.

EASTEAL, P., ed. (1993), *Without Consent: Confronting Adult Sexual Violence*. Canberra: Australian Institute of Criminology.

EDWARDS, A. (1983), 'Sex Roles: A Problem for Sociology and for Women', *Australian and New Zealand Journal of Sociology*, 19: 385–412.

FEELEY, M., and LITTLE, D. (1991), 'The Vanishing Female: The Decline of Women in the Criminal Process, 1687–1912', *Law and Society Review*, 25/4: 719–57.

GEERTZ, C. (1986), *Works and Lives*. Cambridge: Polity Press.

GIBBONS, D. (1992), 'Talking about Crime: Observations on the Prospects for Causal Theory in Criminology', *Criminal Justice Research Bulletin*, 7/6: 1–10.

—— (1993), *Talking about Crime and Criminals*. Englewood Cliffs, NJ: Prentice Hall.

GILMORE, D. (1990), *Manhood in the Making—Cultural Concepts of Masculinity*. London: Yale University Press.

HAMILTON, V., and SANDERS, J. (1992), *Everyday Justice—Responsibility and the Individual in Japan and the United States*. New Haven/London: Yale University Press.

HAZLEHURST, K., ed. (1987), *Migration, Ethnicity and Crime in Australia*. Canberra: Australian Institute of Criminology.

HORSLEY, W., and BUCKLEY, R. (1991), *Nippon—New Superpower*. London: BBC Books.

HOSHINO, K. (1988), 'Organized Crime and its Origins in Japan', paper presented to the 40th Annual Meeting of the American Society of Criminology, Chicago.

HUGHES, R. (1987), *The Fatal Shore. A History of the Transportation of Convicts to Australia 1787–1868*. London: Pan Books.

JAPAN URBAN SECURITY RESEARCH INSTITUTE (1990), *International Forum on Crime Prevention '90*, Conference proceedings. Tokyo: JUSRI.

KERSTEN J. (1991), 'Kriminalität, Kriminalitätsangst und Männlichkeitskultur', *Kriminalsoziologische Bibliografie*, 18/4: 41–64.

—— (1992) 'Beschämung, Verantwortung, Kontrolle? Japan als Referenzpunkt kulturvergleichender Forschung zur Kriminalitätskontrolle', *Monatsschrift für Kriminologie und Strafrechtsreform*, 75/6: 342–57.

—— (1993*a*), 'Crime and Masculinities in Australia, Germany and Japan', *International Sociology*, 8/4: 461–78.

—— (1993*b*), 'Street Youths, *Bosozoku*, and *Yakuza*: Subculture Formation and Societal Reactions in Japan', *Crime and Delinquency*, 39/3: 277–95.

—— (1994*a*), 'Die Neue Unerbittlichkeit—Law and Order und gesellschaftliche Vergeltungsbedürfnisse' in H.-M. Lohmann, ed., *Extremismus der Mitte—Vom rechten Verständnis der Deutschen Nation*, 233–46. Frankfurt: Fischer Taschenbuch.

—— (1994*b*), 'Karoshi—Vom anderen Leben und Sterben in Japan', *Psychologic Heute*, 58–63.

—— (1994*c*), 'Feindbildkonstruktionen und Gewalthandlungen bei Gruppierungen junger Männer' in W. Bergmann and R. Erb, eds., *Neonazismus und Rechte Subkultur*, 125–42. Berlin: Metropol.

—— (1995*a*), 'Junge Männer und Gewalt', *Neue Kriminalpolitik*, 7/1: 22–7.

—— (1995*b*), *Kriminalität, Männlichkeiten und Kultur*. Berlin/New York: Walter de Gruyter (forthcoming).

KÜHNE, H., and MIYAZAWA, K. (1991), *Kriminalität und Kriminalitätsbekämpfung in Japan*. Wiesbaden: Bundeskriminalamt.

LEBRA, T. S. (1976), *Japanese Patterns of Behaviour*. Honolulu: The University Press of Hawaii.

—— (1984) *Japanese Women—Constraint and Fulfillment*. Honolulu: The University Press of Hawaii.

MENKEL-MEADOW, C., and DIAMOND, S. (1991), 'The Content, Method, and Epistomology of Gender in Sociolegal Studies', *Law and Society Review*, 25/2: 221–38.

MESSERSCHMIDT, J. (1993), *Masculinities and Crime*. Lanham, MD: Rowman and Littlefield.

MIYAZAWA, K. (1990), 'The Changing Situation of Crime and Crime Prevention Measures', *International Forum on Crime Prevention*, Conference proceedings, 228–231. Tokyo: JUSRI.

MIYAZAWA, S. (1992), *Policing in Japan—A Study on Making Crime*. Albany: State University of New York Press.

MORAN, A. (1993), 'Patterns of Rape: A Preliminary Queensland Study', in P. Easteal, ed. *Without Consent: Confronting Adult Sexual Violence*, 35–54. Canberra: Australian Institute of Criminology.

MUKHERJEE, S., and DAGGER, K. (1992), *The Size of the Crime Problem in Australia*. Canberra: Australian Institute of Criminology.

NATIONAL COMMITTEE ON VIOLENCE (1990), *Violence: Directions for Australia*. Canberra: Australian Institute of Criminology.

NEWBURN, T., and STANKO, E., eds. (1994), *Just Boys doing Business? Men, Masculinities and Crime*. London/New York: Routledge and Kegan Paul.

POLK, K. (1994), *When Men Kill—Scenarios of Masculine Violence*. Cambridge, UK/ New York/Melbourne: Cambridge University Press.

RENZETTI, C., and CURRAN, D. (1992), *Women, Men, and Society*. Boston: Allyn and Bacon.

RESEARCH AND TRAINING INSTITUTE MINISTRY OF JUSTICE JAPAN (1993) *White Paper on Crime 1992*. Tokyo: RTIMJJ.

SACO, D. (1992), 'Masculinity as Signs: Poststructuralist Feminist Approaches to the Study of Gender' in S. Craig, ed., *Men, Masculinity, and the Media*, 23–40. Newbury Park: Sage.

SAUNDERS, K., and EVANS, R., eds. (1992), *Gender Relations in Australia. Domination and Negotiation*. Marricksville: Harcourt Brace Jovanovich.

SHIMADA, S. (1994), *Grenzgänge—Fremdgänge. Japan und Europa im Kulturvergleich*. Frankfurt/New York: Campus.

SMITH, P. (1993), *Clint Eastwood. A Cultural Production*. London: UCL Press.

SOOTHILL, K. (1991), 'The Changing Face of Rape?', *British Journal of Criminology*, 31/4: 383–92.

SUMMERS A. (1994) *Damned Whores and God's Police. The Colonization of Women in Australia*, updated edn. Ringwood: Penguin:

TAMURA, M. (1992), 'The Yakuza and Amphetamine Abuse in Japan', in H. Traver and M. Gaylord, eds., *Drugs, Law and the State*, 99–118. Hongkong: Hongkong University Press.

TAYLOR, J. (1983), *Shadows of the Rising Sun: A Critical View of the 'Japanese Miracle'*. New York: William Morrow.

VAN WOLFEREN, K. (1989), *The Enigma of Japanese Power*. London: Macmillan.

WALKER, J. *et al.* (1990), 'A Comparison of Crime in Australia and Other Countries', *Trends and Issues*, 23. Canberra: Australian Institute of Criminology.

WESTBURY, V. (1991), 'Women Hating—An Australian Talent', *The Bulletin*, 8 October, 82.

11

HEGEMONIC MASCULINITY

Rethinking the concept

Robert W. Connell and James W. Messerschmidt

Source: *Gender and Society*, 19:6 (2005), 829–59.

Abstract

The concept of hegemonic masculinity has influenced gender studies across many academic fields but has also attracted serious criticism. The authors trace the origin of the concept in a convergence of ideas in the early 1980s and map the ways it was applied when research on men and masculinities expanded. Evaluating the principal criticisms, the authors defend the underlying concept of masculinity, which in most research use is neither reified nor essentialist. However, the criticism of trait models of gender and rigid typologies is sound. The treatment of the subject in research on hegemonic masculinity can be improved with the aid of recent psychological models, although limits to discursive flexibility must be recognized. The concept of hegemonic masculinity does not equate to a model of social reproduction; we need to recognize social struggles in which subordinated masculinities influence dominant forms. Finally, the authors review what has been confirmed from early formulations (the idea of multiple masculinities, the concept of hegemony, and the emphasis on change) and what needs to be discarded (one-dimensional treatment of hierarchy and trait conceptions of gender). The authors suggest reformulation of the concept in four areas: a more complex model of gender hierarchy, emphasizing the agency of women; explicit recognition of the geography of masculinities, emphasizing the interplay among local, regional, and global levels; a more specific treatment of embodiment in contexts of privilege and power; and a stronger emphasis on the dynamics of hegemonic masculinity, recognizing internal contradictions and the possibilities of movement toward gender democracy.

The concept of hegemonic masculinity, formulated two decades ago, has considerably influenced recent thinking about men, gender, and social hierarchy. It has provided a link between the growing research field of men's studies (also known as masculinity studies and critical studies of men), popular anxieties about men and boys, feminist accounts of patriarchy, and sociological models of gender. It has found uses in applied fields ranging from education and antiviolence work to health and counseling.

Database searches reveal more than 200 papers that use the exact term "hegemonic masculinity" in their titles or abstracts. Papers that use a variant, or refer to "hegemonic masculinity" in the text, run to many hundreds. Continuing interest is shown by conferences. In early May 2005, a conference, "Hegemonic Masculinities and International Politics," was held at the University of Manchester, England; in 2004, an interdisciplinary conference in Stuttgart was devoted to the topic "Hegemoniale Männlichkeiten" (Dinges, Ründal, and Bauer 2004).

The concept has also attracted serious criticism from several directions: sociological, psychological, poststructuralist, and materialist (e.g., Demetriou 2001; Wetherell and Edley 1999). Outside the academic world, it has been attacked as—to quote a recent Internet backlash posting—"an invention of New Age psychologists" determined to prove that men are too macho.

This is a contested concept. Yet the issues it names are very much at stake in contemporary struggles about power and political leadership, public and private violence, and changes in families and sexuality. A comprehensive reexamination of the concept of hegemonic masculinity seems worthwhile. If the concept proves still useful, it must be reformulated in contemporary terms. We attempt both tasks in this article.

Origin, formulation, and application

Origin

The concept of hegemonic masculinity was first proposed in reports from a field study of social inequality in Australian high schools (Kessler et al. 1982); in a related conceptual discussion of the making of masculinities and the experience of men's bodies (Connell 1983); and in a debate over the role of men in Australian labor politics (Connell 1982). The high school project provided empirical evidence of multiple hierarchies—in gender as well as in class terms—interwoven with active projects of gender construction (Connell et al. 1982).

These beginnings were systematized in an article, "Towards a New Sociology of Masculinity" (Carrigan, Connell, and Lee 1985), which extensively critiqued the "male sex role" literature and proposed a model of multiple masculinities and power relations. In turn, this model was integrated into a systematic sociological theory of gender. The resulting six pages in *Gender and Power* (Connell 1987) on "hegemonic masculinity and emphasized femininity" became the most cited source for the concept of hegemonic masculinity.

The concept articulated by the research groups in Australia represented a synthesis of ideas and evidence from apparently disparate sources. But the convergence of ideas was not accidental. Closely related issues were being addressed by researchers and activists in other countries too; the time was, in a sense, ripe for a synthesis of this kind.

The most basic sources were feminist theories of patriarchy and the related debates over the role of men in transforming patriarchy (Goode 1982; Snodgrass 1977). Some men in the New Left had tried to organize in support of feminism, and the attempt had drawn attention to class differences in the expression of masculinity (Tolson 1977). Moreover, women of color—such as Maxine Baca Zinn (1982), Angela Davis (1983), and bell hooks (1984)—criticized the race bias that occurs when power is solely conceptualized in terms of sex difference, thus laying the groundwork for questioning any universalizing claims about the category of men.

The Gramscian term "hegemony" was current at the time in attempts to understand the stabilization of class relations (Connell 1977). In the context of dual systems theory (Eisenstein 1979), the idea was easily transferred to the parallel problem about gender relations. This risked a significant misunderstanding. Gramsci's writing focuses on the dynamics of structural change involving the mobilization and demobilization of whole classes. Without a very clear focus on this issue of historical change, the idea of hegemony would be reduced to a simple model of cultural control. And in a great deal of the debate about gender, large-scale historical change is not in focus. Here is one of the sources of later difficulties with the concept of hegemonic masculinity.

Even before the women's liberation movement, a literature in social psychology and sociology about the "male sex role" had recognized the social nature of masculinity and the possibilities of change in men's conduct (Hacker 1957). During the 1970s, there was an explosion of writing about "the male role," sharply criticizing role norms as the source of oppressive behavior by men (Brannon 1976). Critical role theory provided the main conceptual basis for the early antisexist men's movement. The weaknesses of sex role theory were, however, increasingly recognized (Kimmel 1987; Pleck 1981). They included the blurring of behavior and norm, the homogenizing effect of the role concept, and its difficulties in accounting for power.

Power and difference were, on the other hand, core concepts in the gay liberation movement, which developed a sophisticated analysis of the oppression of men as well as oppression by men (Altman 1972). Some theorists saw gay liberation as bound up with an assault on gender stereotypes (Mieli 1980). The idea of a hierarchy of masculinities grew directly out of homosexual men's experience with violence and prejudice from straight men.

The concept of homophobia originated in the 1970s and was already being attributed to the conventional male role (Morin and Garfinkle 1978). Theorists developed increasingly sophisticated accounts of gay men's ambivalent relationships to patriarchy and conventional masculinity (Broker 1976; Plummer 1981).

An equally important source was empirical social research. A growing body of field studies was documenting local gender hierarchies and local cultures of masculinity in schools (Willis 1977), in male-dominated workplaces (Cockburn 1983), and in village communities (Herdt 1981; Hunt 1980). These studies added the ethnographic realism that the sex-role literature lacked, confirmed the plurality of masculinities and the complexities of gender construction for men, and gave evidence of the active struggle for dominance that is implicit in the Gramscian concept of hegemony.

Finally, the concept was influenced by psychoanalysis. Freud himself produced the first analytic biographies of men and, in the "Wolf Man" case history, showed how adult personality was a system under tension, with countercurrents repressed but not obliterated (Freud [1917] 1955). The psychoanalyst Stoller (1968) popularized the concept of "gender identity" and mapped its variations in boys' development, most famously those leading to transsexualism. Others influenced by psychoanalysis picked up the themes of men's power, the range of possibilities in gender development, and the tension and contradiction within conventional masculinities (Friedman and Lerner 1986; Zaretsky 1975).

Formulation

What emerged from this matrix in the mid-1980s was an analogue, in gender terms, of power structure research in political sociology—focusing the spotlight on a dominant group. Hegemonic masculinity was understood as the pattern of practice (i.e., things done, not just a set of role expectations or an identity) that allowed men's dominance over women to continue.

Hegemonic masculinity was distinguished from other masculinities, especially subordinated masculinities. Hegemonic masculinity was not assumed to be normal in the statistical sense; only a minority of men might enact it. But it was certainly normative. It embodied the currently most honored way of being a man, it required all other men to position themselves in relation to it, and it ideologically legitimated the global subordination of women to men.

Men who received the benefits of patriarchy without enacting a strong version of masculine dominance could be regarded as showing a complicit masculinity. It was in relation to this group, and to compliance among heterosexual women, that the concept of hegemony was most powerful. Hegemony did not mean violence, although it could be supported by force; it meant ascendancy achieved through culture, institutions, and persuasion.

These concepts were abstract rather than descriptive, defined in terms of the logic of a patriarchal gender system. They assumed that gender relations were historical, so gender hierarchies were subject to change. Hegemonic masculinities therefore came into existence in specific circumstances and were open to historical change. More precisely, there could be a struggle for hegemony, and older forms of masculinity might be displaced by new ones. This was the element of optimism in an otherwise rather bleak theory. It was perhaps possible that a more humane, less oppressive, means of being a man might become hegemonic, as part of a process leading toward an abolition of gender hierarchies.

Application

The concept of hegemonic masculinity, formulated in these terms, found prompt use. In the late 1980s and early 1990s, research on men and masculinity was being consolidated as an academic field, supported by a string of conferences, the publication of textbooks (e.g., Brod 1987) and several journals, and a rapidly expanding research agenda across the social sciences and humanities.

The concept of hegemonic masculinity was used in education studies to understand the dynamics of classroom life, including patterns of resistance and bullying among boys. It was used to explore relations to the curriculum and the difficulties in gender-neutral pedagogy (Martino 1995). It was used to understand teacher strategies and teacher identities among such groups as physical education instructors (Skelton 1993).

The concept also had influence in criminology. All data reflect that men and boys perpetrate more of the conventional crimes—and the more serious of these crimes—than do women and girls. Moreover, men hold a virtual monopoly on the commission of syndicated and white-collar forms of crime. The concept of hegemonic masculinity helped in theorizing the relationship among masculinities and among a variety of crimes (Messerschmidt 1993) and was also used in studies on specific crimes by boys and men, such as rape in Switzerland, murder in Australia, football "hooliganism" and white-collar crime in England, and assaultive violence in the United States (Newburn and Stanko 1994).

The concept was also employed in studying media representations of men, for instance, the interplay of sports and war imagery (Jansen and Sabo 1994). Because the concept of hegemony helped to make sense of both the diversity and the selectiveness of images in mass media, media researchers began mapping the relations between representations of different masculinities (Hanke 1992). Commercial sports are a focus of media representations of masculinity, and the developing field of sports sociology also found significant use for the concept of hegemonic masculinity (Messner 1992). It was deployed in understanding the popularity of body-contact confrontational sports—which function as an endlessly renewed symbol of masculinity—and in understanding the violence and homophobia frequently found in sporting milieus (Messner and Sabo 1990).

The social determinants of men's health had been raised earlier, but the sex role concept was too diffuse to be very useful. The concepts of multiple masculinities and hegemonic masculinity were increasingly used to understand men's health practices, such as "playing hurt" and risk-taking sexual behavior (Sabo and Gordon 1995). The concepts of hegemonic and subordinated masculinities helped in understanding not only men's exposure to risk but also men's difficulties in responding to disability and injury (Gerschick and Miller 1994).

The concept of hegemonic masculinity also proved significant in organization studies, as the gendered character of bureaucracies and workplaces was increasingly recognized. Ethnographic and interview studies traced the institutionalization of hegemonic masculinities in specific organizations (Cheng 1996; Cockburn 1991) and their role in organizational decision making (Messerschmidt 1995). A particular focus of this research was the military, where specific patterns of hegemonic masculinity had been entrenched but were becoming increasingly problematic (Barrett 1996).

Discussions of professional practice concerned with men and boys also found the concept helpful. Such practices include psychotherapy with men (Kupers 1993), violence-prevention programs for youth (Denborough 1996), and emotional education programs for boys (Salisbury and Jackson 1996).

These are the primary fields where the concept of hegemonic masculinity was applied in the decade following its formulation. But there was also a wider range of application, for instance, in discussions of art (Belton 1995), in academic disciplines such as geography (Berg 1994) and law (Thornton 1989), and in general discussions of men's gender politics and relation to feminism (Segal 1990). We may reasonably conclude that the analysis of multiple masculinities and the concept of hegemonic masculinity served as a framework for much of the developing research effort on men and masculinity, replacing sex-role theory and categorical models of patriarchy.

Eventually, the growing research effort tended to expand the concept itself. The picture was fleshed out in four main ways: by documenting the consequences and costs of hegemony, by uncovering mechanisms of hegemony, by showing greater diversity in masculinities, and by tracing changes in hegemonic masculinities.

Regarding costs and consequences, research in criminology showed how particular patterns of aggression were linked with hegemonic masculinity, not as a mechanical effect for which hegemonic masculinity was a cause, but through the pursuit of hegemony (Bufkin 1999; Messerschmidt 1997). Moreover, the pioneering research of Messner (1992) showed that the enactment of hegemonic masculinity in professional sports, while reproducing steep hierarchies, also comes at considerable cost to the victors in terms of emotional and physical damage.

Research has been fruitful in revealing mechanisms of hegemony. Some are highly visible, such as the "pageantry" of masculinity in television sports broadcasts (Sabo and Jansen 1992) as well as the social mechanisms Roberts (1993) calls "censure" directed at subordinated groups—ranging from informal name calling by children to the criminalization of homosexual conduct. Yet other mechanisms of hegemony operate by invisibility, removing a dominant form of masculinity from the possibility of censure (Brown 1999). Consalvo (2003), examining media reporting of the Columbine High School massacre, notes how the issue of masculinity was withdrawn from scrutiny, leaving the media with no way of representing the shooters except as "monsters."

International research has strongly confirmed the initial insight that gender orders construct multiple masculinities. Valdés and Olavarría (1998) show that even in a culturally homogeneous country such as Chile, there is no unitary masculinity, since patterns vary by class and generation. In another famously homogeneous country, Japan, Ishii-Kuntz (2003) traces the "emergence of diverse masculinities" in recent social history, with changes in child care practices a key development. Diversity of masculinities is also found in particular institutions, such as the military (Higate 2003).

Gutmann (1996), in the most beautifully observed modern ethnography of masculinity, studied a case where there is a well-defined public masculine identity—Mexican "machismo." Gutmann shows how the imagery of machismo developed historically and was interwoven with the development of Mexican nationalism, masking enormous complexity in the actual lives of Mexican men. Gutmann teases out four patterns of masculinity in the working-class urban settlement he studies, insisting that even these four are crosscut by other social divisions and are constantly renegotiated in everyday life.

Finally, a considerable body of research shows that masculinities are not simply different but also subject to change. Challenges to hegemony are common, and so are adjustments in the face of these challenges. Morrell (1998) assembles the evidence about gender transformations in southern Africa associated with the end of Apartheid, a system of segregated and competing patriarchies. Ferguson (2001) traces the decline of long-standing ideals of masculinity in Ireland—the celibate priest and the hardworking family man—and their replacement by more modernized and market-oriented models. Dasgupta (2000) traces tensions in the Japanese "salaryman" model of masculinity, especially after the "bubble economy" of the 1980s: A cultural figure of the "salaryman escaping" has appeared. Taga (2003) documents diverse responses to change among young middle-class men in Japan, including new options for domestic partnership with women. Meuser (2003) traces generational change in Germany, partly driven by men's responses to changes among women. Many (although not all) young men, now expecting women to reject patriarchal social relations, are crafting a "pragmatic egalitarianism" of their own. Morris and Evans (2001), studying images of rural masculinity and femininity in Britain, finds a slower pace of change but an increasing subtlety and fragmentation in the representation of hegemonic masculinity.

From the mid-1980s to the early 2000s, the concept of hegemonic masculinity thus passed from a conceptual model with a fairly narrow empirical base to a widely used framework for research and debate about men and masculinities. The concept was applied in diverse cultural contexts and to a considerable range of practical issues. It is not surprising, then, that the concept has attracted criticism, and to this we now turn.

Critiques

Five principal criticisms have been advanced since debate about the concept began in the early 1990s. In this section, we evaluate each criticism in turn, hoping to discover what is worth retaining from the original conception of hegemonic masculinity and what now needs reformulating.

The underlying concept of masculinity

That the underlying concept of masculinity is flawed has been argued from two different points of view, realist and poststructuralist. To Collinson and Hearn (1994) and Hearn (1996, 2004), the concept of masculinity is blurred, is uncertain in its meaning, and tends to deemphasize issues of power and domination. It is ultimately unnecessary to the task of understanding and contesting the power of men. The concept of multiple masculinities tends to produce a static typology.

To Petersen (1998, 2003), Collier (1998), and MacInnes (1998), the concept of masculinity is flawed because it essentializes the character of men or imposes a false unity on a fluid and contradictory reality. Some versions of this argument criticize masculinity research because it has not adopted a specific poststructuralist tool kit—which would, for instance, emphasize the discursive construction of identities (Whitehead 2002). The concept of masculinity is criticized for being framed within a heteronormative conception of gender that essentializes male–female difference and ignores difference and exclusion within the gender categories. The concept of masculinity is said to rest logically on a dichotomization of sex (biological) versus gender (cultural) and thus marginalizes or naturalizes the body.

No responsible mind can deny that in the huge literature concerned with masculinity, there is a great deal of conceptual confusion as well as a great deal of essentializing. This certainly is common in accounts of masculinity in pop psychology, in the mythopoetic men's movement, and in journalistic interpretations of biological sex-difference research. It is another matter, however, to claim that the concept of masculinity must be confused or essentialist or even that researchers' use of the concept typically is.

We would argue that social science and humanities research on masculinities has flourished during the past 20 years precisely because the underlying concept employed is not reified or essentialist. The notion that the concept of masculinity essentializes or homogenizes is quite difficult to reconcile with the tremendous multiplicity of social constructions that ethnographers and historians have documented with the aid of this concept (Connell 2003). Even further removed from essentialism is the fact that researchers have explored masculinities enacted by people with female bodies (Halberstam 1998; Messerschmidt 2004). Masculinity is not a fixed entity embedded in the body or personality traits of individuals. Masculinities are configurations of practice that are accomplished in social action and, therefore, can differ according to the gender relations in a particular social setting.

The idea that a recognition of multiple masculinities necessarily turns into a static typology is likewise not borne out by the development of research. A paradigmatic example is Gutmann's (1996) Mexican ethnography, already mentioned. Gutmann is able to tease out different categories of masculinity—for example, the macho and the *mandilón*—while recognizing, and showing in detail, that these are not monadic identities but always are relational and constantly are crosscut by other divisions and projects. Warren's (1997) observations in a British elementary school provide another example. Different constructions of masculinity are found, which generate effects in classroom life, even though many boys do not fit exactly into the major categories; indeed, the boys demonstrate complex relations of attachment and rejection to those categories.

Although the idea that the concept of gender embeds heteronormativity is now a familiar criticism (Hawkesworth 1997), it is a contested criticism (Scott 1997). While it correctly identifies a problem in categorical models of gender, it is not a valid criticism of relational models of gender (e.g., Connell 2002; Walby 1997) nor of historical approaches where the construction of gender categories is the object of inquiry. In the development of the concept of hegemonic masculinity, divisions among men—especially the exclusion and subordination of homosexual men—were quite central issues (Carrigan, Connell, and Lee 1985). The policing of heterosexuality has been a major theme in discussions of hegemonic masculinity since then.

The idea that the concept of masculinity marginalizes or naturalizes the body (because it is supposed to rest on a sex-gender dichotomy) is perhaps the most startling of the claims in this critique. Startling, because the interplay between bodies and social processes has been one of the central themes of masculinity research from its beginning. One of the first and most influential research programs in the new paradigm was Messner's (1992) account of the masculinity of professional athletes, in which the use of "bodies as weapons" and the long-term damage to men's bodies were examined. The construction of masculinity in a context of disability (Gerschick and Miller 1994), the laboring bodies of working-class men (Donaldson 1991), men's health and illness (Sabo and Gordon 1995), and boys' interpersonal violence (Messerschmidt 2000) are among the themes in research showing how bodies are affected by social processes. Theoretical discussion has explored the relevance of the "new sociology of the body" to the construction of masculinity (e.g., Connell 1995, chap. 2).

Critiques of the concept of masculinity make better sense when they point to a tendency, in research as well as in popular literature, to dichotomize the experiences of men and women. As Brod (1994) accurately observes, there is a tendency in the men's studies field to presume "separate spheres," to proceed as if women were not a relevant part of the analysis, and therefore to analyze masculinities by looking only at men and relations among men. As Brod also argues, this is not inevitable. The cure lies in taking a consistently relational approach to gender—not in abandoning the concepts of gender or masculinity.

Ambiguity and overlap

Early criticisms of the concept raised the question of who actually represents hegemonic masculinity. It is familiar that many men who hold great social power do not embody an ideal masculinity. On the other hand, Donaldson (1993) remarks that there did not seem to be much masculine substance to those men identified by researchers as hegemonic models. He discusses the case of the Australian "iron man" surf-sports champion described by Connell (1990), a popular exemplar of hegemonic masculinity. But the young man's regional hegemonic status actually prevents him doing the things his local peer group defines as masculine—going wild, showing off, driving drunk, getting into fights, and defending his own prestige.

Martin (1998) criticizes the concept for leading to inconsistent applications, sometimes referring to a fixed type of masculinity and on other occasions referring to whatever type is dominant at a particular time and place. Similarly, Wetherell and Edley (1999) contend that the concept fails to specify what conformity to hegemonic masculinity actually looks like in practice. And Whitehead (1998, 58; 2002, 93) suggests there is confusion over who actually is a hegemonically masculine man—"Is it John Wayne or Leonardo DiCaprio; Mike Tyson or Pele? Or maybe, at different times, all of them?"—and also about who can enact hegemonic practices.

We think the critics have correctly pointed to ambiguities in usage. It is desirable to eliminate any usage of hegemonic masculinity as a fixed, transhistorical model. This usage violates the historicity of gender and ignores the massive evidence of change in social definitions of masculinity.

But in other respects, ambiguity in gender processes may be important to recognize as a mechanism of hegemony. Consider how an idealized definition of masculinity is constituted in social process. At a society-wide level (which we will call "regional" in the framework below), there is a circulation of models of admired masculine conduct, which may be exalted by churches, narrated by mass media, or celebrated by the state. Such models refer to, but also in various ways distort, the everyday realities of social practice. A classic example is the Soviet regime's celebration of the *Stakhanovite* industrial worker, named for the coal miner Aleksandr Stakhanov who in 1935 hewed a world record 102 tons of coal in a single day, triggering a scramble to beat the record. Part of the distortion here was that the famous "shock workers" achieved their numbers with a great deal of unacknowledged help from coworkers.

Thus, hegemonic masculinities can be constructed that do not correspond closely to the lives of any actual men. Yet these models do, in various ways, express widespread ideals, fantasies, and desires. They provide models of relations with women and solutions to problems of gender relations. Furthermore, they articulate loosely with the practical constitution of masculinities as ways of living in everyday local circumstances. To the extent they do this, they contribute to hegemony in the society-wide gender order as a whole. It is not surprising that men who function as exemplars at the regional level, such as the "iron man" discussed by Donaldson (1993), exhibit contradictions.

At the local level, hegemonic patterns of masculinity are embedded in specific social environments, such as formal organizations. There are, for instance, well-defined patterns of managerial masculinity in the British corporations studied by Roper (1994) and Wajcman (1999). Socially legitimated hegemonic models of masculinity are also in play in families. For instance, men's gender strategies shape negotiations around housework and the "second shift" in the U.S. families studied by Hochschild (1989). Hegemonic patterns of masculinity are both engaged with and contested as children grow up. Gender is made in schools and neighborhoods through peer group structure, control of school space, dating patterns, homophobic speech, and harassment (Mac an Ghaill 1994; Thorne 1993). In none of these cases would we expect hegemonic masculinity to stand out as a sharply defined pattern separate from all others. A degree of overlap or blurring between hegemonic and complicit masculinities is extremely likely if hegemony is effective.

The overlap between masculinities can also be seen in terms of the social agents constructing masculinities. Cavender (1999) shows how hegemonic masculine models were constructed differently in feature films in the 1940s compared with the 1980s. This is not just a matter of the characters written into the scripts. Practice at the local level—that is, the actual face-to-face interaction of shooting the film as an actor—ultimately constructs hegemonic masculine fantasy models (in this case, "detectives") at the society-wide or regional level. (We will explore this question of the relations between levels in the Reformulation section of the article.)

The problem of reification

That the concept of hegemonic masculinity reduces, in practice, to a reification of power or toxicity has also been argued from different points of view. Holter (1997, 2003), in the most conceptually sophisticated of all critiques, argues that the concept constructs masculine power from the direct experience of women rather than from the structural basis of women's subordination. Holter believes that we must distinguish between "patriarchy," the long-term structure of the subordination of women, and "gender," a specific system of exchange that arose in the context of modern capitalism. It is a mistake to treat a hierarchy of masculinities constructed within gender relations as logically continuous with the patriarchal subordination of women. Holter (1997) tellingly points to Norwegian survey evidence showing that the gender identities of men do not map directly onto such equality-related practices as attitudes toward violence.

Holter (1997, 2003) certainly is correct that it is a mistake to deduce relations among masculinities from the direct exercise of personal power by men over women. At the least, we also must factor in the institutionalization of gender inequalities, the role of cultural constructions, and the interplay of gender dynamics with race, class, and region.

It is, indeed, research on these issues that shows the concept of hegemonic masculinity is not trapped in reification. Among the fruitful studies of institutional masculinities are those that reveal quite subtle variations, for instance, between the different branches of a single military force, the U.S. Navy (Barrett 1996). There are studies of locally specific hegemonic masculinities constructed in spaces such as a New Zealand country pub, which show the interweaving of masculinity with rural identity (Campbell 2000). Other research, especially studies of school classrooms (Martino 1995; Warren 1997), shows the fine-grained production and negotiation of masculinities (and femininities) as configurations of practice.

Collier (1998) criticizes the concept of hegemonic masculinity through its typical use in accounting for violence and crime. In the "masculinity turn" in criminology, Collier suggests, hegemonic masculinity came to be associated solely with negative characteristics that depict men as unemotional, independent, non-nurturing, aggressive, and dispassionate—which are seen as the causes of criminal behavior. Martin (1998, 473) similarly observes a drift toward a view of hegemonic masculinity not just as a type but as a negative type, for instance, in "saying that defending gun ownership is a defense of hegemonic masculinity."

This criticism has force. It draws on McMahon's (1993) accurate analysis of the psychologism in many discussions of men and masculinity. Men's behavior is reified in a concept of masculinity that then, in a circular argument, becomes the explanation (and the excuse) for the behavior. This can be seen in many discussions of men's health and problems of boys' education—indeed, any of the contemporary troubles assembled under the banner of a "crisis in masculinity." In pop psychology, the invention of new character types is endemic (the alpha male, the sensitive new-age guy, the hairy man, the new lad, the "rat boy," etc.). In this environment, hegemonic masculinity can become a scientific-sounding synonym for a type of rigid, domineering, sexist, "macho" man (in the Anglo usage, e.g., Mosher and Tomkins 1988).

Because the concept of hegemonic masculinity is based on practice that permits men's collective dominance over women to continue, it is not surprising that in some contexts, hegemonic masculinity actually does refer to men's engaging in toxic practices—including physical violence—that stabilize gender dominance in a particular setting. However, violence and other noxious practices are not always the defining characteristics, since hegemony has numerous configurations. Indeed, as Wetherell and Edley (1999) ironically observe, one of the most effective ways of "being a man" in certain local contexts may be to demonstrate one's distance from a regional hegemonic masculinity.

Collier (1998) sees as a crucial defect in the concept of hegemonic masculinity that it excludes "positive" behavior on the part of men—that is, behavior that might serve the interests or desires of women. This hardly is a problem once we get beyond a rigid trait theory of personality. Most accounts of hegemonic masculinity do include such "positive" actions as bringing home a wage, sustaining a sexual relationship, and being a father. Indeed it is difficult to see how the concept of hegemony would be relevant if the only characteristics of the dominant group were violence, aggression, and self-centeredness. Such characteristics may mean domination but hardly would constitute hegemony—an idea that embeds certain notions of consent and participation by the subaltern groups.

Collier (1998, 21) is right in remarking that what actually is being discussed in many accounts of hegemonic masculinity and crime (and, we may add, health and education) is "a range of popular ideologies of what constitute ideal or actual characteristics of 'being a man.'" What Collier misses, however, is that sophisticated research consistently goes on to explore the relationship of those ideologies to the daily lives of boys and men—including the mismatches, the tensions, and the resistances.

It is men's and boys' practical relationships to collective images or models of masculinity, rather than simple reflections of them, that is central to understanding gendered consequences in violence, health, and education. This has been evident since Messerschmidt's (1993) formulation of the idea that different crimes are used by different men in the construction of masculinities. Collier finds this idea unacceptable, either tautological and universalizing, or too multitudinous in what it explains. But there is nothing surprising about the idea of diverse practices' being generated from common cultural templates; there is nothing conceptually universalizing in the idea of hegemonic masculinity. Coordination and regulation occur in the live social practices of collectivities, institutions, and whole societies. The concept of hegemonic masculinity is not intended as a catchall nor as a prime cause; it is a means of grasping a certain dynamic within the social process.

The masculine subject

Several authors have argued that the concept of hegemonic masculinity is based on an unsatisfactory theory of the subject. Wetherell and Edley (1999) develop this critique from the standpoint of discursive psychology, arguing that hegemonic masculinity cannot be understood as the settled character structure of any group of men. We must question "how men conform to an ideal and turn themselves into complicit or resistant types, without anyone ever managing to exactly embody that ideal" (p. 337).

Wetherell and Edley (1999) suggest we should understand hegemonic norms as defining a subject position in discourse that is taken up strategically by men in particular circumstances. Hegemonic masculinity has multiple meanings—a point that some authors have offered as a criticism but that Wetherell and Edley take as a positive point of departure. Men can dodge among multiple meanings according to their interactional needs. Men can adopt hegemonic masculinity when it is desirable; but the same men can distance themselves strategically from hegemonic masculinity at other moments. Consequently, "masculinity" represents not a certain type of man but, rather, a way that men position themselves through discursive practices.

Whitehead (2002, 93) argues that the concept of hegemonic masculinity can "see" only structure, making the subject invisible: "The individual is lost within, or, in Althusserian terms, subjected to, an ideological apparatus and an innate drive for power." To Whitehead, the concept fails to specify how and why some heterosexual men legitimate, reproduce, and generate their dominance and do so as a social minority vis-à-vis women and other men. Consequently, use of the concept results "in obfuscation, in the conflation of fluid masculinities with overarching structure and, ultimately, in 'abstract structural dynamics'" (Whitehead 2002, 93–94). For Whitehead, it is preferable to concentrate on discourse as the means by which men come to know themselves, to practice "identity work," and to exercise gender power and resistance.

A related criticism derives from psychoanalysis. According to this view, the model of hegemonic masculinity presumes a unitary subject; but depth psychology reveals a multilayered or divided subject (Collier 1998; Jefferson 1994). Jefferson (2002) criticizes the "over-socialized view of the male subject" in studies of masculinity, which has resulted in a lack of attention to how men actually relate psychologically to hegemonic masculinity. Given multiple masculinities, Jefferson argues that researchers should ask "how actual men, with their unique biographies and particular psychic formations, relate to these various masculinities" (p. 73). Jefferson suggests that boys and men choose those discursive positions that help them ward off anxiety and avoid feelings of powerlessness.

The argument from discursive psychology is well taken and is well integrated with a fruitful research approach. A good example is Lea and Auburn's (2001) study of the story told by a convicted rapist in a sex-offender program, which shows how the narrating offender moves between conflicting ideologies of sexual interaction in a way that reduces his responsibility for the rape. Another example is Archer's (2001) exploration of the identity talk of young Muslim men in Britain, showing how they use a specific model of hegemonic masculinity ("powerful, patriarchal") to position themselves in relation to Afro-Caribbean men, white men, and Muslim women. From this work, we can learn not only how masculinities are constructed in discourse but also how they are used in discourse. Specifically, we learn how a locally hegemonic version of masculinity can be used to promote self-respect in the face of discredit, for instance, from racist denigration.

Discursive perspectives emphasize the symbolic dimension, whereas the concept of hegemonic masculinity was formulated within a multidimensional understanding of gender. Although any specification of hegemonic masculinity typically involves the formulation of cultural ideals, it should not be regarded only as a cultural norm. Gender relations also are constituted through nondiscursive practices, including wage labor, violence, sexuality, domestic labor, and child care as well as through unreflective routinized actions.

Recognizing the nondiscursive and unreflective dimensions of gender gives us some sense of the limits to discursive flexibility. That there are such limits is a point powerfully made in Rubin's (2003) study of female-to-male transsexual men. One is not free to adopt any gender position in interaction simply as a discursive or reflexive move. The possibilities are constrained massively by embodiment, by institutional histories, by economic forces, and by personal and family relationships. The costs of making certain discursive choices can be extremely high—as shown by the rate of suicide among people involved in transsexual moves.

Constraint also may arise from within the person. Rubin's (2003) respondents act as they do, and face the costs, because of an unshakeable conviction of being men—despite starting out with female bodies and being brought up as girls. They are convinced of being unitary subjects, although they live a contradiction that seems to exemplify Jefferson's (1994, 2002) argument for the divided subject. We agree with Jefferson that psychoanalytic practice and theory are important resources for understanding the complex subject of gender practice. However, Jefferson's particular psychoanalytic approach is not without problems (Messerschmidt 2005), and it is important to recognize the diversity and wealth of the psychoanalytic tradition. Approaches such as Sartre's existential psychoanalysis are helpful for understanding masculinities as projects and a masculine identity as always being a provisional accomplishment within a life course. Adlerian psychoanalysis, with its emphasis on the emotional consequences of gendered power relations in childhood, gave rise to the idea of the "masculine protest," which still resonates with contemporary discussions of marginalized youth.

The concept of hegemonic masculinity originally was formulated with a strong awareness of psychoanalytic arguments about the layered and contradictory character of personality, the everyday contestation in social life, and the mixture of strategies necessary in any attempt to sustain hegemony (Carrigan, Connell, and Lee 1985; Connell 1987). It is somewhat ironic that the concept is criticized for oversimplifying the subject, but it is, of course, true that the concept often has been employed in simplified forms.

Does the concept necessarily erase the subject? We flatly disagree with Whitehead's (2002) claim that the concept of hegemonic masculinity reduces to structural determinism. Masculinity is defined as a configuration of practice organized in relation to the structure of gender relations. Human social practice creates gender relations in history. The concept of hegemonic masculinity embeds a historically dynamic view of gender in which it is impossible to erase the subject. This is why life-history studies have become a characteristic genre of work on hegemonic masculinity.

The concept homogenizes the subject only if it is reduced to a single dimension of gender relations (usually the symbolic) and if it is treated as the specification of a norm. As soon as one recognizes the multidimensionality of gender relations (Connell 2002) and the occurrence of crisis tendencies within gender relations (Connell 1995), it is impossible to regard the subject constituted within those relations as unitary. There are, of course, different ways of representing the incoherence of the subject. The conceptual language of poststructuralism is only one way of doing that; psychoanalysis and the model of agency within contradictory social structures provide others.

The pattern of gender relations

In social theories of gender, there has often been a tendency toward functionalism—that is, seeing gender relations as a self-contained, self-reproducing system and explaining every element in terms of its function in reproducing the whole. Hawkesworth (1997) detects this tendency in most modern theories of gender, and Bourdieu's (2001) late intervention to explain masculine domination has given a new lease on life to functionalism in gender analysis.

The dominance of men and the subordination of women constitute a historical process, not a self-reproducing system. "Masculine domination" is open to challenge and requires considerable effort to maintain. Although this point was made in early statements on the hegemonic masculinity concept, it is not just a theoretical idea. There is detailed work that shows the tactics of maintenance through the exclusion of women, ranging from Bird's (1996) work on homosociality to the organizational research by Collinson, Knights, and Collinson (1990), Cockburn (1991), and Martin (2001).

There exists considerable evidence that hegemonic masculinity is not a self-reproducing form, whether through habitus or any other mechanism. To sustain a given pattern of hegemony requires the policing of men as well as the exclusion or discrediting of women. Evidence of such mechanisms ranges from the discrediting of "soft" options in the "hard" world of international relations, security threats, and war (Hooper 2001), to homophobic assaults and murders (Tomsen 2002), all the way to the teasing of boys in school for "sissiness" (Kimmel and Mahler 2003; Messerschmidt 2000).

In Demetriou's (2001) careful critique of the concept of hegemonic masculinity, the historicity of gender is acknowledged. Demetriou, however, suggests that another kind of simplification has occurred. He identifies two forms of hegemony, internal and external. "External hegemony" refers to the institutionalization of men's dominance over women; "internal hegemony" refers to the social ascendancy of one group of men over all other men. Demetriou argues that the relationship between the two forms is unclear in the original formulation of the concept and unspecified in current usages. Moreover, internal hegemony typically has been understood in an "elitist" way. That is, subordinate and marginalized masculinities are seen as having no impact on the construction of hegemonic masculinity. Nonhegemonic masculinities exist in tension with, but never penetrate or impact, the hegemonic masculinity. There is, then, a dualistic representation of masculinities.

Such a conceptualization, Demetriou (2001) argues, misses the "dialectical pragmatism" of internal hegemony, by which hegemonic masculinity appropriates from other masculinities whatever appears to be pragmatically useful for continued domination. The result of this dialectic is not a unitary pattern of hegemonic masculinity but a "historic bloc" involving a weaving together of multiple patterns, whose hybridity is the best possible strategy for external hegemony. A constant process of negotiation, translation, and reconfiguration occurs.

This conceptualization leads to a different view of historical change in masculinities. Hegemonic masculinity does not simply adapt to changing historical conditions. Rather, the hegemonic masculine bloc is a hybridization whose appropriation of diverse elements makes it "capable of reconfiguring itself and adapting to the specificities of new historical conjunctures" (Demetriou 2001, 355). As an example of this process, Demetriou (2001) discusses the increasing cultural visibility of gay masculinity in Western societies. This has made it possible for certain heterosexual men to appropriate "bits and pieces" of gay men's styles and practices and construct a new hybrid configuration of gender practice. Such an appropriation blurs gender difference but does not undermine patriarchy.

Demetriou's (2001) conceptualization of dialectical pragmatism in "internal hegemony" is useful, and he makes a convincing case that certain representations of masculinity, and some heterosexual men's everyday gender practices, have appropriated aspects of gay masculinities. Clearly, specific masculine practices may be appropriated into other masculinities, creating a hybrid (such as the hip-hop style and language adopted by some working-class white teenage boys and the unique composite style of gay "clones"). Yet we are not convinced that the hybridization Demetriou (2001) describes is hegemonic, at least beyond a local sense. Although gay masculinity and sexuality are increasingly visible in Western societies—witness the fascination with the gay male characters in the television programs *Six Feet Under*, *Will and Grace*, and *Queer Eye for the Straight Guy*—there is little reason to think that hybridization has become hegemonic at the regional or global level.

The concept of a hegemonic bloc brings into focus the issue of multiple hegemonic masculinities. Jefferson (2002, 71) and others have criticized the tendency to speak of just one pattern—"hegemonic masculinity is always used in the singular." There is a paradox here. Because every ethnography discovers a distinctive gender culture, every life-history study uncovers unique trajectories of men's lives, and every structural analysis defines new intersections of race, class, gender, and generation, it is logically possible to define "a thousand and one" variations of masculinity (Meuser and Behnke 1998). This surely is also true of claimants to hegemony. The point is strongly supported by Messner's (1997) mapping of masculinity politics in the United States, which revealed a range of movements with contrasting agendas. Yet when examined closely, most of these movements present a claim to be *the* way for men to think and live. Whatever the empirical diversity of masculinities, the contestation for hegemony implies that gender hierarchy does not have multiple niches at the top. We will return to this issue, which is important for understanding gender politics.

Review and reformulation

We now draw these threads together to suggest how the concept of hegemonic masculinity should be reshaped. We will indicate those features of the original concept that have held up well in the light of research and criticism, those features that should be discarded, and (in greater detail) those areas where the concept is in need of contemporary reformulation.

What should be retained

The fundamental feature of the concept remains the combination of the plurality of masculinities and the hierarchy of masculinities. This basic idea has stood up well in 20 years of research experience. Multiple patterns of masculinity have been identified in many studies, in a variety of countries, and in different institutional and cultural settings. It is also a widespread research finding that certain masculinities are more socially central, or more associated with authority and social power, than others. The concept of hegemonic masculinity presumes the subordination of nonhegemonic masculinities, and this is a process that has now been documented in many settings, internationally.

Also well supported is the idea that the hierarchy of masculinities is a pattern of hegemony, not a pattern of simple domination based on force. Cultural consent, discursive centrality, institutionalization, and the marginalization or delegitimation of alternatives are widely documented features of socially dominant masculinities. Also well supported is the original idea that hegemonic masculinity need not be the commonest pattern in the everyday lives of boys and men. Rather, hegemony works in part through the production of exemplars of masculinity (e.g., professional sports stars), symbols that have authority despite the fact that most men and boys do not fully live up to them.

The original formulations laid some emphasis on the possibility of change in gender relations, on the idea that a dominant pattern of masculinity was open to challenge—from women's resistance to patriarchy, and from men as bearers of alternative masculinities. Research has very fully confirmed the idea of the historical construction and reconstruction of hegemonic masculinities. Both at a local and a broad societal level, the situations in which masculinities were formed change over time. These changes call forth new strategies in gender relations (e.g., companionate marriage) and result in redefinitions of socially admired masculinity (e.g., the domestic partner rather than the Victorian patriarch).

What should be rejected

Two features of early formulations about hegemonic masculinity have not stood up to criticism and should be discarded. The first is a too-simple model of the social relations surrounding hegemonic masculinities. The formulation in *Gender and Power* attempted to locate all masculinities (and all femininities) in terms of a single pattern of power, the "global dominance" of men over women (Connell 1987, 183). While this was useful at the time in preventing the idea of multiple masculinities from collapsing into an array of competing lifestyles, it is now clearly inadequate to our understanding of relations among groups of men and forms of masculinity and of women's relations with dominant masculinities. For instance, dominance in gender relations involves an interplay of costs and benefits, challenges to hegemonic masculinity arise from the "protest masculinities" of marginalized ethnic groups, and bourgeois women may appropriate aspects of hegemonic masculinity in constructing corporate or professional careers. Clearly, better ways of understanding gender hierarchy are required.

Despite the critique of trait psychology in *Gender and Power*, and the appeal to psychoanalytic ideas about unconscious motivation, early statements about hegemonic masculinity, when they attempted to characterize the actual content of different configurations of masculinity, often fell back on trait terminology—or at best failed to offer an alternative to it. The notion of masculinity as an assemblage of traits opened the path to that treatment of hegemonic masculinity as a fixed character type that has given so much trouble and is rightly criticized in recent psychological writing. Not only the essentialist concept of masculinity but also, more generally, the trait approach to gender need to be thoroughly transcended.

What should be reformulated

In light of the research and critiques discussed above, we argue that the concept of hegemonic masculinity is in need of reformulation in four main areas: the nature of gender hierarchy, the geography of masculine configurations, the process of social embodiment, and the dynamics of masculinities. In the following subsections, we offer a line of thought, and some research suggestions, about each of these issues.

Gender hierarchy

Compared with original formulations of the concept, contemporary research has shown the complexity of the relationships among different constructions of masculinity. The recent research in discursive psychology indicates how different constructions of masculinity at the local level may serve as tactical alternatives. Structured relations among masculinities exist in all local settings, motivation toward a specific hegemonic version varies by local context, and such local versions inevitably differ somewhat from each other. Demetriou's (2001) notion of dialectical pragmatism captures the reciprocal influence of masculinities on each other; hegemonic masculine patterns may change by incorporating elements from the others.

Analyses of relations among masculinities now more clearly recognize the agency of subordinated and marginalized groups—often conditioned by their specific location (as discussed below). "Protest masculinity" (Poynting, Noble, and Tabar 2003) can be understood in this sense: a pattern of masculinity constructed in local working-class settings, sometimes among ethnically marginalized men, which embodies the claim to power typical of regional hegemonic masculinities in Western countries, but which lacks the economic resources and institutional authority that underpins the regional and global patterns.

Research has also documented the durability or survivability of non-hegemonic patterns of masculinity, which may represent well-crafted responses to race/ethnic marginalization, physical disability, class inequality, or stigmatized sexuality. Hegemony may be accomplished by the incorporation of such masculinities into a functioning gender order rather than by active oppression in the form of discredit or violence. In practice, both incorporation and oppression can occur together. This is, for instance, the contemporary position of gay masculinities in Western urban centers, where gay communities have a spectrum of experience ranging from homophobic violence and cultural denigration to toleration and even cultural celebration and political representation. Similar processes of incorporation and oppression may occur among girls and women who construct masculinities (Messerschmidt 2004).

The concept of hegemonic masculinity was originally formulated in tandem with a concept of hegemonic femininity—soon renamed "emphasized femininity" to acknowledge the asymmetrical position of masculinities and femininities in a patriarchal gender order. In the development of research on men and masculinities, this relationship has dropped out of focus. This is regrettable for more than one reason. Gender is always relational, and patterns of masculinity are socially defined in contradistinction from some model (whether real or imaginary) of femininity.

Perhaps more important, focusing only on the activities of men occludes the practices of women in the construction of gender among men. As is well shown by life-history research, women are central in many of the processes constructing masculinities—as mothers; as schoolmates; as girlfriends, sexual partners, and wives; as workers in the gender division of labor; and so forth. The concept of emphasized femininity focused on compliance to patriarchy, and this is still highly relevant in contemporary mass culture. Yet gender hierarchies are also affected by new configurations of women's identity and practice, especially among younger women—which are increasingly acknowledged by younger men. We consider that research on hegemonic masculinity now needs to give much closer attention to the practices of women and to the historical interplay of femininities and masculinities.

We suggest, therefore, that our understanding of hegemonic masculinity needs to incorporate a more holistic understanding of gender hierarchy, recognizing the agency of subordinated groups as much as the power of dominant groups and the mutual conditioning of gender dynamics and other social dynamics. We think this will tend, over time, to reduce the isolation of men's studies and will emphasize the relevance of gender dynamics to the problems—ranging from effects of globalization to issues of violence and peacemaking—being explored in other fields of social science.

The geography of masculinities

Change in locally specific constructions of hegemonic masculinity has been a theme of research for the past two decades. But with growing attention to globalization, the significance of transnational arenas for the construction of masculinity has also been argued. Hooper (1998, 2000) describes the deployment of hegemonic and other masculinities in the arenas of international relations, and Connell (1998) proposed a model of "transnational business masculinity" among corporate executives that was connected with neoliberal agendas of globalization.

Whether, or how far, such processes override more local and regional gender dynamics is still being debated. Pease and Pringle (2001), in a recent international collection, argue for a continued focus on understanding masculinities regionally and comparatively. At the least, we must understand that regional and local constructions of hegemonic masculinity are shaped by the articulation of these gender systems with global processes. In this vein, Kimmel (2005) has recently examined how the effects of a global hegemonic masculinity are embedded in the emergence of regional (white supremacists in the United States and Sweden) and global (al Qaeda from the Middle East) "protest" masculinities.

We consider these issues are now unavoidable for studies of masculinity and suggest the following simple framework. Empirically existing hegemonic masculinities can be analyzed at three levels:

1 Local: constructed in the arenas of face-to-face interaction of families, organizations, and immediate communities, as typically found in ethnographic and life-history research;
2 Regional: constructed at the level of the culture or the nation-state, as typically found in discursive, political, and demographic research; and
3 Global: constructed in transnational arenas such as world politics and transnational business and media, as studied in the emerging research on masculinities and globalization.

Not only do links between these levels exist; they can be important in gender politics. Global institutions pressure regional and local gender orders; while regional gender orders provide cultural materials adopted or reworked in global arenas and provide models of masculinity that may be important in local gender dynamics.

Let us consider specifically the relation between regional and local masculinities. Hegemonic masculinity at the regional level is symbolically represented through the interplay of specific local masculine practices that have regional significance, such as those constructed by feature film actors, professional athletes, and politicians. The exact content of these practices varies over time and across societies. Yet regional hegemonic masculinity shapes a society-wide sense of masculine reality and, therefore, operates in the cultural domain as on-hand material to be actualized, altered, or challenged through practice in a range of different local circumstances. A regional hegemonic masculinity, then, provides a cultural framework that may be materialized in daily practices and interactions.

As an illustration of this interplay between regional and local hegemonic masculinities, consider the example of sport. In Western societies, practice at the local level—such as engaging in professional sporting events—constructs hegemonic masculine models (e.g., "star athletes") at the regional level, which in turn affect other local settings. Research on secondary schooling provides a paradigmatic example, indicating that successful participation in sport often is a salient hegemonic masculine practice in this particular local setting (Messner 2002). For example, Light and Kirk (2000) examine an elite Australian high school, finding that a clear structure of masculinities existed at this school in which a specific hegemonic form was shaped through the embodied practice of rugby football—a code that is, of course, not confined to this school—centering on domination, aggression, ruthless competitiveness, and giving all for the school. (Compare the similar findings of Burgess, Edwards, and Skinner 2003.) Thus, regionally significant exemplary masculine models influence—although they do not wholly determine—the construction of gender relations and hegemonic masculinities at the local level.

It is tempting to assume a simple hierarchy of power or authority, running from global to regional to local, but this could be misleading. In discussions of globalization, the determining power of the "global" is often overestimated, while the resistance and capacity of what we are calling the "regional" goes unrecognized (Mittelman 2004). The limited research that has so far been done on masculinities in global arenas (e.g., Connell and Wood 2005; Hooper 2001) does not suggest a powerful formation with the capacity to overwhelm regional or local masculinities. Yet the evidence on global dynamics in gender is growing, and it is clear that processes such as economic restructuring, long-distance migration, and the turbulence of "development" agendas have the power to reshape local patterns of masculinity and femininity (Connell 2005; Morrell and Swart 2005). There is every reason to think that interactions involving global masculinities will become of more importance in gender politics, and this is a key arena for future research on hegemony.

Adopting an analytical framework that distinguishes local, regional, and global masculinities (and the same point applies to femininities) allows us to recognize the importance of place without falling into a monadic world of totally independent cultures or discourses. It also casts some light on the problem of multiple hegemonic masculinities, raised above. Although local models of hegemonic masculinity may differ from each other, they generally overlap. The interplay with society-wide gender dynamics is part of the explanation. Furthermore, hegemonic masculinities are, as we have just argued, to a significant degree constituted in men's interaction with women; therefore, the commonalities in women's gender practices also produce convergence. Accordingly, local constructions of hegemonic masculinity have a certain "family resemblance," to use Wittgenstein's term, rather than logical identity. In this sense, local plurality is compatible with singularity of hegemonic masculinity at the regional or society-wide level. The "family resemblance" among local variants is likely to be represented by one symbolic model at the regional level, not by multiple models.

Social embodiment

That hegemonic masculinity is related to particular ways of representing and using men's bodies has been recognized from the earliest formulations of the concept. Yet the pattern of embodiment involved in hegemony has not been convincingly theorized.

The importance of masculine embodiment for identity and behavior emerges in many contexts. In youth, skilled bodily activity becomes a prime indicator of masculinity, as we have already seen with sport. This is a key way that heterosexuality and masculinity become linked in Western culture, with prestige conferred on boys with heterosexual partners and sexual learning imagined as exploration and conquest. Body practices such as eating meat and taking risks on the road also become linked with masculine identities. This logically results in health promotion strategies that work by degendering—contesting hegemonic masculinity, or moving men in a more androgynous direction. But the difficulties of degendering strategies also are partly based in embodiment, for instance, in the commitment to risk-taking practices as means of establishing masculine reputation in a peer group context.

The common social scientific reading of bodies as objects of a process of social construction is now widely considered to be inadequate. Bodies are involved more actively, more intimately, and more intricately in social processes than theory has usually allowed. Bodies participate in social action by delineating courses of social conduct—the body is a participant in generating social practice. It is important not only that masculinities be understood as embodied but also that the interweaving of embodiment and social context be addressed.

The need for a more sophisticated treatment of embodiment in hegemonic masculinity is made particularly clear by the issue of transgender practices, which are difficult to understand within a simple model of social construction. This issue has been reframed by the rise of queer theory, which has treated gender crossing as a subversion of the gender order or at least as a demonstration of its vulnerability. Sharp debates over transsexualism have arisen, with some psychiatrists' questioning the very possibility of gender change. It is therefore not easy to be confident about the implications of transgender practice for hegemony. With Rubin (2003) and Namaste (2000), we consider that the masculinities constructed in female-to-male transsexuals' life courses are not inherently counterhegemonic. "Self-made men" can pursue gender equality or oppose it, just like nontranssexual men. What the transsexual experience highlights is modernity's treatment of the body as the "medium through which selves interact with each other" (Rubin 2003, 180).

To understand embodiment and hegemony, we need to understand that bodies are both objects of social practice and agents in social practice (Connell 2002). There are circuits of social practice linking bodily processes and social structures—many such circuits, which add up to the historical process in which society is embodied. These circuits of social embodiment may be very direct and simple, or they may be long and complex, passing through institutions, economic relations, cultural symbols, and so forth—without ceasing to involve material bodies. This can readily be illustrated by thinking about the gender patterns in health, illness, and medical treatment.

Among dominant groups of men, the circuits of social embodiment constantly involve the institutions on which their privileges rest. This is dramatically shown in a pioneering study by Donaldson and Poynting (2004) of the daily lives of ruling-class men. This study shows, for instance, how their characteristic sports, leisure, and eating practices deploy their wealth and establish relations of distance and dominance over other men's bodies. A rich field of research opens up here, especially when we consider how expensive technologies—computer systems, global air travel, secure communications—amplify the physical powers of elite men's bodies.

The dynamics of masculinities

Although long acknowledged, the internal complexity of masculinities has only gradually come into focus as a research issue. As indicated by our earlier discussion of the subject in gender practice, we must now explicitly recognize the layering, the potential internal contradiction, within all practices that construct masculinities. Such practices cannot be read simply as expressing a unitary masculinity. They may, for instance, represent compromise formations between contradictory desires or emotions, or the results of uncertain calculations about the costs and benefits of different gender strategies.

Life-history research has pointed to another dynamic of masculinities, the structure of a project. Masculinities are configurations of practice that are constructed, unfold, and change through time. A small literature on masculinity and aging, and a larger one on childhood and youth, emphasize this issue. The careful analysis of life histories may detect contradictory commitments and institutional transitions that reflect different hegemonic masculinities and also hold seeds of change.

Hegemonic masculinities are likely to involve specific patterns of internal division and emotional conflict, precisely because of their association with gendered power. Relationships with fathers are one likely focus of tension, given the gender division of labor in child care, the "long hours culture" in professions and management, and the preoccupation of rich fathers with managing their wealth. Ambivalence toward projects of change on the part of women are likely to be another, leading to oscillating acceptance and rejection of gender equality by the same men. Any strategy for the maintenance of power is likely to involve a dehumanizing of other groups and a corresponding withering of empathy and emotional relatedness within the self (Schwalbe 1992). Without treating privileged men as objects of pity, we should recognize that hegemonic masculinity does not necessarily translate into a satisfying experience of life.

Change over time, while certainly shaped by contradictions within masculinities, may also be intentional. Children as well as adults have a capacity to deconstruct gender binaries and criticize hegemonic masculinity, and this capacity is the basis of many educational interventions and change programs. At the same time, bearers of hegemonic masculinity are not necessarily "cultural dopes"; they may actively attempt to modernize gender relations and to reshape masculinities as part of the deal. A good example is the "new public management" in public-sector organizations, which rejects old-style bureaucracy and believes in "flatter" organizations, equal opportunity, and family-friendly employment policies. Yet even the modernization of masculinities may not solve problems. This too, as Meuser (2001) argues, generates contradictions that may lead to further change.

Gender relations are always arenas of tension. A given pattern of hegemonic masculinity is hegemonic to the extent that it provides a solution to these tensions, tending to stabilize patriarchal power or reconstitute it in new conditions. A pattern of practice (i.e., a version of masculinity) that provided such a solution in past conditions but not in new conditions is open to challenge—is in fact certain to be challenged.

Such contestation occurs continuously, through the efforts of the women's movement (at the local, regional, and global levels), among generations in immigrant communities, between models of managerial masculinity, among rivals for political authority, among claimants for attention in the entertainment industry, and so on. The contestation is real, and gender theory does not predict which will prevail—the process is historically open. Accordingly, hegemony may fail. The concept of hegemonic masculinity does not rely on a theory of social reproduction.

Put another way, the conceptualization of hegemonic masculinity should explicitly acknowledge the possibility of democratizing gender relations, of abolishing power differentials, not just of reproducing hierarchy. A transitional move in this direction requires an attempt to establish as hegemonic among men ("internal hegemony" in Demetriou's [2001] sense) a version of masculinity open to equality with women. In this sense, it is possible to define a hegemonic masculinity that is thoroughly "positive" (in Collier's [1998] sense). Recent history has shown the difficulty of doing this in practice. A positive hegemony remains, nevertheless, a key strategy for contemporary efforts at reform.

Conclusion

Concepts in the social sciences arise in response to specific intellectual and practical problems, and they are formulated in specific languages and intellectual styles. But they also have a capacity to travel and may acquire new meanings as they do. This has certainly happened with the concept of hegemonic masculinity, which has been taken up in fields ranging from education and psychotherapy to violence prevention and international relations. Some of the ambiguities that annoy critics stem from the varied uses that the concept has found and the ways it has been inflected in response to new contexts.

This is perhaps a general problem about conceptualization in the social sciences and humanities. As a theoretical formulation finds application in other settings and by other hands, the concept must mutate—and it may mutate in different directions in different environments. A specific concept may thus transform into a general way of talking, a style of analysis, or a characteristic figure in argument. There is nothing wrong with this process in itself—it is a common way that knowledge in the social sciences and humanities develops. But it means that new usages must also be open to critique and may lack some of the substance or justification of the original.

Thus, while we welcome most of the applications and modifications of the hegemonic masculinity concept as contributions to the understanding of gender dynamics, we reject those usages that imply a fixed character type, or an assemblage of toxic traits. These usages are not trivial—they are trying to name significant issues about gender, such as the persistence of violence or the consequences of domination. But they do so in a way that conflicts with the analysis of hegemony in gender relations and is therefore incompatible with (not just a variation on) both the initial statements and the main developments of this concept.

A renovated analysis of hegemonic masculinities, of the kind suggested above, has a growing relevance in the present moment of gender politics. In the rich countries of the global metropole, the shift from neoliberalism (the radical market agenda formulated in the 1970s) to neoconservatism (adding populist appeals to religion, ethnocentrism, and security) has made gender reaction an important political and cultural issue. In the developing countries, the processes of globalization have opened regional and local gender orders to new pressures for transformation and have also opened the way to new coalitions among groups of powerful men. In the global arenas of transnational corporations, media, and security systems, new patterns of hegemony are being forged. The making and contestation of hegemony in historically changing gender orders is a process of enormous importance for which we continue to need conceptual tools.

Note

The authors are grateful to the journal's reviewers, Pat Martin, Mike Messner, and Kirsten Dellinger, for extremely helpful comments on an earlier draft of this article. We also extend our thanks to John Fisher, whose patient and inventive searching of bibliographical databases provided essential support for this article.

References

Altman, D. 1972. *Homosexual: Oppression and liberation.* Sydney, Australia: Angus and Robertson.

Archer, L. 2001. Muslim brothers, Black lads, traditional Asians: British Muslim young men's constructions of race, religion and masculinity. *Feminism & Psychology* 11 (1): 79–105.

Baca Zinn, M. 1982. Chicano men and masculinity. *Journal of Ethnic Studies* 10 (2): 29–44.

Barrett, F. J. 1996. The organizational construction of hegemonic masculinity: The case of the U.S. Navy. *Gender, Work and Organization* 3 (3): 129–42.

Belton, R. J. 1995. *The beribboned bomb: The image of woman in male surrealist art.* Calgary, Canada: University of Calgary Press.

Berg, L. D. 1994. Masculinity, place and a binary discourse of "theory" and "empirical investigation" in the human geography of Aotearoa/New Zealand. *Gender, Place and Culture* 1 (2): 245–60.

Bird, S. R. 1996. Welcome to the men's club: Homosociality and the maintenance of hegemonic masculinity. *Gender & Society* 10 (2): 120–32.

Bourdieu, P. 2001. *Masculine domination.* Stanford, CA: Stanford University Press.

Brannon, R. 1976. The male sex role: Our culture's blueprint of manhood, and what it's done for us lately. In *The forty-nine percent majority: The male sex role*, edited by D. S. David and R. Brannon. Reading, MA: Addington-Wesley.

Brod, H. 1987. *The making of masculinities: The new men's studies.* Boston: Allen and Unwin.

——. 1994. Some thoughts on some histories of some masculinities: Jews and other others. In *Theorizing masculinities*, edited by D. S. David and R. Brannon. Thousand Oaks, CA: Sage.

Broker, M. 1976. "I may be a queer, but at least I am a man": Male hegemony and ascribed versus achieved gender. In *Sexual divisions and society*, edited by D. Leonard Barker and S. Allen. London: Tavistock.

Brown, D. 1999. Complicity and reproduction in teaching physical education. *Sport, Education and Society* 4 (2): 143–59.

Bufkin, J. L. 1999. Bias crime as gendered behavior. *Social Justice* 26 (1): 155–76.

Burgess, I., A. Edwards, and J. Skinner. 2003. Football culture in an Australian school setting: The construction of masculine identity. *Sport, Education and Society* 8 (2): 199–212.

Campbell, H. 2000. The glass phallus: Pub(lic) masculinity and drinking in rural New Zealand. *Rural Sociology* 65 (4): 562–81.

Carrigan, T., R. W. Connell, and J. Lee. 1985. Toward a new sociology of masculinity. *Theory and Society* 14 (5): 551–604.

Cavender, G. 1999. Detecting masculinity. In *Making trouble: Cultural constructions of crime, deviance and control*, edited by J. Ferrell and N. Websdale. New York: Aldine de Gruyter.

Cheng, C. 1996. "We choose not to compete": The "merit" discourse in the selection process, and Asian and Asian American men and their masculinity. In *Masculinities in organizations*, edited by C. Cheng. Thousand Oaks, CA: Sage.

Cockburn, C. 1983. *Brothers: Male dominance and technological change*. London: Pluto.
——. 1991. *In the way of men: Men's resistance to sex equality in organizations*. London: Macmillan.
Collier, R. 1998. *Masculinities, crime and criminology: Men, heterosexuality and the criminal(ised) other*. London: Sage.
Collinson, D., and J. Hearn. 1994. Naming men as men: Implications for work, organization and management. *Gender, Work and Organization* 1 (1): 2–22.
Collinson, D., D. Knights, and M. Collinson. 1990. *Managing to discriminate*. London: Routledge.
Connell, R. W. 1977. *Ruling class, ruling culture*. Cambridge, UK: Cambridge University Press.
——. 1982. Class, patriarchy, and Sartre's theory of practice. *Theory and Society* 11:305–20.
——. 1983. *Which way is up? Essays on sex, class and culture*. Sydney, Australia: Allen and Unwin.
——. 1987. *Gender and power*. Sydney, Australia: Allen and Unwin.
——. 1990. An iron man: The body and some contradictions of hegemonic masculinity. In *Sport, men and the gender order*, edited by M. Messner and D. Sabo. Champaign, IL: Human Kinetics Books.
——. 1995. *Masculinities*. Cambridge, UK: Polity Press.
——. 1998. Masculinities and globalization. *Men and Masculinities* 1 (1): 3–23.
——. 2002. *Gender*. Cambridge, UK: Polity Press.
——. 2003. Masculinities, change and conflict in global society: Thinking about the future of men's studies. *Journal of Men's Studies* 11 (3): 249–66.
——. 2005. Globalization, imperialism, and masculinities. In *Handbook of studies on men & masculinities*, edited by M. S. Kimmel, J. Hearn, and R. W. Connell. Thousand Oaks, CA: Sage.
Connell, R. W., D. J. Ashenden, S. Kessler, and G. W. Dowsett. 1982. *Making the difference: Schools, families and social division*. Sydney, Australia: Allen and Unwin.
Connell, R. W., and J. Wood. 2005. Globalization and business masculinities. *Men and Masculinities* 7 (4): 347–64.
Consalvo, M. 2003. The monsters next door: Media constructions of boys and masculinity. *Feminist Media Studies* 3 (1): 27–46.
Dasgupta, R. 2000. Performing masculinities? The "salaryman" at work and play. *Japanese Studies* 20 (2): 189–200.
Davis, A. 1983. *Women, race, and class*. New York: Vintage.
Demetriou, D. Z. 2001. Connell's concept of hegemonic masculinity: A critique. *Theory and Society* 30 (3): 337–61.
Denborough, D. 1996. Step by step: Developing respectful and effective ways of working with young men to reduce violence. In *Men's ways of being*, edited by C. McLean, M. Carey, and C. White. Boulder, CO: Westview.
Dinges, M., E. Ründal, and D. Bauer. 2004. Programm. Program for the Hegemoniale Männlichkeiten conference, Stuttgart, Germany, 24–26 June.
Donaldson, M. 1991. *Time of our lives: Labor and love in the working class*. Sydney, Australia: Allen and Unwin.
——. 1993. What is hegemonic masculinity? *Theory and Society* 22:643–57.

Donaldson, M., and S. Poynting. 2004. The time of their lives: Time, work and leisure in the daily lives of ruling-class men. In *Ruling Australia: The power, privilege & politics of the new ruling class*, edited by N. Hollier. Melbourne: Australian Scholarly.

Eisenstein, Z. R. 1979. *Capitalist patriarchy and the case for socialist feminism*. New York: Monthly Review Press.

Ferguson, H. 2001. Men and masculinities in late-modern Ireland. In *A man's world? Changing men's practices in a globalized world*, edited by B. Pease and K. Pringle. London: Zed Books.

Freud, Sigmund. [1917] 1955. *From the history of an infantile neurosis. Complete psychological works*. Standard ed., Vol. 17. London: Hogarth.

Friedman, R. M., and L. Lerner. 1986. Toward a new psychology of men: Psychoanalytic and social perspectives. Special issue, *Psychoanalytic Review* 73 (4).

Gerschick, T. J., and A. S. Miller. 1994. Gender identities at the crossroads of masculinity and physical disability. *Masculinities* 2 (1): 34–55.

Goode, W. 1982. Why men resist. In *Rethinking the family: Some feminist questions*, edited by B. Thorne and M. Yalom. New York: Longman.

Gutmann, M. C. 1996. *The meanings of macho: Being a man in Mexico City*. Berkeley: University of California Press.

Hacker, H. M. 1957. The new burdens of masculinity. *Marriage and Family Living* 19 (3): 227–33.

Halberstam, J. 1998. *Female masculinity*. Durham, NC: Duke University Press.

Hanke, R. 1992. Redesigning men: Hegemonic masculinity in transition. In *Men, masculinity, and the media*, edited by S. Craig. Newbury Park, CA: Sage.

Hawkesworth, M. 1997. Confounding gender. *Signs: Journal of Women in Culture and Society* 22 (3): 649–85.

Hearn, J. 1996. Is masculinity dead? A critique of the concept of masculinity/masculinities. In *Understanding masculinities: Social relations and cultural arenas*, edited by M. Mac an Ghaill. Buckingham, UK: Open University Press.

——. 2004. From hegemonic masculinity to the hegemony of men. *Feminist Theory* 5 (1): 49–72.

Herdt, G. H. 1981. *Guardians of the flutes: Idioms of masculinity*. New York: McGraw-Hill.

Higate, P. R. 2003. *Military masculinities: Identity and the state*. London: Praeger.

Hochschild, A. 1989. *The second shift: Working parents and the revolution at home*. New York: Viking.

Holter, Ø. G. 1997. *Gender, patriarchy and capitalism: A social forms analysis*. Oslo, Norway: University of Olso.

——. 2003. *Can men do it? Men and gender equality—The Nordic experience*. Copenhagen, Denmark: Nordic Council of Ministers.

hooks, b. 1984. *Feminist theory: From margin to center*. Boston: South End.

Hooper, C. 1998. Masculinist practices and gender politics: The operation of multiple masculinities in international relations. In *The "man" question in international relations*, edited by M. Zalewski and J. Parpart. Boulder, CO: Westview.

——. 2000. Masculinities in transition: The case of globalization. *In Gender and global restructuring*, edited by M. H. Marchand and A. S. Runyan. London: Routledge.

——. 2001. *Manly states: Masculinities, international relations, and gender politics*. New York: Columbia University Press.

Hunt, P. 1980. *Gender and class consciousness*. London: Macmillan.

Ishii-Kuntz, M. 2003. Balancing fatherhood and work: Emergence of diverse masculinities in contemporary Japan. In *Men and masculinities in contemporary Japan*, edited by J. E. Roberson and N. Suzuki. London: Routledge Curzon.

Jansen, S. C., and D. Sabo. 1994. The sport-war metaphor: Hegemonic masculinity, the Persian-Gulf war, and the new world order. *Sociology of Sport Journal* 11 (1): 1–17.

Jefferson, T. 1994. Theorizing masculine subjectivity. In *Just boys doing business? Men, masculinities and crime*, edited by T. Newburn and E. A. Stanko. London: Routledge.

——. 2002. Subordinating hegemonic masculinity. *Theoretical Criminology* 6 (1): 63–88.

Kessler, S. J., D. J. Ashenden, R. W. Connell, and G. W. Dowsett. 1982. *Ockers and disco-maniacs*. Sydney, Australia: Inner City Education Center.

Kimmel, M. S. 1987. Rethinking "masculinity": New directions in research. In *Changing men: New directions in research on men and masculinity*, edited by M. S. Kimmel. Newbury Park, CA: Sage.

——. 2005. Globalization and its mal(e)contents: The gendered moral and political economy of terrorism. In *Handbook of studies on men & masculinities*, edited by M. S. Kimmel, J. Hearn, and R. W. Connell. Thousand Oaks, CA: Sage.

Kimmel, M. S., and M. Mahler. 2003. Adolescent masculinity, homophobia, and violence: Random school shootings, 1982–2001. *American Behavioral Scientist* 46 (10): 1439–58.

Kupers, T. A. 1993. *Revisioning men's lives: Gender, intimacy, and power*. New York: Guilford.

Lea, S., and T. Auburn. 2001. The social construction of rape in the talk of a convicted rapist. *Feminism & Psychology* 11 (1): 11–33.

Light, R., and D. Kirk. 2000. High school rugby, the body and the reproduction of hegemonic masculinity. *Sport, Education and Society* 5 (2): 163–76.

Mac an Ghaill, M. 1994. *The making of men: Masculinities, sexualities and schooling*. Buckingham, UK: Open University Press.

MacInnes, J. 1998. *The end of masculinity: The confusion of sexual genesis and sexual difference in modern society*. Buckingham, UK: Open University Press.

Martin. P. Y. 1998. Why can't a man be more like a woman? Reflections on Connell's masculinities. *Gender & Society* 12 (4): 472–74.

——. 2001. "Mobilizing masculinities": Women's experiences of men at work. *Organizations* 8 (4): 587–618.

Martino, W. 1995. Boys and literacy: Exploring the construction of hegemonic masculinities and the formation of literate capacities for boys in the English classroom. *English in Australia* 112:11–24.

McMahon, A. 1993. Male readings of feminist theory: The psychologization of sexual politics in the masculinity literature. *Theory and Society* 22 (5): 675–95.

Messerschmidt, J. W. 1993. *Masculinities and crime: Critique and reconceptualization of theory*. Lanham, MD: Rowman & Littlefield.

——. 1995. Managing to kill: Masculinities and the space shuttle Challenger explosion. *Masculinities* 3 (4): 1–22.

——. 1997. *Crime as structured action: Gender, race, class and crime in the making*. Thousand Oaks, CA: Sage.

Messerschmidt, J. W. 2000. *Nine lives: Adolescent masculinities, the body, and violence.* Boulder, CO: Westview.

——. 2004. *Flesh & blood: Adolescent gender diversity and violence.* Lanham, MD: Rowman & Littlefield.

——. 2005. Men, masculinities, and crime. In *Handbook of studies on men & masculinities*, edited by M. S. Kimmel, J. Hearn, and R. W. Connell. Thousand Oaks, CA: Sage.

Messner, M. A. 1992. *Power at play: Sports and the problem of masculinity.* Boston: Beacon.

——. 1997. *Politics of masculinities: Men in movements.* Thousand Oaks, CA: Sage.

——. 2002. *Taking the field: Women, men, and sport.* Minneapolis: University of Minnesota Press.

Messner, M. A., and D. Sabo, eds. 1990. *Sport, men, and the gender order: Critical feminist perspectives.* Champaign, IL: Human Kinetics Books.

Meuser, M. 2001. "This doesn't really mean she's holding a whip": Transformation of the gender order and the contradictory modernization of masculinity. *Diskurs* 1:44–50.

——. 2003. Modernized masculinities? Continuities, challenges and changes in men's lives. In *Among men: Moulding masculinities*, edited by S. Ervø and T. Johannson. Aldershot, UK: Ashgate.

Meuser, M., and C. Behnke. 1998. Tausendundeine Männlichkeit? Männlichkeitsmuster und socialstrukturelle Einbindungen. *Widersprüche* 67:7–25.

Mieli, M. 1980. *Homosexuality and liberation: Elements of a gay critique*, translated by D. Fernbach. London: Gay Men's Press.

Mittelman, J. H. 2004. *Whither globalization? The vortex of knowledge and ideology.* London: Routledge.

Morin, S. F., and E. M. Garfinkle. 1978. Male homophobia. *Journal of Social Issues* 34 (1): 29–47.

Morrell, R. 1998. Of boys and men: Masculinity and gender in southern African studies. *Journal of Southern African Studies* 24 (4): 605–30.

Morrell, R., and S. Swart. 2005. Men in the Third World: Postcolonial perspectives on masculinity. In *Handbook of studies on men & masculinities*, edited by M. S. Kimmel, J. Hearn, and R. W. Connell. Thousand Oaks, CA: Sage.

Morris, C., and N. Evans. 2001. "Cheese makers are always women": Gendered representations of farm life in the agricultural press. *Gender, Place and Culture* 8 (4): 375–90.

Mosher, D. L., and S. S. Tomkins. 1988. Scripting the macho man: Hypermasculine socialization and enculturation. *Journal of Sex Research* 25 (1): 60–84.

Namaste, V. K. 2000. *Invisible lives: The erasure of transsexual and transgendered people.* Chicago: University of Chicago Press.

Newburn, T., and E. A. Stanko. 1994. *Just boys doing business? Men, masculinities, and crime.* New York: Routledge.

Pease, B., and K. Pringle, eds. 2001. *A man's world? Changing men's practices in a globalized world.* London: Zed Books.

Petersen, A. 1998. *Unmasking the masculine: "Men" and "identity" in a sceptical age.* London: Sage.

——. 2003. Research on men and masculinities: Some implications of recent theory for future work. *Men and Masculinities* 6 (1): 54–69.

Pleck, J. 1981. *The myth of masculinity*. Cambridge, MA: MIT Press.

Plummer, K., ed. 1981. *The making of the modern homosexual*. London: Macmillan.

Poynting, S., G. Noble, and P. Tabar. 2003. "Intersections" of masculinity and ethnicity: A study of male Lebanese immigrant youth in Western Sydney. Unpublished manuscript, University of Western Sydney.

Roberts, P. 1993. Social control and the censure(s) of sex. *Crime, Law and Social Change* 19 (2): 171–86.

Roper, M. 1994. *Masculinity and the British organization man since 1945*. Oxford, UK: Oxford University Press.

Rubin, H. 2003. *Self-made men: Identity and embodiment among transsexual men*. Nashville, TN: Vanderbilt University Press.

Sabo, D., and D. F. Gordon, eds. 1995. *Men's health and illness: Gender, power and the body*. Thousand Oaks, CA: Sage.

Sabo, D., and S. C. Jansen. 1992. Images of men in sport media: The social reproduction of gender order. In *Men, masculinity, and the media*, edited by S. Craig. Newbury Park, CA: Sage.

Salisbury, J., and D. Jackson. 1996. *Challenging macho values: Practical ways of working with adolescent boys*. Washington, DC: Falmer.

Schwalbe, M. 1992. Male supremacy and the narrowing of the moral self. *Berkeley Journal of Sociology* 37:29–54.

Scott, J. W. 1997. Comment on Hawkesworth's "confounding gender." *Signs: Journal of Women in Culture and Society* 22 (3): 697–702.

Segal, L. 1990. *Slow motion: Changing masculinities, changing men*. London: Virago.

Skelton, A. 1993. On becoming a male physical education teacher: The informal culture of students and the construction of hegemonic masculinity. *Gender and Education* 5 (3): 289–303.

Snodgrass, J., ed. 1977. *For men against sexism: A book of readings*. Albion, CA: Times Change Press.

Stoller, R. J. 1968. *Sex and gender: On the development of masculinity and femininity*. New York: Science House.

Taga, F. 2003. Rethinking male socialization: Life histories of Japanese male youth. In *Asian masculinities*, edited by K. Louie and M. Low. London: Routledge Curzon.

Thorne, B. 1993. *Gender play*. New Brunswick, NJ: Rutgers University Press.

Thornton, M. 1989. Hegemonic masculinity and the academy. *International Journal of the Sociology of Law* 17:115–30.

Tolson, A. 1977. *The limits of masculinity*. London: Tavistock.

Tomsen, S. 2002. *Hatred, murder and male honour: Anti-homosexual homicides in New South Wales, 1980–2000*. Vol. 43. Canberra: Australian Institute of Criminology.

Valdés, T., and J. Olavarría. 1998. Ser hombre en Santiago de Chile: A pesar de todo, un mismo modelo. In *Masculinidades y equidad de género en América Latina*, edited by T. Valdés and J. Olavarría. Santiago, Chile: FLACSO/UNFPA.

Wajcman, J. 1999. *Managing like a man: Women and men in corporate management*. Sydney, Australia: Allen and Unwin.

Walby, S. 1997. *Gender transformations*. London: Routledge.

Warren, S. 1997. Who do these boys think they are? An investigation into the construction of masculinities in a primary classroom. *International Journal of Inclusive Education* 1 (2): 207–22.

Wetherell, M., and N. Edley. 1999. Negotiating hegemonic masculinity: Imaginary positions and psycho-discursive practices. *Feminism and Psychology* 9 (3): 335–56.

Whitehead, S. M. 1998. Hegemonic masculinity revisited. *Gender, Work, and Organization* 6 (1): 58–62.

——. 2002. *Men and masculinities: Key themes and new directions*. Cambridge, UK: Polity.

Willis, P. 1977. *Learning to labor: How working class kids get working class jobs*. Farnborough, UK: Saxon House.

Zaretsky, E. 1975. Male supremacy and the unconscious. *Socialist Revolution* 4:7–55.

Part 3

THE AFTERMATH: THE SALIENCE OF GENDER AND THE PROBLEM OF BACKLASH?

12

CHALLENGING ORTHODOXIES IN FEMINIST THEORY

A black feminist critique

Marcia Rice

Source: L. Gelsthorpe and A. Morris (eds), *Feminist Perspectives in Criminology*, Milton Keynes: Open University Press, 1990, pp. 57–70.

Over the past decade feminist criminologists have been challenging stereotypical representations of female offenders. Despite these advances, black women and women from developing countries have been noticeably absent from this discourse. However, in part as a result of a surge of writings by black women (for example, Amos and Parmar, 1984; Carby, 1982; Mama, 1984; Bhavani and Coulson, 1986), there are now attempts to incorporate black women's experiences into feminist writings (Carlen and Worrall, 1987), though few attempt to develop perspectives which take into account race, gender and class simultaneously.

In this chapter I assess the limitations and potential of feminist contributions to these developments. I will focus on feminist criminologists' failure to see that traditional machocentric[1] criminology was constructed on racist as well as sexist ideologies of femininity (and, indeed, of masculinity). I will also show that feminist, just as much as conventional, orthodoxies are based on ethnocentric principles.[2] I will then argue that a broader conceptual framework is necessary which not only acknowledges the triple oppression of race, class and gender but also examines the historical basis of their inter-relationship. Finally I will argue that a black feminist perspective is necessary in order to understand the complexity of the struggles which black women face. I do not intend to present a definitive account of a black feminist perspective, merely one which serves to underline the need to give theoretical consideration to the experiences of black women.

The other dark figure in crime

Traditionally, the phrase the 'dark figure' of crime has been associated with hidden or unreported crime. The term is used here to refer to the way in which black female offenders have been overshadowed by both black men and white women in the criminological literature.[3] Black female offenders are straddled between what I call 'black criminology' (see, for example, the work of Hall *et al.*, 1978; Gilroy, 1982; 1987; Troyna and Cashmore, 1982; Bridges, 1983) which has focused on black men and feminist criminology which is largely concerned with white women. In the next section, I discuss in brief the failings of 'black criminology' and then discuss in more detail my concerns about current feminist criminological writings.

The contribution of 'black criminology'

There is now a significant body of research in Britain which has focused on black men and crime. One of the most popular assertions in conventional wisdom on race and crime is the inherently violent nature of West Indians. Writers such as Gilroy (1987) and Troyna and Cashmore (1982) have disputed this and argue instead that social, political and economic marginalization are of key significance. There is also a considerable amount of research on the experience of black men in the criminal justice system. Studies such as that of Smith and Gray (1983) show that young black men are roughly ten times more likely to be apprehended by the police than their white counterparts. There is also some evidence that black male offenders reach the courts at an earlier stage in their criminal careers (McConville and Baldwin, 1982; Crow, 1987) and are more likely to receive custodial sentences and imprisonment for longer periods than their white counterparts (NACRO, 1989; Crow, 1987).

None of these studies included black women or considered issues of particular relevance for them.[4] For example, concern about the high rates of arrest of black people on the streets does not extend to black women who are harassed by the police on suspicion of soliciting. There can be little justification for this neglect: black women make up over 20 per cent of the prison population, but only around 5 per cent of the general population.

The research which has addressed issues of racial bias in policing and sentencing has targeted particular types of offences and offenders (McConville and Baldwin, 1982; Crow, 1987; NACRO, 1989). The emphasis has been on street crimes and crimes of a predatory and violent nature (Hall *et al.*, 1978; Gilroy, 1982; Troyna and Cashmore, 1982). This discourse has failed to locate black women but, at the same time, has exacerbated the negative image of black men. The seeming invisiblity of black women creates false impressions about the extent and the nature of their involvement in criminal activity although research suggests that they are subjected to similar stereotyping and discriminatory treatment in the criminal justice system as black men (Lewis, 1977; GLC, 1985).

The contribution of feminist criminology

Given the history and theoretical objectives of feminist criminology, one might have assumed that the monolithic, uni-dimensional perspectives employed by traditional theorists would have been abandoned for a more dynamic approach. But, almost without exception, feminist criminological research – from the late 1960s to date – has focused on white female offenders. Pioneering writings by Heidensohn (1968) and Smart (1976) and more recent writings by Carlen and Worrall (1987) and Morris (1987) have all adopted an essentialist position with regards to the construct of 'women' and have paid little attention to the relevance of race. Sexist images of women have been challenged, but racist stereotypes have largely been ignored.

(White) women and crime

Since the 1970s, feminist criminologists have launched a critical attack on male-dominated theoretical premises in criminology. The basic point which they make is that these expositions are not theories of women's crime but stereotypes which perpetuate sexist ideologies of women. Feminists insist that many of the assumptions made about female criminals are incorrect – they are based on middle-class notions of morality and behaviour – and that the focus on biological and social pathologies to explain both crime and conformity is inadequate.

Central to these arguments is the belief that notions such as 'femininity' and 'sexuality' are constructs, not objective givens. But, this said, feminist writers have made little reference to the different cultural experiences and socialization patterns of black women. There is a failure to situate, for example, discussions of sex roles within a structural explanation of the social origins of these roles which are influenced by black women's racial and sexual experiences and their general position in society (Malson, 1983). Gender differences are assumed to be universal, irrespective of race (or class).

This is clearly not so. Despite significant changes in family structures in Britain, the popular representation of the family is the husband/father as the economic supporter of his wife and children and the wife/mother as the full-time domestic worker and child carer. This idealization does not touch on the experiences of black (or working-class) women. It not only excludes them, but distorts the particular gender roles adopted by them (Lewis, 1977; Carby, 1982; Malson, 1983). I provide two examples of this.

First, as a result of economic pressures and cultural distinctions, black women in Britain are more likely than white women to be single and full-time employees on low wages and are less likely to be primarily dependent on a man. Thus, in 1986, 40 per cent of West Indian women worked full-time compared with 20 per cent of white women and 25 per cent of Asian women. Moreover, *Social Trends* (Central Statistical Office, 1988) indicates that most women from ethnic minorities work soon after the birth of their children out of the necessity to provide for their families. Female-headed households are common amongst West Indians; yet the matriarchal family structure (coupled with low rates of marriage and high rates of illegitimacy) is viewed as 'pathological'.

Second, black girls develop early on a particular set of subcultural values which stress strength, independence, resilience and perseverance and which are necessary in the face of a racist and sex-segregated labour market (Riley, 1981; Bryan *et al.*, 1985). However, these qualities, when judged by ethnocentric standards, are viewed as 'unfeminine'. Feminist writers have challenged neither of these steroetypical representations.

(White) women and the criminal justice system

Also since the 1970s a number of feminist researchers have investigated a series of issues pertaining to the discriminatory practices and sexist ideologies present in the criminal justice system. They have covered a range of areas – women as defendants (Edwards, 1984), probationers (Worrall, 1989) and prisoners (Carlen, 1983). While there has been some acknowledgement that black women are not dealt with in the same way as white women (Eaton, 1986; Morris, 1987), no research has been carried out in Britain which compares the sentences of black and white women. This is an important point as a failure to consider the potentially different experiences of black women may invalidate the research findings. Race may be as important as gender, if not more so.

Research into women's imprisonment has covered a range of topics – experiences in prison (Carlen, 1983; O'Dwyer *et al.*, 1987), prison discipline and medical services (Mandaraka-Sheppard, 1986) and post-prison experiences (Wilkinson, 1988). Most of the studies point out that the majority of women are there not because of the seriousness of their offence or their criminal record, but rather as a result of their different and 'unacceptable' lifestyles. Particular emphasis has also been laid on the patriarchal ideologies which attempt to reinforce traditional modes of feminine behaviour on women in prison.

Almost without exception the bulk of the research carried out on women in custody has referred to 'women' (cf GLC, 1985) as a homogeneous category and has ignored the interaction of gender, race and class. For example, there is hardly any recognition of the special problems which black female prisoners encounter during their sentence on remand or after release. There is an assumption that all women are equally disadvantaged. For example, O'Dwyer, Wilson and Carlen write:

> Women in prison suffer all the same deprivation, indignities and degradations as male prisoners. Additionally they suffer other problems that are specific to them as imprisoned women.
>
> (1987: 178)

This statement is inadequate as it stands: it does not acknowledge the added problems of the isolation of and discrimination against black women. Bryan *et al.* (1985), for example, point to the fact that a higher percentage of black than white women in prison are on prescribed psychotropic drugs. This requires explanation. Furthermore, many black women serving long sentences are not indigenous but are from West Africa and are serving sentences for drugs offences. This group of female prisoners, often awaiting deportation, have special needs; for example, contact is usually severed with their families and there are problems of communication.

Feminist criminologists have paid more attention to race in research on women's victimization. Hall (1985), for example, found that black women were much more likely to be assaulted than white women because black women's economic situation tends to exacerbate their vulnerability, particularly as they work unsocial hours and rely on public transport. But while feminists have readily acknowledged that sexism is an important explanatory factor in the physical and sexual assault of any woman, they have been slow to see that racism is a further precipitating factor in attacks on black women. One black woman in Hall's survey sums up the significance of this:

> There's a particular fear of white men that Black girls grow up with. We know they think we're hot, sexual animals, that we're always available. It goes back to slavery. What they think about us sexually is part of the racism.
>
> (1985: 48)

There is another point to be made here. Some feminist criminologists, in arguing for longer sentences for offences against women, have ignored the discriminatory impact this is likely to have on black (and working-class) men.

Feminist research methods

Feminist theories have prided themselves on developing a method of inquiry which reconsiders the relationship between the researcher and the subject (McRobbie, 1982). Therefore, most of the research done by feminists has used methods which allow some participation by subjects in the research process. However, despite claims by feminists to be representing the subjective experiences of *all* women, much of the research has yet to prove its relevance to black women. In hooks's words:

> White women who dominate feminist discourse today rarely question whether or not their perspective on women's reality is true to the lived experience of women as a collective group.
>
> (1984: 3)

Feminist theorists have assumed that, as women, they were qualified to make assertions and generalizations on the grounds that all women's experiences are reducible to gender. However, as McRobbie pointed out in a different (class) context:

> No matter how much our past personal experience figures and feeds into the research programme, we can't possibly assume that it necessarily corresponds in any way to that of the research subjects.
>
> (1982: 52)

This must apply even more so when the researchers are white, middle-class feminists. Ramazanoglu makes clear the reasons for this:

> [They] can live in communities where marriage is unnecessary . . . can choose to avoid families, have the power to counter some of the effects of patriarchy, [can] exercise considerable control over reproduction and their own bodies, [and] are far removed from the experiences of the majority of women. They are unusual in the extent of the choices they can exercise, and in the lack of contradictions in their personal lives – in short, they are highly privileged.
>
> (1986: 85–6)

In sum, feminist criminologists have developed a theoretical approach which emphasizes the significance of patriarchal oppression and sexist ideological practices. The main problem with this is that, in assuming a universal dimension of men's power, this approach has ignored the fact that race significantly affects black women's experiences in the home, in the labour market, of crime and in the criminal justice system.

Ethnocentrism and feminist theory

Black women, like most other women, experience some degree of sexual oppression. However, this fails to acknowledge the complexity of gender considerations and the significance of other social taboos such as ethnicity and economic marginality. Kate Millett defined patriarchy as 'a set of social relations which has a material base in which there are hierarchical relations between men and solidarity among them which enables them in turn to dominate women' (1970: 25). This unqualified focus on men's domination does not allow for the historical specificity of patriarchy which has meant that oppression is not experienced in the same way by all women or expressed by all men (Davis, 1981; Anthias and Davis-Yuval, 1983; Mama, 1984; hooks, 1989).

To take the first point. While accepting that relationships between black men and black women are likely to be as sexually oppressive as those experienced by white women, the historical experiences of black women compound their situation and produce a more complex mesh of struggles both within and outside the family. The experiences of black women as chattels under slavery and colonialism has meant that social relations were often mediated and bound up with economic as much as sexual reproduction. Thus, to understand the unique oppression of black women, we need to consider their experiences as black *people*.

We need to note also that black women do not comprise a homogeneous group, although the majority share a similar class position. Black women are further subdivided in terms of ethnicity. For example, there are differences in histories and experiences between Afro–American, Afro–Caribbean and Asian women (Anthias and Davis-Yuval, 1983). Finally, the relationship between black women and black men is not necessarily analogous to relationships between white women and white men; black women experience sexual and patriarchal oppression by black men but at the same time struggle alongside them against racial oppression (Davis, 1981; hooks, 1982).

With respect to the second point, the hierarchical relationship on which patriarchal oppression is premised assumes that black men naturally occupy a similar economically privileged position to white men. However, in Western industrialized countries black men have been socially and politically disadvantaged to an extent which has limited their power both in the family and in society in general.

One of the consequences of the employment structure in capitalist countries has been reliance on the labour of black women which has reduced their dependency on black men. This has contributed to the complex social and patriarchal relations in which black women are involved and stands in contradiction to the conception of the family which predominantly white feminist academics have endorsed. The traditional model of the family is based on ethnocentric ideals of the dependent married women with a male patriarchal head of the household. Black women's relationship to the family is then presented as deviant or pathological. This is reiterated in discussions of the black family in feminist theory where the dominance of black women in the family is portrayed as both a cause for consternation and an explanation for structural weakness.

An example is the work of Shulamith Firestone (1981) whose theories are based on the ethnocentric assumption that black women's experiences of racism can be understood simply as an extension of sexism (see Simons (1979) for a critique). She denies the significance and impact which the added dimension of racial oppression has for black women. However, the testimony of black women bears witness to the complex interaction of sexist and racist forms of oppression occurring simultaneously. To quote Bryan *et al.*:

> Our relationship with men – both Black and white – has meant that in addition to racism, Black women have had to confront a form of sexism and sexual abuse which is unique to us. But it is impossible to separate our understanding of sexism in our community from its context in a racist society because popular acceptance of racist stereotypes of Black women, Black men and Black juveniles not only compound our sexual oppression but have also become internalised.
> (1985: 212)

Nor does Firestone's thesis acknowledge the status hierarchy which exists between black and white women. hooks explains that white women may be victimized by sexism, but racism enables them to act as exploiters and oppressors of black women (and men):

> Black women are in an unusual position for not only are we collectively at the bottom of the occupational ladder, but the overall social status is lower than that of any other group. Occupying such a position we bear the brunt of sexist, racist and classist oppression. Racist stereotypes of the strong, superhuman black woman are operative myths in the minds of many white women, allowing them to ignore the extent to which black women are likely to be victimised in this society and the role white women play in the maintenance and perpetuation of that victimisation.
> (1984: 14)

Thus it is not just or simply that black women are subject to 'more' disadvantage than white women. Their oppression is of a qualitatively different kind. Women's experiences of oppression in social or patriarchal relations cannot be reduced to those of white middle-class women. Ethnocentric feminist analyses are not adequate. In areas as diverse as women's employment (Barrett, 1980; Beechey and Whitelegg, 1986), the family (Barrett and McIntosh, 1982) and crime (Smart, 1976; Carlen, 1983; Heidensohn, 1985; Morris, 1987), the history of racism and its implications have been ignored. The significance of this intellectual exclusion or marginalization is far reaching. Joseph (1981: 95) has pointed out that to speak of women, all women categorically, is to perpetuate white supremacy because it is white women to whom the comments are addressed and for whom they are most appropriate. Barett and McIntosh recognize this: 'Our work has spoken from an unacknowledged but ethnically specific position: its apparently universal applicability has been specious' (1985: 25). They appreciated the need for such work to be overhauled and re-examined in order to remove ethnocentricism.

Towards a broader framework

Since neither feminist criminologies nor black criminology adequately account for the crimes of black women – the former focuses exclusively on gender and the latter on race – one has to look beyond these perspectives for a more comprehensive understanding. This is not an easy task; it demands a more sensitive and complex set of analytical tools for understanding race and gender relations than currently exists (Brittan and Maynard, 1984).

There are various possible reformulations. First, if the problem is defined in terms of ethnocentricity, then the remedy could be a reconceptualization of the basic notions employed by feminist criminologists. For example, the category of 'women' and characterizations of 'femininity' and 'masculinity' could be constructed in ways which acknowledge black women's experiences (and black men's).[5] The ideology of 'femininity' as it is usually portrayed lends support to the view that women have low crime rates and that women's crimes are trivial and insignificant (Carlen, 1985; Carlen and Worrall, 1987). Neither of these statements is necessarily true of black women.

Second, feminists could simply insert references to black women without altering their underlying theoretical premises. But ethnocentrism is not a 'problem' which can be eradicated simply by grafting black women onto the conceptal framework. Nor do black women want to be grafted on to feminism in a tokenistic manner (Carby, 1982: 232). Black feminists have argued that, by focusing primarily on patriarchal oppression and by not fully considering the significance of race and racism, feminist theory has oversimplified the position of black women who experience the triple oppression of racism, patriarchy and class discrimination. They have argued also that the racism in economic, social and political institutions must be confronted and theories based on cultural pluralism must be developed.

Third – and this is the approach I advocate – the remedy could be to develop a perspective which is both situational and interactive (Bourne, 1984). By this is meant an approach which recognizes that race, class and gender are ideological constructs which overlap and take on particular significances at particular periods in history and which require three levels of analysis: the macro (which involves examination of historical, economic and political influences), the middle-range (which involves consideration of cultural ideologies) and the micro (which includes identification of geographical location, age and other demographic factors).

One of the central elements in developing a black feminist perspective is the development of black consciousness and 'recognising that black women and white women have different histories and different relationships to present (and past) struggles in Britain and internationally' (Bhavani and Coulson, 1986: 82). Black feminists are therefore interested in describing the ways in which racism not only divides but draws together gender identities and how gender is experienced through racism. This particular discourse locates racism as central to feminist theory and practice. Thus a viable black feminist perspective would give full consideration to *all* women. In the words of Smith, a black American feminist:

> Feminism is the political theory and practice that struggles to free *all* women: women of colour, working class women, poor women, disabled women, lesbians, old women – as well as white economically privileged heterosexual women. Anything less than this vision of total freedom is not feminism, but merely female self aggrandizement.
> (1982: 49) (my emphasis)[6]

Taking this wider approach, research would not simply address two race/gender groups (that is, black men and white women) but would include black women and white men (Smith and Stewart, 1983). Thus research into the effects of racism would explore whether or not this is experienced differently by black men and black women and research into the effects of sexism would explore whether or not this is experienced differently by white and black women. It would not assume that the experiences of each group were the same.

A black feminist perspective

By focusing primarily on gender and patriarchy, feminists have been constrained by their own limiting definitions. This stance, as I have shown, omits consideration of the complex process of oppression experienced by women (Brittan and Maynard, 1984). The histories of racism and sexism have meant that, as each social group cuts across racial, ethnic, sex and class lines, experiences vary as to degrees of discrimination and oppression. The forms and intensity of oppression are shaped by relationships between the oppressor and the oppressed and these are constantly renegotiated, reconstructed and re-established in their relative positions. My point is that oppression cannot be conceptualized in abstract and global ethnocentric terms such as patriarchy, but has to be seen as a set of dynamic relations based on concrete and specific situations.

Historically, the struggles of black men and white women have not always signified the liberation of the entire social group which they were representing, that is, black *people* and *all* women. As bell hooks succinctly states:

> White women and black men have it both ways. Black men may be victimised by racism but sexism allows them to act as exploiters and oppressors. White women may be victimised by sexism but racism enables them to act as exploiters and oppressors of black people. Both groups have led liberation movements that favour their interests and support the continued oppression of other groups. Black

> male sexism has undermined struggles to eradicate racism just as white female racism undermines feminist struggle.
>
> (1984: 14–15)

Black feminist politics was constructed out of a disillusionment with the peripheral treatment of black women by black liberation and feminist movements. In Britain, for example, black women committed to improving the quality of life of black women in particular and of black people in general have organized activities around such issues as immigration, employment, housing and education policy (Zhana, 1989). One of the distinguishing features of their work is their definition of feminism. A traditional definition is centred on advocacy of the political, economic and social equality of the sexes. Many black feminists believe this to be inadequate and propose an alternative framework.

Black feminists have been engaged in a process of extending the parameters of conventional definitions of feminism which are alien to many of them into a movement which is more relevant to their experiences (Davis, 1981; hooks, 1984; 1989). For the majority of black women, feminism is not just about equal rights for women but involves a much broader commitment to eradicating oppression in all its forms as it affects the lives of men and women. This approach recognizes the similar economic pressures from the state on black people in developed countries and on those suffering from imperialist oppression.

Drawing on this experience, black feminists in Britain and elsewhere have attempted to develop a theoretical perspective which recognizes the constraints of a racially structured, patriarchal capitalism (Bhavani and Coulson, 1986: 89). The emphasis is on the pervasiveness of racism in economic, social and political institutions through which black women's and black men's oppression is manifested (Bryan *et al.*, 1985). The inclusion of men in a black feminist perspective is based on the realization that the liberation of women through challenges to patriarchal structures cannot be successful unless *all* repressive ideologies and practices are eradicated. Black women have added to the potential power of feminism as they have explored wider collective struggles against imperialism and racism (Hull *et al.*, 1982; hooks, 1984; 1989). What these women have demonstrated is the possibility of a liberating feminist theory capable of being translated into practice.

Conclusion

If feminist criminologists wish to take account of black women's criminality then they must think carefully about the framework which they are using to analyse women's involvement in crime. Feminists must not include black women solely to add an extra edge to the victimization or offending patterns of women. Black women do not represent a homogeneous group and, as such, should not be grouped together and referred to as a common 'other'. Finally, the issues relevant for black women are applicable to the social, economic and political development of all. In essence, then, I would suggest:

1 Theories of black women's criminality should not be based on ethnocentric models or racist stereotypes which construct an inaccurate picture and which ignore important differences between female offenders.
2 Criminology should avoid the use of universal, unspecified categories of 'women' and 'blacks' in theoretical discussions and in research. Homogeneity cannot be assumed.
3 The significance of race and racism must be seen as integral to any analysis of (women's) criminality. There is insufficient research which analyses how gender roles and differential opportunity structures are affected by racism as well as sexism and which considers the implications of this for female offenders.
4 Comparative studies, on the basis of race, sex and class, should be carried out to determine how black and white women (and men) are dealt with in the criminal justice system.
5 Following the sentiments of Smart (1976: 85), studies of (women's) offending should be situated in the wider political, economic and social sphere.
6 The experiences of (black) women should not be investigated in a manner which separates the researcher from the subject. There should be a dynamic exchange which involves participation and consultation at all stages in the research process.

Notes

1 The term 'machocentric' describes a discourse which is male-centred. It represents 'masculinity' as the primary defining characteristic and as qualitatively different from 'femininity', but it is more extreme than the normal usage of masculinity as aggression is central to it. Thus researchers such as Gilroy (1982 and 1987) employ a machocentric perspective when focusing on black men and on particular types of crime with an aggressive imagery – 'black street crime' – to the exclusion of other types of criminal involvement.
2 This concept was coined by Sumner (1906) and was used to criticize sociologists and anthropologists who often imported narrow culturalist assumptions drawn from their own social milieu into their research. According to Troyna and Cashmore 'it refers to a view of the world in which one's self or one's group is at the centre of things: a failure to take into account the perspectives of others' (1982: 45).
3 Brown (1986) employs a similar characterization of women as dark figures in criminology.
4 There are some American theories which purport to explain black women's crimes. Vedder and Somerville (1970), for example, attribute their crime to dilemmas of self-identity, negative feminine narcissism and general physical characteristics. They quote from Mary Harrinton Hall in support of this:

> The black girl is, in fact, the antithesis of American beauty. However loved she may be by her mother, family and community, she has no real basis of feminine attractiveness on which to build a sound feminine narcissism. When to her physical unattractiveness is added a discouraging, depreciating mother–family–community environment, there is a damaged self-concept and an impairment of her feminine narcissism which will have profound consequences for her character development.
>
> (1970: 159)

This explanation of black women's criminality is obviously based on a racist and sexist construction of beauty.

5 Eichler (1980: 120) makes the point that 'masculine' and 'feminine' should only be used as labels for empirically established configurations of variables which are differentiated by sex and never generally as valid descriptions (cf Malson, 1983; Naffine, 1985).

6 This view is echoed by white feminists, Barrett and McIntosh: 'It is not the exclusive responsibility of black women to develop an analysis of the inter-relation of class, race and gender; we see this project as that of white women too (1985: 26).

References

Amos, V. and Parmar, P. (1984). 'Challenging imperial feminism'. *Feminist Review*, 17, 3–19.

Anthias, F. and Davis-Yuval, Y. (1983). 'Contextualising feminism – gender, ethnic and class divisions', *Feminist Review*, 15, 62–77.

Barrett, M. (1980). *Women's Oppression Today*. London: Verso.

Barrett, M. and McIntosh, M. (1982). *The Anti-Social Family*. London: Verso.

Barrett, M. and McIntosh, M. (1985). 'Ethnocentrism and socialist feminist theory', *Feminist Review*, 20, 23–47.

Beechey, V. and Whitelegg, E. (eds) (1986). *Women in Britain Today*. Milton Keynes: Open University Press.

Bhavani, K. and Coulson, M. (1986). 'Transforming socialist feminism: the challenge of racism', *Feminist Review*, 23, 81–91.

Bourne, J. (1984). *Towards an Anti-Racist Feminism*. London: Institute of Race Relations.

Bridges, L. (1983). 'The British Left and law and order', *Sage Race Relations Abstracts*, 8. 1.

Brittan, A. and Maynard, M. (1984). *Sexism, Racism and Oppression*. Oxford: Basil Blackwell.

Brown, B. (1986). 'Women and crime: the dark figures of criminology', *Economy and Society*, **15**, 3, 355–402.

Bryan, B., Dadzie, S. and Scafe, S. (1985). *The Heart of the Race*. London: Virago.

Carby, H. (1982). 'White women listen! Black feminism and the boundaries of sisterhood', in *The Empire Strikes Back*. Birmingham Centre for Contemporary Cultural Studies: Hutchinson.

Carlen, P. (1983). *Women's Imprisonment: A Study in Social Control*. London: Routledge.

Carlen, P. (1985). *Criminal Women: Autobiographical Accounts*. Cambridge: Polity.

Carlen, P. and Worrall, A. (eds) (1987). *Gender, Crime and Justice*. Milton Keynes: Open University Press.

Central Statistical Office (CSO) (1988). *Social Trends*, **18**, London: HMSO.

Crow, I. (1987). 'Black people and criminal justice in the UK', *The Howard Journal of Criminal Justice*, **26**, 4, 303–14.

Davis, A. (1981). *Women, Race and Class.* London: Women's Press.

Eaton, M. (1986). *Justice for Women? Family, Court and Social Control.* Milton Keynes: Open University Press.

Edwards, S. (1984). *Women on Trial.* Manchester: Manchester University Press.

Eichler, M. (1980). *The Double Standard: A Feminist Critique of Feminist Social Science.* London: Croom Helm.

Firestone, S. (1981). *The Dialectic of Sex.* London: Jonathan Cape.

Gilroy, P. (1982). 'The myth of black criminality', in M. Eve and D. Musson (eds), *The Socialist Register.* London: Merlin Press.

Gilroy, P. (1987). *There Ain't No Black in the Union Jack: The Cultural Politics of Race and Nation.* London: Hutchinson.

Greater London Council (GLC) (1985). *Women's Imprisonment: Breaking the Silence.* London: Women's Equality Unit and Strategic Policy Unit.

Hall, R. (1985). *Ask Any Woman: A London Enquiry into Rape and Sexual Assault: Report of the Woman's Safety Survey Conducted by Women Against Rape.* Bristol: Falling Wall Press.

Hall, S., Critcher, C., Jefferson, T., Clarke, J. and Roberts, B. (1978). *Policing the Crisis: Mugging, the State and Law and Order.* London: Macmillan.

Heidensohn, F. (1968). 'The deviance of women: a critique and an enquiry', *British Journal of Sociology*, **19**, 160–75.

Heidensohn, F. (1985). *Women and Crime.* Basingstoke: Macmillan.

hooks, b. (1982). *Ain't I A Woman: Black Women and Feminism.* London: The Women's Press.

hooks, b. (1984). *Feminist Theory: From Margin to Centre.* Boston: South End Press.

hooks, b. (1989). *Talking Black: Thinking Feminist, Thinking Black.* London: Sheba Feminist Publications.

Hull, G., Scott, P. and Smith, B. (1982). *All the Women are White, All the Blacks are Men: But Some of Us Are Brave.* New York: The Feminist Press.

Joseph, G. (1981). 'The incompatible menage à trois: Marxism, feminism and racism', in L. Sargent (ed.), *Women and Revolution.* Boston: South End Press.

Lewis, D. (1977). 'Black women offenders and criminal justice: some theoretical considerations', in M. Warren (ed.), *Comparing Male and Female Offenders.* Beverly Hills, CA: Sage.

Malson, M. (1983). 'Black women's sex roles: the social context for a new ideology', *Journal of Social Issues*, **39**, 3, 101–13.

Mama, A. (1984). 'Black women, the economic crisis and the British State', *Feminist Review*, 17, 20–35.

Mandaraka-Sheppard, A. (1986). *The Dynamics of Aggression in Women's Prisons in England.* Aldershot: Gower.

McConville, M. and Baldwin, J. (1982). 'The influence of race on sentencing in England', *Criminal Law Review*, October, 652–8.

McRobbie, A. (1982). 'The politics of feminist research: between the talk, text and action', *Feminist Review*, 12, 46–57.

Millett, K. (1970). *Sexual Politics.* London: Jonathan Cape.

Morris, A. (1987). *Women, Crime and Criminal Justice.* Oxford: Basil Blackwell.

NACRO (1989). *Some Facts and Figures about Black People in the Criminal Justice System*. London: National Association for the Care and Resettlement of Offenders, Briefing Paper.

Naffine, A. (1985). 'The masculinity–femininity hypothesis', *British Journal of Sociology*, **25**, 4, 365–81.

O'Dwyer, J., Wilson, J. and Carlen, P. (1987). 'Women's imprisonment in England, Wales and Scotland: recurring issues', in P. Carlen and A. Worrall (eds), *Gender, Crime And Justice*. Milton Keynes: Open University Press.

Ramazanoglu, C. (1986). 'Ethnocentrism and socialist feminist theory: a response to Barrett and McIntosh', *Feminist Review*, 22, 83–91.

Riley, K. (1981). 'Black girls speak for themselves', *Multi-racial Education*, **10**, 3, 3–12.

Simons, M. (1979). 'Racism and feminism: a schism in the sisterhood', *Feminist Studies*, **5**, 2, 384–401.

Smart, C. (1976). *Women, Crime and Criminology: A Feminist Critique*. London: Routledge and Kegan Paul.

Smith, A. and Stewart, A. (1983). 'Approaches to studying racism and sexism in Black women's lives', *Journal of Social Issues*, **39**, 3, 1–15.

Smith, B. (1982). 'Racism and women's studies', in G. Hull, P. Scott and B. Smith (eds), *All the Women are White. All the Blacks are Men: But Some of Us Are Brave*. New York: The Feminist Press.

Smith, D. J. and Gray, J. (1983). 'The police in action', in *Police and People in London*, Vol 4. London: Policy Studies Institute.

Sumner, W. (1906). *Folkways*. Boston: Ginn.

Troyna, B. and Cashmore, E. (eds) (1982). *Black Youth in Crisis*. London: Allen and Unwin.

Vedder, C. and Somerville, D. (1970). *The Delinquent Girl*. Springfield, IL: Charles C. Thomas.

Wilkinson, C. (1988). 'The post-release experience of female prisoners', in A. Morris and C. Wilkinson (eds), *Women and the Penal System*. Cambridge: Institute of Criminology, Cropwood Series No. 19.

Worrall, A. (1989). 'Working with female offenders: beyond alternatives to custody', *British Journal of Social Work*, **19**, 1, 77–93.

Zhana, (1989) (ed.) *Sojourn*. London: Methuen.

13

DIFFERENT WAYS OF CONCEPTUALIZING SEX/ GENDER IN FEMINIST THEORY AND THEIR IMPLICATIONS FOR CRIMINOLOGY

Kathleen Daly

Source: *Theoretical Criminology*, 1:1 (1997), 25–51.

Abstract

In the 1980s there were major challenges to feminist theory by women of color and by postmodern/poststructuralist theorists. Three modes of feminist enquiry responded to these challenges: class-race-gender, doing gender, and sexed bodies. I assess the contributions and limits of each to criminological knowledge. Several themes emerge. First, while modern/postmodern boundaries are blurred in feminist knowledge debates, important tensions remain concerning the relationship of a 'real world out there' to 'discourse'. Second, while most feminist scholars are interested in linking sex/gender to class, race-ethnicity, etc., the problem of sex-specific corporeality is receiving renewed attention.

At a recent feminist conference held at the Australian National University, I was struck by the varied vocabularies and assumptions used to discuss sex and gender. There is nothing unusual about seeing differences among women and feminists when we speak and write, but the categories of difference I saw took a new form. They were not marked by the familiar distinctions of liberal, radical and socialist-feminist; nor by identity politics in terms of a speaker's self-declared race-ethnicity, sexuality, nationality, physical ability, and the like. Nor were they ordered—at least not explicitly—by method and epistemology, including feminist arguments 'for' or 'against' postmodern ways of theorizing. What I observed set in motion a rethinking of the ways that sex and gender are conceptualized in feminist theory and in criminology. They can be termed 'class-race-gender', 'doing gender' (and subsequently, 'doing difference'), and 'sexed bodies'. In describing and presenting these modes of feminist enquiry, I do not want to suggest that they cover the field.[1] Rather, I wish to clarify the contributions and limits of each to criminological knowledge.

My essay has two parts. In the first, I sketch major challenges to feminist theory that emerged in the 1980s concerning the production of knowledge and truth claims. This can be termed the 'knowledge problem' for feminism. The second describes three modes of feminist enquiry that responded, in part, to the challenges of the 1980s.

Challenges to feminist theory

Engaging academic feminism in the 1960s and 1970s was how and whether sex, gender and 'women' could be linked or 'added on' to liberal and Marxist theories. A burgeoning literature developed that compared liberal, radical, Marxist and socialist feminist perspectives (see, for example, Jaggar, 1983; Sargeant, 1981). In 'Feminism and Criminology', Meda Chesney-Lind and I appended an overview of these perspectives on the 'causes' of inequality and strategies for social change (Daly and Chesney-Lind, 1988: 536–8). We did so reluctantly: while we wished to show that a range of feminist positions was possible, we worried the typology would become fixed precisely when it was unravelling.[2] It became apparent by the mid-1980s that the task for feminist theory was no longer how 'to remove "biases" [from Marxism and liberalism] but to see this "bias" as intrinsic to the structure of the theories in question' (Gatens, 1996: 60).

Shifting ground in the 1980s

In the 1980s, feminist theory was especially influenced by scholars in philosophy and literature. This signalled a shift from the socio-cultural and historical emphases of the 1970s, when scholars began to 'uncover' women's histories and to reveal ethnographic diversity and commonality in women's lives. Michele Barrett (1992) characterizes this shift as moving from 'things' to 'words'. In the 1970s, feminist scholars had referred to *women* or *women's experiences* unproblematically, and they had stressed the importance of distinguishing biological sex from socio-cultural gender, and of developing a comprehensive feminist theory that might replace liberal, Marxist or psychoanalytical theories. But those efforts became untenable in the 1980s. A related critical challenge came from women marginalized by feminist theory and from a variety of postmodern/poststructuralist texts and theorists.[3] These developments set in motion questions about how feminist knowledge is and should be produced and evaluated.

Early critiques of racism (hooks, 1981) and heterosexism suggested a failure of previous feminist scholarship to reflect on its own 'white solipsism' (Rich, 1979: 299) and 'compulsory heterosexuality' (Rich, 1980). Just when some feminist scholars sought to develop a women's standpoint on knowledge, drawing either from Marxist terminology of proletarian consciousness (Hartsock, 1983) or women's bifurcated consciousness (Smith, 1979, 1987), the grounds for claiming a singular women's standpoint began to dissolve. Increasing attention was given to differences among women, which spawned what was termed *identity politics*: naming who one 'was' in terms of social location or 'identity', with a particular set of experiences and viewpoints, and hence, different knowledges 'about women'. Voices that had been excluded from or ignored within feminist thought—e.g. self-identified radical women of color (Moraga and Anzaldua, 1983) and black feminists (Collins, 1986), among others (Cole, 1986)—gained presence in the 1980s, giving notice to the dominant white, middle-class voices of feminist thought that theirs was not the only feminist analysis in town.[4]

Feminists who drew from postmodern thought also challenged the term *woman*, though for the reason that it lacked a stable and unified referent.[5] But, like the early critiques from women marginalized by feminist thought, which raised questions about whose knowledge or 'experience' was legitimate, feminists working with postmodern texts raised questions about power in the production of knowledge.

Several major feminist literary theorists—Jane Gallop, Marianne Hirsch and Nancy Miller—discussed the role of feminist critique and their fears of being criticized by other scholars. As Gallop admitted,

> I realize that the set of feelings that I used to have about French men I now have about African-American women. Those are the people I feel inadequate in relation to and try to please in my writing.
>
> (Gallop et al., 1990: 363–4)

Gallop's comment suggests that her feminist literary analysis was *first* affected by French men and *then* by black women.[6] I suspect this chronology was common for US feminist literary scholars. Certainly, it was more so for this group than for US feminists in sociology, who responded first to the charge of racism in feminist thought and who were relatively more resistant to postmodern influences. These different histories of coming to terms with 'French men and black women' have important consequences for how we think through the problem of 'difference' (both among and between men and women) and the degree to which postmodern/poststructuralist theoretical terms are embraced.[7]

For feminists in sociology, the problem of difference is commonly understood to mean mapping variation in women's (and men's) lives, of documenting power and resistance in interaction, and of assuming that one's engagement in social structures (and especially, class, race-ethnicity, gender, sexuality and age) matter in shaping one's consciousness, patterns of speech, behavior and capacity to affect social structures. In sociological empirical terms, difference is hardly novel; it is another way to theorize variability and power in social life. For literary scholars, the problem of difference is more often understood primarily as a discursive construction, its elements being binary oppositions in language, the construction of the 'masculine' and 'feminine' as constitutive of hierarchical sexual difference, and for some, an interest in the unconscious psyche. This contrast renders these approaches more oppositional than I would like, but two observations can be made.

First, humanities scholars set the feminist theoretical agenda in the 1980s; they were quicker than social science scholars to work with postmodern texts and theorists and, as such, they were more interested in the ways in which language and discourse set limits on what could be known. One result of the dominance of the humanities in the production of feminist knowledge is that scholars may not appreciate—indeed they may misunderstand—the practices of empirical social research. Another is that the work exhibits a form of theoretical imperialism or theoreticism, where the primary activity is discussion of concepts in the abstract.

Second, and more speculatively, I suspect that many humanities scholars read the race critique through postmodern terms, whereas the order may have been reversed for those in sociology (and kindred social sciences), who read the race critique through modern terms and who took on postmodern texts later. There have, of course, been different directions taken by feminist scholars in response to critique from within and from without. My point here is to note a confluence between the 'problem of difference' in feminist theory and a problem of power in the production of feminist knowledge. It is illustrated by Maria Lugones (a philosopher and Latina), who describes how 'white women' addressed the problem of difference:

> White women conceived [not] noticing us as a theoretical problem, which they label the problem of difference. . . . But white women theorists seem to have worried more passionately about the harm the claim does to theorizing than about the harm the theorizing did to women of color. The 'problem of difference' refers to feminist theories—these theories are the center of concern. The attempted solutions to the 'problem of difference' try to rescue feminist theorizing from several . . . pitfalls that would render it false, trivial, weak, and so on.
>
> (Lugones, 1991: 41)

As Lugones suggests, the problem of difference was framed by many feminist theorists solely as a problem for theory. Whereas she locates this tendency as stemming from 'white women's theorizing', I see it stemming from a disciplinary-based theoreticism, especially evident in philosophy, but which may also have a class and racial nexus.[8] In comparison to philosophy, there was a larger group of feminists in sociology who called for 'incorporating' class-race-gender into the curriculum and research (see Andersen and Collins, 1992).[9] That incorporation is not without problems (see Platt, 1993), but it remains a major theoretical point of entry, especially for feminists of color, and a strategy for coalitional knowledge-building across groups.

Contrary to the claims of radical feminism of the early 1970s, Moira Gatens (1996: 62) suggests that it would be naive to think that feminists can produce 'pure or non-patriarchal theory'. This issue is central to the knowledge problem for feminism: it invites a rethinking of how we adjudicate among competing claims about 'women' or 'women's experiences'. Are some better than others, and how do we decide?

Empiricist-standpoint-postmodern feminisms

In the mid-1980s, Sandra Harding made an important contribution when she compared different epistemologies in producing feminist knowledge: empiricist, standpoint and postmodern (Harding, 1986, 1987). She noted the paradox (Harding, 1986: 24) that feminism was a political movement for social change and yet feminist researchers were producing knowledge in the natural and social sciences that was more 'likely to be confirmed by evidence' than previous scientific claims. Harding wondered, 'How can such politicized research be increasing the objectivity of inquiry? On what grounds should these feminist claims be justified?' She suggested that there were two 'solutions' (empiricism and standpointism) and one 'agenda for a solution' (postmodernism).

By *feminism empiricism*, Harding referred to improvements in knowledge by removing sexist and androcentric biases. This meant to 'correct' but not to transform the methodological norms of science. Such a stance was dominant in 1970s feminist social science work, including criminology; and it remains strong in the 1990s. An unfortunate legacy in Harding's analysis is the choice of the term *empiricism* in light of its connotations in social research.[10] In the social sciences, *empiricist* or *empiricism* are distinguished from *empirical*. The former terms refer to nontheorized empirical enquiry: that which exhibits the 'imperialism of the technique' or that which assumes a firm foundation of knowledge through observation (Wagner, 1992). However, one can do empirical work without being empiricist or without assuming an epistemology of empiricism. It seems crucial, then, that the term empirical not be tied to a particular epistemology. It is as large as 'text', and both can stand in a constructive tension in the practice of social research.

By *feminist standpoint*, Harding (1986: 26) referred to how 'women's subjugated position provides the possibility of more complete and less perverse understandings' than the dominant position of men. This 'standpoint' is informed by women's experiences as understood from the perspective of feminism; thus, it can be taken by both men and women. Several problems are immediately evident. Can there be just one feminist standpoint if subjugated experiences vary by class or race, etc.? And, 'Is it too firmly rooted in a problematic politics of essentialized identities?' (Harding, 1986: 27).

The possibility of a feminist standpoint in law was most explicitly theorized by Catharine MacKinnon (1982, 1983), who contrasted a Marxist ontology of exploited and alienated labor (that of a nongendered proletariat) with a radical feminist ontology of exploited and alienated sexuality (that of women). Her arguments have been discussed and criticized at length by others (see, for example, Smart, 1989) so I will not repeat them here. Despite its problems, the idea of a feminist or women's standpoint remains popular. It has evolved, shifting from an initial justificatory claim of superior feminist knowledge to anti-elitist claims of 'women's gendered experiences' (Fineman, 1994). It continues to resonate with the variety of 'hyphenated' feminisms—black (or African-American) feminism, Native American feminism, and the like—as scholars identify and validate a set of subjugated experiences and knowledges (see, e.g. Collins, 1990); and it is relevant for those examining the consequences of 'lived sexed bodies' for the 'sexualization of all knowledges' (Grosz, 1995: 36, 43). This larger set of positions congenial with standpointism reflects postmodern strains that soon become evident in standpoint thinking (Harding, 1986: 27).

By *feminist postmodernism*, Harding referred to a heterogeneous set of critiques of Enlightenment thought with its associated hierarchical dualisms (mind over body and reason over emotion, among others), disembodied claims of truth 'innocent of power', and assumptions of a stable, coherent self (see Flax, 1990: 41–2). During the 1980s, US feminist engagement with postmodern texts and theorists was emergent; more developed analyses and debates soon followed (e.g. Butler and Scott, 1992; Nicholson, 1990).

One cannot make sense of feminist knowledge debates today without reference to postmodern ways of thinking about multiple and partial knowledges. For example, Harding (1990: 93) suggests that 'the knowing subject of feminist empiricism inadvertently but inevitably is in tension with Enlightenment assumptions', and she views the modernist assumptions embedded in standpoint epistemologies and the postmodern skepticism of science, as reflecting 'converging approaches to a postmodernist world' (Harding, 1987: 295). Like other commentators, she notes that many modernist assumptions are embedded in postmodern texts and that feminist thinkers had already been challenging the assumptions of Enlightenment knowledge without benefit of postmodern thought (see Bordo, 1993; Carrington, 1994; de Lauretis, 1990; Henry and Milovanovic, 1996: Ch. 2; Seidman, 1994).

Discourse and 'a real world out there'

Modern/postmodern boundaries are more often blurred than sharp in feminist knowledge debates. However, for those engaged in social research, important tensions remain concerning the status of 'the real' or the 'extra-discursive' in connection (or disconnection) to 'discourse'. Cain (1995: 70) puts the matter this way:

> Do we emphasize the privilege or necessity of a downsider perspective, or do we buy in to the full postmodern package as a way of dealing with the differences within the downsider group?

By the 'full postmodern package', Cain refers to a tendency to accord 'primal ontological status . . . to texts (or discourses) . . .' (p. 70). She suggests that the fallacies of epistemological primacy ('human knowledge calls the world') and epistemological privilege ('the social world has no potency outside of discourse'), which are present in many postmodern texts, 'arrogant[ly] place human knowledge at the centre of the universe'. Cain argues for

> an autonomous existence for the material world, . . . which . . . include[s] not only untouched stars and virgin forest, artefacts with a knowledge component such as houses, fields, cakes, gardens, radios, bicycles, and income tax forms, but also social relations.
>
> (p. 74)

She envisions an 'empirical argument about the unthought and unspeakable relationships which yet have (so much) power' and thus, she wants to claim an ontology for social relations which 'like discourse . . . exist powerfully in a state of radical and uncaused autonomy' (p. 75). She suggests a methodological strategy of 'mapping . . . the articulations between relationships and knowledge/discourse'. She sees this strategy as implicit in Foucault's earlier work on discourse and the extra-discursive (see also Cain, 1993) and proposes that 'genealogy needs a sociology, as sociology has needed to understand the autonomy and power of the text' (p. 75).

Cain's arguments assist me in several ways. First, she recreates a space within postmodern thought for 'a real world out there', although not a world that is transparent or knowable to an observer in empiricist terms. She terms her approach 'realist feminist', which she links to a relational standpointism that is not given by biology but by social relations and an act of political will (Cain, 1993: 88–94; see also Cain, 1986, 1990). Second, she offers a way to see the limits of discourse analysis and, as such, challenges current hierarchies in feminist knowledge: of words 'over' things and of philosophy and literature 'over' the social sciences.[11] I do not think it is coincidental that Cain's (1995) interest in reconciling 'apparently incompatible ontologies' (p. 73) has been forged from reflecting on the subjugated knowledges both of First World women in the metropole and of Third World men and women in the post-colonial Caribbean.

How has research in criminology been affected by these shifts in feminist thought? In the 1970s and 1980s feminist research on Real Women challenged the androcentrism of the field, as scholars filled knowledge gaps about women law-breakers, victims and criminal justice workers. By the 1990s, several scholars signalled a shift in interest from Real Women to The Woman of criminological or legal discourse (see Smart, 1990a, 1992). This reflected a move toward postmodern thinking on crime, courts and prisons, which is evident in the works of Bertrand (1994), Howe (1990, 1994), Smart (1995), Worrall (1990), and A. Young (1990, 1996). While sympathetic to postmodern texts, others have not wanted to abandon Real Women; they include Cain (1989), Carlen (1985, 1988), Carrington (1990), Daly (1992), Joe and Chesney-Lind (1995), and Maher and Daly (1996). Those studying violence against women may be especially resistant to letting go of Real Women because their voices and experiences have only recently been 'named' (compare Marcus, 1992 and Hawkesworth, 1989; see Radford et al., 1996). I am, of course, simplifying here, but I do so to highlight where feminist debate remains keen, both within and outside criminology, on the politics of knowledge. By retaining Real Women, feminists may take 'the ground of specifically *moral* claims against domination—the avenging of strength through moral critique' (Brown, 1991: 75). Real Women can be mobilized as 'our subject that harbors truth, and our truth that opposes power' (p. 77).[12] But for others, Real Women, their moral grounds and 'truths', must be set aside (Smart, 1990b, as discussed below). Concurring with Smart, Brown asks

> What is it about feminism that fears the replacement of truth with politics . . . privileged knowledge with a cacophony of unequal voices clamoring for position?
>
> (Brown, 1991: 73)

A good deal, many reply (e.g. di Leonardo, 1991; di Stefano, 1990; Harding, 1987). And that is why the knowledge problem continues to be contentious for feminist theory and politics. One response has been sketched by Smart (1995: 230–2), who now admits that while we 'need to address this Woman of legal [or criminological] discourse, . . . this kind of analysis alone gives me cause for concern'. She suggests that discourse analysis of, for example, 'the raped woman is of little value unless we are also talking to women who have been raped' (p. 231). To Smart, this is not the same as asserting some truth about Real Women, but rather to be cognizant that 'women discursively construct themselves' (p. 231).[13]

Let me summarize and reflect on my argument in this first section. I identified problems resulting from a dominance of the humanities in feminist work: theoretical imperialism, insufficient attention to and a misreading of social science enquiry, and analyzing women's 'differences' solely in linguistic or discursive terms. I would not wish to claim superiority of 'the empirical' or of social science enquiry. Such a position does not reflect what I have learned from feminist work in philosophy, literature and media studies. Nor does it reflect my interests to develop interdisciplinary 'hybrid knowledges' that break down disciplinary boundaries (Seidman, 1994: 2). It is to say that social science research has a key role to play in feminist knowledge and that empirical enquiry can be as radical and subversive as deconstruction.

Three modes of feminist enquiry

The challenges to feminist theory in the 1980s, both by women marginalized by its terms and by postmodern texts, were not isolated. They were part of a general mood to unsettle social theory and to re-engage a critique of positivist social science (Seidman, 1994). Thus, we would expect to see reworkings of old concepts and the emergence of new ones. Two ways of reconceptualizing sex/gender in feminist enquiry—'class-race-gender' and 'doing gender'—have been developed by feminists in the social sciences, especially those in sociology. 'Sexed bodies' has been developed by feminists in philosophy, and more generally, by re-readings of Foucault.

Class-race-gender

My work has been most influenced by class-race-gender or what I have come to term *multiple inequalities* (Daly, 1993; 1995a). In the 1980s, it was not French men but black women whose critique of feminist thought had the greater influence on my thinking. Class-race-gender need not be interpreted literally to mean a sole focus on these three relations; its meaning can be stretched to include others, e.g. age, sexuality and physical ability. For many scholars, the term retains an allegiance, though not complete fealty, to notions of determining structures of inequality. For example, Pat Carlen (1994: 139–40) suggests the need to theorize inequalities that 'both recognizes and denies structuralism'. The term varies in application across and within the disciplines: from statistical analyses of wages and law-breaking for particular sub-groups (e.g. King, 1988; Simpson, 1991) to biographical and autobiographical storytelling forms (e.g. Abrams, 1991; Lorde, 1984; Pratt, 1984; Williams, 1991). In the US, class-race-gender is used to denote a more inclusive college-level curricula (see, for example, Belkhir et al., 1994 and the new journal, *Race, Sex & Class*), and it has become a popular title in marketing readers in women's studies (e.g. Andersen and Collins, 1992; Jaggar and Rothenberg, 1993; Ruiz and DuBois, 1994). While, on balance, curricula change and new readers are a good thing,[14] they are but a small slice of a wider class-race-gender project.

Class-race-gender conceptualizes inequalities, not as additive and discrete, but as intersecting, interlocking and contingent. In the US, class-race-gender emerged from the struggles of black women in the Civil Rights Movement; it came into academic institutions (and especially sociology) in the late 1970s through articles and books by women of color. This early body of work not only critiqued ethnocentrism in feminist theory, but also established a rhetorical ground for women of color (see, e.g. Baca Zinn et al., 1986; Combahee River Collective, 1979; Dill, 1983).

Conceptualizing multiple relations of inequality has only just begun (for a recent effort in criminology, see Schwartz and Milovanovic, 1995). It will not take the same form as previous efforts to theorize 'systems of inequality' (as in relationships of capitalism and patriarchy). And while its proponents often claim its 'greater inclusiveness', we should expect that like other ideas, it is 'condemned to be haunted by a voice from the margins . . . awakening us to what has been excluded, effaced, damaged' (Bordo, 1990: 138). Like others (e.g. Anthias and Yuval-Davis, 1992; Collins, 1993) I see the project as mapping the salience and contingency of gender, class, race-ethnicity, and the like, both separately and together. For Floya Anthias and Nira Yuval-Davis (1992: 99), this means 'specify[ing] the mechanisms by which different forms of exclusion and subordination operate'. For Patricia Hill Collins (1990: 226–7), it means showing how social relations operate in a matrix of domination at three levels: personal, group and systemic. Authors' uses of terms such as *power* and *social structure* may vary: they range from earlier, more deterministic understandings of power as something individuals 'possess' in varying degrees, depending on their location in social structures external to them (e.g. Davis, 1981) to recent understandings, which are more context-dependent. These recent ways of conceptualizing social structure as fluid pose major challenges to previous understandings of power, subordination and human emancipation (see Collins, 1990; Henry and Milovanovic, 1996: Chs. 2–3; Yeatman, 1995).

Bordo (1990: 145) observes that the 'analytics of class and race . . . do not seem to be undergoing the same deconstruction' as gender and women. I would agree: relatively less intellectual discussion has been devoted to showing the lack of a unified referent for racial and class categories compared to those for gender. One reason is an under-theorization of race-ethnicity and its links to other social relations, e.g. the 'gendering' of race or the 'racializing' of gender. This is one of several building blocks in developing a class-race-gender analysis in criminology, but as yet, movement has been slow. Discomfort levels are high, not coincidentally because criminologists are so 'white' and advantaged, while the subjects of their crime theories more often are not (despite some attention to organizational crime). Moreover, scholars of color in criminology have only recently been in a position to challenge the white-centered assumptions of the field and to develop anti-racist theoretical and research agendas (see Russell, 1992; Walker and Brown, 1995; Young and Greene, 1995).

There are many ways to work with the idea of multiple inequalities. One is to use it to transform research and writing practices in the social sciences (see Daly, 1993, 1994). For example, to show how racial discrimination 'works', one could use Richard Delgado's (1989) method of presenting multiple accounts of the 'same event'. In this case, Delgado describes what happened when a black man was interviewed for a job at a law school. The multiple perspectives of the participants, as orchestrated by Delgado, bring the white reader into the story in such a way that racial discrimination toward the black man becomes visible to the white reader as part of his/her routine interpretations and practices. Delgado offers a nuanced picture of how race relations routinely work to disadvantage black job applicants through the organizational frame of 'neutral' job criteria. This kind of multi-perspectival approach could also be used by authors in communicating research findings and, as such, class-race-gender can be a vehicle by which to develop collaborations across academic-community locations and identities (see Austin, 1992; Daly and Stephens, 1995).

To date, class-race-gender has been most vividly revealed through literary and storytelling forms (see, for example, Bell, 1987; Delgado, 1989; Jordan, 1985; Lubiano, 1992; Pratt, 1984; Williams, 1991).[15] Unlike a good deal of traditional social science, these works reveal (1) the shifting salience of race, class, gender, nation and sexuality, and the like as one moves through space and time, and (2) the different world-views or lenses that participants bring to social encounters. A major question is whether one can bring these literary or storytelling forms into research practices in sociology and criminology. It may be possible, if researchers use narrative modes of reasoning (see Richardson, 1990; Stivers, 1993; Ewick and Silbey, 1995).

The contribution of class-race-gender to criminology is an insistence that everyone is located in a matrix of multiple social relations, i.e. that race and gender are just as relevant to an analysis of white men as they are to black women. With an emphasis on contingency, one can explore the varied positions of 'black women'—as offenders, victims, and mothers and wives of offenders and victims—to 'white justice' (Daly, 1995b). And as Lisa Maher (1995: Ch. 9) demonstrates in her ethnographic research on women drug-users in New York City, one can reveal varied angles of vision for African- and European-American women and Latinas in neighborhood drug markets. Class-race-gender can also be used to politicize and problematize knowledge in collaboration with others. In this regard, Collins (1993) is right to emphasize the piecing together of work by different scholars as bits in a wider mosaic; the quest to theorize the 'totality' of multiple inequalities is ill-founded. One set of theoretical problems, discussed by Anthias and Yuval-Davis (1992: 17), is how to relate the 'different ontological spheres' of class, race and gender divisions, while simultaneously showing the ways they intermesh in concrete situations. Another challenge is to identify new vocabularies to discuss multiple, intersecting or interlocking inequalities. Otherwise, we may easily slip into additive, mechanical analyses of power, oppression and the heaping of disadvantage and advantage.

Doing gender

Candace West and Donald Zimmerman (1987) coined the construct 'doing gender' to describe gender as a 'situated accomplishment':

> [Gender is not the] property of individuals . . . [but rather] an emergent feature of social situations: . . . an outcome of and a rationale for . . . social arrangements . . . a means of legitimating [a] fundamental division . . . of society. [Gender is] a routine, methodical, and recurring accomplishment (p. 126) . . . not a set of traits, nor a variable, nor a role [but] itself constituted through interaction.
>
> (p. 129)

R. W. Connell (1987, 1995) and James Messerschmidt (1993) have developed linkages between 'doing gender' (more precisely, 'doing masculinity') and gender relations of power. Susan Martin and Nancy Jurik (1996) have also utilized 'doing gender' in their analysis of women and gender in justice system occupations. All four authors have elements of 'class-race-gender' in their work. They view structure as ordering interaction, and interaction as producing structure, drawing on Anthony Giddens' (1984) efforts to transcend the sociological dualism of interaction and social structure.[16]

In 1995, West and Fenstermaker published 'Doing Difference', in which they attempt to incorporate 'doing gender' with 'class-race-gender'. Rather than viewing each relation of class or race or gender as a 'structure of oppression', they propose that the whole be viewed as 'experience'. Thus, every social encounter, no matter who the participants are, can be conceptualized as being classed, raced and gendered. The terms used in 'doing gender' are extended without modification to 'doing race' or class. For example, the authors say that

> the accomplishment of race (like gender) does not necessarily mean 'living up' to normative conceptions of attitudes and activities appropriate to a particular race category; rather, it means engaging in action at the risk of race assessment.
>
> (West and Fenstermaker, 1995: 23–4)

Later that year, several scholars replied to West and Fenstermaker's article (Collins et al., 1995). Critics objected that it ignored power and oppression, as it did resistance and conflict (Collins et al., 1995: 491–4, 497–502).

What vexed the critics, in part, was that the 'isms' of inequality—racism, classism, etc.—were not sufficiently addressed with West and Fenstermaker's version of social constructionism. Also vexing was that gender or race, etc. could be viewed merely as an accomplishment or performance. In this regard, Barrie Thorne (1995: 498–9) noted similarities between 'doing gender' and Judith Butler's (1990) discussion of gender as the performance of sex; both, in her view, neglected the importance of seeing gender (and other social relations) as extending 'deep into the unconscious . . . and outward into social structure and material interests'.[17]

Some feminist skepticism toward 'doing gender' lies in a desire to retain 'structures of power' that both precede and are produced by gender or race, etc. as 'accomplishments'. Whether sex and gender are understood to be produced in interaction or in discourse, feminist critiques (specifically, by sociologists) are based on retaining some semblance of social structure or materialism. As we shall see, some feminists using 'sexed bodies' also wish to include a form of materialism ('materiality'), but its constituents are the body and sexual difference.

Messerschmidt (1993: 85) applied 'doing gender' in his analysis of crime as 'a resource for doing masculinity in specific social settings . . .':

> Crime . . may be invoked as a practice through which masculinities (and men and women) are differentiated from one another. . . . [It] is a resource that may be summoned when men lack other resources to accomplish gender.
>
> (p. 85)

Whereas West and Zimmerman (1987: 137) had focused on how the doing of gender 'creat[es] differences between . . women and men' that materialize as 'essential sexual natures' (p. 138), Messerschmidt suggested that the doing of gender also produces multiple forms of masculinity and crime.

One problem Messerschmidt encounters is how to conceptualize crime as a gendered line of social action without once again establishing boys and men as the norm, differentiating themselves from all that is 'feminine'. Although masculine subjectivity and lines of action may be described with these terms (see Jefferson, 1994), it is disputable that feminine subjectivity and lines of action could be. Specifically, would the claim that crime is a 'resource for doing femininity'—for women and girls 'to create differences from men and boys or to separate from all that is masculine'—have any cultural resonance? Probably not. But nor should theories necessarily have to employ symmetrical sex/gender terms. That is to say, arguments that crime is a resource or situation where masculinities are produced may be useful: they normalize crime but problematize men and masculinity.

In applying 'doing gender' to criminological research, scholars will have to let go of thinking about gender or race etc. as attributes of persons and examine how situations and social practices produce qualities and identities associated with membership in particular social categories. Despite the creative efforts of some to employ doing gender in quantitative analyses of self-reported delinquency (e.g. Simpson and Elis, 1995), it is better suited to analyses of social interaction. Researchers will need to be mindful that categories taken from theorizing masculinity may be inappropriately applied to femininity. Gender categories are not neutral, and the terms used to describe men and women 'doing gender' are not likely to be interchangeable. These are major points for those using the 'sexed bodies' construct.

Sexed bodies

Gatens (1996: 67) observes that 'there is probably no simple explanation for the recent proliferation of writings concerning the body'. She credits Foucault's work on the (male) body as a site of disciplinary practices, coupled with that of feminist social scientists, who showed that even the most privileged women have not attained equality with men in the 'public sphere'.[18] Perhaps feminists would need to face, yet again but in different ways, 'questions of corporeal specificity' (p. 68). The trick, Gatens suggests, is to acknowledge 'historical realities . . . without resorting to biological essentialism' (p. 69):

> The present capacities of female bodies are, by and large, very different from the present capacities of male bodies. It is important to create the means of articulating the historical realities of sexual difference without thereby reifying these differences.
>
> (p. 69)

Feminists have been analyzing a large philosophical literature on 'the body' and its connection with 'the mind' (see, for example, Butler, 1993; Gatens, 1996; Grosz, 1994, 1995). Sexed bodies is theorized in several ways: some emphasize the discursive construction of 'sex', including cultural inscription on bodies, whereas others work at the edges of the 'materiality of sex' and 'culture'. For the moment, I will focus on the latter in reviewing three interrelated themes: the sex/gender distinction, power as productive of gender and sexual difference, and dualisms in western philosophy.

Sex/gender. In 1983 Gatens challenged the familiar distinction between sex (the biological categories of 'male' and 'female') and gender (the social categories of 'masculinity' and 'femininity' that are linked to sex) (reprinted in Gatens, 1996: Ch. 1). She was critical of the assumption that 'the mind of either sex is initially a neutral, passive entity, a blank slate on which are inscribed various social "lessons"'. The 'alleged *neutrality* of the body, the postulated *arbitrary* connection between femininity and the female body, masculinity and the male body' troubled Gatens because it 'encourage[s] . . . a neutralization of sexual difference and sexual politics . . . and the naive solution of resocialization' (p. 4, Gaten's emphasis). Moreover, by denying sex-specific corporeality, key differences are overlooked 'between feminine behavior or experience that is lived out by a female subject and feminine behavior or experience that is lived out by a male subject (and vice versa with masculine behavior)' (p. 9).

Power. Drawing on but moving beyond Foucault's account of 'the manner in which the micropolitical operations of power produce socially appropriate bodies', Gatens (1996: 70) proposes that we view gender as

> not the effect of ideology or cultural values but as the way in which power takes hold of and constructs bodies in particular ways. . . . The sexed body can no longer be conceived as the unproblematic biological and factual base upon which gender is inscribed, but must itself be recognized as constructed by discourses and practices that take the body both as their target and as their vehicle of expression.

Gatens' conceptualization of gender as 'the way in which power takes hold of bodies and constructs them in particular ways' raises questions for the relationship between social construction and materiality, which Butler (1993) takes up:

> To claim that sex is already gendered, already constructed, is not yet to explain in which way the 'materiality' of sex is forcibly produced. What are the constraints by which bodies are materialized as 'sexed', and how are we to understand the 'matter' of sex? . . .
>
> (p. xi)

Butler proposes a 'return to the notion of matter, not as site or surface, but as a process of materialization' (p. 9) and suggests we should ask, 'Through what regulatory norms is sex itself materialized?' (p. 10).

Dualisms. Elizabeth Grosz (1994) argues that current understandings of 'the body' reflect dualisms in western thinking, and by rethinking 'the body', subjectivity can be reconceptualized. She rejects the view of the body as 'natural' or having a 'presocial' existence and, simultaneously, she rejects the view of the body as '*purely* a social, cultural, and signifying effect lacking its own weighty materiality' (p. 21, Grosz's emphasis). (As such, she takes issue with feminist approaches she terms egalitarian and social constructionist.) She wants to

> . . . deny that there is the 'real' material body on the one hand and its various cultural and historical representations on the other. . . . These representations and cultural inscriptions quite literally constitute bodies and help to produce them as such.
>
> (p. x)

Grosz uses the metaphor of a moibus strip to suggest the 'inflection of mind into body and body into mind . . . the torsion of the one into the other . . . [the]

uncontrollable drift of the inside into the outside and outside into the inside' (p. xii). Terms such as 'embodied subjectivity' and 'psychical corporeality' (p. 22) might be used to characterize this inflection.

Why are sexed bodies and corporeality important? When viewing the mind as 'linked to, perhaps even part of, the body' and 'bodies themselves as always sexually (and racially) distinct, . . . then [we can see that] the very forms that subjectivity takes are not generalizable'. We therefore cannot assume 'universalist ideals of humanism' nor can we produce and evaluate knowledges that are not 'sexually determinate, limited, finite' (Grosz, 1994: 20).

'Sexed bodies' is excellent for revealing the 'neutralization and neutering of . . . [sex] specificity' and with it the 'cultural and intellectual effacement of women' (Grosz, 1994: ix). Its practitioners are on weaker ground, however, when they attempt to connect, in a theoretical sense, sexual difference and racial, cultural and class divisions. Grosz suggests that interconnections be viewed as 'interlocking'—using similar terms as Collins (1990) and West and Fenstermaker (1995)—and like these theorists, she is concerned that class, race, etc. should not be conceived as 'autonomous structures which then require external connections' (p. 20). A major difference is what is being explained. For Collins, it is inequality and oppression; for Grosz, it is sexual difference and multiple subjectivities.

Grosz argues (1994: 18) that scholars working with a sexed bodies construct share 'a commitment to a notion of the fundamental, irreducible differences between the sexes' and while they acknowledge that 'class and race differences may divide women, sexual differences demand social recognition and representation'. Arguing against those who say that theirs is an essentialist analysis, Grosz suggests that the task is to undermine the dichotomy between 'sex as an essentialist and gender as a constructionist category' (p. 18).

Grosz and colleagues' work on sexed bodies is one way the construct can be used. Another emphasizes cultural inscription *on* the body (see review in Howe, 1994: 194–205). The work I shall consider is Carol Smart's (1990b) on the production of sexed bodies in legal discourse.

Smart is interested in how 'law constructs and reconstructs masculinity and femininity, and maleness and femaleness' that produce a 'common-sense perception of difference' (p. 201). One sees affinity between Smart's claim that legal discourse produces gender and that of West and Zimmerman for whom situations produce gender; but there are key differences. Smart wants to consider how 'law constructs sexed (and not simply gendered) subjectivities' (p. 202), that is, 'the sexed body' (p. 203).[19] She does so by examining rape and rape trials. Smart's (1990b) article was published at around the same time that analyses of the 'matter' or 'materiality of sex' were emerging; this may explain why she does not engage with authors like Grosz who viewed 'sexed bodies' neither as natural nor as signifying effects of culture. Instead, Smart analyzes the sexed body as produced both by legal and feminist discourse: the 'natural' sexed woman, who during a rape trial becomes a victimized sexed body. In feminist discourse this is the body of the eternal victim, whereas in legal discourse, it is the deserving victim (pp. 207–8). Smart cautions that it will be difficult for feminists to 'construct rape differently' because the effort to 'deconstruct the biological/sexed woman is silenced by the apparition of law's sexed woman to whose survival it is unwillingly tied' (p. 208). In other words, feminist efforts to challenge rape law will be thwarted by law's discursive power.

'Sexed bodies' can contribute to criminology in several ways. We can see that gender categories 'neuter' sexual difference, both in research and in policy. For research, we might explore how the 'sensual attractions' of crime (Katz, 1988) are differently available to and 'experienced' by male/female bodies and masculine/feminine subjectivities. We could analyze the variable production of sexed (and racialized, etc.) bodies across many types of harms (not just rape) or for other sites of legal regulation such as family law. We could take Howe's (1994) theoretical lead by investigating women's bodies as the object of penality. For policy, 'sexed bodies' is useful for showing that reputedly gender-neutral policies are tied to specific male bodies. Sexed bodies may worry some feminists because the construct seems to revisit the spectre of biologism and body types that has long haunted criminology. This need not be the case. Sexed bodies calls attention to how we 'experience' sexual difference and its relationship to gender. It also calls attention to dualisms in western philosophy and how dualisms such as reason/emotion, mind/body and male/female are constituted in and through law, science and criminology.

A problem with sexed bodies is the strong temptation to see social life primarily through a lens of sexual difference. It is not just that feminist analyses may unwittingly collude with say, legal discourse in 'reifying these differences' (Gatens, 1996: 69), as Smart's (1990b) analysis reveals so well. Nor that for those who take 'phallocentric culture' as the start point, the recommended strategy of 'thinking outside the confining concept of the natural/sexed woman' (Smart, 1990b: 208) may be foreclosed by its own terms. From an empirical point of view, the problem is that claims such as 'the utterances of judges constantly reaffirm [the natural/sexed woman]' and 'almost every rape trial tells the same story' (Smart, 1990b: 205–6) are theoretical claims. While they may help us see a pattern of discursive power, they should be seen as open to empirical enquiry not asserted as ahistorical discursive 'fact' (see Carrington, 1994 on this point). A second problem is that variation and particularlity in sexed bodies (e.g. by race or age, etc.) is posited by theorists but not explored with care. As a consequence, sex and gender are foregrounded whereas other socially relevant divisions are accorded secondary status.

Conclusion

I have highlighted the different contributions and trajectories that class-race-gender, doing gender and sexed bodies take, but I have also endeavored to identify points of convergence. 'Class-race-gender' and 'doing gender' share a common sociological heritage, the former emphasizing social relations of inequality and the latter, the production of social categories in interaction. Thus, scholars have drawn from each to get around the sociological 'macro-micro level' problem and the structure–agency dualism. Most feminist scholars today are concerned with linking sex/gender to other social relations and with making particular (not generic) claims about women or men. Those working with 'class-race-gender' have begun to articulate what the linkages might look like and to conduct empirical research along these lines. Those working with 'sexed bodies' continue to challenge the thinking of 'class-race-gender' and 'doing gender' analysts by emphasizing that sexual difference is qualitatively different from other social categories and divisions. The 'sexed bodies' construct takes several forms: one relies on discursive power inscribing 'sex' on bodies (e.g. Butler, 1990), and another aims to bring a 'materiality' to the cultural construction of 'the body' (e.g. Bordo, 1993; Butler, 1993; Grosz, 1994).

Recent interest by feminist philosophers in 'materiality' reflects, I would argue, a recognition of the failure of discourse theory or deconstruction alone to adequately represent social relations and human existence. It also signals a need to rethink the relationship between 'the discursive' and 'the real' in feminist and allied social theories, a development I welcome. Therefore, I would disagree with Charles Lemert (1994: 274), who proposes that sociologists (and criminologists) ignore our 'thirst for reality, and consider it . . as though it were . . . a huge, ugly but plausibly discursive text'. We may do better by working the boundary between 'the discursive' and 'the real world out there', not seeing either as prior or foundational. This would permit greater openness to theoretical and methodological innovation. It may also require reconciling 'apparently incompatible ontologies', as Cain (1995: 73) suggests, and challenging the dominance of the humanities in contemporary feminist and allied social theories. Theoretical space must surely be large enough to include 'French men' and 'black women' and many, many others.

Notes

For their careful reading and comments on an earlier draft, I thank Piers Beirne, Moira Gatens, Stuart Henry, Lisa Maher, Heather Strang and Rebecca Stringer. Portions of this paper were presented at the British Criminology Conference (July, 1995) and the Australian National University, Law Faculty Seminar (October, 1995) (Daly, 1995a), where comments by Angela McRobbie, Rebecca Dobash, Kathy Laster and Barbara Sullivan were especially helpful.

1 Any such typology is likely to reflect one's disciplinary background with its 'core' set of texts and theories; these are modified further by national and academic milieux. Many other typologies are possible, e.g. those arraying psychoanalytical and literary theories, or highlighting disciplinary debates. My typology draws largely from sociology. Readers will appreciate that my sketch of shifts and disciplinary differences in feminist thought is done with broad brush strokes.

2 Even in the better discussions in US undergraduate textbooks and readers (Beirne and Messerschmidt, 1995: 550–61; Price and Sokoloff, 1995: 1–3), this typology remains in place.

3 Following Seidman (1994: 2) I use the terms *modern* and *postmodern* 'to refer to broad social and cultural patterns and sensibilities that can be analytically distinguished for the purpose of highlighting social trends'. Elements of each may be embedded in the other, but among those associated with *modern* are 'the claim of the exclusive truth-producing capacity of science', centered and transcendental subjects and causal relations; for *postmodern*, a rejection of Enlightenment theories of knowledge, decentered subjects or multiple subject positions, and non-causal relations. Most scholars working with a postmodern sensibility term their analyses 'poststructuralist', which signals an interest to deconstruct hierarchical binary oppositions in language and to analyze the role of discourse in 'shaping subjectivity, social institutions, and politics' (Seidman, 1994: 18). I shall use postmodern and poststructuralist loosely and interchangeably, although others have suggested ways of distinguishing them (see Smart, 1995: 1–15; see also Henry and Milovanovic, 1996: 1–15; Schwartz and Friedrichs, 1994).

4 As Lise Vogel (1991) suggests, some members of the second generation of feminist scholars, who came into the academy in the mid-1980s, can also be criticized for their poor revisionist history of 1960s and 1970s feminist thought, one major strand of which *did* address class and racial-ethnic divisions.

5 Also raised was the problem of *essentialism* in feminist thought (see de Lauretis, 1990; Grosz, 1990; Martin, 1994). I see this problem as far more relevant for feminist philosophers than for social researchers. Whereas the former reflect on 'woman' or 'women' as analytical categories, the latter assume and describe variability in particular women studied (see Roseneil, 1995, on this point).

6 Her particular reference is to Jacques Lacan and Deborah McDowell (Gallop et al., 1990: 364). There are, of course, several 'French women' who have been highly influential in feminist thought (see Spivak, 1992).

7 This claim is impressionistic and is based on reading the major US feminist journals (*Signs* and *Feminist Studies*) in the past two decades; it could be explored empirically. Many feminist scholars might also say that 'French men and black women' had a simultaneous impact on their thinking.

8 Major feminist philosophers themselves have made the same point (Bordo, 1993: 285–300; Young, 1994: 717).

9 Evidence for this claim comes from several sources. First, sociology has been the disciplinary home for more feminists of color than has philosophy; and it was feminists of color who put race (and class-race-gender) on the agenda. Second, institutional support, including materials for curriculum integration, was developed by sociologists at a key US center in Memphis State University. In general, 'incorporation' of race-ethnicity did not require a fundamental rethinking of the canon in sociology (or in history or anthropology) to the same degree as it did in philosophy and literature.

10 Naffine (1994: xi–xxx) has developed a modified version of this knowledge typology; she uses the terms empiricism and empirical interchangeably.

11 This hierarchy is also in place when one says that words 'contain' things. See Norris (1992: 28–31) for other critical realist arguments and Bordo's (1993: 291) critique of discursive foundationalism in which 'language swallows everything up, voraciously, a theoretical pasta machine through which the categories of competing frameworks are pressed and reprocessed as "tropes"'.

12 Brown (1991) gives a good characterization of how Real Women is mobilized by feminists, but she argues that it should be set aside.

13 One problem with positing The Woman of legal or criminological discourse is the assumption of a single or overarching discourse. I prefer the notion of discordant discourses; but in any event, this should be open to empirical enquiry, not presupposed.

14 In the readers just cited, articles describe a particular group at a particular time, but the editors identify no historical or relational linkages between them. These readers tend to reinforce notions of 'experience' and 'identity politics', which have been ably challenged by postmodern feminist scholars (e.g. Scott, 1992).

15 To me these are excellent examples of class-race-gender in action, but the authors may not claim them as such.

16 As such, I see more discussion of 'structure' in Connell, Messerschmidt, and Martin and Jurik than in the original West and Zimmerman (1987) article.

17 Thorne (1995: 498) said that 'Butler [who] writes within the tradition of post-structuralism seems to be unaware of sociological analyses of . . . gender, which predated her work by more than a decade' (see also Epstein, 1994). Young's (1994) philosophical argument of gender as 'seriality' has affinities with 'doing gender'.

18 By contrast, Bordo (1993: 17) suggests that 'the body' was a preoccupation of feminist scholars prior to the influence of Foucault.

19 In a more recent essay, Smart (1995: 228–30) discusses law as a 'gendering practice' and a 'sexing practice', which 'work alongside' each other. The former 'render[s] women as perpetually feminine, [and the latter makes] women perpetual "biological" women' (p. 229). Smart uses 'sexed bodies' to refer to the ways that women (more often than men) are constructed as 'sex' or simply as 'mere bodies' by legal discourse. Grosz (1994) discusses the women/body equivalence as one of several elements of 'sexed bodies'.

References

Abrams, Kathryn (1991) 'Hearing the Call of Stories', *California Law Review* 79(4): 971–1052.

Andersen, Margaret L. and Patricia Hill Collins (eds) (1992) *Race, Class, and Gender: An Anthology*. Belmont, CA: Wadsworth.

Anthias, Floya and Nira Yuval-Davis (1992) *Racialized Boundaries: Race, Nation, Gender, Colour and Class and the Anti-Racist Struggle*. New York: Routledge.

Austin, Regina (1992) '"The Black Community," Its Lawbreakers, and A Politics of Identification', *Southern California Law Review* 65: 1769–1817.

Baca Zinn, Maxine, Lynn Weber Cannon, Elizabeth Higginbotham, and Bonnie Thornton Dill (1986) 'The Costs of Exclusionary Practices in Women's Studies', *Signs: Journal of Women in Culture and Society* 11(2): 290–303.

Barrett, Michele (1992) 'Words and Things: Materialism and Method in Contemporary Feminist Analysis', in Michele Barrett and Anne Phillips (eds) *Destabilizing Theory*, pp. 201–19. Stanford: Stanford University Press.

Beirne, Piers and James W. Messerschmidt (1995, 2nd edn) *Criminology*. San Diego: Harcourt Brace Jovanovich.

Belkhir, Jean, Suzanne Griffith, Christine Sleeter and Carl Allsup (1994) 'Race, Sex, Class & Multicultural Education: Women's Angle of Vision', *Race, Sex & Class* 1(2): 7–22.

Bell, Derrick (1987) *And We Are Not Saved*. New York: Basic Books.

Bertrand, Marie-Andree (1994) '1893–1993: From La Donna Delinquente to a Post-modern Deconstruction of the "Woman Question" in Social Control Theory', *The Journal of Human Justice* 5(2): 43–57.

Bordo, Susan (1990) 'Feminism, Postmodernism, and Gender-Scepticism', in Linda J. Nicholson (ed.) *Feminism/Postmodernism*, pp. 133–56. New York: Routledge.
Bordo, Susan (1993) *Unbearable Weight: Feminism, Western Culture, and the Body*. Berkeley: University of California Press.
Brown, Wendy (1991) 'Feminist Hesitations, Postmodern Exposures', *differences: A Journal of Feminist Cultural Studies* 3(1): 63–84.
Butler, Judith (1990) *Gender Trouble: Feminism and the Subversion of Identity*. New York: Routledge.
Butler, Judith (1993) *Bodies That Matter: On the Discursive Limits of 'Sex'*. New York: Routledge.
Butler, Judith and Joan W. Scott (eds) (1992) *Feminists Theorize the Political*. New York: Routledge.
Cain, Maureen (1986) 'Realism, Feminism, Methodology, and Law', *International Journal of the Sociology of Law* 14: 255–67.
Cain, Maureen (ed.) (1989) *Growing Up Good*. Newbury Park: Sage.
Cain, Maureen (1990) 'Realist Philosophy and Standpoint Epistemologies or Feminist Criminology as a Successor Science', in Loraine Gelsthorpe and Allison Morris (eds) *Feminist Perspectives in Criminology*, pp. 124–40. Philadelphia: Open University Press.
Cain, Maureen (1993) 'Foucault, Feminism and Feeling: What Foucault Can and Cannot Contribute to Feminist Epistemology', in Caroline Ramazanoglu (ed.) *Up Against Foucault*, pp. 73–96. New York: Routledge.
Cain, Maureen (1995) 'Horatio's Mistake: Notes on Some Spaces in an Old Text', *Journal of Law and Society* 22(1): 68–77.
Carlen, Pat (ed.) (1985) *Criminal Women: Autobiographical Accounts*. Cambridge: Polity Press.
Carlen, Pat (1988) *Women, Crime and Poverty*. Philadelphia: Open University Press.
Carlen, Pat (1994) 'Gender, Class, Racism, and Criminal Justice: Against Global and Gender-Centric Theories, For Poststructuralist Perspectives', in George S. Bridges and Martha A. Myers (eds) *Inequality and Social Control*, pp. 134–44. Boulder: Westview Press.
Carrington, Kerry (1990) 'Aboriginal Girls and Juvenile Justice: What Justice? What Justice', *Journal for Social Justice Studies* 3: 1–18.
Carrington, Kerry (1994) 'Postmodern and Feminist Criminologies: Disconnecting Discourses?', *International Journal of the Sociology of Law* 22: 261–77.
Cole, Johnetta B. (ed.) (1986) *All American Women: Lines That Divide, Ties that Bind*. New York: Free Press.
Collins, Patricia Hill (1986) 'Learning From the Outsider Within: The Sociological Significance of Black Feminist Thought', *Social Problems* 33(6): 14–32.
Collins, Patricia Hill (1990) *Black Feminist Thought: Knowledge, Consciousness, and the Politics of Empowerment*. London: Unwin Hyman.
Collins, Patricia Hill (1993) 'Toward a New Vision: Race, Class, and Gender as Categories of Analysis and Connection', *Race, Sex, and Class* 1(1): 25–45.
Collins, Patricia Hill, Lionel A. Maldonado, Dana Y. Takagi, Barrie Thorne, Lynn Weber and Howard Winant (1995) 'Symposium: On West and Fenster-maker's "Doing Difference"', *Gender & Society* 9(4): 491–506.
Combahee River Collective (1979) 'The Combahee River Collective Statement', in Zillah Eisenstein (ed.) *Capitalist Patriarchy and the Case for Socialist Feminism*, pp. 362–72. New York: Monthly Review Press.

Connell, R. W. (1987) *Gender and Power*. Stanford: Stanford University Press.
Connell, R. W. (1995) *Masculinities*. St Leonards, NSW: Allen & Unwin.
Daly, Kathleen (1992) 'Women's Pathways to Felony Court: Feminist Theories of Lawbreaking and Problems of Representation', *Southern California Review of Law and Women's Studies* 2(1): 11–52.
Daly, Kathleen (1993) 'Class-Race-Gender: Sloganeering in Search of Meaning', *Social Justice* 20(1–2): 56–71.
Daly, Kathleen (1994) 'Criminal Law and Justice System Practices as Racist, White, and Racialized', *Washington & Lee Law Review* 51(2): 431–64.
Daly, Kathleen (1995a) 'Where Feminists Fear to Tread? Working in the Research Trenches of Class-Race-Gender', paper presented at the annual meeting of the British Criminology Conference, Loughborough, July.
Daly, Kathleen (1995b) 'Black Women, White Justice', paper presented to the Law and Society Summer Institute, Niagara-on-the-Lake, Ontario, June.
Daly, Kathleen and Meda Chesney-Lind (1988) 'Feminism and Criminology', *Justice Quarterly* 5(4): 497–538.
Daly, Kathleen and Deborah Stephens (1995) 'The "Dark Figure" of Criminology: Toward a Black and Multi-Ethnic Feminist Agenda for Theory and Research', in Nicole Hahn Rafter and Frances Heidensohn (eds) *International Feminist Perspectives in Criminology*, pp. 189–215. Philadelphia: Open University Press.
Davis, Angela (1981) *Women, Race, and Class*. New York: Vintage.
de Lauretis, Teresa (1990) 'Upping the Anti (Sic) in Feminist Theory', in Marianne Hirsch and Evelyn Fox Keller (eds) *Conflicts in Feminism*, pp. 255–70. New York: Routledge.
Delgado, Richard (1989) 'Storytelling for Oppositionists and Others: A Plea for Narrative', *Michigan Law Review* 87: 2411–41.
di Leonardo, Micaela (1991) 'Introduction', in Micaela di Leonardo (ed.) *Gender at the Crossroads of Knowledge: Feminist Anthropology in the Postmodern Era*, pp. 1–48. Berkeley: University of California Press.
Dill, Bonnie Thornton (1983) 'Race, Class, and Gender: Prospects for an All-Inclusive Sisterhood', *Feminist Studies* 9: 131–50.
di Stefano, Christine (1990) 'Dilemmas of Difference: Feminism, Modernity, and Postmodernism', in Linda J. Nicholson (ed.) *Feminism/Postmodernism*, pp. 63–82. New York: Routledge.
Epstein, Steven (1994) 'A Queer Encounter: Sociology and the Study of Sexuality', *Sociological Theory* 12: 188–202.
Ewick, Patricia and Susan S. Silbey (1995) 'Subversive Stones and Hegemonic Tales: Toward a Sociology of Narrative', *Law & Society Review* 29(2): 197–226.
Fineman, Martha (1994) 'Feminist Legal Scholarship and Women's Gendered Lives', in Maureen Cain and Christine B. Harrington (eds) *Lawyers in a Postmodern World*, pp. 229–46. Buckingham: Open University Press.
Flax, Jane (1990) 'Postmodernism and Gender Relations in Feminist Theory', in Linda Nicholson (ed.) *Feminism/Postmodernism*, pp. 39–62. New York: Routledge.
Gallop, Jane, Marianne Hirsch and Nancy K. Miller (1990) 'Criticizing Feminist Criticism', in Marianne Hirsch and Evelyn Fox Keller (eds) *Conflicts in Feminism*, pp. 349–69. New York: Routledge.
Gatens, Moira (1996) *Imaginary Bodies: Ethics, Power, and Corporeality*. New York: Routledge.

Giddens, Anthony (1984) *The Constitution of Society: Outline of the Theory of Structuration*. Oxford: Polity Press.

Grosz, Elizabeth (1990) 'A Note on Essentialism and Difference', in Sneja Gunew (ed.) *Feminist Knowledge: Critique and Construct*, pp. 332–44. London: Routledge.

Grosz, Elizabeth (1994) *Volatile Bodies: Toward a Corporeal Feminism*. St Leonards, NSW: Allen & Unwin.

Grosz, Elizabeth (1995) *Space, Time and Perversion: The Politics of Bodies*. St Leonards, NSW: Allen & Unwin.

Harding, Sandra (1986) *The Science Question in Feminism*. Ithaca: Cornell University Press.

Harding, Sandra (1987) 'The Instability of the Analytical Categories of Feminist Theory', in Sandra Harding and Jean F. O'Barr (eds) *Sex and Scientific Inquiry*, pp. 283–302. Chicago: University of Chicago Press.

Harding, Sandra (1990) 'Feminism, Science, and the Anti-Enlightenment Critiques', in Linda J. Nicholson (ed.) *Feminism/Postmodernism*, pp. 83–106. New York: Routledge.

Hartsock, Nancy (1983) 'The Feminist Standpoint: Developing the Ground for a Specifically Feminist Historical Materialism', in Sandra Harding and Merrill Hintikka (eds) *Discovering Reality*, pp. 283–310. Dordrecht: Reidel.

Hawkesworth, Mary E. (1989) 'Knowers, Knowing, Known: Feminist Theory and Claims of Truth', *Signs: Journal of Women in Culture and Society* 14(3): 533–57.

Henry, Stuart and Dragan Milovanovic (1996) *Constitutive Criminology: Beyond Postmodernism*. London: Sage.

hooks, bell (1981) *Ain't I a Woman? Black Women and Feminism*. Boston: South End Press.

Howe, Adrian (1990) 'Prologue to a History of Women's Imprisonment: In Search of a Feminist Perspective', *Social Justice* 17(2): 5–22.

Howe, Adrian (1994) *Discipline and Critique: Towards a Feminist Analysis of Penality*. New York: Routledge.

Jaggar, Alison (1983) *Feminist Politics and Human Nature*. Totowa, NJ: Rowman & Allenheld.

Jaggar, Alison and Paula Rothenberg (eds) (1993, 3rd edn) *Feminist Frameworks*. New York: McGraw-Hill.

Jefferson, Tony (1994) 'Theorizing Masculine Subjectivity', in Tim Newburn and Elizabeth A. Stanko (eds) *Just Boys Doing Business? Men, Masculinities and Crime*, pp. 10–31. New York: Routledge.

Joe, Karen A. and Meda Chesney-Lind (1995) '"Just Every Mother's Angel": An Analysis of Gender and Ethnic Variations in Youth Gang Membership', *Gender & Society* 9(4): 408–30.

Jordan, June (1985) 'Report from the Bahamas', in June Jordan (ed.) *On Call: Political Essays*, pp. 39–49. Boston: South End Press.

Katz, Jonathan (1988) *Seductions of Crime: Moral and Sensual Attractions of Doing Evil*. New York: Basic Books.

King, Deborah K. (1988) 'Multiple Jeopardy, Multiple Consciousness: The Context of a Black Feminist Ideology', *Signs: Journal of Women in Culture and Society* 14(1): 42–72.

Lemert, Charles C. (1994) 'Post-Structuralism and Sociology', in Steven Seidman (ed.) *The Postmodern Turn: New Perspectives on Social Theory*, pp. 265–81. New York: Cambridge University Press.

Lorde, Audre (1984) *Sister Outsider*. Trumansburg, NY: The Crossing Press.

Lubiano, Wahneema (1992) 'Black Ladies, Welfare Queens, and State Minstrels: Ideological War by Narrative Means', in Toni Morrison (ed.) *Race-ing Justice, Engender-ing Power*, pp. 323–63. New York: Pantheon.

Lugones, Maria C. (1991) 'On the Logic of Pluralist Feminism', in Claudia Card (ed.) *Feminist Ethics*, pp. 35–44. Lawrence: University Press of Kansas.

MacKinnon, Catharine (1982) 'Feminism, Marxism, Method, and the State: An Agenda for Theory', *Signs: Journal of Women in Culture and Society* 7(3): 515–44.

MacKinnon, Catharine (1983) 'Feminist, Marxism, Method, and the State: Toward Feminist Jurisprudence', *Signs: Journal of Women in Culture and Society* 8(4): 635–58.

Maher, Lisa (1995) 'Dope Girls: Gender, Race and Class in the Drug Economy', PhD Thesis, Rutgers University, New Jersey.

Maher, Lisa and Kathleen Daly (1996) 'Women in the Street-Level Drug Economy: Continuity or Change?', *Criminology* 34(4): in press.

Marcus, Sharon (1992) 'Fighting Bodies, Fighting Words: A Theory and Politics of Rape Prevention', in Judith Butler and Joan W. Scott (eds) *Feminists Theorize the Political*, pp. 385–403. New York: Routledge.

Martin, Jane Roland (1994) 'Methodological Essentialism, False Difference, and Other Dangerous Traps', *Signs: Journal of Women in Culture and Society* 19(3): 630–57.

Martin, Susan E. and Nancy C. Jurik (1996) *Doing Justice, Doing Gender*. Newbury Park: Sage.

Messerschmidt, James W. (1993) *Masculinities and Crime: Critique and Reconceptualization of Theory*. Lanham, MD: Rowman & Littlefield Publishers.

Moraga, Cherrie and Gloria Anzaldua (eds) (1983, 2nd edn) *This Bridge Called My Back: Writings by Radical Women of Color*. New York: Kitchen Table Press.

Naffine, Ngaire (1994) 'Introduction', in Ngaire Naffine (ed.) *Gender, Crime and Feminism*, pp. xi–xxx. Brookfield, VT: Dartmouth Publishing Company.

Nicholson, Linda (ed.) (1990) *Feminism/Postmodernism*. New York: Routledge.

Norris, Christopher (1992) *Uncritical Theory: Postmodernism, Intellectuals and the Gulf War*. London: Lawrence & Wishart.

Platt, Anthony M. (1993) 'Beyond the Canon, with Great Difficulty', *Social Justice* 20(1–2): 72–81.

Pratt, Minnie Bruce (1984) 'Identity: Skin Blood Heart', in Elly Bulkin, Minnie Bruce Pratt and Barbara Smith (eds) *Yours in Struggle*, pp. 11–63. Ithaca, NY: Firebrand Books.

Price, Barbara Raffel and Natalie J. Sokoloff (eds) (1995, 2nd edn) *The Criminal Justice System and Women*. New York: McGraw-Hill.

Radford, Jill, Liz Kelly and Marianne Hester (1996) 'Introduction', in Marianne Hester, Liz Kelly and Jill Radford (eds) *Women, Violence and Male Power*, pp. 1–16. Philadelphia: Open University Press.

Rich, Adrienne (1979) 'Disloyal to Civilization: Feminism, Racism, Gynophobia', in Adrienne Rich (ed.) *On Lies, Secrets, and Silence*, pp. 275–310. New York: Norton.

Rich, Adrienne (1980) 'Compulsory Heterosexuality and Lesbian Existence', *Signs: Journal of Women in Culture and Society* 5(4): 631–60.

Richardson, Laurel (1990) 'Narrative and Sociology', *Journal of Contemporary Ethnography* 19(1): 116–35.

Roseneil, Sasha (1995) 'The Coming of Age of Feminist Sociology: Some Issues of Practice and Theory for the Next Twenty Years', *British Journal of Sociology* 46(2): 191–205.

Ruiz, Vicki L. and Ellen Carol DuBois (eds) (1994, 2nd edn) *Unequal Sisters*. New York: Routledge.

Russell, Katheryn K. (1992) 'Development of a Black Criminology and Role of the Black Criminologist', *Justice Quarterly* 9: 667–83.

Sargeant, Lydia (ed.) (1981) *Women and Revolution: A Discussion of the Unhappy Marriage of Marxism and Feminism*. Boston: South End Press.

Schwartz, Martin D. and David O. Friedrichs (1994) 'Postmodern Thought and Criminological Discontent: New Metaphors for Understanding Violence', *Criminology* 32(2): 221–46.

Schwartz, Martin D. and Dragan Milovanovic (eds) (1995) *Race, Gender, and Class in Criminology: The Intersections*. New York: Garland.

Scott, Joan W. (1992) '"Experience"', in Judith Butler and Joan W. Scott (eds) *Feminists Theorize the Political*, pp. 22–40. New York: Routledge.

Seidman, Steven (1994) 'Introduction', in Steven Seidman (ed.) *The Postmodern Turn: New Perspectives on Social Theory*, pp. 1–23. New York: Cambridge University Press.

Simpson, Sally S. (1991) 'Caste, Class, and Violent Crime: Explaining Differences in Female Offending', *Criminology* 29(1): 115–35.

Simpson, Sally S. and Lori Elis (1995) 'Doing Gender: Sorting Out the Caste and Crime Conundrum', *Criminology* 33(1): 47–81.

Smart, Carol (1989) *Feminism and the Power of Law*. New York: Routledge.

Smart, Carol (1990a) 'Feminist Approaches to Criminology, or Postmodern Woman Meets Atavistic Man', in Loraine Gelsthorpe and Allison Morris (eds) *Feminist Perspectives in Criminology*, pp. 70–84. Philadelphia: Open University Press.

Smart, Carol (1990b) 'Law's Power, the Sexed Body, and Feminist Discourse', *Journal of Law and Society* 17: 194–210.

Smart, Carol (1992) 'The Woman of Legal Discourse', *Social and Legal Studies* 1(1): 29–44.

Smart, Carol (1995) *Law, Crime and Sexuality: Essays in Feminism*. London: Sage.

Smith, Dorothy E. (1979) 'A Sociology for Women', in Julia A. Sherman and Evelyn Torton Beck (eds) *The Prism of Sex: Essays in the Sociology of Knowledge*, pp. 135–87. Madison: University of Wisconsin Press.

Smith, Dorothy (1987) *The Everyday World as Problematic: A Feminist Sociology*. Toronto: University of Toronto Press.

Spivak, Gayatri Chakravorty (1992) 'French Feminism Revisited: Ethics and Politics', in Judith Butler and Joan W. Scott (eds) *Feminists Theorize the Political*, pp. 54–85. New York: Routledge.

Stivers, Camilla (1993) 'Reflections on the Role of Personal Narrative in Social Science', *Signs: Journal of Women in Culture and Society* 18(2): 408–25.

Thorne, Barrie (1995) Symposium participant, *Gender & Society* 9(4): 497–9.

Vogel, Lise (1991) 'Telling Tales: Historians of Our Own Lives', *Journal of Women's History* 2(winter): 89–101.

Wagner, David G. (1992) 'Daring Modesty: On Metatheory, Observation, and Theory Growth', in Steven Seidman and David G. Wagner (eds) *Postmodernism and Social Theory*, pp. 199–220. Cambridge, MA: Blackwell.

Walker, Samuel and Molly Brown (1995) 'A Pale Reflection of Reality: The Neglect of Racial and Ethnic Minorities in Introductory Criminal Justice Textbooks', *Journal of Criminal Justice Education* 6(1): 61–83.

West, Candace and Sarah Fenstermaker (1995) 'Doing Difference', *Gender & Society* 9(1): 8–37.

West, Candace and Don H. Zimmerman (1987) 'Doing Gender', *Gender & Society* 1(2): 125–51.

Williams, Patricia J. (1991) *The Alchemy of Race and Rights: Diary of a Law Professor*. Cambridge: Harvard University Press.

Worrall, Anne (1990) *Offending Women*. New York: Routledge.

Yeatman, Anna (1995) 'Interlocking Oppressions', in Barbara Caine and Rosemary Pringle (eds) *Transitions: New Australian Feminisms*, pp. 42–56. Sydney: Allen & Unwin.

Young, Alison (1990) *Femininity in Dissent*. London: Routledge.

Young, Alison (1996) *Imagining Crime*. London: Sage.

Young, Iris Marion (1994) 'Gender as Seriality: Thinking About Women as a Social Collective', *Signs: Journal of Women in Culture and Society* 19(3): 713–38.

Young, Vernetta D. and Helen Taylor Greene (1995) 'Pedagogical Reconstruction: Incorporating African-American Perspectives into the Curriculum', *Journal of Criminal Justice Education* 6(1): 85–104.

14

INTERSECTIONS OF RACE, CLASS, GENDER, AND CRIME

Future directions for feminist criminology

Amanda Burgess-Proctor

Source: *Feminist Criminology*, 1:1 (2006), 27–47.

Abstract

More than 30 years after the first scholarship of its kind was produced, feminist studies of crime are more commonplace than ever before. Two recent milestone events—the 20th anniversary of the American Society of Criminology's Division on Women and Crime and the creation of this journal, the official publication of the division—provide the perfect opportunity to reflect on what lies ahead for feminist criminology. In this article, the author argues that the future of feminist criminology lies in our willingness to embrace a theoretical framework that recognizes multiple, intersecting inequalities. Specifically, the author maintains that to advance an understanding of gender, crime, and justice that achieves universal relevance and is free from the shortcomings of past ways of thinking, feminist criminologists must examine linkages between inequality and crime using an interactional theoretical framework that is informed by multiracial feminism.

Feminist criminology has survived the growing pains of its development during the 1970s to emerge as a mature theoretical orientation. Thanks to the pioneering generation of feminist criminologists who insisted that women's deviance was worthy of academic inquiry, as well as to the contemporary generation of feminist criminologists who have contributed immensely to our understanding of women as victims, offenders, and practitioners of the criminal justice system, feminist criminology now is routinely recognized by the broader discipline as a legitimate theoretical perspective (or more accurately, set of perspectives). More than 30 years after the first scholarship of its kind was produced, feminist studies of crime are more commonplace than ever before.

Two recent milestone events remind us of just how powerful an influence feminists have had in criminology during the past three decades. First, 2004 marked the 20th anniversary of the Division on Women and Crime, the unit of the American Society of Criminology whose members are dedicated to feminist criminology and to the study of issues related to women, gender, and crime. Second, the creation of this journal, the official publication of the Division on Women and Crime, serves as a testament to the demand that exists for feminist criminological scholarship. Together, these two important achievements provide the perfect opportunity to reflect on what lies ahead for feminist criminology. Now is the time to ask ourselves, In what direction is contemporary feminism heading, and how will developments in the broader feminist movement influence the future of feminist criminology in particular? How will the work of feminist criminologists be defined in the 21st century, and what opportunities exist for the advancement of feminist criminology in the coming years?

Throughout this article, I argue that the future of feminist criminology lies in our willingness to embrace a theoretical framework that recognizes multiple, intersecting inequalities. Contemporary feminist criminologists bear the responsibility of advancing an inclusive feminism, one that simultaneously attends to issues of race, class, gender, sexuality, age, nationality, religion, physical ability, and other locations of inequality as they relate to crime and deviance. Put simply, to advance an understanding of gender, crime, and justice that achieves universal relevance and is free from the shortcomings of past ways of thinking, feminist criminologists must examine linkages between inequality and crime using an intersectional theoretical framework that is informed by multiracial feminism.

To present a persuasive argument for using an intersectional approach in feminist studies of crime, I have divided this article into four sections. First, I start by tracing the development of feminist criminology from its inception in the early 1970s. This section begins with a brief discussion of various feminist perspectives and then outlines the development of feminist criminology within the context of the broader feminist movement. Second, I describe the evolution of feminist approaches to gender that occurred during second-wave feminism of the 1970s and 1980s. Specifically, this section considers the transition from "sameness" and "difference" models, which are informed by liberal feminism, to a "dominance" model informed by radical feminism. Third, I discuss the emergence during contemporary third-wave feminism of an alternative approach to gender: an intersectional model informed by multiracial feminism. Fourth, I underscore the importance of this intersectional model for feminist criminology by highlighting its theoretical, methodological, and praxis-related relevance, and I suggest future directions for feminist criminology with respect to intersections of race, class, gender, and crime.

Feminist perspectives and the development of feminist criminology

Overview of feminist perspectives

Before summarizing the development of feminist criminology, it is first necessary to point out that *feminism* does not refer to a unitary theory. Rather, there are multiple perspectives that fall under the rubric of *feminism*, each of which involves different assumptions about the source of gender inequality and women's oppression (Barak, Flavin, & Leighton, 2001; Daly & Chesney-Lind, 1988: Price & Sokoloff, 2004). Accordingly, feminist theory traditionally is divided into five major perspectives.[1]

First, *liberal feminism* regards gender role socialization as the primary source of women's oppression. In other words, men's social roles (e.g., competitive and aggressive) are afforded more social status and power than women's roles (e.g., nurturing and passive). Consequently, liberal feminists emphasize political, social, legal, and economic equality between women and men. Within criminology, liberal feminists view women's offending as a function of gender role socialization as well; that is, women offend at a lower rate than men because their socialization provides them with fewer opportunities to engage in deviance.

Second, *radical feminism* identifies patriarchy, or male dominance, as the root cause of women's oppression. In other words, women experience discrimination because social relations and social interactions are shaped by male power and privilege. Within criminology, radical feminists often focus on manifestations of patriarchy in crimes against women, such as domestic violence, rape, sexual harassment, and pornography, and recognize that women's offending often is preceded by victimization, typically at the hands of men.[2]

Third, *Marxist feminism* attributes women's oppression to their subordinate class status within capitalist societies. In other words, the capitalist mode of production shapes class and gender relations that ultimately disadvantage women because women occupy the working class instead of the ruling class. Within criminology, Marxist feminists theorize that women's subordinate class status may compel them to commit crime as a means of supporting themselves economically.

Fourth, *socialist feminism* combines radical and Marxist perspectives to conclude that women's oppression results from concomitant sex- and class-based inequalities. In other words, class and gender work in tandem to structure society, and socialist feminists call for an examination of the ways in which gender relations are shaped by class and vice versa. Within criminology, socialist feminists examine causes of crime within the context of interacting gender- and class-based systems of power.

Fifth, *postmodern feminism* departs from the other feminist perspectives by questioning the existence of any one "truth," including women's oppression. In other words, postmodern feminists reject fixed categories and universal concepts in favor of multiple truths, and as such examine the effects of discourse and symbolic representation on claims about knowledge. Within criminology, postmodern feminists interrogate the social construction of concepts such as "crime," "justice," and "deviance" and challenge accepted criminological truths.

Although these are the five most commonly identified feminist perspectives, other perspectives are equally important to feminist theory. *Black feminism* and *critical race feminism* are centered on the experiences of Black women and women of color, and as such view women's oppression in terms of simultaneous gender- and race-based disadvantage (Collins, 2000; Crenshaw, 1991). As I discuss more fully in the third section of this article, this focus on intersecting systems of race and class makes Black and critical race feminism (along with socialist feminism) the precursors to multiracial feminism. Within criminology, Black and critical race feminists call attention to the discriminatory treatment of non-White women in the criminal justice system, such as judicial instructions to juries in rape trials to forgo the assumption that Black women are chaste (Crenshaw, 1991).

Alternatively, *lesbian feminism* links women's oppression to heterosexism and men's control of women's social spaces by "[taking] the radical feminist pessimistic view of men to its logical conclusion," whereas *Third World feminism* views women's oppression as a function of the economic exploitation of women in developing nations (Lorber, 2001, p. 99; see also Belknap, 2001). Examples of these latter two perspectives are not as common in criminology as examples of the previous perspectives, although this appears to be changing. For example, the past decade has seen an increase in domestic violence research that examines the experiences of lesbian (Renzetti, 1992), immigrant (Bui, 2004), and Muslim (Hajjar, 2004) battered women.

It is clear that each of these feminist perspectives represents a unique way of theorizing about women's oppression and about the linkages between inequality and crime. However, as I argue throughout this article, it is not any of these perspectives but the perspective of *multiracial feminism* that is most relevant to feminist criminology in the 21st century.

The emergence of feminist criminology

Having outlined these feminist perspectives, it is now possible to trace the emergence of feminist criminology. Historically, the feminist movement is divided into three eras or waves. The first wave of feminism began in the United States with the birth of the abolitionist and women's suffrage movements in the mid-to-late 1800s. Criminology itself was still developing at this time, as scholars such as Lombroso and Durkheim (in Europe) and Kellor (in the United States) began theorizing about crime and deviance (Beirne & Messerschmidt, 2000). Some 100 years later, the women's liberation and civil rights movements of the 1960s and 1970s marked the genesis of second-wave feminism. It is during this era that feminism made its appearance in criminology.

Theoretically speaking, feminist criminology developed because (primarily liberal) feminist scholars objected to the exclusion of gender from criminological analyses, an omission that seemed particularly glaring given that gender is such a strong predictor of offending (Blumstein, Cohen, Roth, & Visher, 1986; Steffensmeier & Allan, 1996), arrest (Stolzenberg & D'Alessio, 2004), and sentencing outcomes (Daly, 1994; Daly & Tonry, 1997). Feminist scholars were dissatisfied with the failure of mainstream criminology to recognize issues of gender inequality at all, as well as with the failure of critical and radical criminology to consider the relationship between inequality and crime outside of the narrow context of economic disparities, under which were subsumed issues of race and gender (see Beirne & Messerschmidt, 2000). In particular, feminist criminologists protested the exclusion of women's experiences in emerging "general" theories of crime, which were being developed by mainstream criminologists using almost exclusively male samples to predict patterns of male delinquency (Barak, 1998; Belknap, 2001; Chesney-Lind & Pasko, 2004; Daly & Chesney-Lind, 1988; Flavin, 2004; Miller, 2004; Milovanovic & Schwartz, 1996; Morash, 1999). These early feminist criminologists demanded that analyses of crime include consideration of gender in ways that had not occurred before.

It is important to note here that feminist criminology was born during a crucial juncture of the feminist movement. Shortly after the beginning of the second wave in the 1970s, feminists of minority-group status found that their experiences were underrepresented in mainstream feminism and subsequently levied sharp criticism toward their majority-group counterparts whose voices were purported to speak on behalf of all women. Feminists of color, lesbian feminists, Third World feminists, and feminists from other marginalized groups condemned the hegemony of White, middle-class, heterosexual experience that characterized mainstream second-wave feminism at that time. As I discuss more fully in the following section, it is against this backdrop that feminist criminology emerged, and claims of essentialism and reductionism soon plagued the broader feminist movement as well as feminist criminology in particular.

Finally, second-wave feminism gave way to third-wave feminism during the 1980s and 1990s. A defining feature of third-wave feminism is its focus on multiplicities or the belief that there exist multiple genders, races, and sexualities. With this idea in mind and echoing earlier criticisms, many third-wave feminists expressed dissatisfaction with the insufficient treatment of race, class, sexuality, and other locations of inequality in mainstream feminist scholarship. As a result, it is during contemporary third-wave feminism that intersectionality first appeared (Price & Sokoloff, 2004).[3] Intersectionality recognizes that systems of power such as race, class, and gender do not act alone to shape our experiences but rather, are multiplicative, inextricably linked, and simultaneously experienced. Feminist criminologists writing at this time also recognized the need for intersectionality (Daly, 1993; Daly & Stephens, 1995). For example, Daly and Stephens (1995) observed that an intersectional approach to studying crime explores

> how class, gender, and race (and age and sexuality) construct the normal and deviant . . . how these inequalities put some societal members at risk to be rendered deviant or to engage in law-breaking, and . . . how law and state institutions both challenge and reproduce these inequalities.
>
> (p. 193)

This timeline of events allows for a more thorough understanding of the development of feminist thought during second-wave and early third-wave feminism. In the following section, I describe in detail how feminist approaches to studying gender have evolved in the past 30 years, largely in response to the events outlined above.

The evolution of feminist approaches to gender: sameness, difference, and dominance

Shortly after the inception of second-wave feminism, one question divided feminists more sharply than perhaps any other: Are women essentially similar to men such that the sexes should be treated equally (i.e., the sameness approach) or do women have distinctive characteristics that require special treatment to overcome their gender-based discrimination (i.e., the difference approach)? This question loomed large among feminists, with proponents of each side lamenting the threat posed by the opposing viewpoint to the advancement of women's rights. For example, opponents of the difference approach argued that *difference* often is nothing more than a euphemism for *discrimination*, as well as that championing women's differences ultimately leads to their exclusion from certain roles, particularly within the workplace (MacKinnon, 1991; Nagel & Johnson, 2004; Williams, 1991). Conversely, opponents of the sameness approach believed in a gender dichotomy and claimed that women suffer from an equal-treatment model because, under the guise of gender neutrality, women's status ultimately is measured against a dominant male norm (Daly & Chesney-Lind, 1988; MacKinnon, 1991; Nagel & Johnson, 2004).

The sameness/difference debate that surfaced in the broader feminist movement also appeared in feminist criminology. For example, advocates of the sameness approach supported gender-neutral, "equal treatment under the law" measures, such as symmetrical correctional programming meant to guarantee male and female inmates access to the same vocational and educational resources (Barak et al., 2001). Furthermore, supporters of this equal-treatment model worried about the hidden dangers of the difference approach, wherein women's difference from men translates into their need for greater legal protection, as in the case of statutory rape laws:

> Statutory rape is, in criminal law terms, a clear instance of a victimless crime, since all parties are, by definition, voluntary participants. In what sense, then, can [Supreme Court Justice] Rehnquist assert [in a 1981 decision upholding California's statutory rape law] that the woman is victim and the man offender? One begins to get an inkling when, later, the Justice explains that the statutory rape law is "protective" legislation. . . . The notion that men are frequently the sexual aggressors and that the law ought to be able to take that reality into account in very concrete ways is hardly one that feminists could reject out of hand . . . it is therefore an area . . . in which we need to pay special attention to our impulses lest we inadvertently support and give credence to the very social constructs and behaviors we so earnestly mean to oppose.
>
> (Williams, 1991, pp. 20–21)

However, critics of the sameness approach argued that this model actually harms women because the law is not gender neutral but in fact assumes a male standard (MacKinnon, 1991; Williams, 1991). Given this male standard, women's legal claims have the potential to be regarded as requiring special or preferential treatment (Daly & Chesney-Lind, 1998). For example, considering parenthood as a mitigating factor in sentencing decisions, although applied "equally" to all defendants, disproportionately benefits female defendants with children (or "familied" women) and unintentionally punishes childless women (Barak el al., 2001; Daly, 1989; Daly & Tonry, 1997). Furthermore, critics recognized that the desire to standardize sentencing practices in the name of "equal justice" may carry unintended consequences for women:

> A major problem is that [equal-treatment] sentencing reforms are designed to reduce race- and class-based disparities in sentencing men. Their application to female offenders may yield equality with a vengeance: a higher rate of incarceration and for longer periods of time than in the past. Like reforms in divorce . . . and in child custody . . . devised with liberal feminist definitions of equality, sentencing reform also may prove unjust and may work ultimately against women.
>
> (Daly & Chesney-Lind, 1988, p. 525)

Despite the stark contrast in the orientation of the sameness and difference models, both approaches share a commonality: They are rooted in simplistic notions of women's and men's equality that are characteristic of liberal feminism. Recall that liberal feminism emphasizes political, social, legal, and economic equality between the sexes. Therefore, theoretical paradigms such as the sameness and difference models that fail to place gender relations in the context of patriarchy fit squarely within the perspective of liberal feminism. Furthermore, as many feminists have observed, the sameness and difference models also share the same fundamental flaw: They essentially ignore issues of power and privilege (Barak et al., 2001; MacKinnon, 1991; Sokoloff, Price, & Flavin, 2004). Put differently, both approaches fail to acknowledge disparities in power between the sexes; consequently, sameness and/or difference cannot be considered meaningfully without regard for women's subordinate status in a patriarchal society. As MacKinnon (1991) noted, although "men's differences from women are equal to women's differences from men . . . the sexes are not socially equal" (p. 85).

In an effort to improve upon previous models that were informed by liberal feminism and that offered elementary comparisons of men and women without regard for the effects of patriarchy, radical feminists writing at the beginning of the third wave argued for the adoption of a dominance approach to studying gender. The dominance approach is informed by radical feminism because it recognizes how patriarchy shapes gender relations and considers gender differences within the context of power and oppression (Barak et al., 2001; MacKinnon, 1991). "For women to affirm difference, when difference means dominance, as it does with gender, means to affirm the qualities and characteristics of powerlessness" (MacKinnon, 1991, p. 86). Moreover, supporters argued that the dominance approach was the only truly feminist paradigm. According to radical feminists, the sameness and difference approaches are masculinist insomuch as they use a male referent, whereas the dominance approach, "in that it sees the inequalities of the social world from the standpoint of the subordination of women to men, is feminist" (MacKinnon, 1991, p. 86).

Feminist criminologists also recognized the value of using the dominance approach. For example, Barak et al. (2001) maintain that the utility of the dominance model for feminist criminologists rests in its attention to power: "For example, proponents of the dominance approach have been instrumental in pressuring the legal system to abandon its 'hands-off' attitude toward domestic violence and to define wife battering and marital rape as crimes" (p. 154). Furthermore, the dominance approach has value for feminist criminologists because its emphasis on power and privilege dovetails with related issues of inequality in the criminal justice system.

However, despite its appeal, the dominance approach was criticized by many early third-wave feminists—primarily women of color, lesbian women, and women from other marginalized groups—for essentializing women (Andersen

& Collins, 2004; Baca Zinn, Hondagneu-Sotello, & Messner, 2000; Barak et al., 2001; Belknap, 2001; Daly & Chesney-Lind, 1988). "Essentialism occurs when a voice—typically a white, heterosexual, and socioeconomically privileged voice—claims to speak for everyone" (Sokoloff et al., 2004, p. 12). By asserting that women universally suffer the effects of patriarchy, the dominance approach rests on the dubious assumption that all women, by virtue of their shared gender, have a common "experience" in the first place. In short, the dominance approach is reductionist because it assumes that all women are oppressed by all men in exactly the same ways or that there is one unified experience of dominance experienced by women. Soon after these criticisms first emerged in the broader feminist movement, feminist criminologists began contemplating their own acts of essentialism. In the words of Daly and Chesney-Lind (1988), "One of the many challenges for feminism in general and feminist criminology in particular is the paradox of acknowledging diversity among women while claiming women's unity in experiences of oppression and sexism" (p. 502).

To summarize, although the sameness and difference approaches to gender that characterized second-wave feminism were replaced by the dominance model during early third-wave feminism, this approach also has serious flaws. What the dominance approach leaves out, of course, is the idea of multiple, intersecting sites of dominance that include, but are not limited to, gender. Moreover, this approach leaves many questions unanswered, and indeed unanswerable: Do women of color or lesbian women who are "multiply burdened" experience dominance in the same ways as straight White women? What about women victims and offenders? How do they experience dominance, both by perpetrators and by practitioners of the criminal justice system? Although these questions are rendered rhetorical using the dominance approach, they may be answered using a theoretical orientation that recognizes issues of power and privilege without assuming a monolithic women's experience: multiracial feminism.

Beyond dominance: multiracial feminism and intersections of race, class, and gender

As discussed in the previous section, the promise of the dominance approach was not shared by women who felt marginalized by "the hegemony of feminisms constructed primarily around the lives of white–middle class women" (Baca Zinn & Thornton Dill, 1996, p. 321).[4] Moreover, the dominance approach, for all of its positive attributes, is unidimensional in the sense that it merely examines women's experiences vis-à-vis men's experiences. In contrast, contemporary feminists now face a more multidimensional question: How do we move away from the "false universalism embedded in the concept 'woman'" toward an examination of gender in the context of other locations of inequality (Baca Zinn & Thornton Dill, 1996, p. 322)?

This question is not easily answered, and previous attempts by feminist scholars to acknowledge systems of power other than gender resulted in a rather benign emphasis on "diversity." As Baca Zinn and Thornton Dill (1996) comment,

> Despite the much heralded diversity trend within feminist studies, difference is often reduced to mere pluralism; a "live and let live" approach where principles of relativism generate a long list of diversities which begin with gender, class, and race and continue through a range of social structural as well as personal characteristics. . . . The major limitation of these approaches is the failure to attend to the power relations that accompany difference. Moreover, these approaches ignore the inequalities that cause some characteristics to be seen as "normal" while others are seen as "different" and thus, deviant.
> (p. 323)

For example, as "outsiders within" the feminist movement, women of color protested the complicity of "unitary theories of gender" in mainstream feminism (Baca Zinn & Thornton Dill, 1996, p. 321; see also Collins, 2000). Building on the criticisms wielded by feminists of color, a new paradigm has emerged in contemporary third-wave feminism that advances feminist thought beyond issues of sameness, difference, or dominance.[5] The "intersectional" model, informed by multiracial feminism, has succeeded in examining gender through the lens of difference while at the same time acknowledging the instrumental role of power in shaping gender relations. That is, guided by the perspective of multiracial feminism, the intersectional approach successfully attends to issues of power and dominance while achieving a universal relevance that has eluded previous approaches to studying gender.

It is sometimes difficult to disentangle concepts embedded in multiracial feminism from concepts embedded in intersections of race, class, and gender. In an attempt to elucidate these ideas, I have divided the following section in half. The first half describes key conceptual features of multiracial feminism. The second half discusses the advantages of adopting an intersectional (or "race-class-gender") approach to studying gender that is informed by multiracial feminism. Together, both halves of the following section are intended to highlight the importance of intersectionality for feminist criminology.

Multiracial feminism

Multiracial feminism was pioneered by women of color who recognized the need to construct approaches to studying gender that attended to issues of power and difference in ways that previous models had not (Baca Zinn & Thornton Dill, 1996). Although this perspective is known by a variety of names, including intersectionality theory and multicultural feminism, the term *multiracial feminism* is preferred because it emphasizes "race as a power system that interacts with other structured inequalities to shape genders" (Baca Zinn & Thornton Dill, 1996, p. 324). Still, the main focus is on interlocking and multiple inequalities (Baca Zinn & Thornton Dill, 1996; Thompson, 2002).

Multiracial feminism has several key conceptual features that distinguish it from other feminist perspectives and that make it ideal for promoting theoretical advancement for feminist criminology. First, multiracial feminism proposes that gender relations do not occur in a vacuum but, instead, that men and women also are characterized by their race, class, sexuality, age, physical ability, and other locations of inequality (Baca Zinn & Thornton Dill, 1996). Put differently, this perspective emphasizes that a power hierarchy—what Collins (2000) calls the "matrix of domination"—exists in which people are socially situated according to their differences from one another. Feminists who operate within this perspective interpret gender as being *socially constructed* through interlocking systems of race, class, gender, and other sources of inequality (Baca Zinn & Thornton Dill, 1996). In turn,

> this structural pattern affects individual consciousness, group interaction, and group access to institutional power and privileges . . . within this framework, [the focus is] less on the similarities and differences among race, class, and gender than on patterns of connection that join them.
>
> (Andersen & Collins, 2004, p. 7)

In a related manner, multiracial feminism proposes that these intersections occur simultaneously and, therefore, create a distinct *social location* for each individual (Baca Zinn & Thornton Dill, 1996). In other words, the various axes of the matrix of domination intersect to create a particular status within the broader social structure, which constitutes one's social location (Andersen & Collins, 2004). "A key element to class-race-gender is that social relations are viewed in multiple and interactive terms—not as additive" (Daly, 1993, p. 56). Thus, the main point here is that these elements work multiplicatively to shape one's social location. Although at a given time race, class, or gender might feel more relevant, "they are overlapping and cumulative in their effect on people's experience" (Andersen & Collins, 2004, p. 7).

Second, multiracial feminism calls attention to the ways in which intersecting systems of power act on all social-structural levels:

> Class, race, gender, and sexuality are components of *both* social structure *and* social interaction. Women and men are differently embedded in locations created by these cross-cutting hierarchies. As a result, women and men throughout the social order experience different forms of privilege and subordination.
>
> (Baca Zinn & Thornton Dill, 1996, p. 327, italics added)[6]

One important concept of multiracial feminism that underscores this point is *both/and* (e.g., see Collins, 2000). That is, all people simultaneously experience both oppression and privilege; no individual or group can be entirely privileged or entirely oppressed. In other words,

> the theoretical starting point [of this perspective] is that there are multiple and cross-cutting relations of class, race-ethnicity, gender, sexuality and age. This produces a matrix of domination taking a "both/and" form . . . not a simple additive model of structural subordinate relations.
>
> (Daly & Stephens, 1995, pp. 206–207)

Third, multiracial feminism is centered on the concept of *relationality*; that is, it assumes that groups of people are socially situated in relation to other groups of people based on their differences. "This means that women's differences are *connected* in systematic ways" (Baca Zinn & Thornton Dill, 1996, p. 327, emphasis in original). More important, relationality should not be thought of as a unilateral concept. To illustrate, multiracial feminism assumes that the experiences of women are structurally linked, such that some women benefit from the oppression of other women who occupy a lower social position, even when (or perhaps especially when) the former are not cognizant of the benefits that their privileged status provides. In this way, multiracial feminism retains an emphasis on power and privilege but avoids essentializing women's experiences. As Baca Zinn and Thornton Dill (1996) observe, "Multiracial feminism highlights the relational nature of dominance and subordination. Power is the cornerstone of women's differences" (p. 327).

Last, other key conceptual features of multiracial feminism include a focus on the interaction of social structure and women's agency, a reliance on a variety of methodological approaches, and an emphasis on understandings grounded in the lived experiences of dynamic groups of women (Baca Zinn & Thornton Dill, 1996). Together, these features distinguish multiracial feminism from other feminist perspectives. Although some feminist perspectives share certain of these conceptual features (e.g., postmodern feminism's emphasis on the social construction of reality, socialist, Black, and critical race feminism's attention to interacting systems of power), taken in total these characteristics make multiracial feminism truly unique among feminist perspectives.

The intersectional approach to gender: using a race-class-gender framework

Feminists who operate from the perspective of multiracial feminism advocate for an intersectional approach to studying gender. The intersectional approach recognizes that race, class, gender, sexuality, and other locations of inequality are dynamic, historically grounded, socially constructed power relationships that simultaneously operate at both the micro-structural and macro-structural levels (Andersen & Collins, 2004; Weber, 2001; Weber & Parra-Medina, 2003).

In many ways, the development of this intersectional approach to studying gender may be viewed as a natural progression of feminist thought. Recall that the sameness and difference approaches, which are informed by liberal feminism, were criticized by radical feminists who favored the dominance approach because it attends to issues of power and privilege. Likewise, feminists dissatisfied with the primacy of gender in the dominance approach have advocated for the adoption of the intersectional approach, which is informed by multiracial feminism and which does not prioritize gender over other systems of power. Thus, applying a race-class-gender framework to the study of gender may be regarded as the next step in the evolution of feminist thought.

An example from the sentencing literature helps to clarify this point. According to Daly and Tonry (1997), criminologists and legal scholars have adopted three modes of conceptualizing race and gender in criminal law and criminal justice practice: (a) law and practices as racist/sexist, (b) law and practices as White/male, and (c) law and practices as racialized/gendered. The first mode (racist/sexist) parallels the sameness approach because "differential treatment is seen as synonymous with discrimination" and because liberal feminists would "be most comfortable" with this mode (p. 236). The second mode (White/male) is equivalent to the dominance approach because it is concerned with challenging the use of a White, male referent. As Daly and Tonry note,

> Virtually all empirical work on race and gender disparities (and our assessment of it) is framed within a racist/sexist perspective in that the research centers on whether sanctions are applied differently across varied racial-ethnic, gender groups. However, a new generation of feminists and critical race scholars has raised questions about the limits this conceptualization imposes on theory, research and policy . . . [and] are more likely to embrace the latter two modes.
> (p. 235)

The third mode (racialized/gendered) corresponds to the intersectional approach because it "assumes that race and gender relations structure criminal law and justice system practices" in important ways (p. 237). Thus, the third (intersectional) mode of conceptualizing race and gender has evolved in response to the inadequacies of previous paradigms.

For these reasons, the intersectional approach that is informed by multiracial feminism offers feminists the broadest, richest, and most complete theoretical framework for studying gender. Because all social relations are racialized, including those that appear not to be, multiracial feminism achieves a universal relevance that remains elusive to other feminist perspectives. In Daly and Stephens's (1995) words,

> Although many claim that black women are at the intersection of class, race, and gender, that statement is misleading. Black women are *marked* at the intersection as being on the subordinate side of these three relations, but all social groups (including middle-class white men) are at the intersection.
>
> (p. 205)

A race-class-gender framework is applicable to the lives of all people, regardless of their social location:

> At the same time that structures of race, class, and gender create disadvantages for women of color, they provide unacknowledged benefits for those who are at the top of these hierarchies—Whites, members of upper classes, and males. Therefore, multiracial feminism applies not only to racial ethnic women but also to women and men of all races, classes, and genders.
>
> (Baca Zinn & Thornton Dill, 1996, p. 327)

It is clear, then, that multiracial feminism and the intersectional framework through which it operates hold great promise for contemporary feminist scholarship.

Multiracial feminism and criminology: intersections of race, class, gender, and crime

For several reasons, multiracial feminism and the intersectional approach can make important contributions to feminist criminology. Although still an emerging body of scholarship, some feminists (as well as some nonfeminists) have already begun urging the adoption of an intersectional approach to studying crime (e.g., Barak et al., 2001; Belknap, 2001; Britton, 2004; Daly, 1993, 1997; Daly & Chesney-Lind, 1988; Daly & Stephens, 1995; Flavin, 2004; Lynch, 1996; Milovanovic & Schwartz, 1996; Price & Sokoloff, 2004; Sokoloff & Dupont, 2005; Zatz, 2000). However, despite this support for a race-class-gender framework, to date few feminist criminologists have embraced the intersectional approach. Below I outline several reasons why contemporary third-wave feminist criminologists should adopt an intersectional framework.

The theoretical relevance of intersections

Criminologists have begun to recognize the importance of developing integrated criminological theories. As Barak (1998) argues, criminology stands to benefit from the integration of criminological perspectives. Although a thorough discussion of integrating criminologies is beyond the scope of this article, Barak's overall point helps justify the use of the intersectional approach and multiracial feminism. For example, Barak observes that race, class, and gender have been "autonomously" applied to the study of crime, whereas in the past decade feminist criminologists have begun to focus on the interaction between two or more of these variables as they relate to crime (p. 251). According to Barak, an integrated theoretical perspective "incorporates an appreciation of differences in the patterns of crime attributed to socialization, opportunities, and bias in the context that everyone's life is framed by inequalities of race, class, and gender" (p. 251).

In a similar manner, multiracial feminism emphasizes that intersecting systems of race, class, and gender act as "structuring forces" affecting how people act, the opportunities that are available to them, and the way in which their behavior is socially defined (Lynch, 1996, p. 4). For criminologists, this includes examining how the legal system responds to individual offenders based on their social locations (Barak et al., 2001). For example, Steffensmeier, Ulmer, and Kramer (1998) studied the interaction of race, gender, and age in sentencing decisions and discovered that outcomes are most punitive for defendants whose social locations place them at the margins of race, age, and gender systems—in other words, young Black men. The findings of Steffensmeier et al. "demonstrate the importance of considering the joint effects of race, gender, and age on sentencing, and of using interactive rather than additive models" (p. 763). In a similar manner, Spohn and Holleran (2000) discovered that punishment penalties also are paid by defendants in other marginalized social locations: young, unemployed Black and Hispanic men.

Therefore, concepts and propositions found in multiracial feminism may be integrated with concepts and propositions found in existing criminological theories to achieve the type of integrated perspective that Barak (1998) described. To illustrate, the preceding examples from the sentencing literature represent conceptual theoretical integration. That is, the concept of social location from multiracial feminism and the concept (or "focal concern") of *offender blameworthiness* from sentencing theory overlap in a meaningful, theoretical way to explain how defendants' demographic characteristics influence judicial decision making (Steffensmeier et al., 1998).

Moreover, initial attempts at theorizing about inequality and crime using an intersectional framework have already occurred. For example, Sampson and Wilson (1995) developed their theory of race, crime, and urban inequality by examining intersecting race and class inequalities. Taking this approach one step further, Lynch (1996) has attempted to develop a theory of race, class, gender inequality, and crime in four ways by (a) "linking race, class, and critical criminology to life course or life history research"; (b) "connecting race, class, and gender to the types of choices that are structured into people's lives"; (c) "demonstrating life course and structured choice effects by reviewing data on income, wealth, and power disparities that arise from race, gender and class inequality"; and (d) "examining how race, class and gender intersect to affect the production of crime" (p. 3).

Finally, several feminist criminologists have used intersectionality to theorize about the relationship between inequality and crime. For example, Richie (1996) shows how intersecting systems of race, class, and gender can lead battered Black women to commit criminal offenses. In her analysis, Richie uses the concept of *gender entrapment* to explain how "some women are forced or coerced into crime by their culturally expected gender roles, the violence in their intimate relationships, and their social position in the broader society" (p. 133). In a similar manner, Maher (1997) explores intersections of race, class, and gender in the lives of women who participate in the street-level drug economy. In her study, Maher describes how explanations of women's involvement with the drug economy have shifted from "primarily class-based explanations towards acknowledgement of a more complex set of cross-cutting influences—race/ethnicity, sex/gender, age, immigrant status, and other social relations" (p. 169). Most recently, Sokoloff and Dupont (2005) argue for the use of an intersectional framework in developing theories of domestic violence (see also Sokoloff & Pratt, 2005). Sokoloff and Dupont observe that intersectional approaches to domestic violence

> question the monolithic nature of woman battering, call for a greater emphasis on the structural causes of woman battering, caution against disempowering representations of marginalized battered women, and explore the complex role of culture in understanding woman abuse and our responses to it.
>
> (p. 40)

As these examples illustrate, an intersectional theoretical framework that is informed by multiracial feminism can be instrumental to the advancement of criminological theory.

The methodological relevance of intersections

In addition to the unique theoretical contributions that this framework can make to feminist criminology, the intersectional approach offers feminist criminologists the opportunity to interrogate crime and deviance in a manner that goes beyond regression models and statistical analyses (Daly, 1993; Daly & Stephens, 1995; Lynch, 1996; Weber & Parra-Medina, 2003). Of course, this does not mean that quantitative methods have no place in intersectional analyses. On the contrary, the aforementioned studies conducted by Steffensmeier et al. (1998) and Spohn and Holleran (2000) use quantitative methods to investigate the effect of social location on sentencing outcomes and make important contributions to intersectional scholarship. Rather, the important point here is that the intersectional approach invites researchers to use empirical methods that can explore what it is like to "live as" a victim or offender in a particular social location (Lynch, 1996). In other words, feminist criminologists seeking to move beyond strictly quantitative investigations of population data to identify ways in which individual characteristics mediate intersecting systems of inequality such as race, class, and gender may wish to use qualitative or mixed-methods designs (Weber & Parra-Medina, 2003).

To illustrate, qualitative methodologies such as ethnography and neighborhood studies allow us to understand "processes of conformity and deviance are gendered and racialized, the conditions of street life and illicit work for women, and how once they are immersed in the street life and subject to criminalization, women's options are narrowed" (Daly & Stephens, 1995, p. 207; e.g., see Maher, 1997; Richie, 1996). In addition, Way (2004) has suggested that historical institulionalism, a qualitative empirical method that examines how institutional structures influence a phenomenon with time, is particularly well suited for conducting intersectional analyses. Guided by the multiracial feminist proposition that individuals are situated in the hierarchical social order based on their social locations, the use of historical institutionalism to place "women within a historical and institutional context may help researchers flesh out female lawbreakers' intersectional existence" (Way, 2004, p. 88).

Perhaps most befitting of the intersections approach, mixed-methods designs that employ both quantitative and qualitative analyses have much to offer feminist criminologists wishing to produce intersectional scholarship. First, quantitative and qualitative strategies frequently grant access to different types of data. For example, quantitative methods are especially useful for uncovering macro-level social processes, whereas qualitative methods are especially useful for uncovering micro-level social processes. Given concern for the simultaneity of micro- and macro-level systems that characterizes the intersectional approach, analyses of the ways in which these processes are concurrently produced may be best achieved by combining qualitative and quantitative data.[7]

Second, qualitative methods are particularly advantageous when the topic of interest is sensitive or difficult to discuss (Rosenblatt & Fischer, 1993); thus, a combined strategy may be more successful in exploring personal experiences with social power, and privilege than a purely quantitative design. In a similar manner, qualitative interview questions are especially useful for gathering detailed information from participants. Therefore, in-depth follow-up questions that antecede more general, broad-based interview questions may grant researchers greater insight into participants' self-reported experiences with intersecting race, class, and gender systems (Fisher & Cullen, 2000; Huizinga & Elliott, 1986).

For example, Bridges and Steen (1998) used a mixed-methods design to examine racial disparities in probation officers' assessments of juvenile offenders.

Although the quantitative analysis reveals that differential attributions about the causes of crime mediate the relationship between race and officers' sentencing recommendations, a qualitative analysis of officers' narrative reports suggests that "aspects of social context" are as important to officers as are legal variables such as prior criminal history (Bridges & Steen, 1998, p. 558). From the results of the qualitative data analysis, Bridges and Steen conclude, "Some offenders are perceived as threatening and at risk of reoffending because their personal characteristics [i.e., their social location] and their behavior are salient in officials' working explanations of criminal behavior" (p. 567).[8] In this instance, the combination of quantitative and qualitative methods offers unique insight into the ways in which race (and other aspects of a defendant's social location) influences his or her treatment in the criminal justice system. As this example illustrates, a research design that uses a qualitative or mixed-methods approach can be particularly relevant to producing intersectional scholarship.

The praxis-related relevance of intersections

Finally, multiracial feminism and the intersectional approach offer feminist criminologists the chance to translate theory into action. Perhaps the most important opportunity for praxis concerns the pursuit of social justice that forms the cornerstone of the intersectional approach (Andersen & Collins, 2004; Thompson, 2002; Weber, 2001; Weber & Parra-Medina, 2003). Specifically, intersectional scholarship can advance social justice goals by providing insight into social and political contexts that reinforce power relations and by uncovering processes of resistance that can alter hierarchical systems of inequality (Weber, 2001). Put differently,

> by placing primary attention on the construction of multiple social inequalities as they are simultaneously produced, [intersectional] research is particularly well-suited to addressing the question of disparities in our social worlds . . . and seeks activism for social justice . . . for all people as an integral part of the knowledge acquisition process.
> (Weber & Parra-Medina, 2003, p. 185)

With respect to multiracial feminism, some feminists have argued that its commitment to social justice distinguishes it entirely from alternative feminist perspectives:

> There are multiple strategies for social justice embedded in multiracial feminism. . . . Multiracial feminism is not just another brand of feminism that can be taught alongside liberal, radical, and socialist feminism. Multiracial feminism is the heart of an inclusive women's liberation struggle. The race-class-gender-sexuality-nationality framework

> through which multiracial feminism operates encompasses and goes way beyond liberal, radical, and socialist feminist priorities—and it always has.
>
> (Thompson, 2002, p. 349)

In addition, unlike other feminist perspectives, one hallmark of multiracial feminism is its emphasis on forming coalitions across racial divides. Indeed, coalition building is a theme often echoed by scholars who advocate for an intersectional framework (e.g., Collins, 2000; Thompson, 2002). For example, Daly and Stephens (1995) note that as is the case with multiracial feminism, promising transformative coalition opportunities exist when dominance-based feminist perspectives are combined with critical race perspectives that reflect the experiences of people of color, and that "the need to build such coalitions could not be more urgent" (p. 208). Opportunities for coalition building coupled with commitment to social justice make multiracial feminism and the intersectional approach a crucial strategy for achieving feminist criminologist praxis.

Conclusion

For the reasons outlined in this article, feminist criminologists wishing to advance inclusive analyses of race, class, gender, and crime would do well to adopt an intersectional framework that is informed by multiracial feminism. In one of the few existing criminological texts advocating the use of the intersectional approach, Barak et al. (2001) noted several promising developments for intersectionality in criminology. Of these, perhaps most relevant to feminist criminology is "scholarship that shifts the emphasis [of criminology] on identifying systems of privilege that support existing systems of oppression but are rarely acknowledged by those who reap the benefits" (p. 234).

Indeed, feminist criminologists have long been critical of scholarship that remains blind to issues of power and privilege. For contemporary third-wave feminist criminologists, the time has come to build on the foundation that has been laid for us by our predecessors and to advance a feminist criminology that embraces all sources of oppression without prioritizing gender. After all, as multiracial feminism reveals, power, privilege, and oppression are multiplicative and intersecting according to race, class, gender, sexuality, nationality, age, and other defining social characteristics. As we take stock of our field and look ahead to the future, the words of Daly and Chesney-Lind (1988) are instructive:

> Turning to the future, we wonder what will happen as increasing numbers of white women, as well as men and women of color, enter the discipline and try to find their place in it. One cannot expect that the first generation of new scholars will be confident or sure-footed after centuries of exclusion from the academy. One might

> expect, however, that we will ask different questions or pursue problems which our discipline has ignored.
>
> (p. 506)

In the coming years, successful examination of the ways in which women (and men) in the criminal justice system experience oppression by virtue of their race, class, and gender characteristics must be grounded in an intersectional framework that is informed by multiracial feminism:

> Research and theorizing must continue to reject the essentialism inherent in treating women as a unitary category. . . . We already know much about the ways in which race, class, and sexual inequality interweave with women's experiences as victims, offenders, and workers. The challenge for feminist criminology in the years to come lies in formulating theory and carrying out empirical studies that prioritize all of these dimensions, rather than relegating one or more of them to the background for the sake of methodological convenience.
>
> (Britton, 2004, p. 71)

In time, such advances will no doubt constitute the very core of feminist criminology in the 21st century.

Notes

Many thanks to Maxine Baca Zinn and to the editor and anonymous reviewers whose comments and suggestions greatly improved the quality of this article. An earlier draft of this article was presented as part of the Division on Women and Crime's 20th anniversary featured panel, "Past, Present, and Future: The Study of Gender and Crime," at the 2004 annual meeting of the American Society of Criminology, Nashville, Tennessee.

1 See Daly and Chesney-Lind (1988) for a thoughtful comparison of these feminist perspectives.

2 For example, recent feminist research identifies the concept of "blurred boundaries" between women's victimization and offending experiences (e.g., Daly & Maher, 1998; Gaarder & Belknap, 2002; Moe, 2004).

3 According to Thompson (2002), intersectionality actually emerged during the 1970s. That is, at the beginning of the second wave of the feminist movement, women of color (as well as White antiracist women and others who felt marginalized by mainstream feminism) began calling for scholarship that simultaneously attended to issues of race, class, gender, and sexuality. However, the concept of intersecting inequalities first appeared in criminology during the 1980s, corresponding to feminism's third wave. Therefore, for the purposes of this article, intersectionality is presented as a product of third-wave feminism.

4 In fact, the mainstream second-wave feminist movement was labeled "hegemonic feminism" by some women of color and White antiracist women for its exclusive use of a White, middle-class, heterosexual female standard (Thompson, 2002).

5 Again, see Thompson (2002) for a discussion of the timing of the emergence of multiracial feminism.

6 However, Sokoloff and Dupont (2005) have argued that social structure is "rarely" the focus of analyses rooted in multiracial feminism.
7 However, as one anonymous reviewer correctly noted, some strictly quantitative techniques such as nested modeling are similarly useful for these types of analysis because they make it possible to explore variation in individual-level variables (such as race, class, or gender) across community- or neighborhood-level contexts.
8 This finding also supports the integration of social location and offender blameworthiness discussed previously.

References

Andersen, M., & Collins, P. H. (2004). *Race, class, and gender* (5th ed.). Belmont, CA: Wadsworth.

Baca Zinn, M., Hondagneu-Sotello, P., & Messner, M. A. (Eds.). (2000). *Gender through the prism of difference* (2nd ed.). Boston: Allyn & Bacon.

Baca Zinn, M., & Thornton Dill, B. (1996). Theorizing difference from multiracial feminism. *Feminist Studies, 22*, 321–331.

Barak, G. (1998). *Integrating criminologies.* Boston: Allyn & Bacon.

Barak, G., Flavin, J., & Leighton, P. S. (2001). *Class, race, gender, and crime: Social realities of justice in America.* Los Angeles: Roxbury.

Beirne, P., & Messerschmidt, J. (2000). *Criminology* (3rd ed.). Boulder, CO: Westview.

Belknap, J. (2001). *The invisible woman: Gender, crime, and justice* (2nd ed.). Belmont, CA: Wadsworth.

Blumstein, A., Cohen, J., Roth, J. A., & Visher, C. (1986). Introduction: Studying criminal careers. In A. Blumstein, J. Cohen, J. A. Roth, & C. Visher (Eds.), *Criminal careers and "career criminals"* (pp. 12–30). Washington, DC: National Academy Press.

Bridges, G., & Steen, S. (1998). Racial disparities in official assessments of juvenile offenders: Attributional stereotypes as mediating mechanisms. *American Sociological Review, 63*, 554–570.

Britton, D. M. (2004). Feminism in criminology: Engendering the outlaw. In P. J. Schram & B. Koons-Witt (Eds.), *Gendered (in)justice: Theory and practice in feminist criminology* (pp. 49–67). Long Grove, IL: Waveland Press.

Bui, H. (2004). *In the adopted land: Abused immigrant women and the criminal justice system.* Westport, CT: Praeger.

Chesney-Lind, M., & Pasko, L. (Eds.). (2004). *Girls, women, and crime.* Thousand Oaks, CA: Sage.

Collins, P. H. (2000). *Black feminist thought: Knowledge, consciousness, and the politics of empowerment* (2nd ed.). New York: Routledge.

Crenshaw, K. (1991). Demarginalizing the intersection of race and sex: A Black feminist critique of antidiscrimination doctrine, feminist theory, and antiracist politics. In K. Bartlett & R. Kennedy (Eds.), *Feminist legal theory* (pp. 57–80). Boulder, CO: Westview.

Daly, K. (1989). Rethinking judicial paternalism: Gender, work-family relations, and sentencing. *Gender & Society, 3*, 9–36.

Daly, K. (1993). Class-race-gender: Sloganeering in search of meaning. *Social Justice, 20*, 56–71.

Daly, K. (1994). Gender and punishment disparity. In M. Myers & G. Bridges (Eds.), *Inequality, crime, and social control* (pp. 117–133). Boulder, CO: Westview.

Daly, K. (1997). Different ways of conceptualizing sex/gender in feminist theory and their implications for criminology. *Theoretical Criminology*, *1*, 25–51.

Daly, K., & Chesney-Lind, M. (1988). Feminism and criminology. *Justice Quarterly*, *5*, 497–538.

Daly, K., & Maher, L. (1998). Crossroads and intersections: Building from feminist critique. In K. Daly & L. Maher (Eds.), *Criminology at the crossroads: Feminist readings in crime and justice* (pp. 1–17). New York: Oxford University Press.

Daly, K., & Stephens, D. J. (1995). The "dark figure" of criminology: Towards a Black and multi-ethnic feminist agenda for theory and research. In N. Hahn Rafter & F. Heidensohn (Eds.), *International feminist perspectives in criminology: Engendering a discipline* (pp. 189–215). Philadelphia: Open University Press.

Daly, K., & Tonry, M. (1997). Gender, race, and sentencing. In M. Tonry (Ed.), *Crime and justice: An annual review of research* (Vol. 22, pp. 201–252). Chicago: University of Chicago.

Fisher, B. S., & Cullen, F. T. (2000). Measuring the sexual victimization of women: Evolution, current controversies, and future research. In D. Duffee, D. McDowall, L. G. Mazerolle, & S. Mastrofski (Eds.), *Measurement and analysis of crime and justice* (pp. 317–390). Washington, DC: National Institute of Justice.

Flavin, J. (2004). Feminism for the mainstream criminologist: An invitation. In P. J. Schram & B. Koons-Witt (Eds.), *Gendered (in)justice: Theory and practice in feminist criminology* (pp. 68–92). Long Grove, IL: Waveland Press.

Gaarder, E., & Belknap, J. (2002). Tenuous borders: Girls transferred to adult court. *Criminology*, *40*, 481–518.

Hajjar, L. (2004). Religion, state power, and domestic violence in Muslim societies: A framework for comparative analyses. *Law & Social Inquiry*, *29*, 1–38.

Huizinga, D., & Elliott, D. S. (1986). Reassessing the reliability and validity of self-report delinquency measures. *Journal of Quantitative Criminology*, *2*, 293–327.

Lorber, J. (Ed.). (2001). *Gender inequality: Feminist theories and politics* (2nd ed.). Los Angeles: Roxbury.

Lynch, M. J. (1996). Class, race, gender and criminology: Structured choices and the life course. In D. Milovanovic & M. D. Schwartz (Eds.), *Race, gender, and class in criminology: The intersections* (pp. 3–28). New York: Garland.

MacKinnon, C. A. (1991). Difference and dominance: On sex discrimination. In K. T. Bartlett & R. Kennedy (Eds.), *Feminist legal theory* (pp. 81–94). Boulder, CO: Westview.

Maher, L. (1997). *Sexed work: Gender, race, and resistance in a Brooklyn drug market*. Oxford, UK: Oxford University Press.

Miller, J. (2004). Feminist theories of women's crime: Robbery as a case study. In B. R. Price & N. Sokoloff (Eds.), *The criminal justice system and women* (3rd ed., pp. 51–67). New York: McGraw-Hill.

Milovanovic, D., & Schwartz, M. D. (Eds.). (1996). *Race, gender, and class in criminology: The intersections*. New York: Garland.

Moe, A. (2004). Blurring the boundaries: Women's criminality in the context of abuse. *Women's Studies Quarterly*, *32*, 116–138.

Morash, M. (1999). A consideration of gender in relation to *Social learning and social structure: A general theory of crime and deviance. Theoretical Criminology*, *3*, 451–462.

Nagel, I., & Johnson, B. (2004). The role of gender in a structured sentencing system: Equal treatment, policy choices, and the sentencing of female offenders. In P. J.

Schram & B. Koons-Witt (Eds.), *Gendered (in)justice: Theory and practice in feminist criminology* (pp. 198–235). Long Grove, IL: Waveland Press.

Price, B. R., & Sokoloff, N. (2004). *The criminal justice system and women* (3rd ed.). New York: McGraw-Hill.

Renzetti, C. (1992). *Violent betrayal: Partner abuse in lesbian relationships*. Newbury Park, CA: Sage.

Richie, B. (1996). *Compelled to crime: The gender entrapment of Black battered women*. New York: Routledge.

Rosenblatt, P., & Fischer, L. R. (1993). Qualitative family research. In P. G. Boss, W. J. Doherty, R. LaRossa, W. R. Schumm, & S. K. Steinmetz (Eds.), *Sourcebook of family theories and methods: A contextual approach* (pp. 167–177). New York: Plenum.

Sampson, R., & Wilson, W. J. (1995). Toward a theory of race, crime, and urban inequality. In J. Hagan & R. D. Peterson (Eds.), *Crime and inequality* (pp. 37–54). Stanford, CA: Stanford University Press.

Sokoloff, N., & Dupont, I. (2005). Domestic violence at the intersections of race, class, and gender. *Violence Against Women, 11*, 38–64.

Sokoloff, N., & Pratt, C. (2005). *Domestic violence at the margins: Readings on race, class, gender, and culture*. New Brunswick, NJ: Rutgers University Press.

Sokoloff, N., Price, B. R., & Flavin, J. (2004). The criminal law and women. In B. R. Price & N. Sokoloff (Eds.), *The criminal justice system and women* (3rd ed., pp. 11–29). New York: McGraw-Hill.

Spohn, C., & Holleran, D. (2000). The imprisonment penalty paid by young, unemployed Black and Hispanic male offenders. *Criminology, 38*, 281–306.

Steffensmeier, D., & Allan, E. (1996). Gender and crime: Toward a gendered theory of female offending. *Annual Review of Sociology, 22*, 459–487.

Steffensmeier, D., Ulmer, J., & Kramer, J. (1998). The interaction of race, gender, and age in criminal sentencing: The punishment cost of being young, Black, and male. *Criminology, 36*, 763–793.

Stolzenberg, L., & D'Alessio, S. (2004). Sex differences in the likelihood of arrest. *Journal of Criminal Justice, 32*, 443–454.

Thompson, B. (2002). Multiracial feminism: Recasting the chronology of second wave feminism. *Feminist Studies, 28*, 337–360.

Way, L. B. (2004). Missing faces: Is historical institutionalism the answer for conducting intersectional research? *Women & Criminal Justice, 15*, 81–98.

Weber, L. (2001). *Understanding race, class, gender, and sexuality: A conceptual framework*. Boston: McGraw-Hill.

Weber, L., & Parra-Medina, D. (2003). Intersectionality and women's health: Charting a path to eliminating health disparities. In M. Texler Segal, V. Demos, & J. Jacobs Kronenfeld (Eds.), *Gender perspectives on health and medicine: Key themes* (pp. 181–229). Oxford, UK: Elsevier.

Williams, W. (1991). The equality crisis: Some reflections on culture, courts, and feminism. In K. T. Bartlett & R. Kennedy (Eds.), *Feminist legal theory* (pp. 15–34). Boulder, CO: Westview.

Zatz, M. (2000). Convergence of race, ethnicity, and class on court decision-making: Looking toward the 21st century. In J. Horney (Ed.), *Policies, process, & decisions of the criminal justice system: Criminal justice 2000* (Vol. 3, pp. 503–552). Washington, DC: U.S. Department of Justice.

15

PATRIARCHY, CRIME, AND JUSTICE

Feminist criminology in an era of backlash

Meda Chesney-Lind

Source: *Feminist Criminology*, 1:1 (2006), 6–26.

Abstract

Feminist criminology, as an outgrowth of the second wave of feminism, came of age during a period of considerable change and political optimism. As a mature field, it now inhabits a social and political landscape radically altered and increasingly characterized by the politics of backlash. Given feminist criminology's dual focus on gender and crime, it is uniquely positioned to respond to two core aspects of the current backlash political agenda: racism and sexism. To do this effectively, feminist criminology must prioritize research on the race/gender/punishment nexus. This article provides three examples of how such a focus exposes the crucial roles played by constructions of the crime problem as well as current crime-control strategies in the ratification and enforcement of antifeminist and racist agendas. Finally, the field must seek creative ways to blend scholarship with activism while simultaneously providing support and encouragement to emerging feminist criminologists willing to take such risks.

A product of the second wave of the women's movement, feminist criminology has been in existence now for more than three decades. Although any starting point is arbitrary, certainly one could point to the publication of key journal issues and books in the 1970s,[1] and it is clear that a signal event was the founding of the Women and Crime Division of the American Society of Criminology in 1982 (Rafter, 2000, p. 9). Since that time, the field has grown exponentially, which makes it increasingly impossible to do justice to all its dimensions in the space of an article. This article, instead, focuses on the challenges facing our important field as we enter a millennium characterized by a deepening backlash against feminism and other progressive movements and perspectives.

Feminist criminology in the 20th century: looking backward, looking forward

The feminist criminology of the 20th century clearly challenged the overall masculinist nature of theories of crime, deviance, and social control by calling attention to the repeated omission and misrepresentation of women in criminological theory and research (Belknap, 2001; Cain, 1990; Daly & Chesney-Lind, 1988). Turning back the clock, one can recall that prior to path-breaking feminist works on sexual assault, sexual harassment, and wife abuse, these forms of gender violence were ignored, minimized, and trivialized. Likewise, girls and women in conflict with the law were overlooked or excluded in mainstream works while demonized, masculinized, and sexualized in the marginalized literature that brooded on their venality. Stunning gender discrimination, such as the failure of most law schools to admit women, the routine exclusion of women from juries, and the practice of giving male and female "offenders" different sentences for the same crimes went largely unchallenged (see Rafter, 2000, for a good overview of the history in each of these areas).

The enormity of girls' and women's victimization meant that the silence on the role of violence in women's lives was the first to attract the attention of feminist activists and scholars. Because of this, excellent work exists on the problem of women's victimization—especially in the areas of sexual assault, sexual harassment, sexual abuse, and wife battery (see, e.g., Buzawa & Buzawa, 1990; Dziech & Weiner, 1984; Estrich, 1987; D. Martin, 1977; Rush, 1980; Russell, 1986; Schechter, 1982; Scully, 1990).

In retrospect, the naming of the types and dimensions of female victimization had a significant impact on public policy, and it is arguably the most tangible accomplishment of both feminist criminology and grassroots feminists concerned about gender, crime, and justice. The impact on the field of criminology and particularly criminological theory was mixed, however, in part because these offenses did not initially seem to challenge androcentric criminology per se. Instead, the concepts of "domestic violence" and "victimology," although pivotal in the development of feminist criminology, also supplied mainstream criminologists and some criminal justice practitioners with a new area in which to publish, "new" crimes to study (and opportunities to secure funding), and new men to jail (particularly men of color and other marginalized men). More recent, the field of domestic violence has even been home to a number of scholars who have argued that women are as violent as men (for critical reviews, see DeKeseredy, Sanders, Schwartz, & Alvi, 1997; DeKeseredy & Schwartz, 1998; S. Miller, 2005). In part because of these trends, the focus on girls' and women's victimization has produced a range of challenges for feminist criminology and for feminist activists that have become even more urgent as we move into the new century.

Compared to the wealth of literature on women's victimization, interest in girls and women who are labeled, tried, and jailed as "delinquent" or "criminal" was slower to fully develop[2] in part because scholars of "criminalized" women and girls had to contend early on with the masculinization (or "emancipation") hypothesis of women's crime, which argues in part that "in the same way that women are demanding equal opportunity in the fields of legitimate endeavor, a similar number of determined women are forcing their way into the world of major crimes" (Adler, 1975, p. 3; see also Simon, 1975). Feminist criminologists, as well as mainstream criminologists, debated the nature of that relationship for the next decade and ultimately concluded it was not correct (Chesney-Lind, 1989; Steffensmeier, 1980; Weis, 1976), but this was a costly intellectual detour (and also a harbinger of things to come, as it turned out).

The 1980s and 1990s, however, would see breakthrough research on the lives of criminalized girls and women. Rich documentation of girls' participation in gangs, as an example, challenges earlier gang research that focuses almost exclusively on boys (see Chesney-Lind & Hagedorn, 1999; Moore, 1991). Important work on the role of sexual and physical victimization in girls' and women's pathways into women's crime (see Arnold, 1995; Chesney-Lind & Rodriquez, 1983; Chesney-Lind & Shelden, 1992; Gilfus, 1992) began to appear, along with work that suggests unique ways in which gender and race create unique pathways for girl and women offenders into criminal behavior, particularly in communities ravaged by drugs and overincarceration (Bourgois & Dunlap, 1993; Joe, 1995; Maher & Curtis, 1992; Richie, 1996). Needless to say, the focus on girls' and women's gender also highlights the fact that masculinity and crime need to be both theorized and researched (Bowker, 1998; Messerschmidt, 2000).

Instead of the "add women and stir" (Chesney-Lind, 1988) approach to crime theorizing of the past century (which often introduces gender solely as a "variable" if at all), new important work on the gender/crime nexus *theorizes gender*. This means, for example, drawing extensively on sociological notions of "doing gender" (West & Zimmerman, 1987) and examining the role of "gender regimes" (Williams, 2002) in the production of girls' and women's behavior. Contemporary approaches to gender and crime (see Messerschmidt, 2000; J. Miller, 2001) tend to avoid the problems of reductionism and determinism that characterize early discussions of gender and gender relations, stressing instead the complexity, tentativeness, and variability with which individuals, particularly youth, negotiate (and resist) gender identity (see Kelly, 1993; Thorne, 1993). J. Miller and Mullins (2005), in particular, have argued for the crafting of "theories of the middle range" that recognize that although society and social life are patterned on the basis of gender, it is also the case that the *gender order* (Connell, 2002) is "complex and shifting" (J. Miller & Mullins, 2005, p. 7).

Feminist criminology and the backlash

Feminist criminology in the 21st century, particularly in the United States, finds itself in a political and social milieu that is heavily affected by the backlash politics of a sophisticated and energized right wing—a context quite different from the field's early years when the initial intellectual agenda of the field evolved. Political backlash eras have long been a fixture of American public life, from reconstruction after the Civil War to the McCarthy era of the 1950s. Most of these have certain common characteristics, including a repression of dissent, imperialistic adventure, a grim record of racism, and "resistance to extending full rights to women" (Hardisty, 2000, p. 10).

The current backlash era, however, uses crime and criminal justice policies as central rather than facilitating elements of political agenda—a pattern clearly of relevance to feminist criminology. The right-wing intent to use the "crime problem" became evident very early. Consider Barry Goldwater's 1964 unsuccessful presidential campaign where he repeatedly used phrases such as *civil disorder* and *violence in the streets* in a "covertly racist campaign" to attack the civil rights movement (Chambliss, 1999, p. 14). Both Richard Nixon and Ronald Reagan refined the approach as the crime problem became a centerpiece of the Republican Party's efforts to wrest electoral control of southern states away from the Democratic Party. Nixon's emphasis on *law and order* and Reagan's *war on drugs* were both built on "white fear of black street crime" (Chambliss, 1999, p. 19). With time, crime would come to be understood as a code word for race in U.S. political life, and it became a staple in the Republican attacks on Democratic rivals. When Reagan's former vice president, George Bush Sr., ran for office, he successfully used the Willie Horton incident (where an African American on a prison furlough raped and murdered a woman) to derail the candidacy of Michael Dukakis in 1988 (Chambliss, 1999).

His son, George W. Bush, would gain the presidency as a direct result of backlash criminal justice policies, because felony disenfranchisement of largely African American voters in Florida was crucial to his political strategy in that state (Lantigua, 2001). In Bush's second election campaign, however, another feature would be added to the Republican mix: an appeal to "moral values." Included in the moral values agenda, designed to appeal to right-wing Christians, is the rolling back of the gains of the women's movement of the past century, including the recriminalization of abortion and the denial of civil rights to gay and lesbian Americans. Bush's nominee to the Supreme Court, John Roberts, has even questioned "whether encouraging homemakers to become lawyers contributes to the public good" (Goldstein, Smith, & Becker, 2005).

The centrality of both crime and gender in the current backlash politics means that feminist criminology is uniquely positioned to challenge right-wing initiatives. To do this effectively, however, the field must put an even greater priority on *theorizing patriarchy and crime*, which means focusing on the ways in which the definition of the crime problem and criminal justice practices support patriarchal practices and worldviews.

To briefly review, patriarchy is a sex/gender system[3] in which men dominate women and what is considered masculine is more highly valued than what is considered feminine. Patriarchy is a system of social stratification, which means that it uses a wide array of social control policies and practices to ratify male power and to keep girls and women subordinate to men (Renzetti & Curran, 1999, p. 3). Often, the systems of control that women experience are explicitly or implicitly focused on controlling female sexuality (such as the sexual double standard; Renzetti & Curran, 1999, p. 3). Not infrequently, patriarchal interests overlap with systems that also reinforce class and race privilege, hence, the unique need for feminist criminology to maintain the focus on intersectionality that characterizes recent research and theorizing on gender and race in particular (see Crenshaw, 1994).

Again, in this era of backlash, the formal system of social control (the law and criminal justice policies) play key roles in eroding the rights of both women and people of color, particularly African Americans but increasingly, other ethnic groups as well. Feminist criminology is, again, uniquely positioned to both document and respond to these efforts. To theorize patriarchy effectively means that we have done cutting-edge research on the interface between patriarchal and criminal justice systems of control and that we are strategic about how to get our findings out to the widest audience possible, issues to which this article now turns.

Race, gender, and crime

If feminist criminology is to fully understand the interface between patriarchal control mechanisms and criminal justice practices in the United States, we must center our analysis on the race/gender/punishment nexus. Specifically, America's long and sordid history of racism and its equally disturbing enthusiasm for imprisonment must be understood as intertwined, and both of these have had a dramatic effect on African American women in particular (Bush-Baskette, 1998; Horton & Horton, 2005; Johnson, 2003; Mauer, 1999).

More than a century ago, W. E. B. Du Bois saw the linkage between the criminal justice system and race-based systems of social control very clearly. Commenting on the dismal failure of "reconstruction," he concluded,

> Despite compromise, war, and struggle, the Negro is not free. In well-nigh the whole rural South the black farmers are peons, bound

> by law and custom to an economic slavery from which the only escape is death or the penitentiary.
>
> (as quoted in Johnson, 2003, p. 284)

Although the role of race and penal policy has received increased attention in recent years, virtually all of the public discussion of the issues has focused on African American males (see, e.g., Human Rights Watch, 2000). More recent, the significant impact of mass incarceration on African American and Hispanic women has received the attention it deserves. Current data show that African American women account for "almost half (48 percent)" of all the women we incarcerate (Johnson, 2003, p. 34). Mauer and Huling's (1995) earlier research adds an important perspective here; they noted that the imprisonment of African American women grew by more than 828% between 1986 and 1991, whereas that of White women grew by 241% and of Black men by 429% (see also Bush-Baskette, 1998; Gilbert, 2001). Something is going on, and it is not just about race or gender; it is about both—a sinister synergy that clearly needs to be carefully documented and challenged.

Feminist criminologist Paula Johnson (2003), among others, advocated a "Black Feminist analysis of the criminal justice system." An examination of Black women's history from slavery through the Civil War and the postwar period certainly justifies a clear focus on the role that the criminal justice system played in the oppression of African American women and the role of prison in that system (Rafter, 1990). And the focus is certainly still relevant because although women sometimes appear to be the unintended victims of the war on drugs, this "war" is so heavily racialized that the result can hardly be viewed as accidental. African American women have always been seen through the "distorted lens of otherness," constructed as "subservient, inept, oversexed and undeserving" (Johnson, 2003, pp. 9–10), in short, just the "sort" of women that belong in jail and prison. Hence, any good work on criminalized women must also examine the ways in which misogyny and racism have long been intertwined themes in the control of women of color (as well as other women) in the United States, as the next section demonstrates.

Media demonization and the masculinization of female offenders

As noted earlier, the second wave of feminism had, by the 1980s, triggered an array of conservative political, policy, and media responses. In her book *Backlash: The Undeclared War Against American Women*, Susan Faludi (1991), a journalist, was quick to see that the media in particular were central, not peripheral, to the process of discrediting and dismissing feminism and feminist gains. She focused specific attention on mainstream journalism's efforts to locate and publicize those "female trends" of the 1980s that would undermine and indict the feminist agenda. Stories about "the failure to get husbands, get pregnant, or properly bond with their children" were suddenly everywhere, as were the very first stories on "bad girls"; Faludi noted that "NBC, for instance, devoted an entire evening news special to the pseudo trend of 'bad girls' yet ignored the real trends of bad boys: the crime rate among boys was climbing twice as fast as for girls" (p. 80).

Faludi's (1991) recognition of the media fascination with bad girls was prescient. The 1990s would produce a steady stream of media stories about violent and bad girls that continues unabated in the new millennium. Although the focus would shift from the "gansta girl," to the "violent girl," to the "mean girl" (Chesney-Lind & Irwin, 2004), the message is the same: Girls are bad in ways that they never used to be. As an example, the Scelfo (2005) article titled "Bad Girls Go Wild," published in the June 13, 2005, issue of *Newsweek*, describes "the significant rise in violent behavior among girls" as a "burgeoning national crisis" (p. 1).

Media-driven constructions such as these generally rely on commonsense notions that girls are becoming more like boys on both the soccer field and the killing fields.[4] Implicit in what might be called the "masculinization" theory (Chesney-Lind & Eliason, in press; Pollock, 1999) of women's violence is the idea that contemporary theories of violence (and crime more broadly) need not attend to gender but can, again, simply add women and stir. The theory assumes that the same forces that propel men into violence will increasingly produce violence in girls and women once they are freed from the constraints of their gender. The masculinization framework also lays the foundation for simplistic notions of "good" and "bad" femininity, standards that will permit the demonization of some girls and women if they stray from the path of "true" (passive, controlled, and constrained) womanhood.

Ever since the first wave of feminism, there has been no shortage of scholars and political commentators issuing dire warnings that women's demand for equality would result in a dramatic change in the character and frequency of women's crime (Pollak, 1950; Pollock, 1999; Smart, 1976). As noted earlier, in the 1970s, the notion that the women's movement was causing changes in women's crime was the subject of extensive media and scholarly attention (Adler, 1975; Chesney-Lind, 1989; Simon, 1975). Again, although this perspective was definitely refuted by the feminist criminology of the era (see Gora, 1982; Steffensmeier & Steffensmeier, 1980; Weis, 1976), media enthusiasm about the idea that feminism encourages women to become more like men and, hence, their "equals" in crime, remains undiminished (see Chesney-Lind & Eliason, in press).

As examples, *Boston Globe Magazine* proclaimed in an article as well as on the issue's cover, over the words *BAD GIRLS* in huge red letters, that "girls are moving into the world of violence that once belonged to boys" (Ford, 1998). And from *San Jose Mercury News* came a story titled "In a New Twist on Equality, Girls' Crimes Resemble Boys'" that features an opening paragraph arguing that

> juvenile crime experts have spotted a disturbing nationwide pattern of teenage girls becoming more sophisticated and independent criminals. In the past, girls would almost always commit crimes with boys or men. But now, more than ever, they're calling the shots.
>
> (Guido, 1998, p. 1B)

In virtually all the stories on this topic (including the Scelfo, 2005, article appearing in *Newsweek*), the issue is framed as follows. A specific and egregious example of female violence is described, usually with considerable, graphic detail about the injury suffered by the victim—a pattern that has been dubbed "forensic journalism" (Websdale & Alvarez, 1997, p. 123). In the *Mercury News* article, for example, the reader hears how a 17-year-old girl, Linna Adams, "lured" the victim into a car where her boyfriend "pointed a .357 magnum revolver at him, and the gun went off. Rodrigues was shot in the cheek, and according to coroner's reports, the bullet exited the back of his head" (Guido, 1998, p. 1B). Websdale and Alvarez (1997) noted that this narrative style, while compelling and even lurid reading, actually gives the reader "more and more information about less and less" and stresses "individualistic explanations that ignore or de-emphasize the importance of wider social structural patterns of disadvantage" (p. 125).

These forensic details are then followed by a quick review of the Federal Bureau of Investigation's arrest statistics showing what appear to be large increases in the number of girls arrested for violent offenses. Finally, there are quotes from "experts," usually police officers, teachers, or other social service workers, but occasionally criminologists, interpreting the narrative in ways consistent with the desired outcome: to stress that girls, particularly African American and Hispanic girls whose pictures often illustrate these stories, are getting more and more like their already demonized male counterparts and, hence, becoming more violent (Chesney-Lind & Irwin, 2005).

There are two problems with this now familiar frame: One, there are considerable reasons to suspect that it is demonstrably wrong (i.e., that girls' violence is not increasing) and two, it has created a "self-fulfilling prophecy" that has had dramatic and racialized effects on girls' arrests, detentions, and referrals to juvenile courts across our country.

Although arrest data consistently show dramatic increases in girls' arrests for "violent" crimes (e.g., arrests of girls for assault climbed an astonishing 40.9%, whereas boys' arrests climbed by only 4.3% in the past decade; Federal Bureau of Investigation, 2004), other data sets, particularly those relying on self-reported delinquency, show no such trend (indeed they show a decline; Chesney-Lind, 2004; Chesney-Lind & Belknap, 2004; Steffensmeier, Schwartz, Zhong, & Ackerman, 2005). It seems increasingly clear that forces other than changes in girls' behavior have caused shifts in girls' arrests (including such forces as zero-tolerance policies in schools and mandatory arrests for domestic violence; Chesney-Lind & Belknap, 2004). There are also indications that although the hype about bad girls seems to encompass all girls, the effects of enforcement policies aimed at reducing "youth violence" weigh heaviest on girls of color whose families lack the resources to challenge such policies (Chesney-Lind & Irwin, 2005).

Take juvenile detention, a focus of three decades of deinstitutionalization efforts. Between 1989 and 1998, girls' detentions increased by 56% compared to a 20% increase seen in boys' detentions, and the "large increase was tied to the growth in the number of delinquency cases involving females charged with person offenses (157%)" (Harms, 2002, p. 1). At least one study of girls in detention suggests that "nearly half" the girls in detention are African American girls, and Latinas constitute 13%; Caucasian girls, who constitute 65% of the girl population, account for only 35% of those in detention (American Bar Association & National Bar Association, 2001, pp. 20–21).

It is clear that two decades of the media demonization of girls, complete with often-racialized images of girls seemingly embracing the violent street culture of their male counterparts (see Chesney-Lind & Irwin, 2004), coupled with increased concerns about youth violence and images of "girls gone wild," have entered the self-fulfilling prophecy stage. It is essential that feminist criminology understand that in a world governed by those who self-consciously manipulate corporate media for their own purposes, newspapers and television may have moved from simply covering the police beat to constructing crime "stories" that serve as a "nonconspiratorial source of dominant ideology" (Websdale & Alvarez, 1997, p. 125). Feminist criminology's agenda must consciously challenge these backlash media narratives, as well as engage in "newsmaking criminology" (Barak, 1988), particularly with regard to constructions of girl and women offenders. The question of how to do this is one that must also engage the field. As a start on such a discussion, consider the advice of Bertold Brecht (1966):

> One must have the courage to write the truth when the truth is everywhere opposed; the keenness to recognize it, and although it is everywhere concealed; the still to manipulate it as a weapon; the judgment to select in whose hands it will be effective, and the cunning to spread the truth among such persons.
>
> (p. 133)

The advocacy work coupled with excellent research that one sees with reports issued by The Sentencing Project and the Center for Juvenile and Criminal Justice provide models of how this work might be done. It certainly requires that we work more closely with progressive journalists than many academics are used to, but given the success of these agencies in doing just that, feminist criminologists should consider this a priority and use our national and regional meetings, as a start, to develop strategies toward this end.

Criminalizing victimization

Many feminist criminologists have approached the issue of mandatory arrest in incidents of domestic assault with considerable ambivalence (see Ferraro, 2001). On one hand, as noted earlier, the criminalization of sexual assault and domestic violence was in one sense a huge symbolic victory for feminist activists and criminologists alike. After centuries of ignoring the private victimizations of women, police and courts were called to account by those who founded rape crisis centers and shelters for battered women and those whose path-breaking research laid the foundation for major policy and legal changes in the area of violence against women (see Schecter, 1982).

On the other hand, the insistence that violence against women be handled as a criminal matter threw victim advocates into an uneasy alliance with police and prosecutors—professions that feminists had long distrusted and with good reason (see Buzawa & Buzawa, 1990; Heidensohn, 1995; S. Martin, 1980). The criminal justice approach, however, was bolstered in the mid-1980s by what appeared to be overwhelming evidence that arrest decreased violence against women (Sherman & Berk, 1984). Although subsequent research would find that arrest was far less effective than originally thought (see Ferraro, 2001; Maxwell, Garner, & Fagan, 2002), for the policy world, the dramatic early research results seemed to ratify the wisdom of a law enforcement–centered approach to the problem of domestic violence. Ultimately, the combined effects of the early scientific evidence; political pressure from the attorney general of the United States, the American Bar Association, and others; and the threat of lawsuits against departments who failed to protect women from batterers "produced nearly unanimous agreement that arrest was the best policy for domestic violence" (Ferraro, 2001, p. 146).

As the academic debate about the effectiveness of arrest in domestic violence situations continued unabated, the policy of "mandatory arrest" became routinized into normal policing and quite quickly, other unanticipated effects began to emerge. When arrests of adult women for assault increased by 30.8% in the past decade (1994 to 2003), whereas male arrests for this offense fell by about 5.8% (Federal Bureau of Investigation, 2004, p. 275), just about everybody from the research community to the general public began to wonder what was happening. Although some, such as criminologist Kenneth Land, quoted in a story titled "Women Making Gains in Dubious Profession: Crime," attributed the increase to "role change over the past decades" that presumably created more females as "motivated offenders" (Anderson, 2003, p. 1), others were not so sure. Even the Bureau of Justice Statistics looked at a similar trend (increasing numbers of women convicted in state courts for "aggravated assault") and suggested the numbers might be "reflecting increased prosecution of women for domestic violence" (Greenfeld & Snell, 1999, pp. 5–6).

Much like the increases seen in girls' assaults, this trend requires critical review, a process that takes the reader through the looking glass to a place that the feminists who worked hard to force the criminal justice system and the general public to take wife battery seriously could never have imagined. In this world, as in California recently, the female share of domestic violence arrests tripled (from 5% in 1987 to 17% in 1999; S. Miller, 2005, p. 21); and as it turned out, it was not just a California phenomenon.

Despite the power of the stereotypical scenario of the violent husband and the victimized wife, the reality of mandatory arrest practices has always been more complicated. Early on, the problem of "mutual" arrests—the practice of arresting both the man and the woman in a domestic violence incident if it is not clear who is the "primary" aggressor—surfaced as a concern (Buzawa & Buzawa, 1990). Nor has the problem gone away, despite efforts to clarify procedures (Bible, 1998; Brown, 1997); indeed, many jurisdictions report similar figures. In Wichita, Kansas, for example, women were 27% of those arrested for domestic violence in 2001 (Wichita Police Department, 2002). Prince William County, Maryland, saw the number of women arrested for domestic violence triple in a 3-year period, with women going from 12.9% of those arrested in 1992 to 21% in 1996 (Smith, 1996). In Sacramento, California, even greater increases were observed; there the number of women arrested for domestic violence rose by 91% between 1991 and 1996, whereas arrests of men fell 7% (Brown, 1997).

A Canadian study (Comack, Chopyk, & Wood, 2000) provides an even closer look at the impact of mandatory arrest on arrests of women for crimes of violence. Examining the gender dynamics in a random sample of 1,002 cases (501 men and 501 women) involving charges filed by the Winnipeg, Manitoba, police services for violent crimes during the period 1991 through 1995, the researchers found that the "zero-tolerance" policy implemented by the police force in 1993 had a dramatic effect on women's arrest patterns. Although the policy resulted in more arrests of both men and women for domestic violence, the impact on women's arrests was most dramatic. In 1991, domestic violence charges represented 23% of all charges of violence against women; by 1995, 58% of all violent crime charges against women were for partner violence (Comack et al., 2000, p. ii). Most significant, the researchers found that in 35% of the domestic violence cases involving women, the accused woman had actually called the police for help (only 5% of male cases showed this pattern; Comack et al., 2000, p. 15).

Susan Miller's (2005) study of mandatory arrest practices in the state of Delaware adds an important dimension to this discussion. Based on data from police ride-alongs, interviews with criminal justice practitioners, and observations of groups run for women who were arrested as offenders in domestic violence situations, Miller's study comes to some important conclusions about the effects of mandatory arrest on women.

According to beat officers S. Miller (2005) and her students rode with, in Delaware, they do not have a "pro-arrest policy, we have a pro-paper policy" (p. 100) developed in large part to avoid lawsuits. What initially surfaces as a seemingly minor, and familiar, lament begins to take on far more meaning. It emerges that at least in Delaware (but one suspects elsewhere), police departments, often in response to threatened or real lawsuits, have developed an "expansive definition" (S. Miller, 2005, p. 89) of domestic violence, including a wide range of family disturbances. As a consequence, although the officers "did not believe there was an increase in women's use of violence" (S. Miller, 2005, p. 105), "her fighting back now gets attention too" (S. Miller, 2005, p. 107) because of this sort of broad interpretation of what constitutes domestic violence.

Another significant theme in police comments reflects male batterers' increased skill in deploying the criminal justice system to further intimidate and control their wives. Officers reported that men are now more willing to report violence committed by their wives and more willing to use "cross-filings" in securing protective orders against their wives and girlfriends. Police particularly resent what they regard as "bogus" violations of protective orders that are actually just harassment (S. Miller, 2005, p. 90).

None of the social service providers and criminal justice professionals S. Miller (2005) spoke with felt women had become more aggressively violent; instead, they routinely called the women "victims." They noted that at least in Delaware, as the "legislation aged," the name of the game began to be "get to the phone first" (S. Miller, 2005, p. 127). Social service workers noted that male batterers tended to use their knowledge of the criminal justice system and process as a way to threaten their wives with the loss of the children, particularly if they had managed to get the woman placed on probation for abuse. Workers echoed the police complaints about paperwork, noting it takes 8 hours to do the paperwork if an arrest is made, but then they made a crucial link to the arrest of women, noting that police, weary of being told they were the problem, have channeled at least some of their resentment into making arrests of women who act out violently (regardless of context or injury) because "according to police policy," they have to make an arrest.

Essentially, it appears that many mandatory arrest polices have been interpreted on the ground to make an arrest if any violent "incident" occurs, rather than considering the context within which the incident occurs (Bible, 1998). Like problematic measures of violence that simply count violent events without providing information on the meaning and motivation, this definition of *domestic violence* fails to distinguish between aggressive and instigating violence from self-defensive and retaliatory violence. According to S. Miller (2005) and other critics of this approach, these methods tend to produce results showing "intimate violence is committed by women at an equal or higher rate than by men" (p. 35). Although these findings ignited a firestorm of media attention about the "problem" of "battered men" in the United States (Ferraro, 2001, p. 137), the larger question of how to define *domestic violence* in the context of patriarchy is vital. Specifically, much feminist research of the sort showcased here is needed on routine police and justice practices concerning girls' and women's "violence." In particularly short supply are studies of girls' arrests, particularly those of girls of color (who are often detained for "assault"), although indirect evidence certainly suggests this is happening (see Chesney-Lind & Irwin, 2005). The evidence to date suggests the distinct possibility that in addition to the well-documented race and class problems, with draconian criminal justice approaches to domestic violence (S. Miller, 1989; Richie, 1996), we have a gender issue: Are these policies criminalizing women's (and girls') attempts to protect themselves?

Women's imprisonment and the emergence of vengeful equity

When the United States embarked on a policy that might well be described as mass incarceration (Mauer & Chesney-Lind, 2002), few considered the impact that this correctional course change would have on women. Yet the number of women in jail and prison continues to soar (outstripping male increases for most of the past decade), completely untethered from women's crime rate, which has not increased by nearly the same amount (Bloom & Chesney-Lind, 2003). The dimensions of this shift are staggering: For most of the 20th century, we imprisoned about 5,000 to 10,000 women. At the turn of the new century, we now have more than 100,000 women doing time in U.S. prisons (Harrison & Beck, 2004, p. 1). Women's incarceration in the United States not only grew during the past century but also increased tenfold; and virtually all of that increase occurred in the final two decades of the century.

The number of women sentenced to jail and prison began to soar at precisely the same time that prison systems in the United States moved into an era that abandoned any pretense of rehabilitation in favor of punishment. As noted earlier, decades of efforts by conservative politicians to fashion a crime policy that would challenge the gains of the civil rights movement as well as other progressive movements in the 1960s and 1970s had, by the 1980s, born fruit (Chambliss, 1999). Exploiting the public fear of crime, particularly crime committed by "the poor, mostly nonwhite, young, male inner-city dwellers" (Irwin, 2005, p. 8), all manner of mean-spirited crime policies where adopted. The end of the past century saw the war on drugs and a host of other "get tough" sentencing policies, all of which fueled mass imprisonment (see Mauer, 1999). The period also saw the development of what Irwin (2005) has called "warehouse prisons," a correctional regime that focuses on a physical plant designed to control (not reform), rigid enforcement of extensive rules, and easy transfer of unruly prisoners to even more draconian settings.

Although feminist legal scholars can and do debate whether equality under the law is necessarily good for women (see Chesney-Lind & Pollock-Byrne,

1995), a careful look at what has happened to women in U.S. prisons might serve as a disturbing case study of how correctional equity is implemented in practice. Such a critical review is particularly vital in an era where decontextualized notions of gender and race "discrimination" are increasingly and successfully deployed against the achievements of both the civil rights and women's movements (Pincus, 2001/2002).

Consider the account of Martha Sierra's experience of childbirth. As she

> writhed in pain at a Riverside hospital, laboring to push her baby into the world, Sierra faced a challenge not covered in the childbirth books: her wrists were shackled to the bed. Unable to roll on her side or even sit straight up, Sierra managed as best she could. The reward was fleeting . . . she watched as her daughter, hollering and flapping her arms, was taken from the room.
>
> (Warren, 2005, p. A1)

As difficult as it was to talk about giving birth while serving time in prison, Sierra was particularly "distressed and puzzled" by her medical treatment: "Did they think I was going to get up and run away?" asked the 28-year-old California prisoner (Warren, 2005, p. A1).

Sierra's story is unfortunately all too familiar to anyone who examines gender themes in modern correctional responses to women inmates. In fact, her experience is less horrific than the case of Michelle T., a former prisoner from Michigan who told Human Rights Watch (1996) that she was accompanied by two male correctional officers into the delivery room:

> According to Michelle T., the officers handcuffed her to the bed while she was in labor and positioned themselves where they could view her genital area while giving birth. She told [Human Rights Watch] they made derogatory comments about her throughout the delivery.
>
> (p. 249)

Basically, male prisoners have long used visits to hospitals as opportunities to escape, so correctional regimes have generated extensive security precautions to assure that escapes do not occur, including shackling prisoners to hospital beds (Amnesty International, 1999, p. 63). This is the dark side of the equity or parity model of justice—one which emphasizes treating women offenders as though they were men, particularly when the outcome is punitive, in the name of equal justice—a pattern that could be called vengeful equity.

Vengeful equity could have no better spokesperson than Sheriff Joe Arpaio who, when he defended his controversial chain gang for women in Maricopa County, Arizona, proclaimed himself an "equal opportunity incarcerator" and went on to explain his controversial move by saying,

> If women can fight for their country, and bless them for that, if they can walk a beat, if they can protect the people and arrest violators of the law, then they should have no problem with picking up trash in 120 degrees.
>
> (Kim, 1996, p. A1)

Other examples of vengeful equity can be found in the creation of women's boot camps, often modeled on the gender regimes found in military basic training. These regimes, complete with uniforms, shorn hair, humiliation, exhausting physical training, and harsh punishment for even minor misconduct have been traditionally devised to "make men out of boys." As such, feminist researchers who have examined them contended, they "have more to do with the rites of manhood" than the needs of the typical woman in prison (Morash & Rucker, 1990).

Although these examples might be seen as extreme, legal readings by correctional administrators and others that define any attention to legitimate gender differences as "illegal" have clearly produced troubling outcomes. It is obviously misguided to treat women as if they were men with reference to cross-gender supervision, strip searches, and other correctional regimes while ignoring the ways in which women's imprisonment has unique features (such as pregnancy and vulnerability to sexual assault). Recently, this approach has been correctly identified by Human Rights Watch (1996) as a major contributing factor to the sexual abuse of women inmates.

Reviewing the situation of women incarcerated in five states (California, Georgia, Michigan, Illinois, and New York) and the District of Columbia, Human Rights Watch (1996) concluded,

> Our findings indicate that being a woman prisoner in U.S. state prisons can be a terrifying experience. If you are sexually abused, you cannot escape from your abuser. Grievance or investigatory procedures where they exist, are often ineffectual, and correctional employees continue to engage in abuse because they believe they will rarely be held accountable, administratively or criminally. Few people outside the prison walls know what is going on or care if they do know. Fewer still do anything to address the problem.
>
> (p. 1)

Human Rights Watch also noted that their investigators were "concerned that states' adherence to U.S. anti-discrimination laws, in the absence of strong safeguards against custodial sexual misconduct, has often come at the fundamental rights of prisoners" (p. 2).

Institutional subcultures in women's prisons, which encourage correctional officers to "cover" for each other, coupled with inadequate protection accorded women who file complaints, make it unlikely that many women prisoners will formally complain about abuse. In addition, the public stereotype of women in prison as bad makes it difficult for a woman inmate to support her case against a correctional officer in court. Finally, what little progress has been made is now threatened by recent legislation that curtails the ability of prisoners and advocates to commence a legal action concerning prison conditions (Stein, 1996, p. 24).

Finally, it appears that women in prison today are also recipients of some of the worst of the more traditional, separate-spheres approach to women offenders (which tends to emphasize gender difference and the need to focus on "saving" women by policing even minor behaviors, particularly sexual behaviors; Rafter, 1990). Correctional officers often count on the fact that women prisoners will complain, not riot, and as a result, often punish women inmates for offenses that would be ignored in male prisons. McClellan (1994) found this pattern quite clearly in her examined disciplinary practices in Texas prisons. Following up two cohorts of prisoners (one male and one female), she found most men in her sample (63.5%) but only a handful of women (17.1%) had no citation or only one citation for a rule violation. McClellan found that women prisoners not only received numerous citations but also were charged with different infractions than men. Most frequent, women were cited for "violating posted rules," whereas males were cited most often for "refusing to work" (McClellan, 1994, p. 77). Women were more likely than men to receive the most severe sanctions.

McClellan (1994) noted that the wardens of the women's prisons in her study stated quite frankly that they demand total compliance with every rule on the books and punish violations through official mechanisms. McClellan concluded by observing that there exists

> two distinct institutional forms of surveillance and control operating at the male and female facilities. . . . This policy not only imposes extreme constraints on adult women but also costs the people of the State of Texas a great deal of money.
>
> (p. 87)

Much good, early feminist criminology focuses on the conditions of girls and women in training schools, jails, and prisons (see Burkhart, 1976; Carlen, 1983; Faith, 1993; Freedman, 1981). Unfortunately, that work is now made much harder by a savvy correctional system that is extremely reluctant to admit researchers, unless the focus of the research is clearly the woman prisoner and not the institution. That said, there is much more need for this sort of criminology in the era of mass punishment, and the work that is being done in this vein (see Bloom, 2003; Owen, 1998) points to the need for much of the same. Huge numbers of imprisoned girls and women are targeted by male-based systems of "risk" and "classification" (Hannah-Moffat & Shaw, 2003) and then subjected to male-based interventions such as "cognitive behaviorism" to address their "criminal" thinking as though they were men (Kendall & Pollack, 2003). Good work has also been done on the overuse of "chemical restraints" with women offenders (Auerhahn & Leonard, 2000; Leonard, 2002). In short, as difficult as it might be to do, in this era of mass imprisonment, feminist criminology needs to find creative ways to continue to engage core issues in girls' and women's carceral control as a central part of our intellectual and activist agenda. As Adrian Howe (1994) put it, "Academics must not let 'theoretical rectitude' deter them from committing themselves as *academics* and *feminists* to campaigns on behalf of women lawbreakers" (p. 214).

Theorizing patriarchy: concluding thoughts

In 1899, Jane Addams was asked to address the American Academy of Political and Social Science. She took the occasion to reflect on the role of the social science of her day:

> As the college changed from teaching theology to teaching secular knowledge the test of its success should have shifted from the power to save men's souls to the power to adjust them in healthful relations to nature and their fellow men. But the college failed to do this, and made the test of its success the mere collecting and dissemination of knowledge, elevating the means unto an end and falling in love with its own achievement.
>
> (Addams, 1899, pp. 339–340)

Perhaps Addams's use of the generic *he* to describe the universities of her day was more a simple convention. Recall that when Addams worked in Chicago, criminology as a discipline was taking shape at the University of Chicago, whose researchers often relied heavily on contacts made at Hull House while systematically excluding women from its faculty ranks and distancing themselves from the female-dominated field of social work (see Deegan, 1988).

How do we avoid the pitfalls Addams (1899) observed in the male-dominated criminology of her day? This article argues that although feminist criminology has made a clear contribution to what might be described as the criminological project, it is positioned to play an even more central role in the era of political backlash. Certainly, we, as feminist scholars, shoulder many burdens, but perhaps the most daunting is the one articulated by Liz Kelly (as quoted in Heidensohn, 1995): "Feminist research investigates aspects of women's oppression while seeking at the same time to be a part of the struggle against it" (p. 71).

For feminist criminology to remain true to its progressive origins in very difficult times, we must seek ways to blend activism with our scholarship (and senior scholars, in particular, need to make the academy safe for their junior colleagues to do just that by redefining tenure criteria to make this work a part of "scholarship"). We must discuss the many tensions and difficulties with this work, again in an era of backlash when the right is actively patrolling faculty behavior (Horowitz & Collier, 1994), and be honest about the many challenges ahead. We must create venues for feminist criminology, including peer-reviewed journals (such as *Critical Criminology*, *Feminist Criminology*, and *Women & Criminal Justice*) while also writing for broader audiences, particularly practitioners and policy makers (see *Women, Girls & Criminal Justice*). We must engage in continued activism on the part of girls and women who are the victims of crimes and whose very experiences are being trivialized by well-funded backlash research (Hoff Sommers, 1994) while also documenting the problems those same girls and women have when they take their cases to court (see Estrich, 1987; Matoesian, 1993). It means close attention and continued vigilance about the situations of women working in various aspects of the criminal justice system, particularly as the right wing cynically appropriates concepts such as discrimination. Finally, and most important, it means activism on behalf of criminalized girls and women, the least powerful and most marginalized of all those we study.

Again, given the focus of the backlash, this article argues that feminist criminology is uniquely positioned to do important work to challenge the current political backlash. To do so effectively, however, it is vital that in addition to documenting that gender matters in the lives of criminalized women, we engage in exploration of the interface between systems of oppression based on gender, race, and class. This work will allow us to make sense of current crime-control practices, particularly in an era of mass incarceration, so that we can explain the consequences to a society that might well be ready to hear other perspectives on crime control if given them (consider the success of drug courts and some initiatives that encourage alternatives to incarceration; Mauer, 2002). Researching as well as theorizing both patriarchy and gender is crucial to feminist criminology so that we can craft work, as the right wing does so effectively, that speaks to backlash initiatives in smart, media-savvy ways. To do this well means foregrounding the role of race and class in our work on gender and crime, as the work showcased here makes clear. There is simply no other way to make sense of key trends in both the media construction of women offenders and the criminal justice response that increasingly awaits them, particularly once they arrive in prison.

Finally, we must also do work that will document and challenge the policy and research backlash aimed at the hard fought and vitally important feminist and civil rights victories of the past century. To do any less would be unthinkable to those who fought so long to get us where we are today, and so it must be for us.

Notes

The author thanks Lisa Jean Pasko for early conversations on topics addressed in this article as well as Susan Sharp and three anonymous referees for their very useful suggestions on earlier drafts of this article.

1 One might cite the appearance of the classic special issue on women and crime of *Issues in Criminology*, edited by Dorie Klein and June Kress (1973); two important books on the topic of women and crime by Rita Simon (1975) and Freda Adler (1975); and the publication of Del Martin's (1977) *Battered Wives* and Carol Smart's (1976) *Women, Crime and Criminology*.

2 Early but important exceptions to this generalization are Klein and Kress (1973), Smart (1976), Crites (1976), Bowker, Chesney-Lind, and Pollock (1978), Chapman (1980), and Jones (1980). There has also been an encouraging outpouring of more recent work on women offenders in the past decade. See Belknap (2001), Chesney-Lind and Pasko (2004), and DeKeseredy (1999) for reviews of this recent work.

3 Sex-gender systems include the following elements: (a) the social construction of gender categories on the basis of biological sex, (b) a sexual division of labor in which specific tasks are allocated on the basis of sex, and (c) the social regulation of sexuality, in which particular forms of sexual expression are positively and negatively sanctioned (Renzetti & Curran, 1999, p. 3).

4 I owe this analogy to Frank Zimring who, in response to a question from a reporter, quipped, "Women's liberation didn't turn girls into boys—violence is still particularly male. There has been much more diversification of gender roles on the soccer field than the killing field" (Ryan, 2003, p. 2).

References

Addams, J. (1899). A function of the social settlement. *Annals of the Academy of Political and Social Science*, *13*, 323–345.

Adler, F. (1975). *Sisters in crime*. New York: McGraw-Hill.

American Bar Association and the National Bar Association. (2001, May 1). *Justice by gender: The lack of appropriate prevention, diversion and treatment alternatives for girls in the justice system*. Retrieved from http://www.abanet.org/crimjust/juvjus/justicebygenderweb.pdf

Amnesty International. (1999). *Not part of my sentence: Violations of the human rights of women in custody*. Washington, DC: Author.

Anderson, C. (2003, October 28). Women making gains in dubious profession: Crime. *Arizona Star*, p. A1.

Arnold, R. (1995). Processes of criminalization: From girlhood to womanhood. In M. B. Zinn & B. T. Dill (Eds.), *Women of color in American society* (pp. 136–146). Philadelphia: Temple University Press.

Auerhahn, K., & Leonard, E. (2000). Docile bodies? Chemical restraints and the female inmate. *The Journal of Criminal Law and Criminology*, *90*(2), 599–634.

Barak, G. (1988). Newsmaking criminology: Reflections on the media, intellectuals, and crime. *Justice Quarterly*, *5*(4), 565–587.

Belknap, J. (2001). *The invisible woman: Gender, crime and justice* (2nd ed.). Belmont, CA: Wadsworth.

Bible, A. (1998). When battered women are charged with assault. *Double-Time*, *6*(1/2), 8–10.

Bloom, B. (Ed.). (2003). *Gendered justice*. Durham, NC: Carolina Academic Press.

Bloom, B., & Chesney-Lind, M. (2003). Women in prison: Vengeful equity. In R. Muraskin (Ed.), *It's a crime: Women and the criminal justice system* (pp. 175–195). New Jersey: Prentice Hall.

Bourgois, P., & Dunlap, E. (1993). Exorcising sex–for crack: An ethnographic perspective from Harlem. In M. Ratner (Ed.), *The crack pipe as pimp* (pp. 97–132). New York: Lexington Books.

Bowker, L. (Ed.). (1998). *Masculinities and violence*. Thousand Oaks, CA: Sage.

Bowker, L., Chesney-Lind, M., & Pollock, J. (1978). *Women, crime, and the criminal justice system*. Lexington, MA: D. C. Heath.

Brecht, B. (1966). *Galileo* (E. Bentley, Ed., C. Laughton, Trans.). New York: Grove.

Brown, M. (1997, December 7). Arrests of women soar in domestic assault cases. *Sacramento Bee*. Retrieved July 31, 2005, from http://www.sacbee.com/static/archive/news/projects/violence/part12.html

Burkhart, K. W. (1976). *Women in prison*. New York: Popular Library.

Bush-Baskette, S. (1998). The war on drugs as a war against Black women. In S. L. Miller (Ed.), *Crime control and women* (pp. 113–129). Thousand Oaks, CA: Sage.

Buzawa, E., & Buzawa, C. G. (1990). *Domestic violence: The criminal justice response*. Newbury Park, CA: Sage.

Cain, M. (1990). Realist philosophy and standpoint epistemologies or feminist criminology as a successor science. In L. Gelsthorpe & A. Morris (Eds.), *Feminist perspectives in criminology* (pp. 124–140). Buckingham, UK: Open University Press.

Carlen, P. (1983). *Women's imprisonment: A study in social control*. London: Routledge.

Chambliss, W. (1999). *Power, politics and crime*. Boulder, CO: Westview.

Chapman, J. R. (1980). *Economic realities and the female offender*. Lexington: Lexington Books.

Chesney-Lind, M. (1988, July–August). Doing feminist criminology. *The Criminologist, 13*, 16–17.

Chesney-Lind, M. (1989). Girls' crime and woman's place: Toward a feminist model of female delinquency. *Crime & Delinquency, 35*(10), 5–29.

Chesney-Lind, M. (2004, August). Girls and violence: Is the gender gap closing? *National Electronic Network on Violence Against Women*. Retrieved from http://www.vawnet.org/DomesticViolence/Research/VAWnetDocs/ARGirlsViolence.php

Chesney-Lind, M., & Belknap, J. (2004). Trends in delinquent girls' aggression and violent behavior: A review of the evidence. In M. Putallaz & P. Bierman (Eds.), *Aggression, antisocial behavior and violence among girls: A development perspective* (pp. 203–222). New York: Guilford.

Chesney-Lind, M., & Eliason, M. (in press). From invisible to incorrigible: The demonization of marginalized women and girls. *Crime, Media, Culture: An International Journal*.

Chesney-Lind, M., & Hagedorn, J. M. (Eds.). (1999). *Female gangs in America: Essays on gender and gangs*. Chicago: Lakeview Press.

Chesney-Lind, M., & Irwin, K. (2004). From badness to meanness: Popular constructions of contemporary girlhood. In A. Harris (Ed.), *All about the girl: Culture, power, and identity* (pp. 45–56). New York: Routledge.

Chesney-Lind, M., & Irwin, K. (2005). Still "the best place to conquer girls": Gender and juvenile justice. In J. Pollock-Byrne & A. Merlo (Eds.), *Women, law, and social control* (pp. 271–291). Boston: Allyn & Bacon.

Chesney-Lind, M., & Pasko, L. (2004). *The female offender*. Thousand Oaks, CA: Sage.

Chesney-Lind, M., & Pollock-Byrne, J. (1995). Women's prisons: Equality with a vengeance. In J. Pollock-Byrne & A. Merlo (Eds.), *Women, law, and social control* (pp. 155–176). Boston: Allyn & Bacon.

Chesney-Lind, M., & Rodriguez, N. (1983). Women under lock and key. *The Prison Journal, 63*, 47–65.

Chesney-Lind, M., & Shelden, R. G. (1992). *Girls, delinquency and juvenile justice*. Belmont, CA: Wadsworth.

Comack, E., Chopyk, V., & Wood, L. (2000). *Mean streets? The social locations, gender dynamics, and patterns of violent crime in Winnipeg*. Ottawa, Ontario: Canadian Centre for Policy Alternatives.

Connell, R. W. (2002). *Gender*. Cambridge, UK: Polity.

Crenshaw, H. (1994). Mapping the margins: Intersectionality, identity politics, and violence against women of color. In M. A. Fineman & R. Mykitiuk (Eds.), *The public nature of private violence* (pp. 93–118). New York: Routledge.

Crites, L. (Ed.). (1976). *The female offender*. Lexington, MA: Lexington Books.

Daly, K., & Chesney-Lind, M. (1988). Feminism and criminology. *Justice Quarterly, 5*(4), 497–538.

Deegan, M. J. (1988). *Jane Addams and the men of the Chicago School, 1892–1918*. New Brunswick, NJ: Transaction Books

DeKeseredy, W. (1999). *Women, crime, and the Canadian criminal justice system*. Cincinnati, OH: Anderson.

DeKeseredy, W., Sanders, D., Schwartz, M., & Alvi, S. (1997). The meanings and motives for women's use of violence in Canadian college dating relationships. *Sociological Spectrum, 17*, 199–222.

DeKeseredy, W., & Schwartz, M. (1998, February). *Measuring the extent of woman abuse in intimate heterosexual relationships: A critique of the conflict tactics scales*. Retrieved from VAWnet Web site: http://www.vawnet.org/DomesticViolence/Research/VAWnetDocs/AR_ctscrit.php

Dziech, B. W., & Weiner, L. (1984). *The lecherous professor*. Boston: Beacon.

Estrich, S. (1987). *Real rape*. Cambridge, MA: Harvard University Press.

Faith, K. (1993). *Unruly women: The politics of confinement & resistance*. Vancouver, British Columbia, Canada: Press Gang.

Faludi, S. (1991). *Backlash: The undeclared war against American women*. New York: Anchor Doubleday.

Federal Bureau of Investigation. (2004). *Crime in the United States, 2003*. Washington, DC: Government Printing Office.

Ferraro, K. (2001). Women battering: More than a family problem. In C. Renzetti & L. Goodstein (Eds), *Women, crime and criminal justice* (pp. 135–153). Los Angeles: Roxbury.

Ford, R. (1998, May 24). The razor's edge. *Boston Globe Magazine*, pp. 3, 22–28.

Freedman, E. (1981). *Their sisters' keepers: Women and prison reform, 1830–1930*. Ann Arbor: University of Michigan Press.

Gilbert, E. (2001). Women, race, and criminal justice processing. In C. Renzetti & L. Goodstein (Eds.), *Women, crime and criminal justice* (pp. 222–231). Los Angeles: Roxbury.

Gilfus, M. (1992). From victims to survivors to offenders: Women's routes of entry into street crime. *Women & Criminal Justice, 4*(1), 63–89.

Goldstein, A., Smith, J., & Becker, J. (2005, August 19). Roberts resisted women's rights. *Washington Post*, p. A1.

Gora, J. (1982). *The new female criminal: Empirical reality or social myth*. New York: Praeger.

Greenfeld, A., & Snell, T. (1999). *Women offenders: Bureau of Justice Statistics, special report*. Washington, DC: U.S. Department of Justice.

Guido, M. (1998, June 4). In a new twist on equality, girls' crimes resemble boys'. *San Jose Mercury News*, p. 1B–4B.

Hannah-Moffat, K., & Shaw, M. (2003). The meaning of "risk" in women's prisons: A critique. In B. Bloom (Ed.), *Gendered justice* (pp. 25–44). Durham, NC: Carolina Academic Press.

Hardisty, J. V. (2000). *Mobilizing resentment*. Boston: Beacon.

Harms, P. (2002, January). *Detention in delinquency cases, 1989–1998* (OJJDP Fact Sheet No. 1). Washington, DC: U.S. Department of Justice.

Harrison, P. M., & Beck, A. J. (2004). *Prisoners in 2003*. Washington, DC: U.S. Department of Justice, Bureau of Justice Statistics.

Heidensohn, F. (1995). Feminist perspectives and their impact on criminology and criminal justice in Britain. In N. H. Rafter & F. Heidensohn (Eds.), *International feminist perspectives in criminology* (pp. 63–85). Buckingham, UK: Open University Press.

Hoff Sommers, C. (1994). *Who stole feminism? How women have betrayed women*. New York: Simon & Schuster.

Horowitz, D., & Collier, P. (1994). *The heterodoxy handbook: How to survive the PC campus*. Lanham, MD: National Book Network.

Horton, J. O., & Horton, L. (2005). *Slavery and the making of America*. Oxford, UK: Oxford University Press.

Howe, A. (1994). *Punish and critique: Towards a feminist analysis of penality*. London: Routledge.

Human Rights Watch. (1996). *All too familiar: Sexual abuse of women in U.S. state prisons*. New York: Human Rights Watch.

Human Rights Watch. (2000, May). Punishment and prejudice: Racial disparities in the war on drugs. *Human Rights Watch Reports*, *12*(2). Available from http://www.hrw.org/reports/2000/usa/

Irwin, J. (2005). *The warehouse prison*. Los Angeles: Roxbury.

Joe, K. (1995). Ice is strong enough for a man but made for a woman: A social cultural analysis of methamphetamine use among Asian Pacific Americans. *Crime, Law and Social Change*, *22*, 269–289.

Johnson, P. (2003). *Inner lives: Voices of African American women in prison*. New York: New York University Press.

Jones, A. (1980). *Women who kill*. New York: Fawcett Columbine.

Kelly, D. M. (1993). *Last chance high: How girls and boys drop in and out of alternative schools*. New Haven, CT: Yale University Press.

Kendall, K., & Pollack, S. (2003). Cognitive behaviorism in women's prisons. In B. Bloom (Ed.), *Gendered justice* (pp. 69–96). Durham, NC: Carolina Academic Press.

Kim, E.-K. (1996, August 26). Sheriff says he'll have chain gangs for women. *Tuscaloosa News*, p. A1.

Klein, D., & Kress, J. (Eds.). (1973). Women, crime and criminology [Special issue]. *Issues in Criminology*, *8*(3).

Lantigua, J. (2001, April 30). How the GOP gamed the system in Florida. *The Nation*, pp. 1–8.

Leonard, E. (2002). *Convicted survivors: The imprisonment of battered women*. New York: New York University Press.

Maher, L., & Curtis, R. (1992). Women on the edge: Crack cocaine and the changing contexts of street-level sex work in New York City. *Crime, Law and Social Change*, *18*, 221–258.

Martin, D. (1977). *Battered wives*. New York: Pocket Books.

Martin, S. (1980). *Breaking and entering: Police women on patrol*. Berkeley: University of California Press.

Matoesian, G. (1993). *Reproducing rape domination through talk in the courtroom*. Chicago: University of Chicago Press.

Mauer, M. (1999). *Race to incarcerate*. New York: New Press.

Mauer, M. (2002). State sentencing reforms: Is the "get tough" era coming to a close? *Federal Sentencing Reporter*, *15*, 50–52.

Mauer, M., & Chesney-Lind, M. (Eds.). (2002). *Invisible punishment: The collateral consequences of mass imprisonment*. New York: New Press.

Mauer, M., & Huling, T. (1995). *Young Black Americans and the criminal justice system: Five years later*. Washington, DC: The Sentencing Project.

Maxwell, C., Garner, J. H., & Fagan, J. A. (2002). The preventive effects of arrest on intimate partner violence: Research, policy and theory. *Criminology & Public Policy*, *2*(1), 51–80.

McClellan, D. S. (1994). Disparity in the discipline of male and female inmates in Texas prisons. *Women & Criminal Justice*, *5*(20), 71–97.

Messerschmidt, J. W. (2000). *Nine lives: Adolescent masculinities, the body, and violence*. Boulder, CO: Westview.

Miller, J. (2001). *One of the guys: Girls, gangs, and gender*. New York: Oxford University Press.

Miller, J., & Mullins, C. (2005). *Taking stock: The status of feminist theories in criminology*. Unpublished manuscript.

Miller, S. (1989). Unintended side effects of pro-arrest policies and their race and class implications for battered women: A cautionary note. *Criminal Justice Policy Review*, *3*, 299–317.

Miller, S. (2005). *Victims as offenders: Women's use of violence in relationships*. New Brunswick, NJ: Rutgers University Press.

Moore, J. (1991). *Going down to the barrio: Homeboys and homegirls in change*. Philadelphia: Temple University Press.

Morash, M., & Rucker, L. (1990). A critical look at the idea of boot camp as a correctional reform. *Crime & Delinquency*, *36*(2), 204–222.

Owen, B. (1998). *"In the mix": Struggle and survival in a women's prison*. Albany: State University of New York Press.

Pincus, F. (2001/2002). The social construction of reverse discrimination: The impact of affirmative action on Whites. *Journal of Inter-Group Relations*, *38*(4), 33–44.

Pollak, O. (1950). *The criminality of women*. Philadelphia: University of Pennsylvania Press.

Pollock, J. (1999). *Criminal women*. Cincinnati, OH: Anderson.

Rafter, N. H. (1990). *Partial justice: Women, prisons and social control*. New Brunswick, NJ: Transaction Books.

Rafter, N. H. (Ed.). (2000). *Encyclopedia of women and crime*. Phoenix, AZ: Oryx Press.

Renzetti, C., & Curran, D. J. (1999). *Women, men and society*. Boston: Allyn & Bacon.

Richie, B. (1996). *Compelled to crime: The gender entrapment of battered Black women*. New York: Routledge.

Rush, F. (1980). *The best kept secret: Sexual abuse of children*. New York: McGraw-Hill.

Russell, D. (1986). *The secret trauma*. New York: Basic Books.

Ryan, J. (2003, September 5). Girl gang stirs up false gender issue: Data show no surge in female violence. *San Francisco Chronicle*, p. 2.

Scelfo, J. (2005, June 13). Bad girls go wild. *Newsweek*. Retrieved July 31, 2005, from http://www.msnbcnsn.com/id.8101517/site/newsweek/page/2/

Schecter, S. (1982). *Women and male violence: The visions and struggles of the battered women's movement*. Boston: South End.

Scully, D. (1990). *Understanding sexual violence*. Boston: Unwin Hyman.

Sherman, L. W., & Berk, R. A. (1984). The specific deterrent effects of arrest for domestic assault. *American Sociological Review*, *49*(1), 261–272.

Simon. R. (1975). *Women and crime*. Lexington, MA: Lexington Books.

Smart, C. (1976). *Women, crime and criminology: A feminist critique*. London: Routledge Kegan Paul.

Smith, L. (1996, November 18). Increasingly, abuse shows a female side: More women accused of domestic violence. *Washington Post*, p. B1.

Steffensmeier, D. J. (1980). Sex differences in patterns of adult crime, 1965–1977. *Social Forces*, *58*, 1080–1108.

Steffensmeier, D. J., Schwartz, J., Zhong, H., & Ackerman, J. (2005). An assessment of recent trends in girls' violence using diverse longitudinal sources. *Criminology*, *43*, 355–406.

Steffensmeier, D. J., & Steffensmeier, R. H. (1980). Trends in female delinquency: An examination of arrest, juvenile court, self-report, and field data. *Criminology*, *18*, 62–85.

Stein, B. (1996, July). Life in prison: Sexual abuse. *The Progressive*, 23–24.

Thorne, B. (1993). *Gender play*. New Brunswick, NJ: Rutgers University Press.

Warren, J. (2005, June 19). Rethinking treatment of female prisoners. *Los Angeles Times*, p. A1.

Websdale, N., & Alvarez, A. (1997). Forensic journalism as patriarchal ideology: The newspaper construction of homicide-suicide. In D. Hale & F. Bailey (Eds.), *Popular culture, crime and justice* (pp. 123–141). Belmont, CA: Wadsworth.

Weis, J. G. (1976). "Liberation and crime": The invention of the new female criminal. *Crime and Social Justice*, *6*, 17–27.

West, C., & Zimmerman, D. H. (1987). Doing gender. *Gender & Society*, *1*, 125–151.

Wichita Police Department. (2002). *Domestic violence statistics: 2001*. Retrieved from http://wichitapolice.com/DV/DV_statistics.htm

Williams, L. S. (2002). Trying on gender, gender regimes, and the process of becoming women. *Gender & Society*, *16*, 29–52.